PRAISE FOR
BIPOLAR DISORDER DEMYSTIFIED

"Lana Castle has written from experience in providing an 'owner's manual' for bipolar disorder. And what a resource—not only has she presented helpful information, including an extensive glossary and index, but she has identified a number of web and print resources for further understanding, treating, and living with manic depression. Indispensable!"

—Pierce J. Howard, Ph.D., Director of Research,
Center for Applied Cognitive Studies, Charlotte, North Carolina;
author of *The Owner's Manual for the Brain*

"Lana Castle has written a very thorough book that includes the latest treatments for bipolar disorder, as well as giving readers an idea of the subjective experience of being bipolar. I would recommend this book for nursing students and other medical professionals, for clients who suffer from this illness, and for their families."

—Donna Poole, R.N., M.S.N., A.P.N.,
Austin Community College

"In solid, concise language devoid of professional jargon, Castle helps readers understand the true nature of bipolar disorder. . . . What sets this book apart from the growing number of titles on the topic is the winning combination of Castle's life-long experience with the disorder and her professional yet accessible writing. Valuable for both mental health professionals and those dealing with the disease, this information-rich title is highly recommended for all libraries."

—Dale Farris, *Library Journal*

Bipolar Disorder
Demystified

Bipolar Disorder Demystified

MASTERING THE TIGHTROPE

OF MANIC DEPRESSION

Lana R. Castle

Foreword by Peter C. Whybrow, M.D.

MARLOWE & COMPANY ■ NEW YORK

BIPOLAR DISORDER DEMYSTIFIED:
  Mastering the Tightrope of Manic Depression
Copyright © 2003 by Lana R. Castle
Foreword copyright © 2003 by Peter C. Whybrow, M.D.
Illustrations copyright © Mercedes Newman

"A Place in the Choir" © Bill Staines.
On *The Whistle of the Jay*, FSI-70.
Lyrics reprinted by permission.

Published by
Marlowe & Company
An Imprint of Avalon Publishing Group Incorporated
245 West 17th Street, 11th Floor
New York, NY 10011-5300

Library of Congress Cataloging-in-Publication Data

Castle, Lana R.
  Bipolar disorder demystified : mastering the tightrope
of manic depression / by Lana Castle.
    p. cm.
  Includes bibliographical references.
  ISBN 1-56924-558-4 (trade paper)
  1. Manic-depressive illness—Popular works. I. Title.
RC516.C342002
616.89'5—dc21
                                    2002071844

20 19 18 17 16 15 14 13 12 11 10

Designed by Pauline Neuwirth, Neuwirth & Associates, Inc.

Printed in the United States of America
Distributed by Publishers Group West

*This book is dedicated to all of those challenged
by mood disorders and to their loved ones.*

∞

In loving memory of my sister Barbara Jean,
whose spirit now soars among the butterflies

CONTENTS

Foreword by Peter C. Whybrow, M.D.   xvii

Author's Note   xx

PART ONE: Living the Bipolar Life   1

Introduction: Welcome to the Tightrope   3
- Mental Illness Myths   4
- A Word or Two About Language   5
- Why I Wrote This Book   6
- Who Can Benefit From This Book   6
- How This Book Is Organized   7
- My Hopes   7

ONE: Strutting on the Tightrope: 9
Mania and Hypomania
- What Are Mania and Hypomania?   10
- The Beginning Strands of Mania   22

TWO: Descending into Darkness: Depression   23
- What Is Clinical Depression?   24
- The Beginning Strands of Depression   34

THREE: Losing All Hope: Suicide   36
- The Permanent "Solution" to Your   37
  Temporary Problem
- The Folks You Leave Behind   42

FOUR: Realizing There's a Problem: Recognition   48
- Risks of Not Seeking Treatment   49

■ "Coming to Terms" With Your Condition 51

■ Reasons People Put Off Treatment 53

■ Admitting You Need Help 55

■ Helping Others Recognize Your Need for Treatment 55

■ Finding Effective Treatment and Sticking With It 58

■ Hospitalization 59

PART TWO: Separating Strands 63

FIVE: Probing the Pathology: Diagnosis 65

■ What Is a Mood Disorder? 66

■ Getting a Diagnosis 67

■ Types of Mood Disorders 71

■ Diagnostic Complications 81

■ Watching for Early Warning Signs 81

SIX: Untangling Complications: Mimicking and Co-occurring Conditions 84

■ Autoimmune Disorders 85

■ Cancer and Tumors 87

■ Endocrine Disorders 89

■ Infectious Diseases 92

■ Neurological Disorders 93

■ Other Psychiatric Disorders 95

■ Unexplained Conditions 101

■ Are Co-Occurring Conditions Related? 101

SEVEN: Uncovering Root Causes: Biochemistry and Genetics 103

■ Basic Brain Structure 104

■ Biochemistry 110

■ The Endocrine System 116

■ The Flexible Brain 119

■ Genetics 119

EIGHT: Delving Deep Inside: Personality 124

■ Temperament 124

■ Personality 125

■ Personality Theories 125

■ Genetic Contributions to Personality and Temperament 126

- How Personality and Temperament 127
  Relate to Bipolar Disorder
- Personality Disorders 128
- Five Important Personality Concepts 130

NINE: Reflecting on Childhood: Upbringing 137
- The "Bad Parenting" Myth 137
- What Makes a Family "Functional"? 138
- What Makes a Family "Dysfunctional"? 139
- Types of Dysfunctional Families 139
- Analyzing My Own Family 141
- Family Communication 143
- Family Discipline 145

TEN: Encountering Snarls: Stress and Trauma 151
- Stress 151
- Trauma 159
- My Experiences of Stress and Trauma 161

PART THREE: Maintaining Balance 165

ELEVEN: Building a Foundation: 167
First Things First
- Maslow's Hierarchy of Needs 167
- Sleep and Biorhythms 169
- Nutrition 172
- Drugs, Alcohol, and Nicotine 182
- Exercise 183
- Making Changes Gradually 185

TWELVE: Seeking Medical Treatment: 187
Medications and Procedures
- Finding the Right Doctor 188
- Changing Doctors 190
- Medication 190
- Managing Medications 202
- Electroconvulsive Therapy 205
- Transcranial Magnetic Stimulation 206
- Vagal Nerve Stimulation 207
- Hospitalization 207

THIRTEEN: Expressing Your Emotions: "Talk Therapy" 209
- What's Involved in Psychotherapy 210
- Individual Therapy 210
- Group Therapy 219

■ Support Groups   220

FOURTEEN: Exploring Nonmedical Options: 224
Alternatives and Complements
■ Dietary Supplements   225
■ Bodywork Options   243
■ Special Devices and Other Treatments   245

FIFTEEN: Finding Firmer Footing: 251
Lifestyle Adjustments
■ Where Do I Start?   252
■ Living and Working in Safe   253
Environments
■ Increasing Your Sense of Belonging   260
■ Developing a New Routine   262

SIXTEEN: Shifting Your Perspective: 270
From Wishes to Reality
■ Setting Goals   271
■ Affirmations   276
■ Visualization   281

SEVENTEEN: Being All That You Can Be: 284
Creativity and Self-Fulfillment
■ Creativity and Madness   285
■ Creative or Expressive Therapies   294
■ Nonpsychiatric Options   298
■ Self-Fulfillment   299

EIGHTEEN: Taking Leaps of Faith: 303
Spirituality and Transcendence
■ Organized Religion   304
■ Religious Beliefs and Mood Disorders   305
■ Religious Approaches to   306
Peer Support Groups
■ My Religious Upbringing   309
■ My Evolving Religious Views   310
■ Connecting with Your Spiritual Side   311
■ Transcendence   317

NINETEEN: Helping Others: When Someone   318
You Know Has a Mood Disorder
■ Showing Concern and Support   319
■ How to Tell When It's Time   320
to Seek Help
■ Helping Someone Get Treatment   321

■ When Hospitalization Becomes   323
Necessary

■ Helping Someone Cope   326
After Hospitalization

TWENTY: Living Beyond Labels: Overcoming   331
Stigma and Advocating for Change

  ■ Stigma from a Historical Perspective   332

  ■ Stigma in the Present   334

  ■ What Are the Results of Stigma?   337

  ■ Limitations Society Must Soon Resolve   339

  ■ Advocating for Better Treatment   342

EPILOGUE: Moving Toward Solid Ground   345

  ■ Mental Illness Myths Demystified   345

  ■ Reasons for Hope   350

Medications Appendix   352

  ■ Dosage Determinations   352

  ■ Half-Life Determinations   353

  ■ How to Use These Tables   354

Notes   361

Bibliography   372

Resources   385

Glossary   396

Acknowledgments   415

Index   419

FOREWORD:
Of Tightropes and Safety Nets

THOUGHTS ABOUT TIGHTROPES conjure up images of risk, of lurking tragedy, and of daring human exploit. For me, and probably for many others, the word tightrope summons the memories of youth and the throbbing excitement of a summer evening spent within the magic of the circus. For Lana Castle, however, tightrope is a metaphor that symbolizes a life of unpredictable challenge of deftly learning to balance herself on the high wire of manic depression. Those who suffer similarly, or who have watched others do so, will immediately appreciate her meaning, and her story.

Mania and depression are disorders of the brain's emotional gyroscope—that balancing bar that enables us to navigate the high wire of the circus that is human society. Our emotions, a preverbal system of social communication that we share with our mammalian forebears, monitor the stress and strain of an ever-changing world and orchestrate the body's ancient mechanisms of survival. Thus, shifting moods, and the emotions that feed them, are part of normal experience. We each value our emotional life as the essential quality of being alive—as the passionate pith of ourselves.

Without emotion the everyday world would be reduced to a series of random events with no point of reference. Life would be without personal meaning, and for this reason we defend the emotions we experience as the essence of who we are. And in consequence we find it hard to accept that such an intimate part of being can fall victim to stress and disease. Thus, when mania or depression strike as an alien shift in the climate of customary emotion, we are first inclined to see moral weakness rather than illness.

The explanation for this unhappy state of affairs is distinctively human. The confusion arises because the experience of manic depression is simultaneously both unique and similar to other illness. Manic depression is not simply a biological irregularity that has invaded a body organ as an illness might invade the liver, for the organ of disability here is the brain: In disturbing the chemical regulation and integrity of the brain's emotional gyroscope, manic depression enters and disturbs the person. Manic depression is a brain disorder that afflicts the integrity of the self—that collection of vital feelings, behaviors, and beliefs that together shape each of us a unique human being.

Lana Castle learned these truths the hard way—through the personal experience of suffering the illness—but with grit and determination she has mastered the high wire of manic depression. *Bipolar Disorder Demystified* is the personal story of a woman who has walked the tightrope and returned to offer a helping hand to those who still struggle to find their balance. The missteps and the mysteries, the doubts and the decisions, the indignities and the insights, the tragedies and the triumphs that have been part of her daily diet since a teenager, are all elaborated upon here in this unusual volume. But you will find the book to be more than a compelling saga: It is also a compendium of intriguing dimension. From diagnosis to diet, from glutamate to ginkgo, from choosing a psychotherapist to the art of public speaking and the value of Toastmasters in building self-confidence, you will be both amazed and amused by Lana Castle's insight and understanding. Read the book from cover to cover in one sitting, as did I, or dig into its pages as one might use a thesaurus. Regardless of method, you will discover threads of practical advice drawn intelligently from a lifetime of experience and presented succinctly in easily accessible prose. Lana Castle deserves our collective thanks, for it is through the insightful weaving of resilient threads of knowledge such as these that personal safety nets are constructed. And such nets of knowledge can be of special comfort when treading the tightrope.

—*Peter C. Whybrow,* M.D.

PETER C. WHYBROW, M.D., is the director of the Neuropsychiatric Institute and Judson Braun Professor and Executive Chair of the Department of Psychiatry and Biobehavioral Sciences at UCLA. An international authority on depression and manic-depressive disease and the effects of thyroid hormone on brain and human behavior, he is the author of numerous scientific papers and five books, the latest of which, *A Mood Apart: A Thinker's Guide to Emotion and Its Disorder,* has been widely acclaimed as the definitive guide to the experience and science of mood disorder written expressly for the general public.

AUTHOR'S NOTE

THIS BOOK RELAYS my personal experience of and perspective on mood disorders, combined with clinical and scientific information. I encourage medication, therapy, and support groups because that's what finally moved me closer to solid ground. But everyone's experience of bipolar disorder differs. Everyone's biochemical makeup and experiences differ. I therefore have not disclosed what medications I've tried nor those I currently take because I don't want you to conclude the same ones will work for you.

Many other treatment options are available to use in place of or along with conventional approaches. I'll describe many options I've tried, as well as many I have not but seem to work well for others. *I will not recommend any specific treatment because what works for me may not work for you.*

I am not a counselor, therapist, psychologist, psychiatrist, or any other type of medical professional. What I *am* is a mental health patient, a suicide survivor, a concerned family member, and an advocate for early treatment, suicide prevention, and better mental health services.

I've done my best to research this book as carefully as I could and to confirm my own speculations with facts. Much of my information comes from notable books and publications about mood and brain disorders. Some comes from authoritative Web sites. Some comes from attending four annual conferences of the National Depressive and Manic-Depressive Association (now known as the Depression and Bipolar Support Alliance). Some comes from my participation in local mental health organizations and support groups, and talking with concerned family members and other mental health patients. Some comes from conversing and corresponding with doctors and other mental health professionals. Much comes from my own therapy and continuing recovery.

Several experts in psychiatry, neurology, and pharmacology have assisted with technical portions of this book. They include

- CHARLES L. BOWDEN, M.D., Karren Professor and Chairman of the Department of Psychiatry at the University of Texas Health Science Center in San Antonio;
- LAUREN B. MARANGELL, M.D., Director of Mood Disorders Research, Director of Clinical Psychopharmacology, Department of Psychiatry, Baylor College of Medicine in Houston, Texas;
- JIM VAN NORMAN, M.D., Medical Director of Austin Travis County Mental Health Mental Retardation Center;
- RICHARD E. WILCOX, PH.D., Professor and Doluisio Fellow, Division of Pharmacology and Toxicology and Neuropharmacology Program Head, Institute for Neuroscience at the University of Texas at Austin, who patiently explained basic pharmacology concepts to me and made extraordinary contributions to the Medications Appendix;
- M. THERESA VALLS, M.D., a Board Certified psychiatrist in private practice in Austin, whose specialty is treating children, adolescents, and adults with mood and anxiety disorders;
- CAROL PIERCE-DAVIS, PH.D., a Licensed Psychologist, with HSP Certification, Board Certified Diplomate-Fellow in Psychopharmacology, Board Certified Diplomate-Fellow in Serious Mental Illness; and

- PETER C. WHYBROW, M.D., Director of the Neuropsychiatric Institute and Judson Braun Professor and Executive Chair of the Department of Psychiatry and Biobehavioral Sciences at University of California at Los Angeles, and author of the book's foreword.

I'm deeply indebted to each and every one.

Living the Bipolar Life

INTRODUCTION

Welcome to
the Tightrope

LIVING WITH BIPOLAR disorder is much like living your life on a tightrope—not because you choose to walk that tightrope but because *it's the only available surface upon which you can walk*. One false step, one impulsive moment, could easily end your life. Imagine being destined to walk that rope forever—either romping ecstatically across it or fighting a force that's pulling you down, and rarely achieving that elusive level ground. This is the experience of bipolar disorder (formerly called manic depression).

Sometimes it feels *great* to be up on that rope. Incredible surges of energy and power make you think you're invincible. You believe wholeheartedly that you can pull off any trick you try. You know with certainty that you'll walk away unscathed.

Other times, you'll find you've fallen from your rope. You may lie tangled in the net or stuck in a dark abyss below. Or the tightrope you've been walking may now bind your body and threaten to cut you in half.

Untreated, bipolar disorder can put you one story or even five stories up when you're high and one story or even five stories down when you're low. If you're lucky, you may experience balance for a while. But you can never fully trust your next step. You can never fully trust your own mind.

Mental Illness Myths

This book demystifies the true nature of mood disorders (also called affective disorders) as we now know them, and based on current understanding, dispels common myths about mental illness. Here are some examples:

- There's no good reason for the mentally ill to act so crazy. They just need to learn some self-control.
- We all get depressed from time to time. Positive thinking should be enough to turn things around.
- Lots of people think about suicide at times but don't actually attempt it. Those who say they want to kill themselves are just seeking sympathy.
- The mentally ill are eccentrics who crave attention. They aren't sick, and many of them don't want treatment.
- Psychiatric diagnoses involve a lot of guesswork. They're not made scientifically. "Shrinks" are quacks.
- Lots of people with "mental illness" have some unrelated physical illness. When that gets treated, the "mental illness" should go away.
- Mental illness is all in your head. It has no physical basis.
- The mentally ill have warped personalities.
- People with mental illness come from bad families.
- The mentally ill are weak. They're just overreacting to normal stress.
- The mentally ill just won't take responsibility and help themselves.
- If "imbalanced brain chemistry" causes mental illness, then medication should rebalance it and cure the problem.
- Talking about problems won't solve them. It only makes you dwell on them more. Instead of yammering endlessly

in therapy, these people should take action.

- The mentally ill can do nothing to help themselves other than find good mental health professionals, take the right medications, and undergo lengthy hospitalizations.
- Once they get effective treatment, the mentally ill should be able to get right back into normal life.
- The mentally ill just need to change their attitudes and be more realistic.
- The mentally ill are immature and self-absorbed. They just need to grow up and become responsible.
- Those people are sick because they have no faith in God. All they really need is religious commitment and prayer.
- Friends and relatives often overreact and push those who "march to a different drummer" into unnecessary treatment.
- The mentally ill are too undependable, weird, or violent to function well in society.

A Word or Two About Language

You may have noticed, particularly if you have a mental illness, that I've used the phrase "the mentally ill" in many of the preceding statements. I've done this only because it reflects the language people often use when making such statements, but I don't condone it. Many of us affected by mental illness strongly prefer people-first language.

People-first language emphasizes *individuals* rather than illnesses, disorders, and disabilities. I don't object to someone saying I'm bipolar any more than I would to someone saying I'm diabetic (if I were), but I *do* object to being called *a bipolar* and prefer that groups of people with mood disorders not be called *bipolars* or *depressives*. We amount to much more than our illness.

I feel the same way about other ailments, injuries, and procedures. People-first language may be less succinct, but I'm offended when medical professionals say things like "the hysterectomy in Room 2" rather than *at least* "the hysterectomy *patient* in Room 2." We are all human beings, not ailments, injuries, or procedures. And all patients deserve as much respect as people blessed with the best of health. People-first language is a more humanistic way of talking about those who are ill or face a disability.

Although the terms consumer, client, and patient are all used to describe those affected by mental illness, I'm using patient to emphasize that mood disorders are *medical illnesses*. As you read this book, please focus on the content rather than get hung up on the terminology.

Why I Wrote This Book

Writing this book has been nothing short of an obsession ever since I lost my sister Barbara to suicide. Her death shook me to the core. In many ways, I'm here today only because she took her life. I had attempted suicide a mere ten days before, and I would undoubtedly have tried again had her death not opened my eyes and helped turn my life around.

I have since embraced the mission to communicate openly and honestly my thoughts, feelings, and experiences related to mental health and suicide prevention in the interest of helping as many people as I can.

Who Can Benefit from This Book

My primary concern in writing this book is to reach those affected by mood disorders (and their loved ones and associates) and to encourage them to seek and stick with treatment. These include

- people with *any* form of bipolar disorder or mood-related illness—already diagnosed or merely suspected, and
- families, friends, and employers of people with bipolar disorder or a mood-related illness.

In addition, I want to help those who work with—or plan to work with—mental health patients to better understand and have compassion for them. These might include

- professionals: psychiatrists, psychologists, psychiatric nurses, social workers, counselors, clergy, and general practitioners;
- workers in hospitals and treatment facilities; and
- teachers and students of psychiatry and psychology.

How This Book Is Organized

The organization throughout this book is topical rather than chronological to help you more quickly access the information you need. I've omitted specific dates and time frames both out of memory lapses and out of privacy concerns.

Part One focuses primarily on my own experiences with depression and bipolar disorder. In addition, this part includes a small amount of clinical information. The last chapter in Part One (chapter 4) provides information to help you or those concerned about you recognize when it's time to seek treatment.

Part Two addresses diagnosis and illnesses that complicate diagnoses, and describes the roles that brain structure, biochemistry, and genetics play in mood disorders. This part also discusses how personality, upbringing, stress, and trauma can affect or trigger mood disorders in those with a genetic predisposition for them.

Part Three offers strategies to help you better cope—or even thrive—with depression or bipolar disorder. In addition, this part shares ways to help others with mood disorders—either directly, or by educating society about mental illness and advocating for more effective treatment.

Following a brief epilogue are a Medications Appendix; Notes and Bibliography sections; a listing of Resources you may find useful; and a comprehensive index.

Terms that appear in boldface indicate words that are defined in the Glossary.

My Hopes

In writing this book, I've learned far more than I ever expected about handling my own disorder. I've changed medications, adjusted my diet, and adopted new routines. Even after many years of treatment, I've discovered negative thinking patterns and withheld feelings that I still want to work on.

I've read about new treatment possibilities I haven't yet had time to try but soon will. In the meantime, it comforts me to know that so many options are out there and that our knowledge about what's most effective is growing rapidly.

I hope this book will benefit you and your loved ones, your friends, and your associates. I hope the information it contains will lead you to a more stable, fulfilling, and happier life.

I also hope you'll share this book with others—including mental health treatment teams—to help educate as many people as possible. As soon as you feel able, I hope you'll also reach out to others who need treatment. You may very well help save their lives.

We've made tremendous progress in informing the general public about mental illness in the last decade or so, but we still have a long, long way to go.

ONE

Strutting on the Tightrope: Mania and Hypomania

SUPPOSE THE TIGHTROPE *you've been walking on suddenly rises, and you find yourself three stories above the floor. While this might frighten a lesser person, you are perfectly at ease. You are in control. Every cell of your being pulses with power. Your sense of everything is "heightened."*

Each fiber of the taut rope stretched before you caresses your flexed arches. As you glide fearlessly across the rope, it dips precariously with your weight. Other people sit far below you. You cannot see their eyes, yet you sense the anxious upward tilt of their faces. You know that sweat drips from their hands while yours remain dry. You can taste their nervousness; it tingles on your tongue. But there's not a nervous bone in your body. Other people are fearful for your life, but you have no fear. Fear is silly! Fear is for fools! There's no need to be afraid.

Sure, you may have fallen from the tightrope in the past. You may have plunged into the net repeatedly. But today will be different. You know it, absolutely. Today you will not fall; you won't so much as slip! Today you will perform as no one has before.

You execute a dozen death-defying cartwheels, brushing the rope ever so lightly with your hands. Others were certain you would fall, but you never doubted yourself for a second. You may even try it blindfolded or with your hands behind your back next time!

At long last, your life is working! In your joy, you don't sense your rope rising higher. You feel such freedom that you think you could fly! But you won't. Not just yet. It's time for your surprise finale. Arms outstretched, you perform a series of perfect somersaults. Your admirers rise and go absolutely wild! But, by then, they do so only in your mind.

Particularly when your normal mode of operation is depression, a manic episode can bring sweet relief. Marvelous surges of adrenaline fuel your boundless enthusiasm. You're full of energy, creativity, and optimism, ready to embrace life and everyone you meet. This, you think, is the "real me." This, you think, is who I want to be. It's as if you hadn't been *present* in your life before.

If you've experienced mania or hypomania (mild mania), you may identify with the previous description. Or your experience may be somewhat different. In any case, you're probably familiar with many of these thoughts and sensations.

What Are Mania and Hypomania?

Mania involves extreme changes of moods, thoughts, and feelings; appetite and sleep patterns; energy and activity levels; self-esteem and confidence; and concentration and decision-making abilities.

The signs and symptoms of **hypomania** are, for the most part, the same as mania but are less severe. Symptoms and mood-shift patterns vary with each individual and appear in differing degrees. Some people plunge directly from an extreme high to severe depression. For others, the change occurs more gradually. Some people have manic episodes but no depressive episodes at all.

TYPICAL SIGNS AND SYMPTOMS OF MANIA AND HYPOMANIA

- Extreme optimism and euphoria
- Anger and aggression

- Inflated self-esteem and confidence
- Appetite changes and decreased need for sleep
- Elevated energy and activity
- Lack of focus and distractibility
- Racing thoughts and rapid, erratic speech
- Impulsiveness and lack of inhibition
- Risky behaviors
- Substance abuse
- Bizarre thoughts and behaviors

I'm one of the lucky ones who has rarely gone beyond the hypomanic state. I've never attempted to fly off a rooftop, thought I was some celebrity, or gambled away the family fortune—the classic symptoms you often hear about. My manic symptoms were generally much more subtle. I have had strong sensations of being *capable* of flying. At times, I've been convinced that I had psychic powers. And I've spent more than a thousand dollars on stationery when I didn't know where the next month's groceries were coming from.

Chapter 5 further clarifies the line between mania and hypomania and how diagnoses are made.

Optimism and Euphoria

A hypomanic state can actually make you quite productive—at least in the beginning. You're bombarded by clever ideas and great inspirations. You make lofty plans. You get all geared up to head in exciting new directions. Your infatuation with *everything* drives you to wring out every little drop of life you can. It's just wonderful for a while!

But, inevitably, things get out of control, even ugly, and someone or something drives you back down. Your jokes become insults. Your openness becomes rudeness. Your laughter becomes too loud and lasts too long. Your bottled emotions strain to blast forth. Eventually, your mood either escalates into mania or you burn yourself out and fall into depression.

MANIC EUPHORIA VERSUS "NORMAL" HAPPINESS

> UNLIKE TRUE happiness, manic euphoria tends to leave shame, humiliation, broken relationships, lost jobs, injuries, debt, and pain.

My childhood highs were always followed by depression or a more "legitimate" disease. Strep throat, tonsillitis, bronchitis, and bronchial pneumonia were my standard repertoire. Occasionally, my energetic flurries produced a minor injury to a knee or an ankle, or even to my head. People considered me clumsy and accident-prone.

While I was growing up, no one in the family seemed especially concerned, though my parents sometimes tried to constrain me. Mother would say, "You're trying to do too much. You're going to make yourself sick!" And, when I was a bit too rambunctious, Daddy would warn, "Calm down now. Don't get too happy!"

Don't get too happy? This admonishment seemed designed to spoil my fun. The times when I was "all stirred up" were the only times I felt alive and vital—the only times I *liked* myself or found my life worth living. Most of the time, I was a shy, introverted child. People were always trying to bring me out of my shell. Why did my joy on these rare occasions make others so nervous? Why were folks always trying to bring me down?

People often see **bipolar disorder** only as a dichotomy of ecstatic highs and melancholic lows. And that matched my experience of it for at least a decade. My life mimicked the "comedy" and "tragedy" masks that hung on my parents' basement wall.

But sometimes mania takes a different direction.

Anger and Aggression

Although euphoric mania is more common, some manic episodes bring volcanic anger and aggression. When this happens, you become impatient, demanding, easily provoked, argumentative, obnoxious, or enraged. You pick fights or make scenes in public. You risk being arrested and thrown in jail. Your friends and family "walk on eggshells" when you're around, in fear of your next "explosion."

VIOLENCE AND MANIA

ALTHOUGH SOME people do become violent when manic, most of us with bipolar disorder are much less likely to harm others than to harm ourselves. Despite sensational media coverage of "psycho" crimes, we're no more violent than the general public. And adequate treatment can decrease the risk of violence considerably.

For years, I knew only about the bright side of mania. I equated bipolar disorder only with deep depression or with euphoria and fun. I never knew that anger might be a symptom.

When I experienced rages later in my illness, I shattered our best dishes and beat the walls and floors and sofa with a broom. The intensity of these episodes terrified me. Influenced by our society's mores and media horror stories, I feared I might be capable of murder, even though I've never physically harmed anyone. Although I'd dreamed of having a large, happy family, I tabled my desire to bear children because I feared I might harm my own baby.

Self-Esteem and Confidence

During euphoric mania or hypomania, *everything* becomes possible. You embrace each challenge with open arms. Life is simpler and clearer, as if it's channeling directly through you. Your heightened senses may make every color seem brighter, every smell stronger, every sound clearer. You feel an exuberant connection to the entire universe.

Even if you're normally withdrawn and uncertain of yourself, you become extraordinarily self-assured. You're highly sociable and outgoing, and bring smiles to everyone's faces. You're fun, witty, a delight to be around. Attracted to your exuberance, people willingly follow your lead. And you may feel such a direct connection that you're certain you can read their minds.

After a long depression, the euphoria of hypomania makes me feel like someone has sandblasted the rust off me. The charismatic individual who emerges is such a refreshing change from the mousy, morose little person I am when I'm depressed.

For some, however, this heightened self-esteem becomes superiority. Highly manic people can become grandiose and believe God has chosen them for a special mission, or that they're royalty or some deity.

Appetite Changes and Decreased Need for Sleep

When in a manic or hypomanic state, you may lose your appetite, forget to eat, or consider your new projects too important to stop for meals. Hours, or even full days, may fly by before you consume a bite of anything.

Or, delighting in the taste, smell, and texture of everything that goes into your mouth, you may begin to eat compulsively. All control may disappear, even if you normally watch what and when you eat quite carefully.

During both mania and hypomania, frenetic thoughts and creative inspirations often won't let you wind down and sleep, so insomnia is common. In fact, it's one of the first signs of such episodes. It's not unusual during an episode to get by with three or four hours' sleep, to stay up all night, or to go for days on end without sleeping. And, unlike most people, you won't feel tired until the episode subsides.

As early as grade school, I had frequent bouts of insomnia and racing thoughts—a sensation I now call "brain spin." I'd lie awake at night with my body in first gear but my brain stuck in fifth. I simply couldn't wind down until something yanked my "tightrope" out from under me.

Elevated Energy and Activity

When you're manic or hypomanic, you become like the Energizer bunny on speed. You're fueled by the need for action. Life suddenly holds all kinds of new possibilities. You take on new commitments with great fervor.

You become the ultimate "multitasker"—surfing the Web, reading e-mails, printing files, writing checks, sending faxes, and returning calls simultaneously. You may begin ambitious projects or even start a new business with very little planning, and then drop them at any time for entirely new ventures.

Over the years, I've invested extraordinary amounts of time, energy, and money in projects I suddenly abandoned and forgot about entirely. When I was a child, Mother claimed I lacked "stick-to-itiveness."

Lack of Focus and Distractibility

When manic or hypomanic, your ability to concentrate and focus on priorities often becomes impaired. It may be impossible to sit in one place for more than a few minutes and to concentrate on one task at a time. You become like a distracted smoker with multiple cigarettes lit up in every room.

Say you try to gain control by listing what you need to do. You're likely to misplace your list, forget within minutes that you've made it, or make essentially the same list repeatedly. Filing papers or paying bills during such a state may lead to illogical decisions that take months to straighten out.

Racing Thoughts and Rapid, Erratic Speech

When you're manic or hypomanic, thoughts bombard you so rapidly that you can't keep up with them. Thoughts whiz through your brain like enormous meteor showers. When I'm in this state, I feel as if my brain is spinning, trying to gather all the thoughts before they disintegrate.

As a child, I sometimes experienced brain spin at school. Although I'd sit there quietly, thoughts kept colliding in my mind. When asked a question, it was as if I'd had a mental blackout. I had no idea what had been going on in class. More than one teacher scolded me for my excessive "daydreaming."

As an adult, if I tried to record my thoughts, I couldn't keep up with all that flashed through my mind. I often got up while my husband was soundly sleeping and wrote for hours at a time. I sometimes produced pages of overlapping scribbles or cryptic notes I later could not begin to decipher.

In the press to share their brilliance, people who are manic or hypomanic often

- interrupt others and take over conversations,
- talk incessantly,
- jump from one idea to another,
- leave their thoughts unfinished, and
- answer simple questions at great length.

Other people are usually pressed to get a word in, which quickly becomes frustrating for them. Until the conversation is over (or well afterward), the hypomanic or manic individual often won't recognize that a one-sided interchange has taken place. This gives others the impression that people with bipolar disorder are totally self-centered. And, during such episodes, we may very well be.

Impulsiveness and Lack of Inhibition

During manic and hypomanic states, judgment takes a backseat to impulsive urges. Very little stops you from letting it all hang out. You might decide to test-drive a new car by driving hundreds of miles, to join a performer onstage completely uninvited, or to coax a friend to hop on a plane with you solely to dine outside the country.

You may decide to "set things right" by telling off your boss or disrupting an important meeting. You may make a radical lifestyle change, like leaving a long-term relationship to marry a virtual stranger, giving away all of your belongings, or joining a cult.

Risky Behaviors

Mania and hypomania bring the urge to take risks you'd never consider in your normal state. You may drive a car at its maximum speed, scale the outside of a multistory building, or stroll across a busy highway with one arm raised in the expectation that you can part oncoming traffic like Moses parted the Red Sea.

Or, like many people with this illness, you may lose all control of your libido.

HYPERSEXUALITY AND PROMISCUITY DURING HYPOMANIC AND MANIC EPISODES

- on average, occur in about 57 percent of those with more severe mania
- occur in about 40 percent of those with **cyclothymia** (mild but chronic bipolar disorder)

In my late teens and early twenties, I was barely aware that something was wrong. My moods surged up and down frequently, and I was up for longer intervals. It's hard to say whether these mood swings came from illness or from normal hormonal change, but when not slowed by depression and hiding out from others, I became a sexual dynamo. Because of my age, our country's loosening morals, and my shifting social circles, few people took notice.

When I started college at Kansas State University in the late sixties, open premarital sex was just coming into vogue. I'd grown up in a conservative churchgoing family in which "nice girls" saved themselves for marriage, but being away from strict parental control left nothing between me and all sorts of new possibilities.

Even in childhood I'd had a high sex drive, but in college I became insatiable. There were spells during which I had sex or masturbated several times a day. I was multiorgasmic but never satisfied. The sex I craved when hypomanic was not at all like the tender lovemaking I desired at other times. I suppressed lovers' attempts to be tender with my urgency to get straight to "the act." I became driven to penetrate myself with whoever or whatever came along. I lived in fear that newspapers would one day announce: WOMAN DIES IMPALED ON STICK SHIFT! These sexual exploits later intensified my depressions. For three decades I chastised myself for my "weak will" and told no one about my misadventures.

During the first two years that I was sexually active with others, much of the sex was unprotected. I approved of sex only in a committed, monogamous relationship and was even shocked by friends who weren't virgins, but I was way past saving myself for some future husband. I could tolerate my behavior only by convincing myself that each new conquest was my one true love. These strings of one-night stands with virtual strangers brought me much private pain.

At one point later in graduate school at the University of Texas at Austin, I was simultaneously seeing three different men. I stuffed myself with sex much like children stuff themselves with candy. For almost a decade, the "notches on my bedpost" mounted up so fast that I could neither say how many men I'd slept with nor recall many of their names. At one point, an old "regular" at a café where I waitressed shared that my "fiancé" had proclaimed me "a really great lay." I was horrified.

But I was one of the lucky ones. I walked away with only a brief chlamydia infection contracted from a bisexual houseguest I'd harassed into servicing me. Had my escapades occurred after AIDS got its foothold, I might not be alive today.

For years, I thought I was merely oversexed. The idea that my behavior could relate to an illness never crossed my mind. I thought I was simply a bad person. That I was outrageously undisciplined. And I was so certain my family would agree that I never even hinted at what was going on. Short of the telling grass stains Mother found on some slacks I'd worn to a formal banquet, I doubt my family had a clue.

Fortunately, now that I'm fairly well stabilized, my sexual frenzies have more or less subsided. I still experience intense sexual urges on those rare occasions when I'm hypomanic. But, incredibly, a small adjustment to my mood stabilizer shifts me from wanting to jump the next deliveryman who arrives at my door to having barely any interest in sex.

Substance Abuse

Even if you're normally not a drinker and take only the occasional aspirin, alcohol and illicit drugs may become attractive during mania or hypomania.

ALCOHOL ABUSE

The second semester of my first year of college, I switched from my parent-sanctioned "nice girl" major of interior design to theater. This impractical, racy major helped downplay my illness. "Theater freaks" were *supposed* to be different, bizarre, expansive. Manicky behavior fit right in. All but those few people who knew me well in high school found my antics fairly normal—for a theater freak.

I also began drinking—often heavily. My parents had never had alcohol in the house, and I hadn't drunk in high school. When my high school steady had brought a bottle of booze along on a date, I'd been incensed. But once away from my sheltered upbringing, the situation changed. I discovered a talent for holding my liquor. At those theater gatherings I wasn't too depressed to attend, I often became the life of the party. I experienced a marvelous popularity I had never known.

ALCOHOL ABUSE

CURRENTLY, THE most common form of substance abuse is *alcohol abuse*—the overuse of beer, wine, or liquor. Alcohol abuse occurs frequently and leads to many problems in people with mood disorders.

I started off one party by splitting a fifth of rum with a friend. When that was gone, I downed another partygoer's vodka. Then I switched to wine for a while. All the time, I was singing, dancing, entertaining. Other partygoers were placing bets on when I'd finally pass out. I concluded the evening by polishing off the host's scotch. I didn't throw up until we left the party and the fresh air hit me. My poor, conservative roommate, Beth, wound up bathing me, brushing my teeth, and tucking me into bed.

DRUG ABUSE

I fooled around with drugs in college, too, though rarely with the hard stuff. I smoked marijuana and hashish when offered, but thanks to a meager budget never bought drugs on my own. During my junior year, one of my boyfriends turned out to be a pusher, and he introduced me to speed. He'd dole out a couple of dozen little white cross pills like a parent paying an allowance. I liked speed—a lot. It helped me feel productive and fully alive. Suddenly, I had the power to create or extend highs on my own. It was one of the few times I felt in control—at least until the speed led to the shakes.

> DRUG ABUSE may involve the overuse or misuse of prescribed or over-the-counter medications (particularly sleeping pills) or illicit drugs. *Stimulants* (cocaine, "Ecstasy," "speed," and other *amphetamines*), *opioids* (heroin, morphine, and other sleep-inducing narcotics), and marijuana are currently the most widely abused illicit drugs.

During this same period, I also began smoking cigarettes, which appeal to me only when I'm up. The manic urge to breathe in life's essence—to get it while you can—is much like the drive to inhale deep drags from a cigarette. Even though I quit smoking fairly easily—perhaps the sole benefit of my depressions—I still get the urge for a deep drag when I'm even slightly up.

Envisioning myself as a great playwright, I'd sit at my desk for hours, popping speed, chain-smoking, and pecking away at my Smith-Corona.

Bizarre Thoughts and Behaviors

Sometimes bizarre thoughts plague people, especially during more severe manic or depressive states. Such thoughts often produce bizarre behaviors. You may be convinced that you've developed the power to heal others with your touch, or that the devil's come to drag you down to hell. You may think you hear plants or animals speak or believe you can read their minds. You may spend days creating strange inventions. Clothing may suddenly seem too restrictive, and you may get picked up for public nudity.

Comparatively speaking, my thoughts and behaviors were pretty mild. Sometimes the intensity of my senses was so heightened that I felt I could see individual cells, or feel my hand "melt" through my cat's fur to massage his muscles when I stroked him. Sometimes I was convinced I could read others' thoughts and became a self-appointed interpreter for the people around them.

During high school, I had predictive dreams of other people's deaths, which later actually occurred. I could pass the first two off to coincidence, as the victims were elderly. But the third dream was inexplicable. I shared it the next day with my science lab partner, who had become a regular confidant. In the dream, a crowd surrounded a blank-faced dying man. When I described my dream, I could recall only one of the people in the crowd—my lab partner. He disappeared the very next day, and when he returned about two weeks later, he accused me of being a witch. His father had died suddenly, and he'd been out for the funeral. The experience made me unreceptive to any further "psychic" input.

It never occurred to me at the time, but there's a chance I lost my coveted summer job as a counselor at Camp Ko-Ha-Me because of bipolar disorder. Employment was by invitation only, and even though I'd worked there several summers, I wasn't asked back after my junior year.

Perhaps it was my behavior the summer before. I spent one entire session speaking with a cockney accent and told all the campers I was from England. I didn't begin this with the intention of speaking cockney every day; I just got stuck in that mode and couldn't seem to turn it around. I didn't know squat about England's geography or culture, and somehow I dodged the campers' curiosity. I have no memory of what I said. The rest of the staff knew I was a native Kansan, but for some unknown reason, no one broke the pretense— at least not in front of me. They were all strangely mute about the subject, as if counselors changed their country of origin every day.

Another time, I knocked myself out on a thick iron bedpost while performing Shakespearean lines for my campers. The camp administrators rushed me to the nearest hospital, where I was admitted overnight. But, other than a small tender bump, the doctors found no sign of a head injury. Were my actions merely those of an over-enthusiastic theater buff, or were they symptoms of bipolar disorder?

The Beginning Strands of Mania

Only recently has bipolar disorder been diagnosed before late adolescence. The most common age of onset is in the late teens, but it has been diagnosed even in toddlers. Doctors often have more difficulty diagnosing bipolar disorder in children and adolescents because their symptoms are often hard to distinguish from age-related behavior. Sometimes the illness is mistaken for something else, such as attention deficit hyperactivity disorder or oppositional defiant disorder.

I can't say precisely when my hypomanic tendencies emerged. They were certainly there by my late teens, and a tendency toward manic moments seems to have been present most of my life. It's just that no one recognized the symptoms as such when they first occurred. When I was hypomanic, I felt as if the "real me" had emerged from my depression or my normal quiet state, but I recognized these patterns only in retrospect.

Mania and hypomania can be so exhilarating! So dangerously seductive! When you're cavorting across your tightrope, you're having the time of your life. You want to keep feeling confident, outgoing, talkative. You want to feel that power forever. You want to keep thinking you can do anything and that you'll do it with ease.

You try to cram all the living you've missed into the time that you're up. You begin to think nothing can stop you—that you truly can have it all. You become so certain that you convince others you can nearly walk on water.

It's a challenge to slow down, to not overcommit. You keep nurturing the hopeful thought that maybe this time no dark pain will follow. You desperately want to believe your life has changed. Yet you hear your loved ones' warnings, and underneath lies a sense of impending doom, a knowledge that you're just fooling yourself. In some far recess of your mind, you know that the tightrope will soon deposit you in the depressive hell that waits hungrily to devour you once again.

TWO

Descending into Darkness: Depression

THERE YOU ARE, *scampering across your tightrope without a care in the world, when the rope slips suddenly from beneath you. Without warning, you plunge into darkness, nothingness, into a choking void. When you awaken from the impact, you're in agony, your head throbbing as if your brain's about to burst. You ache all over but don't remember why.*

A horrific stench fills your nostrils and plugs your every pore. You can't shut it out. You crave air, but your tortured lungs will not expand. Something is crushing the very life out of you. No matter which way you turn, you can't slip from its toxic grip. Every move you make sucks you farther down.

A clutching blackness surrounds you. You try to escape, but it's as if your legs are encased in thick cement. All is darkness, grief, and pain. Tears flow in rivulets from your eyes. The only relief you can imagine is sleep—or, better yet, death. Whatever have you done to deserve this?

Then you recognize that you've been here before. You know the place well. You should have seen this coming. You are such an ass! How many times must you go through this before you get it in your head? You've fallen from your tightrope and have landed three stories underground. Once again you've confirmed your diagnosis. You and your damned bipolar life.

If you've experienced clinical depression, you may identify with the previous description. Or your experience may differ. In any case, you're probably familiar with some of these thoughts and sensations.

What Is Clinical Depression?

Everyone gets down from time to time and occasionally gets the blues. If you break up with a loved one, get laid off from your job, or suffer some other disappointment, it's natural to feel bad—at least for a while. Even a reconciled relationship, a healthy new baby, or an outstanding accomplishment can lead to the blues. But **clinical depression** affects cognitive, physical, and/or social functioning.

Authorities used to explain the difference between "the blues" and clinical depression by calling them *reactive* (event based) versus *endogenous* (biologically based) depression. But in the past decade or two, we've learned that both types can intertwine. A long-lasting reactive depression that retains its impact or intensifies will become a clinical depression. And in those of us genetically predisposed for a mood disorder, emotional or stressful events often trigger episodes.

As with mania and hypomania, people with clinical depression experience significant changes of their moods and feelings; sleep patterns and appetite; energy and activity levels; self-esteem and confidence; and thinking, concentration, and decision-making abilities.

TYPICAL SIGNS AND SYMPTOMS OF DEPRESSION

- Inexplicable aches and pains
- Indecisiveness and feeling overwhelmed
- Despondency or a total lack of feeling
- Sleep and appetite changes
- Poor self-esteem and lack of confidence
- Dragging through life and talking at a slower pace
- Performing useless actions
- Anger and frustration
- Substance abuse
- Self-destructive thoughts and actions

Like mania and hypomania, depression surfaces in varying degrees and displays different symptoms in different individuals.

Inexplicable Aches and Pains

Depression often brings physical symptoms such as constipation, fatigue, headaches, and stomachaches. Many depressed people completely lose interest in sex. If you don't realize you're experiencing depression, you may attribute your symptoms to stress. Women may acknowledge that they feel "down" but discount the depth of their feelings. Men may hide their emotional pain and reveal only their physical symptoms.

HYPOSEXUALITY AND REDUCED LIBIDO DURING DEPRESSION

- occur in about 75 percent of those experiencing depression
- may be further aggravated by many **psychotropic** medications (those that affect the mind)

When you're depressed, other people may think you're "neurotic" and discount the seriousness of your situation. This is true even of medical professionals. Particularly if you bring doctors a "laundry list" of physical complaints for which they can find no clinical explanation, your condition may go undiagnosed.

Many times during my twenties and thirties, I sought medical help for symptoms that concerned only me. Doctors had done everything from advising me to "just cut back" my schedule to suggesting I see the movie *Chariots of Fire*! But very few people can shrug off depression or turn their lives around by just thinking positively.

On the day I was forced to admit that I needed psychiatric help, I was at the office of a family doctor I'd seen twice before. On my first visit, four months earlier, I'd dragged myself to the doctor's office, thoroughly exhausted. I'd had headaches, dizziness, erratic sleep, difficulty concentrating, and a growing sense of disorganization.

This time I suspected *hypoglycemia,* a likely culprit, as I'd had blood sugar problems in the past. I'd taken birth control pills for nearly ten years but discontinued them after developing borderline diabetes.

After a series of lab tests, the doctor explained that my blood work showed no evidence of hypoglycemia or diabetes. He then prescribed a mild tranquilizer to quell my anxieties and an antidepressant to improve my mood.

After four months on these two medications, I felt no better. If anything, I felt worse. The doctor then prescribed a different anti-depressant and suggested I see a psychiatrist. A psychiatrist! I could not believe he'd said it. I left his office in shock.

I sat in the parking lot and fingered the page from his prescription pad. He'd written down the names of three psychiatrists. It was a pleasant spring afternoon without a cloud in the sky, a day on which I should have been grateful to be alive. But all I could do was sit in my Mazda and sob.

I'd had a few encounters with mental health professionals before. I had seen one psychologist briefly for counseling as an undergrad-uate at the university health center, and I'd seen a social worker a dozen or so times at a county mental health facility. But both of these individuals had seemed far more disturbed than I was. Then there was the social worker who ran the assertiveness group I'd attended for six or eight weeks. I'd sought help for common relationship problems and the residue of a failed first marriage. But a psychiatrist! Only the "deeply disturbed" saw "shrinks."

In desperation six years before, I had seen a doctor who almost immediately pronounced me manic depressive and recommended electric shock. I couldn't have been *that* bad off. It seemed uncon-scionable to make that diagnosis based on one visit, so I didn't return.

Why was this happening? What was wrong with me? Could "Dr. Shock" have been right?

QUESTIONING THE CAUSE
OF DEPRESSION

WHEN FIRST diagnosed with depression, you may tend to look for an outside cause. Did your depression come from a recent illness, a stressful home life, or a rotten job? Are you depressed because your parent mistreated you or because you have hardly any friends? Or are you just incredibly unlucky?

I saw my first psychiatrist later that month. After a few appointments and more lab work, he concluded that I had **dysthymic disorder**, a mild form of clinical depression. He switched me to yet another tranquilizer and a different antidepressant. In addition to weekly sessions with my psychiatrist, I began seeing a social worker for individual and group therapy.

After six weeks of psychiatric treatment, I had barely improved. Getting up and dressed for work was a major effort. When the alarm rang, I'd burrow deeper under the covers, nearly merging into the mattress. My husband, Ralph, had to pry me out of bed and help me dress. I was increasingly late to work and highly agitated by the traffic.

Indecisiveness and Feeling Overwhelmed

My worst "fall from the tightrope" was especially confusing because, for the past few years, I'd felt better than ever, full of energy and highly active. I was in a happy second marriage to a saint of a man. I got along well with my stepchildren, Tom and Joy, who lived with us half the time. I had a full-time career, served on the board of directors for my professional organization, and was involved in committee work. Friends, teachers, and coworkers from grad school days held me up as an example of success. For once in my life, I felt well liked. At times, I brimmed over with so much happiness that I cried tears of joy on my daily commute. And although the job I'd had just over a year was challenging, it still held much promise. It strongly matched my skills and values.

I had been hired for one of two newly created managerial positions. I was to handle organizational communications in the long term but also to fill another manager's role "until they hired someone else." My primary task initially was to prepare for a major anniversary event for the organization. I was alarmed to learn that nothing substantive had been done, but I hit the ground running and never looked back. I worked fifty- and sixty-hour weeks and often lunched at my desk. My boss kept assuring me that things would calm down after the big celebration, but they didn't. More than a year later, I was still wearing both hats.

My boss was no help at all. When I'd go in with a list of my top dozen "urgent" assignments and ask for help in prioritizing them, I would invariably leave with three or four additional tasks. I was so overwhelmed, I could accomplish almost nothing.

My boss appeared supportive on the surface but was relentlessly controlling, demanding, and difficult to please underneath—just like my father. When I discussed this with my therapist, she explained that people often re-create their dysfunctional childhood relationships repeatedly. This revelation confused me. Why would I re-create something I found so painful?

I dealt with my exhaustion and the pressures at work by consuming as many as three pots of coffee a day, topped off with diet sodas in the afternoon. All this caffeine compounded my problems.

Despondency or a Total Lack of Feeling

People in depressive states tend to withdraw from others and to isolate themselves. Self-hatred and pessimism overtake their lives. They spend enormous amounts of time "awfulizing" about their situation. Rather than the "rose-colored glasses" of mania and hypomania, the "lenses" of depressive "glasses" are coated with shit.

Rather than feeling despondent, some clinically depressed individuals feel completely numb. They're bored and disinterested in life and lack motivation.

When I finally left my "dream job," I felt thoroughly defeated. Not having an active, productive life, I became a total recluse. Once a supportive wife and stepmother, I now barely acknowledged my family's existence. My anxieties verged on paralysis. I stayed locked in a dark house all day, venturing out only for therapy. My routine consisted of visits to my psychiatrist, therapist, and therapy group.

Sleep and Appetite Changes

In nearly everyone with clinical depression, sleep patterns and appetite change significantly. Some people get insomnia and toss and turn all night with great frustration. Others simply want to hibernate until this monstrous presence goes away.

During that same long depression, I spent the summer and fall sleeping twelve to sixteen hours a day. When out of bed, I usually sat in my easy chair, crying and contemplating suicide, or on better days, devouring self-help books. I had begun serious self-examination while in grad school, when I'd purchased the first of more than sixty self-help books I now own. I borrowed and read dozens more from my few remaining friends and from the public library.

A lack of appetite is common. Some people have no interest whatsoever in eating when they're depressed. Fixing a meal isn't worth the effort. Everything tastes bland and boring. But others crave carbohydrates and sweets, especially chocolates. These individuals tend to binge until they can hold no more.

If I went out, I'd guiltily stuff my face with junk food, consuming several candy bars at a time or wolfing down an entire package of cookies. For years I'd followed low-sugar diets, which always made me feel much better. Usually, a single candy bar gave me a headache, and too much sugar made my stomach ache. But when depressed, I sought sugar like an addict seeking heroin. A single bite of something sweet would set off a craving.

Poor Self-Esteem and Lack of Confidence

Deep depression has a way of erasing your past successes and accomplishments. No matter how outstanding they were, you may be unable to recall them. No matter how happy you may have once been, you can no longer remember ever feeling good. Or, if you can somehow dredge up pleasant memories, you'll be convinced that further happiness for you is lost forever.

During depressive states, you may chastise yourself repeatedly and dwell on every little failure throughout your entire life. Even if you're normally optimistic and outgoing, you may become pessimistic, withdrawn, and morose. A fall from mania or hypomania may make you particularly despondent, partly because of the stark contrast in mood, and partly out of embarrassment about your recent behavior.

Dragging Through Life

During severe depression, the slightest decision, like what to eat or what to wear, become herculean tasks. Eating, bathing, and getting dressed don't seem worth the bother or are jobs you're no longer able to fulfill. In *The Noonday Demon: An Atlas of Depression,* Andrew Solomon describes a time when the thought of putting on not *one* sock but *two* was more than he could bear.

Your abilities to set goals, make plans, and set priorities often vanish. Household chores and bill-paying are too complex, difficult, or pointless. Dirty dishes, unwashed laundry, overflowing ashtrays, and stacks of dusty magazines and newspapers accumulate everywhere. The clutter may be so thick, it's hard to move from room to room.

During my worst depression, some days I managed to pull on some jeans and a T-shirt. Other days I never shed my nightgown and robe. Occasionally I could pull myself together long enough to cook a simple family dinner. Other times I left Ralph and the kids on their own. Ralph kept hoping I'd snap out of it and return to work.

Performing Useless Actions

I developed the habit of picking at the dead skin on my heels, peeling it off until the heels became as red and raw as my emotions. I doctored my concerns about unemployment by overeating—terribly self-indulgent for a happily married woman with two wonderful stepchildren living in a nice home in suburban Austin. I berated myself constantly for behaving as I did, and my guilt sucked me further into my deep black hole.

On my more energetic days, I'd pull the weeds and grass roots from the ten-foot oval bed in which we'd planted a small redbud, some live oaks, and a sprinkling of yaupon. By the time I'd worked my way around the bed a few days later, the weeds I'd started with had grown back. Sweating through one-hundred-degree heat to pull up grass roots was a thankless task, but I thought it might purge my pain. Instead, this activity became a metaphor for my life.

Anger and Frustration

Many experts define depression as anger turned inward, and I've seen some evidence of that in my life. Most depressed people wonder what they've done to deserve such pain. The illness frustrates them, and they become angry that they have it. Sometimes they take that anger out on others.

When I lived with my parents and entered a depressive state, I'd complain endlessly to my mother about every little thing. My moods were so hard for her to live with that I often secluded myself in the basement for hours.

Shortly after my worst suicide attempt, I developed a theory about the source of my depression. As a child, I was so angry and frustrated by my father's controlling, unpredictable behavior that I wanted to kill him. But through my Christian upbringing, I'd learned that you must honor your parents and never kill another human being. I knew I could never do it. Still, my evil thoughts made me conclude that I was extraordinarily bad.

I often prayed my parents would divorce so my sisters and I could live with Mother. When I was eight or nine, they nearly did, but I don't recall the discussion. Apparently, my sisters talked them into staying together "for my sake."

> *I FEEL* like stabbing myself over and over and over and over, severing my hands from my body, slamming my head against the wall until my skull's crushed to a pulp and there's nothing left of this selfish, cold, thoughtless, unloving, humorless, klutzy, inept, immature, unprofessional, disgusting, despicable, hideous, asinine, spineless, slutty, lush-faced, pathetic excuse for a human being.

In deep depression, I lose all control of my emotions and go into these awful states of grief. The slightest emotional experience produces violent sobs. Appearing in public is awful. Even joyful celebrations or cheerful music can unleash cascades of tears. It becomes impossible to attend an entire church service or a sports event without making several trips to a bathroom to cry and freshen up.

I've cried unceasingly for hours when I've been depressed. Such behavior baffled other people. They initially showed concern. Then they tried to cheer me up. Finally, most became impatient and disgusted and left me with a sorrow I couldn't even name.

I'd often wake up from dreams convulsing with grief. If I could, I'd isolate myself in a bathroom so my crying wouldn't disturb anyone. But when the crying came on too rapidly, my muffled sobs would wake up Ralph, who would do his best to comfort me. He often talked with me and held me for hours.

Substance Abuse

Many people numb depression with alcohol or drugs. Alcohol and drugs are *exceedingly dangerous* if you're suicidal, because they impair your judgment and loosen your inhibitions. Lots of depressed individuals also smoke excessively to quell anxieties or use caffeine in the attempt to chase away fatigue and boost their energy.

My alcohol and drug use occurred mostly in my hypomanic states, partially because I was more prone to party then. When depressed and alone, however, I sometimes drank an entire six-pack or a bottle of wine. Because my funds were usually limited and drinking gave me headaches fairly quickly, I rarely had more. And I never sprang for drugs.

But even television can become a sort of drug when you're depressed, because it helps your mind go numb. You may while away hours watching aimlessly and absorbing nothing. Or you may watch TV to remind yourself what "normal" life was like or to search for clues as to how "normal" people interact.

When I was severely depressed, television became my "drug" of choice. My habitual viewing got so out of control that I devised a system to ration my viewing time. At the start of each week, I'd place plastic tabs from bread packages in a pimento jar. Each tab represented one half hour of viewing time. Then, when each program started, I'd move a bread tab for each half hour it ran into a second jar. When I began running low on bread tabs, I'd turn off the TV. This seemed the only way to regain control.

Self-Destructive Thoughts and Actions

Suicidal thoughts, attempts, and "gestures" (halfhearted attempts) are the hallmarks of depression, as, of course, are "successful" suicides. Sometimes attempts are skillfully executed after months of careful planning; other times the person acts on impulse. Some methods require incredible strength and effort, as when someone crushes their own head in a vise. Other methods take little effort, as when a person sits in a running car and inhales its poisonous exhaust.

Much of my life, I've contemplated suicide. My suicidal thinking became so deeply engraved that it became like repeating lyrics on a vinyl record that kept the needle from finishing a song. At times, the thought comforted me enormously. I'd stretch out on my parents' living room carpet and practice being a corpse, willing my mind to blank and my breath to stop, and remaining incredibly still.

As an adult, I'd get powerful urges on the freeway to ram my car into the overpass support. I'd imagine the comforting crush of metal, the cheerful tinkling of glass, my soul happily escaping its fleshy prison.

Or I'd think about our house being just one lot away from the railroad tracks on which Amtrak trains and freight cars rumble by several times a day. I'd dream of lurking in the bushes at the edge of the track and waiting for the next train. I'd simply dart out in front of a passing locomotive and end it all.

Or perhaps I'd drown myself. Just the other side of our back fence is a spring-fed lake that formed in an old stone quarry. When the stone workers unearthed the spring, the lake filled up so fast that they couldn't retrieve the equipment. I'd envision myself with cinder blocks tied to my ankles, wading deeper and deeper into the quarry's waters on a moonless night. My body wedged amid the rusting machinery eighty feet down.

But what always stopped my "suicidal ideation," as the pros call it, was the thought of traumatizing highway drivers or the engineer who hit me. Or the idea that I might be rescued from the water but live on for years as a vegetable. How could I do that to my family?

I have my mother to thank for these conclusions. When I had shared my childhood sorrows with her, she'd point out a child who'd had polio and now walked with braces and crutches, or a child who was deaf or blind. I should be thankful. My parents could see nothing wrong with me; why couldn't I just be happy?! But happiness was not part of my repertoire. Sometimes I yearned for a more "respectable" affliction. Sometimes I needed someone who could understand my pain.

The Beginning Strands of Depression

When depression strikes alone, without mania or hypomania, it commonly surfaces between the ages of twenty and fifty. But it's also common in older adults and can even appear in infancy. Early-onset bipolar disorder often starts with a depressive episode. As with mania, depression in children, adolescents, and teens may be hard to distinguish from other disorders, such as social phobia or antisocial personality disorder.

When I was a child, my parents gently tried to humor me out of my dark moods by singing "Let the Sun Shine In," a song popular in the 1950s. Even total strangers would coax me to smile and "let the sun shine in." Their efforts only made me feel defective and pushed me further down.

I can't say for certain when my depressions started. I know only that it was quite early in life. Nor can I say precisely *why*. It wasn't as if my parents had beaten me or I'd come from a broken family. But, somehow, during my depressions, I just felt hopeless, weird, substandard. Starting in childhood and continuing into my thirties, I cried myself to sleep more often than not, sobbing silently into my pillow to muffle the sound, all the while being unable to understand why I felt so bad. And when I said my nightly prayers, I often prayed for release by having some tragic accident or getting some fast-acting incurable disease.

THREE

Losing All Hope: Suicide

YOU'VE BEEN STUCK *in this blackness, it seems, your whole life. Was life ever worth living? You can barely recall. If it once was, it was all an illusion. Or something has changed and your life will never be the same. The future holds nothing but pain for you. You can bring only sorrow to those you love. Clearly, they'd be better off without you.*

The mere idea of positive thinking—of trying to be optimistic—is a crock. Those who think otherwise are simply deluded. You cannot think yourself out of this illness, this curse. You will wear this albatross forever.

Whether you've fallen from three or four or five stories—or from solid ground to five stories under—you're at the bottom now. You can fall no farther. Life holds no promise. Nada. You can't walk that tightrope even one more time. For you, no solid ground exists. It never will. You're so tired of the struggle. So weary of having so little control. You've lost all hope. Admit it. It's time to check out.

The Permanent "Solution" to Your Temporary Problem

Although I had often thought of suicide—actually dwelled on it repeatedly—I never quite believed I would attempt it. I thought everyone considered suicide when they got depressed. I had made a halfhearted effort in college during my first year, when I tried to hang myself from the dorm stairwell. My roommate, Beth, came and pulled me back to safety. But that attempt was more an expression of anguish over a lost love than a sincere desire to die.

TEEN AND ADOLESCENT SUICIDE

BECAUSE TEENS and adolescents tend to be impulsive, they're at great risk of taking their lives. Their suicides may be triggered by

- Breakups with girlfriends or boyfriends
- Humiliating experiences
- Disciplinary action at school
- Trouble with the law
- "Unacceptable performance" in high-achieving perfectionists

My one serious attempt came much later. It was the summer after I left my "dream job." I'd been out of work for several months, with no good prospects in sight. Yet, I'd have been incapable of holding even a part-time job then had someone offered one.

What finally pushed me over the edge was a devastating piece of mail: My unemployment income was in jeopardy. We'd already been struggling because of my illness; without my unemployment checks, we couldn't make ends meet. When Ralph and I married, I was a vital young woman with a promising career, someone he doted on who could enhance his children's lives. Without this income, I'd be totally dependent—almost a parasite, in my view. Although Ralph's health insurance covered about half of my psychiatric care—a luxury compared to many insurance plans—we were falling deeper in debt with no end in sight, all because of me. We'd even had to refinance the house. How long would it be before Ralph would divorce me and I'd wind up alone on the street?

SOME WARNING SIGNS OF SUICIDE

- Depression accompanied by severe anxiety, agitation, or rage
- A previous suicide attempt
- Statements about wanting to die or being tired of living
- Giving away possessions, paying off debts, or updating a will
- Physical or emotional illness
- Loss of a spouse, child, or close friend, particularly if unexpected and sudden
- Excessive use of alcohol or drugs
- But, most important, a sense of hopelessness and helplessness

Earlier that spring, my favorite cat, Harriet, had turned up dead. Ralph found her when he went out for the morning paper. Harriet had been my special "baby." She snuggled on my lap each morning as I ate breakfast and read the paper—whether I invited her to or not. It was our little ritual, and here she was, dead on our front lawn. As I stood over her twisted little body, it became clear she hadn't been hit by a car. Our driveway bore signs of a scuffle—large paw prints mixed among bloody-looking streaks. Ralph said he'd seen a pair of German shepherds trotting down the block just as he came outside. The vet surmised that a "big playful dog" had shaken Harriet until her neck snapped. My "baby's" final moments must have been filled with horror.

My old friend Janet had called a couple of months before to break the news that our friend Meta had committed suicide. She'd made two other attempts before, and she'd finally succeeded. Third time's the charm, right? I could barely believe my ears. I thought Meta was so much better adjusted than I was. A child of divorce, she'd seen psychiatrists for years. I regretted that I'd turned down Meta's last invitation—to a barbecue at her new place. I had pretty well abandoned her once I'd married Ralph. And I never got around to returning her copy of *I'm OK—You're OK*. Perhaps Janet was mistaken. I called

Meta's old number and found it disconnected. When I phoned the bookstore where she had worked, her former coworker tearfully confirmed it. Meta really was gone. Perhaps she had the right idea.

As my spirits sank further, I attempted to reach my psychiatrist. It was late on a Friday afternoon, and he had left for the day. Then I tried to reach my therapist and got her answering machine. I hung up. No matter. What could they possibly have said to help me? That things would get better? They wouldn't. I was certain. I felt cursed, doomed. It would be this way forever.

IF YOU FEEL SUICIDAL

SUICIDAL FEELINGS are nothing to take lightly. If you feel strongly that life is no longer worth living, get help immediately.

- If you're in treatment, contact your psychiatrist or therapist. If they're unavailable, speak with one of their associates.
- Talk with your family doctor or a clergy member.
- Talk with a relative, neighbor, or trusted friend.
- If you attend a support group, contact a trusted group member.
- Ask someone to drive you to a psychiatric facility or the emergency room of a hospital.
- Contact a community mental health center or a mental health organization.
- Speak to someone at a suicide hotline, such as the National Hopeline Network: 1-800-784-2433 (1-800-SUICIDE), 1-888-784-2433 (1-888-SUICIDE), or the Girls and Boys Town National Hotline: 1-800-448-3000.
- If you're alone or severely agitated, call 911.

I concluded that Ralph and the kids would be better off without me. Much better off, actually, without this albatross in their lives. No great loss, really. And my parents had other daughters, who also had each other. Everybody would get over it in no time.

With scientific detachment, I determined a potentially fatal amount of medication by thumbing through a family prescription guide. I counted out just the right number of antidepressants from those I had on hand. Not so many that I'd throw up. Not so few that they'd merely sedate me.

I began a note, but I couldn't put my feelings into words. I was so damned inadequate, I couldn't do anything right. The mere effort of breathing exhausted me. But soon it would no more.

I set the reddish-brown tablets in a neat little row on my pillow and prepared to go to sleep for good. With long sips of ice water, I downed a few pills at a time and then stopped to see if I felt different. Nothing. I swallowed a few more, and then a few more until all of the pills were gone. Then I tossed in a couple of tranquilizers for good measure.

Even in the process of drugging myself, I couldn't completely understand my decision. Why was this happening *now*? I'd been through harder times, through much more traumatic experiences. Why hadn't I tried to kill myself then? My suicidal urges had poured out with so much emotion in the past. With such terrible intensity. Now I felt only bland resignation. I closed my eyes and envisioned my peaceful, cold corpse.

At the same time that I was wondering why I was trying to kill myself *that* day, I felt a sense of fulfilling destiny—I had no doubt I would take my life eventually. It seemed all I had to look forward to was a shallow obituary.

A HIGH-RISK TIME

PEOPLE JUST recovering from depression are at higher risk for suicide than when they're deeply depressed because they have more initiative and energy to act on suicidal thoughts.

About fifteen minutes later, I noticed with great irritability that I had to pee. Not about to die with wet pants, I got up and staggered to the bathroom. For a moment, my dizziness pleased me, and then I began to worry that I'd taken too few pills. That perhaps I'd botched the job, and I'd wind up a vegetable. A burden forever. I should have thought this through more carefully! What a screwup!

I stuck my finger down my throat, but I couldn't throw up. Still dizzy and nauseated, I panicked and called Ralph at work. He arranged for an ambulance, then called me right back. He kept me on the phone until EMS showed up.

By the time the ambulance arrived, I had managed to retch up a minuscule amount—unfortunately, at the foot of our bed on our beige carpet. One more thing to feed my guilt.

When the EMS staff took my vital signs and reported cardiac arrhythmia and central nervous system depression, I made a foggy mental note of my progress. They strapped me to a gurney, hooked me up to a portable oxygen unit, and rolled me out the door, through a gaggle of gawking neighbors. All nine miles to the hospital, the crew bombarded me with questions: "What's your name?" "What day is this?" "How many pills did you take?" "What were they?"

When Ralph met us at the emergency room, I was overcome with shame. One look at his face revealed that I'd done the last thing on earth I'd ever want to do—hurt the only human being from whom I'd ever experienced unconditional love. I felt like scum, yet Ralph stood by my side and held my hand at every opportunity.

The emergency room staff first gave me ipecac syrup to induce vomiting. When that failed, they had me drink a hideous activated charcoal solution to absorb the drugs. When I threw up the first cup, they gave me a second, but I couldn't hold anything down. So, a dour nurse prepared me for a gastric lavage to suction out my stomach. She attempted to thread a fat tube through one nostril, but it wouldn't go in. By the time she'd forced the tube through the other nostril and down into my gut, I felt like I'd been raped. When I complained, she scolded me for causing a scene and for all this "unnecessary trouble." At some point, one of my psychiatrist's associates had me admitted to the coronary care unit.

By morning, my vital signs had stabilized. Apparently, I hadn't done much damage. The admitting psychiatrist considered sending me to a local psychiatric hospital. But Ralph assured him that wasn't necessary, that he'd watch me closely the rest of the weekend. I rapidly agreed, both because of the stigma and because of the expense. I'd been so worried about being a burden, and here I was chalking up a big hospital bill. Although I promised both the doctor and Ralph that I'd never, ever try this again, at the time I meant only that I wouldn't try again with pills.

THE GRAVE DECEPTION

IT'S NOT that hard to convince others you're not suicidal when you actually are. In fact, nursing and medical staffs have considered more than half of those who killed themselves in psychiatric hospitals as "clinically improved" or "improving" just before their suicides.

Ralph took me home, and we spent the remainder of the weekend reconnecting. He showered me with so much love and attention that over the next several days, I became grateful I'd been saved.

The Folks You Leave Behind

Ten days later, I got the news about my sister Barbara, just after I got home from the gym. When Ralph greeted me in the driveway, I knew something was terribly wrong. "Your father just called," he said, carefully studying my face. I shifted my workout bag to my other hip and waited for him to continue. "He's got bad news about Barbara."

"Did she kill herself?" I blurted out. The conclusion came like a reflex; there was no real question in my mind. It felt odd that I didn't need to ask him to confirm it.

Waves of pain and guilt overcame me. I'd never consciously thought that Barbara might commit suicide, but at that moment it made perfect sense. She had written me several months before, clearly in need of help, but I'd been too steeped in my own troubles to respond. Could I have done something to save her? Could her death have been my fault?

I wondered how Mother was taking it and how long she and Daddy had known before they'd called. When I phoned back, Daddy said there would be two memorial services. One was to be at a church in Stillwater, Oklahoma, where Barbara and her new husband had been living. The other memorial was to be at my parents' house in Wichita, Kansas. Because Barbara had willed her body to science, there would be no burial. And because there'd be no body, her daughter, then married and living back east, decided not to attend either service. The first memorial would take place the following week.

Planning Barbara's memorial was like grasping at straws. No one in the family knew her well. Barbara was my half sister, the first of two children from my mother's first marriage. When Mother and her first husband divorced, she took Kay, who was then an infant, and her ex took Barbara, who was five. My father adopted Kay, who always lived with us. The following year my parents had my sister Jo. Then eight years after that, they had me.

Barbara had grown up spending some time with her father, who often left her behind in foster homes. Mother often didn't know just where Barbara was. But, off and on, they corresponded. After Barbara married, Mother visited her and her family. But because they lived out of state and travel was expensive, Mother always traveled alone.

Although Barbara never lived with my immediate family, I considered her just as much my sister as I did Kay and Jo. As I write these words, my grief floods back. I feel her loss as deeply as I would have had it been any other member of my family. No matter what sort of sister Barbara was, she was a sister of my soul.

I remember meeting her for the first time the summer after my senior year of high school. She and her adolescent daughter came to Wichita to visit, and Barbara and I bonded immediately. I felt as if I'd known her my entire life. Who could resist her warmth? Her expansive personality? She was such a free spirit, so much fun. A super seamstress, she stayed up all night and whipped up a bright red suit for me to wear at college. I had no clue she was probably in a hypomanic or manic state at the time.

When I was just out of grad school, Barbara came to visit me in Austin. We stayed up until all hours, comparing our love lives, our divorces, and our health problems. We shared the same challenges of severe mood swings and food addictions. In addition to having bipolar disorder, Barbara was challenged by alcoholism and was attending

AA meetings. She said I was the only person in the family who understood what she was going through.

SUBSTANCE ABUSE AND SUICIDE

- The majority of suicides involve a combination of alcohol and depression.
- Nondrinkers often drink to numb their pain and then indulge in risky actions, such as driving recklessly or playing Russian roulette.
- Alcohol and drugs increase impulsive behavior, and thereby the risk of suicide.
- *Suicidal people are not safe without sobriety.*

When I arrived in Wichita for the memorials, I had another shock in store. One of my nieces had slit her wrists in a suicide attempt a few weeks before mine and was now in a psychiatric facility. She and Barbara had also corresponded, and after Barbara's move to Stillwater, they learned that they, too, had much in common. Concerned about the way my niece would take the news of Barbara's death, my family decided not to tell her until she was "well enough to handle it." Of course, I felt too weak not to join in this deception, but I despised myself for hiding Barbara's death from my niece.

For Barbara's first memorial, my parents, my sister Kay, and I drove to Stillwater from Wichita in a tense little knot. My maternal grandmother's sister, Aunt Jeannette, then in her nineties, had come along as well. Although we'd spoken about the logistics of the memorials, we had not shared our feelings about Barbara's suicide. By the time we reached the small, stark church, some of my mother's brothers and their families and a few friends and parishioners sat scattered in the pews.

After the service, I made my way through the church pews to introduce myself to Barbara's husband. He was a Vietnam vet who had developed schizophrenia during the war, and I was concerned about how he was coping with her death. A few days before, I'd sent him some books about dealing with grief. Even though we'd never met, I felt an instant bond. We had both lost Barbara, and we both struggled with mental illness.

We'd barely begun to speak, when Aunt Jeannette's blue-gray head popped up between us. She grabbed his arm and asked, "What did Barbara die from?" I nearly fainted from shock that she had no idea! How could my parents not have told Aunt Jeannette what happened? Were they trying to "protect her," like they had my niece? Barbara's poor husband had problems enough. How horrible to be asked how his wife had died. Had I been in his shoes, I'd have felt like I'd been shot.

And what about the others? What had my parents told Mother's brothers and their families? Had they evaded the truth or lied to them too? How could they try to keep Barbara's suicide a secret?

Yet, wasn't I part of the conspiracy? Hadn't I always been? Certainly, in keeping her death a secret from my niece, I was covering up as much as they were.

Barbara's poor husband went white. For a while, he seemed to struggle to absorb the question. Then he gently replied, "She shot herself." And tears filled his eyes. "I didn't know she had a gun. . . . She seemed fine when I left for work. Then when I got home . . ." He shrugged and shook his head, "I didn't know. I didn't know she had a gun."

PASSING FOR "NORMAL"

SUICIDAL PEOPLE often appear normal shortly before they take their lives. Some potential reasons include:

- Once they've decided to kill themselves, they may foresee an end to their pain and anxiety.
- They may feel genuine relief during recovery but quickly switch to severe depression or a mixed mood during which they take their life.
- They may lie about their feelings so they'll be left alone to carry out their plans.

When the other guests had left the church, my family decided to go out for ice cream. That struck me as a bit incongruous. Then again, hadn't we always stuffed our faces to suppress our feelings? Barbara's husband came with us. At Braum's Ice Cream parlor, my relatives sat in close familial clumps while I visited with Barbara's husband across the room. After that awful night, I wrote him for a while, as did Mother, but he never wrote back, and eventually we all lost touch.

THE LEGACY OF SUICIDE

- Most people can't understand why someone would commit suicide. They're horrified and plagued by questions like "Why'd she do it?"
- Then there are those of us who understand this decision all too well.
- Others are angry at the person's "selfishness" or consider suicide an affront to God.
- Those left behind often feel rejected and bitter or helpless and lost.
- Many loved ones are left with unrelenting regret, pain, and guilt.
- And those who find the victim are left with unerasable images of horror.

The second memorial, which took place at my parents' home in Wichita three days later, was a more personal affair. We'd put it together long distance, each of us contributing a part. My family's beloved minister, Dr. Ronald Meredith, shared a few words of wisdom. Daddy did the introductions. Mother wrote a brief biography, from which we learned that Barbara loved the color blue, that her favorite creature was the butterfly, and that she was a free spirit who flitted wherever her spirit moved her.

I'd typed up the program on my computer and assembled small booklets before leaving Austin. They were hand-stitched, with a pale blue cover sporting a butterfly.

Since my sister Jo could not fly up from Florida, she sent a poem, "She's Only Gone On," by Helen Steiner Rice. I read one prayer and sang an adaptation of "Corner of the Sky" from my favorite musical, *Pippin*, accompanying myself on the piano. Aunt Jeannette played "How Great Thou Art" while everyone sang. Kay read a poem my niece once wrote, then played "Give Your Heart a Home," a Don

Francisco song she and her children treasured. Finally, Kay read the closing prayer. We adjourned and consumed a sheet cake.

BRINGING UP THE "S" QUESTION

PEOPLE OFTEN don't ask if someone is suicidal out of fear of the results. But letting the matter slide can be disastrous. When you suspect someone's considering suicide

- Take the person's feelings seriously.
- Reach out and listen without interrupting.
- Calmly ask questions without judging.
- Maintain eye contact and comfort the person.
- Don't try to argue the person out of it.
- Don't promise to keep the person's plans secret.
- Persuade the person to get help.
- If the person refuses help, arrange help on your own. If suicide seems imminent, call 911.

Barely a day passes when I don't think of Barbara and wonder if she might still be alive today had I been well enough to offer my support. Sometimes I feel that if we had only stayed in closer contact, it might have made a difference. It means a lot when someone fully accepts you—particularly someone aware of your imperfections and challenges. Had Ralph not been there for me, I could have easily wound up in Barbara's shoes.

While I'm no longer consumed with guilt over Barbara's death, I do believe that, as a society, we're all partially responsible. I can't help but think that if the world were more accepting of mental illness, we could all express ourselves more honestly and receive better treatment sooner. It just might help prevent such tragedies.

I like to think that when Barbara died, her spirit scattered and now empowers all the butterflies.

FOUR

Realizing There's a Problem: Recognition

Ever find yourself thinking things like . . .

I simply can't be sick or crazy, like everyone is saying. It's those people who are out of their minds! Can't they see I'm just trying to have a little fun? Everybody needs to cut loose sometimes.

There's nothing wrong with my judgment. Other people just don't happen to agree. They're too concerned with "being safe" to truly live their lives!

And it's a waste of time to go to bed when you're not the least bit tired. I've accomplished more in the last ten days than in the last ten months! I'll slow down when I'm ready. Others are jealous because they can't keep up with me. I'm fine.

If they can't understand what I'm saying, that's their problem. They're not listening carefully enough. I've never been so lucid. My thoughts so wonderfully clear. No one recognizes my brilliance. They just think I'm out of control. No one ever has any faith in me. And it's not as if their lives worked. They're like the walking dead! I'm perfectly all right. Better than all right. Fantastic! It's time they leave me the hell alone!

My boss can take that job and shove it. That anal-retentive asshole! I'd never have lost my temper if the rules weren't so ridiculous. That job's not good enough for me anyway. I have plenty of better options.

And that car wreck was an accident. Why can't people get that? Sure, maybe I was speeding, but it was clearly the other driver's fault. The fool practically stopped in the middle of the intersection! I never get a break. Everyone's against me.

Or have you ever thought . . .

Why won't they just let me sleep! Anyone who's been feeling the way I have would need a break too. It's natural to feel sad or cry occasionally. Everybody gets down sometimes. If they'd just let me be, I'd get over this. I've always survived these downers in the past.

And people should eat only when they're hungry. They should listen to their bodies. If I don't feel like eating, then I shouldn't! I could probably stand to lose the weight. And when I'm ravenous, it's because my body needs the fuel. People need food for energy. Don't these folks know anything?

What's the point in looking for a job when there's nothing out there? I wish these people would stop hassling me! I'm always too "underqualified" or too "overqualified" or too this or that. You only get hired if you fit people's exact requirements. No one's willing to give you a break.

It's the same with relationships. Everyone's looking for someone perfect. No one will give me a chance. No one has ever truly loved me. And no one ever will. Those who say that they're "concerned" don't really care. They just feel guilty. They'd probably be relieved if I were gone.

Life is so boring. So pointless. If only this horror would end.

If you identify with any of the previous thoughts, it's probably time—or past time—to seek treatment. *Don't stop reading now. This may be the most important information of your life.*

Risks of Not Seeking Treatment

Untreated or undertreated mood disorders bring all types of devastating consequences. Because mood disorders distort self-concept, attitudes, thinking, behaviors, relationships, perception, judgment, and reactions to every situation you encounter, they change the very essence of what makes you "you."

Common Risks

If your mood disorder goes untreated or undertreated for too long, you risk

- having your spouse or significant other get fed up and leave you;
- losing your children or your right to see them;
- having your family disown you;
- having your friends desert you;
- becoming socially isolated;
- missing work and getting fired, or missing school and getting expelled;
- having massive financial problems;
- losing all of your possessions;
- becoming dependent on underfunded government assistance;
- developing or worsening a substance abuse problem;
- winding up in jail; and
- becoming homeless and living on the street.

I personally know people who have faced every one of these problems. And a few of my family members and I have experienced some of these situations ourselves.

Deadly Risks

Suppose, for just a moment, that the people who've been "hassling" you have a point. That there's a valid reason for their concern. Suppose that they're seeing things more clearly than you are just now.

Do you plan to keep "walking your tightrope" over and over, never knowing when or how far it will rise and fall? Facing the same problems repeatedly?

And what if you *can't* manage your mood on your own this time? If you do have a mood disorder, you're at very high risk for suicide. This is *not* an exaggeration.

Is your resistance to treatment worth risking your *life*? Do you truly want to *die*? Don't you actually just want to escape your mood shifts and your pain?

MENTAL ILLNESS AND SUICIDE

- Without effective treatment, people with bipolar disorder commit suicide *at least fifteen to twenty times more often* than the general population, and those with unipolar disorder do so at least *twenty times more often.*
- Someone who has made a previous serious attempt is *at least thirty-eight times more likely* to commit suicide.
- Of those who commit suicide, at least *90 percent have a diagnosable—and often highly treatable—mental disorder.*

These are shocking statistics, because they represent a terrible waste of potentially productive and happy lives.

Those of us who have mood disorders now are much more fortunate than those who struggled with them in the past. Current treatments can significantly improve our lives and often prevent future episodes. And doctors are learning more about brain disorders every day.

"Coming to Terms" with Your Condition

Part of the stigma of mental illness relates to terminology.

Illness, Disease, and Disorder

We often associate the terms illness, disease, and disorder with bacteria, viruses, and germs. If you're sick, we say you have a "bug." But illnesses, diseases, and disorders are also associated with the following:

- Impairment, damage, or weakness of the body or mind
- Trouble, disquiet, lack of ease (*dis*–ease)
- An altered state that disrupts a bodily function
- A functional disturbance of the body and/or mind

Mood, Emotion, State, and Trait

Similarly, people confuse the terms mood, emotion, state, and trait. Here are some clarifications: While your *mood* may last from days to months, an *emotion* lasts only seconds to hours. A *state* describes your current frame of mind, and a *trait* describes a consistent characteristic of your personality.

Clinical Depression and the Blues

All too often people confuse the term depression with merely feeling "down" or having the blues. A more accurate name for mood disorders might be hypothalamic-pituitary-adrenal disorders. But that's a bit too tongue-twisting for everyday use.

What Is "Mental Illness"?

Mental illnesses involve behaviors, thinking, and perceptions that fall outside the bounds of what a particular culture or society perceives as "normal." They produce extreme moods and behaviors, confusion and chaos, faulty memories and perceptions, desperation and hopelessness.

Because mental illnesses also produce physical symptoms and often verifiable changes in the body, they're also clearly medical disorders. By bringing your brain to a normal state, treatment can greatly improve your life.

What Is "Normal" Anyway?

So how can you tell what's "normal" versus what's "mentally ill"? It's far from an either/or situation. All of us are saddened by a loss or elated by good news—at least for a while. But there's a chance you have a mood disorder if your moods

- are significantly different from the usual,
- are out of proportion or unrelated to what's happening in your life,
- keep you from functioning effectively, and
- last an unusually long time.

In such cases, it's probably time for treatment, but unfortunately, many people put it off.

Reasons People Put Off Treatment

The very thought of having a mood disorder brings up all sorts of questions and emotions.

FEAR—Your brain represents your very essence and identity. And virtually no one finds the term mentally ill a compliment. "Brain disorder" takes away some of the sting, yet it's still terrifying to realize that something may be wrong with your mind. But not seeking treatment won't make a mood disorder disappear.

STIGMA—You may worry about what others will think and be concerned that you'll be labeled "crazy." You may fear that others—even family members and close friends—will reject you. Or you may think you'll lose your job. It's true that many people still don't realize that mood disorders are physical illnesses just as deserving of treatment and respect as other medical conditions. But we're slowly educating our society on that fact.

Other conditions have brought similar public relations problems. Reading almost like the alphabet, a few include asthma, cancer, diabetes, epilepsy, hypertension, mental retardation, and ulcers. As people learn more about conditions, they tend to fear them less, and their stigma begins to fade. People become more compassionate and understanding.

EMOTIONS—You may be ashamed or embarrassed that you can't control your moods. That's a common reaction. But please realize that you are much more than your moods, and *mood disorders are nobody's fault*. Plus, it's not as if you're alone. Mental illness is almost epidemic. Each year, more than one quarter of the adults eighteen and over in the United States experience some type of mental disorder. Rather than the rarities many people think they are, mental illnesses are among the most common health conditions today.

MEDICATION—You may dislike or fear taking medication. Particularly if your disorder is bipolar rather than unipolar, you may believe that medication will drain the joy from life. But *real* joy comes from having a healthy body, safety and security, loving relationships, realistic self-esteem, growth and learning, self-expression, peace, and contributing to society. And more and better medications are appearing all the time.

COST—You may be concerned about managing the costs of doctors, medications, and possibly hospitalizations. Can you meet out-of-pocket costs? If you have insurance that covers treatment, are there limitations you must consider? It's true that care is expensive and that in many states mental health coverage tends to lag behind that for other physical illnesses. But we're coming closer to obtaining *parity*—equal coverage for both mental and physical illnesses.

Or you may wonder how to get coverage if you don't have health insurance at all. If that's your situation, the Resources section at the back of this book suggests some starting points.

DISBELIEF—You may not believe that what's troubling you is actually a mood disorder. And it may very well not be. A number of other medical conditions can cause signs and symptoms of mood disorders. Chapter 6 describes many of them. It's possible you have something much more benign or much more serious, but unless you seek treatment, you may never know.

GRIEF—In some ways, accepting mental illness is like accepting death. People go through stages of grief similar to those that Dr. Elisabeth Kübler-Ross described: denial and isolation, anger and rage, bargaining (by delaying treatment), depression (in the sense of feeling loss and helplessness), and finally accepting reality.

Admitting You Need Help

For most of us, actually coming out and asking for help is extremely difficult. Forty-four percent of the respondents to a National Depressive and Manic-Depressive Association survey waited at least five years before they sought treatment. That's *five years* during which they might have been productive, stable, and less disturbed. Quite a high price to pay. The sooner you get effective treatment, the sooner you get your life back.

If you're like most of us, during depression you're more likely to acknowledge you're not feeling well and to seek treatment. But during mania or hypomania, you may feel so good, so right, it's hard to believe something is wrong. You may be convinced it's everyone else who has the problem.

Helping Others Recognize Your Need for Treatment

Sometimes people don't recognize mental illness at all, particularly if symptoms aren't pronounced. People in full-blown episodes are more likely to get treated. But less conspicuous forms of mood disorders often go unnoticed.

Acknowledging "Milder" Forms of Mood Disorders

You can be thoroughly depressed and miserable or mildly hypomanic for *years* without anybody knowing. It's akin to having "walking pneumonia." Your symptoms may not be apparent, but you don't feel like yourself. You may be up and around and not realize that you're sick. But you certainly don't feel normal.

Until signs and symptoms become severe, depression and hypomania may be nearly invisible. So you struggle on alone. Oddly enough, the people you interact with may be less distressed when you're depressed. But hypomania often bothers them more because you may become impatient and criticize them rather than yourself. I sometimes resent the fact that my husband is more comfortable with me when I'm down.

Early episodes of bipolar disorder all too frequently go undiagnosed. But early diagnosis and treatment are crucial to stave off or reduce the intensity of future episodes. Without effective treatment, mood disorders nearly always worsen.

Discounting Labels and Judgments

People around you view your symptoms as shortcomings: "It's always about you you you. . . . Must you always draw attention to yourself? . . . Go away. You're scaring me!"

Or discount your feelings: "You're making mountains out of molehills. . . . Just get over it! . . . Cheer up and give us a smile."

Or label and judge you: "You're immature . . . undisciplined . . . lazy. You idiot! You crybaby. You slob."

Then there are those who offer unrealistic "solutions": "Start a family so you won't be so self-absorbed. . . . Just take time to smell the roses. . . . Come pray with me and you'll soon feel fine."

EDUCATING OTHERS ABOUT YOUR NEED FOR TREATMENT

LEARN EVERYTHING you can about mental illness and mood disorders. Then share it with those you trust. This book offers a starting point.

If you can't get treatment on your own, ask someone you trust to help you. Try statements like "I really need some help. I think I have a mood disorder. I need to see someone about it as soon as possible."

If necessary, have the person set up an appointment with a mental health professional for you and even accompany you if you prefer not to go alone.

Dealing with Naysayers

Admittedly, not everyone believes that mental illness even *exists* or that psychiatry is a viable option. They may find doctors and medications suspect. Opponents often argue that psychiatrists and drug companies exploit patients, that medications cause brain damage, that psychiatric treatment destroys religion, or that those with mental illness can cure themselves by tapping the power of their brains.

Based on my own experience, however, I strongly disagree. My life has improved tremendously since I've been receiving regular treatment. And the same is true for many other patients that I know.

At any rate, you may run into opponents like the following.

FORMER PATIENTS

Some naysayers have been treated for mental illness themselves. Frequently, they were hospitalized long ago, were overmedicated, or restrained or isolated too long during hospitalization. A couple of decades ago, my niece experienced some of these problems when hospitalized, which made her resist further treatment for many years. Sometimes patients do receive higher doses of medications to get them out of a severe episode when they first enter the hospital. Psychiatrists generally reduce such doses, however, as quickly as they can.

Treatment methods and patients' rights have improved significantly in the past decade or so. We've learned so much more about the brain and biochemistry, and we're constantly learning more. Now, most psychiatrists prescribe the lowest amount of medication a patient needs to manage his or her disorder. Hospitals treat patients with greater respect and let them retain more rights. But many former patients still view psychiatry with suspicion and advocate actively against any form of psychiatric treatment.

SCIENTOLOGISTS

One well-known critic of psychiatry is L. Ron Hubbard, author of *Dianetics* and founder of the Church of Scientology. Hubbard views psychiatric professionals as aliens out to control our minds.

Scientologists blame psychiatry for destroying religion and for the demise of education. They claim that large numbers of psychiatrists and psychologists are seriously mentally ill atheists who sexually abuse their patients. The Scientology-affiliated Citizens Commission on Human Rights (CCHR) advocates against psychiatrists and psychotropic medications and adamantly opposes the use of psychotropic medications for children. Unfortunately, such scare tactics spread misinformation that discourages patients from getting treatment and blocks advocacy efforts for services they sorely need.

"NEW AGE" THINKERS

"New Age" movements often oppose treatment too. Some discourage psychotropic medications and encourage followers to rely on the power of their brains. These movements may rely extensively on affirmations and visualizations. These are powerful techniques when you're well enough to access them, but using affirmations and visualizations is virtually impossible when your brain is malfunctioning.

Finding Effective Treatment and Sticking with It

Assuming you get into treatment, the next hurdle is to find what options work best for you. Most often, the most effective treatment involves a combination of medication, psychotherapy, and lifestyle changes. You should examine the suggestions from which you can pick and choose. Don't let the possibilities overwhelm you. Add them only when you feel ready, and don't add too many at a time.

The trickiest hurdle for most of us is complying with a treatment regimen. Once you've been in treatment and you're feeling better, it's easy to believe you're "cured." You may doubt you had a mental illness in the first place. You may be tempted to stop taking medication to test whether you really need it. But *don't just stop treatment on your own!* Psychiatric wards and morgues are full of folks who have done just that.

Hospitalization

Although community-based treatment is often preferable, sometimes a hospital is the safest place to be.

Two Kinds of Hospitalization

If you clearly need hospitalization, you can admit yourself voluntarily, or in extreme circumstances, be forced to go.

VOLUNTARY COMMITMENT

When you sign into a hospital voluntarily, you can leave shortly after the treating psychiatrist feels it will be safe. Some states require a written release; others don't. Given patients' rights and the difficulty of keeping people in the hospital due to insurance limitations, it's unlikely you'll be forced to stay unless you really need to.

INVOLUNTARY COMMITMENT

In the past, involuntary commitment may have been a way to get rid of an embarrassing or difficult relative. But because of greater sensitivity to patients' rights, it's a rarity these days. You generally must be considered a danger to yourself or to others to be involuntarily admitted to a psychiatric unit. At most facilities, symptoms must be quite severe for an involuntary commitment. And once you've been admitted, procedures are in place to ensure that you're not detained unnecessarily.

Protecting Your Rights When You Are Ill

Thanks to mental health patients and advocates, people with mental illness now retain extensive rights during hospital stays. And if you feel those rights have been violated, you have several options for addressing your concerns.

If you have a mood disorder and don't trust that you'll be treated appropriately if you become severely ill, you have some legal options for maintaining some control. Two of these, for which you should consult a lawyer are 1) a Power of Attorney for Health Care, and 2) an Advance Directive for Mental Health Treatment.

POWER OF ATTORNEY FOR HEALTH CARE

This document allows you to appoint a person you trust to act on your behalf and make health care decisions for you if you become too incapacitated to make them yourself. This is one simple way to communicate your wishes about mental health treatment.

ADVANCE DIRECTIVE FOR MENTAL HEALTH TREATMENT

If you have recurrent episodes, particularly if severe and likely to require hospitalization, it's a good idea to obtain an Advance Directive. This legal document outlines your treatment preferences if you become incapable of expressing them at some point in the future.

Some of major points an Advance Directive may cover include

- what **psychotropic medications** (medications that affect the mind) you will accept, if any,
- whether you will allow **electroconvulsive therapy** (shock therapy), and
- your preference for emergency treatment, such as restraint, seclusion, or medication.

Advance Directives are sometimes more complex and complicated. Some states place a limit on the length of time such a document is in effect. In Texas the limit is three years. As long as you're not incapacitated, you may revoke an Advance Directive at any time.

You must take responsibility for your disorder—not in the sense that it's your fault, because it isn't—but in the sense that your recovery is ultimately on *your* shoulders. No doctor, medicine, or treatment facility can cure a severe mood disorder. They can only help you manage your disorder.

Continued compliance with treatment is the best way to control a mood disorder. Most of the time, this requires a lifelong commitment. But, trust me, it's well worth it. With the right combination of medication, diet, exercise, sleep, therapy, and stress reduction, you can very likely lead a productive—or even extraordinary—life.

If you're not sure what symptoms should concern you, chapter 5 should help clarify when it's time to seek help.

PART TWO

Separating Strands

FIVE

Probing the Pathology: Diagnosis

GETTING TO THE HEART of bipolar disorder can be like teasing knots out of a rope. If you're experiencing depression when you first see a doctor, a history of **mania** or **hypomania** may be overlooked. Or, if you're having a psychotic episode or displaying paranoia, your doctor may misdiagnose you as having *schizophrenia* (a thought disorder characterized by false beliefs and *hallucinations*). The fact that stressful situations often launch depressive, hypomanic, or manic episodes also complicates diagnosis. It can be hard to separate a **pathological** (abnormal or disease-related) response from a normal reaction to a stressful situation—like a divorce, a death in the family, or a challenging job. What's more, such situational or normal moods can become abnormal if they last too long.

Dr. Peter Whybrow clarifies that it's time to seek treatment

- when your sadness or joy persists for days or even weeks;
- when your mood colors everything you do; and
- when your sleep, appetite, and even thoughts become disturbed.

What's important in diagnosis is the overall picture, or *syndrome* (combined signs and symptoms that point to one cause), rather than isolated symptoms. This chapter will help you decide if you or a loved one should seek help. But *don't* use it as a substitute for professional diagnosis and treatment. *Never take this illness lightly!* Doing so can be a *fatal* mistake.

What Is a Mood Disorder?

Bipolar disorder is a **mood disorder**—a condition whose primary feature is a disturbance of mood. You may feel euphoric, angry, or irritable; you may feel dejected, hopeless, or apathetic. All of these are normal feelings, but they often indicate a mood disorder when their intensity and duration differ significantly from "the norm." Even though mood disorders primarily affect moods, they also produce significant physical symptoms and affect thinking and behavior.

Who Should You See for Treatment?

If you suspect you have a mood disorder, you'll most likely need a professional to confirm it. This may be a *general practitioner* (such as your family physician) or a *psychiatrist*.

General practitioners vary widely in their knowledge about mental illness. Few have the time or interest to keep up on new developments with all of the medications and other treatments available for mood disorders. I therefore strongly recommend that you see a psychiatrist, at least initially.

Don't put off getting help in the hope that your symptoms will simply disappear, even if other people think your symptoms are "no big deal." You'll only cause yourself needless suffering.

Initially, my depressions limited my everyday activities only slightly. When I tried to discuss my moods with friends and family, they would blame the moods on stressful situations, advise me to lighten up or change my attitude, or simply laugh them off. But it's the rare person who can just *will* this illness away.

As I became more impaired, I was consumed—and even comforted—by my suicidal thoughts. If things got too unbearable, I thought, I'd simply "check out."

How Should You Prepare for Your Appointment?

Before you see your doctor, list and prioritize your symptoms. Ask those you live with to contribute to the list. They may have observed symptoms you're unaware of, particularly if you're currently experiencing an episode.

Force yourself to discuss what's bothering you most early on in your appointment. If you put it off, you may run out of time and not get a chance to bring it up.

You can help your doctor diagnose you more quickly and accurately if you chart your mood symptoms, the traumatic events you've experienced, any diet and exercise changes you've made, and the medications, drugs, and alcohol you've used throughout your life. Such visual records often reveal significant patterns.

Getting a Diagnosis

As of this writing, no definitive test can confirm bipolar disorder nor reveal how severe your illness is. Getting an accurate diagnosis can therefore take awhile—particularly if you're not in the grips of a severe episode. Remember, each doctor visit reveals only a snapshot of your thoughts, feelings, and behaviors, not the full-length version of your life. Unless you or someone else reveals *all* of your symptoms, no one can get a clear picture of everything that's going on. This is one reason hospitalization can be helpful; someone will be observing you daily.

Communicating Your Symptoms

Even when you try to convey everything to a doctor, revealing every single symptom is a formidable task. Most doctor visits are limited these days, so it's a challenge to fit in everything. Don't expect the doctor to ask about every possible symptom. A National Depressive and Manic-Depressive Association study found that the majority of doctors ask fewer than half of their depressed patients if they've also experienced manic symptoms. You must take responsibility for making all of your symptoms known.

One reason people don't communicate all of their symptoms to their doctors is that they may not even *know* that some symptoms relate to the illness. When I first sought treatment, it was for the depressions I'd experienced over many years. Because I'd experienced so much low-grade depression, I viewed my hypomanic episodes as my natural, normal, healthy state. As a result, I didn't even think of mentioning hypomanic symptoms to most of the doctors and therapists I saw. In some cases, I didn't even recognize my experiences as symptoms. This book will help you determine what symptoms you need to bring up.

Particularly with less flagrant forms of bipolar disorder, some of us put on a front—even for our doctors. After all, we don't want them to think we're crazy. We may be embarrassed by our condition or fear they'll put us away forever. Both of these concerns are unfounded. There's no need to be embarrassed. *This illness is not your fault—or anyone else's.* If you go into a hospital, it's unlikely you'll be there very long. Today's treatments are much more effective than they were even a decade or two ago. And bipolar disorder is so treatable that many of us receive treatment entirely on an outpatient basis.

Working with Your Doctor

There's a real art to talking effectively with medical professionals. Often they are short of time, impatient, and speak in acronyms and technical terms unfamiliar to those outside the medical profession. Don't let the doctor intimidate you. Ask questions when you need to, and get clarifications when you don't understand the answers. If the doctor uses acronyms and technical language, request definitions and restatements in simpler terms.

Remember that *you* are the client here, so you need to take charge.

charge. (But if you need to remind the doctor of that fact, do so in a respectful and pleasant manner.) Think of you and your doctor in terms of a partnership working together to help you get better.

Take careful notes and verify that you understood the doctor correctly. Enter the relationship in a spirit of mutual respect and cooperation. If the doctor won't work with you on that basis, it's time to move on.

Factors Doctors Consider in Making Psychiatric Diagnoses

Medical professionals characterize illnesses by their *symptoms* (the typical problems they cause) and *signs* (the doctors' physical findings). Symptoms alone aren't enough to rely on for three primary reasons:

- Other illnesses often share similar symptoms.
- Different people perceive and explain the same symptoms in different ways.
- Sex, age, personality, upbringing, culture, memory, and recent experiences affect what symptoms get reported and their severity.

A psychiatric diagnosis therefore usually involves a combination of factors:

- **WHAT YOU AND YOUR FAMILY COMMUNICATE ABOUT YOUR THOUGHTS, FEELINGS, AND BEHAVIORS.** How are you different from your usual self? Or, if you've gone untreated for years and have had few periods of normalcy, how do you differ from other people? Do your friends and family members describe you as mercurial or having a split personality?
- **A THOROUGH HISTORY OF YOUR OWN HEALTH AND THAT OF YOUR RELATIVES.** Researchers have identified eight separate chromosomes that they currently believe link to bipolar disorder and make people more vul-

nerable to emotional and physical stress. Such stresses often trigger depressive, hypomanic, or manic episodes.

- **A COMPLETE PHYSICAL EXAM AND LABORATORY TESTS.** Your doctor will need to rule out other conditions that can cause depressive symptoms (such as thyroid disease, immune system disorders, cancer, nutritional deficiencies, toxicities, and drug or alcohol problems). Your lab tests might include a complete blood count; tests to check your thyroid, kidney, and liver functions; chemistry panels to check your electrolytes, glucose, and vitamin and mineral levels; a urinalysis and stool exam; and so on.

- **ELECTRONIC AND COMPUTERIZED BRAIN SCANS.** Several noninvasive electronic or computerized technologies may help reveal functional or structural irregularities in the brain. Common tests include the **EEG (electroencephalogram)**, which measures brain wave activity, and **CT (computed tomography)**, **MRI (magnetic resonance imaging)**, **PET (positron-emission tomography)**, and **SPECT (single photon-emission computed tomography)**, all of which produce computerized images of the brain. Unfortunately, most functional brain irregularities tend to be visible only when you're in the midst of an episode. And researchers don't yet know whether such irregularities contribute to or result from mood disorders.

- **PSYCHOLOGICAL ASSESSMENT RESULTS.** Mental health professionals often rely on written tests, scales, and interview tools to gather information about your thoughts, feelings, and behaviors.

- **DSM-IV.** Since 1952, doctors have relied on a book called the *Diagnostic and Statistical Manual of Mental Disorders* to diagnose mental illnesses. This book, often referred to as the DSM, is currently in its fourth and fourth revised editions: *DSM-IV* and *DSM-IV-TR* (Text Revision). A committee of doctors and scientists write each edition of the DSM and revise the book as their knowledge about psychiatry and brain disorders grows. The DSM lists criteria that tend to accompany different psychiatric disorders. These criteria relate to mood, feelings, activity level, energy, sleep, appetite, self-esteem, thinking, decision making, concentration, and so on. The charts later in this chapter list some of the criteria for depressive and manic disorders, based on *DSM-IV*.

- **THE DOCTOR'S CLINICAL OPINION ABOUT YOUR PRESENT STATE.** Of course, this is subjective and varies with individual doctors. And symptoms aren't always thoroughly defined. The DSM does not, for instance, precisely explain what counts as a spending spree or a sexual indiscretion—two potentially risky activities that frequently occur with hypomanic and manic states.

Types of Mood Disorders

Let's take a closer look at the major types of mood disorders: unipolar and bipolar disorder. With a **unipolar disorder**, you have depressive episodes but no manic or hypomanic episodes. With a **bipolar disorder**, you have manic or hypomanic episodes. And usually, but not always, you have depressive episodes of varying intensity as well.

Manic and Depressive Episodes

People tend to consider mania and depression to be exact opposites, just as the term bipolar (two poles) and the following diagram imply. And, for many people with the illness, that's fairly accurate.

I used to think that bipolar disorder involved *constant* flip-flops between mania and depression with no normal periods in between. That's how it often felt to me. But most adults with bipolar disorder function normally between episodes, even for years at a time. An average number of episodes over a ten-year period is four depressive and/or manic (or hypomanic) episodes.

THE BIPOLAR MOOD CONTINUUM

Mania

Hypomania
(mild to moderate mania)

Joyfulness
"Normal"/ "Balanced" Mood
"The Blues"

Mild to Moderate Depression

Severe Depression

A CLOSER LOOK AT DEPRESSIVE EPISODES

The two basic types of unipolar disorder are major depressive disorder and dysthymic disorder. **Major depressive disorder** tends to be more severe and episodic; **dysthymic disorder** tends to be a milder, chronic form. The following chart, based on *DSM-IV,* lists the major signs and symptoms for both unipolar and bipolar depressive episodes, and distinguishes between those for major depression and dysthymia. The authors of *DSM-IV* chose these signs and symptoms primarily with adults in mind.

TABLE 1

Depression in Unipolar or Bipolar Disorder

Major Signs and Symptoms	Major Depression	Dysthymia
■ Sadness, emptiness, and/or tearfulness (Children and adolescents may be irritable instead.) ■ Significantly decreased interest or pleasure in all or nearly all of your usual activities (Subjective or observed by others)	Consists of first or second symptom, plus four or more others	Consists of first or second symptom, plus two or more others
■ Decreased energy or fatigue ■ Sleeping significantly more or less than usual ■ Decrease or increase in appetite and/or loss or gain of more than 5 percent of body weight within a month without dieting (Children may not weigh enough to meet expected standards.)	Symptoms present most of the day nearly every day for at least two weeks	Symptoms present most of the day nearly every day for at least two years without subsiding for more than two months
■ Difficulty thinking, concentrating, or making decisions ■ Slowed body movements, or an increase in nonproductive, repetitious actions (like fidgeting, hand wringing, and pulling on clothes or hair, etc.) (Must be observed by others) ■ Feelings of worthlessness or excessive or inappropriate guilt (Not just because you're depressed) ■ Suicidal thoughts, plans, or attempts	Focus is more on actions.	Focus is more on thoughts.

Note that these signs and symptoms must represent an uncharacteristic change from your normal state and be intense enough to prevent you from functioning effectively, either socially or at work or school.

Although psychiatrists once thought that children were too emotionally immature to develop clinical depression, they now know that even infants can be significantly depressed. More than half of the adults with depression experienced their first episode before they turned twenty, and the majority experienced their first depressive episode by adolescence.

CHILDHOOD AND ADOLESCENT DEPRESSION

IN ADDITION to the signs and symptoms that adults with unipolar disorder have, children and adolescents may

- Lack enthusiasm or motivation
- Be unusually clingy or have separation anxiety
- Cry easily or excessively
- Be fascinated by morbid topics
- Complain frequently of physical problems, such as headaches and stomachaches

An estimated one-third of children and adolescents with clinical depression in the United States may actually be displaying the early onset of bipolar disorder.

A Closer Look at Manic and Hypomanic Episodes

The three basic types of bipolar disorder are

- **bipolar I** (the classic florid form that people tend to associate with the term manic depression);
- **bipolar II** (sometimes called soft bipolar, in which hypomania occurs in place of mania); and
- **cyclothymic disorder** (a mild but chronic form of the illness).

The following chart, also based on *DSM-IV,* lists the major signs and symptoms of manic and hypomanic episodes, again chosen primarily with adults in mind.

TABLE 2

Manic and Hypomanic Episodes in Bipolar (but Not Unipolar) Disorder

Major Signs and Symptoms	Mania	Hypomania
■ Exaggerated self-confidence and optimism	Consists of three or more symptoms if mood is elated or expansive, or four or more if mood is irritable	Consists of three or more symptoms if mood is elated or expansive, or four or more if mood is irritable
■ Decreased need for sleep without loss of energy		
■ More talkative than usual		
■ Sense that thoughts are racing	May or may not include delusions or hallucinations	May not include delusions or hallucinations
■ Distractibility and difficulty focusing	May or may not require hospitalization to prevent harming yourself or others	
■ Increase in goal-directed activities or nonproductive activities like pacing, squirming, and so on		
■ Planning and carrying out potentially risky activities (foolish business investments, reckless driving, sexual indiscretions, spending sprees)	Without hospitalization, symptoms must be present for at least one week; with hospitalization, symptoms may be present for anylength of time.	Symptoms present for at least four days

Just as young children can develop unipolar disorder, they can also develop bipolar disorder. When the illness begins in childhood or early adolescence, it tends to be slightly different and sometimes more severe. Providing your doctor with a thorough family history is crucial. When children display even subclinical signs and symptoms of bipolar disorder, early treatment can be beneficial and may offset the disorder's typical worsening course.

IN ADDITION to the signs and symptoms that adults with bipolar disorder display, children and adolescents may show

- Significant hyperactivity and distractibility
- Excessive involvement in multiple projects and activities
- Explosive, lengthy tantrums and rages
- Daredevil behaviors and play that involves excessive aggression or sad themes
- Defiance of authority and serious acting-out behaviors, such as stealing and vandalism
- Strong and frequent cravings, often for carbohydrates and sweets

In children and young adolescents, bipolar disorder often begins with major depression. They may display more irritability and disruptive behaviors, particularly initially, making their illness hard to distinguish from developmental problems and other disorders. Their mood may also shift rapidly from mania to depression several times a day.

Older adolescents and adults tend to first have a manic episode. Their illness is usually more episodic, with stable periods in between.

Age of Onset

While unipolar disorders tend to emerge between one's twenties and fifties, they also occur in up to one-third of children and 12 to 13 percent of adolescents. Bipolar disorders usually emerge earlier. Historically, the average age at which bipolar disorder has been diagnosed was eighteen to twenty-four. But, nearly 90 percent now report that their symptoms began before the age of twenty or even during childhood. The disorder rarely emerges after one's fifties.

Researchers believe that early-onset and late-onset bipolar disorder may involve different factors or even be entirely different disorders. In one study comparing older adults with late-onset versus early-onset bipolar disorder, those with the late-onset form reported

- fewer family histories of psychiatric problems,
- less frequent stressful life events,
- better social support systems, and
- more problems with *vascular* (blood-vessel-related) disease.

It appears that physical illnesses are a significant contributor to late-onset bipolar disorder.

Differences Between the Sexes

Although bipolar disorder is equally distributed between the sexes, women with the illness typically have more depressive episodes and men have more manic episodes. The hormonal fluctuations that come with menstruation, oral contraception, fertility treatments, childbirth, and menopause may at least in part explain this difference.

Criteria for Bipolar Diagnoses

The following table, based on *DSM-IV* as well, summarizes the distinctions among the three basic types of bipolar disorders. These criteria were formed primarily with adults in mind.

TABLE 3

Basic Types of Bipolar Disorders

Type	Duration	Symptoms
BIPOLAR I	One week if not hospitalized, or any length of time if hospitalization is necessary	One or more manic or mixed episodes, usually with major depressive episodes
BIPOLAR II	Four days	One or more major depressive episodes, with at least one hypomanic episode
CYCLOTHYMIA	Two or more years	Several hypomanic episodes and periods of depressive symptoms, without meeting the criteria for major depressive episodes

Because bipolar II and cyclothymia produce less-dramatic symptoms, they're more likely to go unrecognized. People in full-blown episodes tend to seek help themselves or have others seek it for them. But people who display milder symptoms tend to struggle on alone, frustrating themselves as well as their friends and families, who don't understand what's going on. Meanwhile, the disorders become more severe. One-third of those with cyclothymic disorder, for instance, tend to develop a more serious form of bipolar disorder in time.

Bipolar I and cyclothymia are fairly equally distributed in men and women, but more women than men have bipolar II disorder.

Two other forms of bipolar disorder are especially challenging to diagnose and to treat. These are the mixed and rapid cycling forms.

MIXED EPISODES

People having **mixed episodes** may feel sad, hopeless, and suicidal as well as extremely energized. The following diagram illustrates where a mixed episode might fit on a mood continuum. Mixed episodes involve both depression and mania nearly every day for at least one consecutive week.

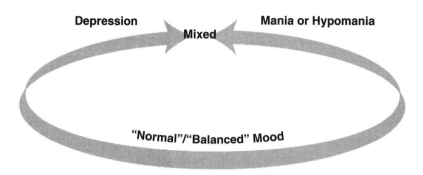

MIXED EPISODES

Depression   Mixed   Mania or Hypomania

"Normal"/"Balanced" Mood

People in mixed episodes may be particularly in danger because they have enough energy to act on any suicidal feelings.

RAPID CYCLING

Rapid cycling involves manic or hypomanic and depressive symptoms that alternate as often as several times a year, several times a month, or even several times a day. A diagnosis of rapid cycling involves having four or more depressive, manic, hypomanic, and/or mixed episodes in any combination within a single year. Most people who rapid–cycle do so sporadically rather than continuously. Rapid cycling complicates diagnosis, especially when stress triggers an episode.

Up to half of those with bipolar disorder experience temporary rapid cycling at some point, but most can be stabilized with treatment. Some people rapid cycle for a while when their illness starts, but rapid cycling is most common in those who have gone far too long without treatment or with inadequate treatment. Tricyclic antidepressants can shift some people with less recurrent forms of bipolar disorder into rapid cycling.

Women may be slightly more likely to rapid cycle, perhaps because of their monthly hormonal fluctuations. However, the *DSM-IV-TR* cautions doctors not to diagnosis rapid cycling when a woman's mood shifts appear to link only to a phase of menstruation.

Children with bipolar disorder tend to experience more mixed episodes, more rapid cycling, and less level time between episodes.

Other Variations

Seasonal Affective Disorder

In **seasonal affective disorder (SAD)**, symptoms vary with the season, weather, and level of light. Many people with SAD sink into depression during dark, dreary weather (November through March in many United States climates), and then brighten up on sunny days. The most likely causes of SAD are an out-of-sync internal body clock and an imbalance of hormones and **neurotransmitters** in the brain.

> HORMONES—chemical regulators that work constantly to keep the body in a state of stability and balance, or **homeostasis**. Hormones control growth and development, sexual activity and reproduction, blood pressure, heart rate, body temperature, appetite, energy level, and stress response.
>
> NEUROTRANSMITTERS—chemical messengers that relay signals between adjacent nerve cells in the body

People with SAD often find that light therapy relieves or improves SAD symptoms. Chapter 14 has more on light therapy.

Schizoaffective Disorder

Psychosis (losing touch with reality) sometimes accompanies severe manic or depressive episodes. Psychotic symptoms include **hallucinations** (sensing things that aren't actually there) and **delusions** (fixed false beliefs that others can't reason you out of despite evidence that they're not true). It's common to be misdiagnosed with schizophrenia when you're experiencing severe bipolar mania. But when people with bipolar or unipolar disorder experience psychotic symptoms even after their moods stabilize, they may actually have **schizoaffective disorder**—schizophrenia plus a mood disorder.

DSM-IV also includes some catch-all labels that doctors use when symptoms don't meet the criteria for any of these disorders: depressive disorder not otherwise specified, bipolar disorder not otherwise specified, mood disorder not otherwise specified, and so on. And it's possible to suffer simultaneously from more than one psychiatric disorder at a time.

Diagnostic Complications

One further factor that complicates diagnosis is the way that mood disorders tend to change over time. Untreated or undertreated, they tend to worsen with age. People who have dysthymia in childhood tend to get more severely depressed in adolescence, and many develop bipolar disorder later on.

This seems to have been the case for me. Over the years during which I've been in ongoing treatment, my diagnosis has changed from dysthymia to cyclothymia to bipolar I/mixed state, to bipolar II/rapid cycling. Whether these changes reflect misdiagnoses, shifts in the course of my illness, the effects of medication, or something still unknown is anybody's guess. I suspect it's a little of each.

Many people have different diagnoses over the years. It's not at all unusual to be diagnosed initially with unipolar disorder rather than bipolar II disorder when your hypomanic episodes have gone unrecognized. In fact, bipolar II disorder may be the most unrecognized and undertreated mood disorder that medical professionals encounter.

Some of us with bipolar disorder have *co-occurring conditions* or *comorbid conditions* (those that occur simultaneously with other health conditions) that complicate diagnosis. *Hypothyroidism* (low thyroid), premenstrual problems, an autoimmune disorder, and a series of stressors complicated my own diagnosis. I'll explain more about co-occurring conditions and stress in chapters 6 and 10.

Watching for Early Warning Signs

To cope with bipolar disorder, it's important to monitor your thoughts, feelings, and behaviors regularly. Knowing the early warning signs of impending depression or mania helps you address problems before they get out of control. The following table lists some common early warning signs. You may wish to add others, based on your own patterns. For instance, when I start getting extremely anxious about making simple phone calls, I'm probably drifting into a depression. And when I repeatedly interrupt my husband or try to complete his sentences, which I rarely do otherwise, it often signals oncoming hypomania.

Note that anxiety and nervousness, difficulty concentrating, confusion and disorganization, irritability, and increased alcohol consumption may signal a depressed, hypomanic, or manic state.

TABLE 4
Early Warning Signs

Depression	Mania/Hypomania
■ Despondency	■ Euphoria
■ Low self-esteem	■ Feelings of superiority
■ Excessive sleep or insomnia	■ Insomnia
■ Staying in bed for long periods	■ Staying up all night
■ Poor appetite	■ Compulsive eating
■ Inactivity	■ Overambitiousness
■ Low energy level	■ Surges of energy
■ Frequent frustration	■ Impatience with others
■ Inability to show affection	■ Inappropriate anger, outbursts of temper
■ Low libido	■ Increased sexual activity
■ Self-destructive thoughts or actions	■ Excessive spending
■ Inability to experience pleasure	■ Inability to keep up with own thoughts
■ Withdrawal	■ Increased but often unfocused creativity
■ Feelings of boredom	■ Bizarre ideas or thoughts

As you become more familiar with your own patterns, you may wish to record your own warning signs and familiarize your friends and family with them. That way, they can bring them to your attention, and if necessary, intervene on your behalf.

If you suspect that you—or a friend or loved one—might have a mood disorder, no matter how mild or how severe, it's important to get treatment. The right treatment can not only save your life but can take you off the tightrope and place you on solid ground.

SIX

Untangling Complications: Mimicking and Co-Occurring Conditions

OTHER PHYSICAL AND psychiatric conditions often mimic or accompany bipolar disorder. In such a case, you may experience symptoms of a mood disorder but have an entirely different illness. For instance, your moods and feelings may shift wildly. Your sleep and appetite may differ dramatically. Your energy and activity levels may rise or fall. And your self-esteem, confidence, thinking, concentration, and decision-making abilities may change.

Just as you might have a punctured lung and a broken leg simultaneously, you might have bipolar disorder *along with* another condition. When you have two entirely different conditions simultaneously, doctors call them *co-occurring* or *comorbid conditions*. For instance, you may have both bipolar disorder and a thyroid disorder. Or both bipolar disorder and a **substance abuse disorder**—an addiction to alcohol, medications, or illicit drugs.

Additional mimicking and co-occurring conditions include

- Autoimmune disorders
- Cancer and tumors
- Endocrine disorders
- Infectious diseases
- Neurological disorders
- Other psychiatric disorders
- Unexplained conditions

And, of course, any condition that affects the brain can cause mood and behavioral changes. This includes incompatible medications, illicit drugs and alcohol, vitamin deficiencies, toxicities, and head trauma.

Mimicking and co–occurring conditions complicate both diagnosis and treatment significantly. The good news is that by taking a thorough history, performing a physical exam, and obtaining the right laboratory tests, doctors can usually rule out most of these problems.

Autoimmune Disorders

When functioning properly, your **immune system** protects your body from outside invaders like bacteria and viruses. But when it malfunctions, your body attacks its own cells, just as your mind turns on you during a depression. When this happens, you may develop an *autoimmune disease.*

Autoimmune factors are present in many diseases. For instance, the endocrine disorder *Hashimoto's disease,* in which the thyroid secretes too little thyroid hormone, is also an autoimmune disorder. Scientists believe that some psychiatric disorders may be autoimmune disorders as well.

Acquired Immune Deficiency Syndrome

Acquired immune deficiency syndrome (AIDS) results from an infection with the *human immunodeficiency virus (HIV),* usually through sexual contact. This virus attacks cells of the immune, nervous, and other systems and impairs proper functioning. An HIV infection may damage the brain and spinal cord, causing *encephalitis* (inflammation of the brain), *meningitis* (inflammation of the membranes surrounding it), and nerve damage. AIDS-related cancers such as *lymphoma* (cancer of the lymph nodes or other lymphoid tissues) and other infections may further affect the nervous system and produce behavioral changes.

Psychiatric symptoms may be mild in the early stages of AIDS but later become severe, due to increasing brain damage. This may lead to lethargy, weakness, and difficulty thinking. Some patients experience seizures. People who are HIV-positive but do not yet display other AIDS symptoms may be excessively moody and irritable, or display memory loss and confusion.

Lupus

Lupus, also known as *systemic lupus erythematosus (SLE),* is a rheumatic (or arthritic) disease that attacks and inflames the connective tissues throughout the body.

> RHEUMATIC DISEASES attack the joints, tendons, muscles, bones, or nerves, bringing pain and often disability. Rheumatic disease can also produce depressive or manic symptoms.

People with lupus often display symptoms ranging from mild anxiety to severe psychosis. Fatigue, weakness, lack of appetite, weight loss, and inability to concentrate may be some of the first symptoms. Rapid mood changes and abnormal behavior are also common.

And just as people with bipolar disorder have depressive or manic episodes alternating with stable periods, people with lupus have alternating flares and remissions. This makes the early stages of lupus hard to diagnose.

In my early forties, while spending two weeks at a writers' retreat in the woods of northeast Texas, I had a bizarre experience. First the knee on one leg and the ankle on the other would swell up inexplicably; then it would be the other way around. Sometimes both joints on one leg were swollen, but the other leg was fine. Luckily, not every joint was swollen simultaneously; rather, I resembled a balloon animal being squeezed at different points.

I hobbled around my little cabin for a couple of days, wondering what to do if my condition worsened. The nearest person was a mile away, and I didn't have a phone. On one of my better days, I finally managed to drive to the main house to call my husband. He notified the doctor, who advised me to take Advil and come in as soon as I returned home. After ruling out Lyme disease—a strong possibility since I'd been out in the woods—my doctor concluded I had SLE and referred me to a rheumatologist. I've had other flare-ups since then, but with fewer joints simultaneously involved.

Because the lupus surfaced several years after I'd started taking psychotropic medications, and joint problems weren't a potential side effect, the lupus appears to be a co-occurring condition. Plus, several of my family members had some form of arthritis.

I'm still a bit uncertain about my condition because I've always been one criterion short of a formal diagnosis. Similar to a bipolar diagnosis, a lupus diagnosis requires that at least four out of eleven criteria be present at once. Even in episodes during which I had to use a cane or crutches to get around, I experienced only three official symptoms. It's possible I have a different form of arthritis, but until I have another episode, which I'm hoping won't occur, my rheumatologist is sticking with the lupus diagnosis.

Cancer and Tumors

Cancer

Cancer is closely associated with psychiatric symptoms, particularly depression. One-fourth to one-half of people who have cancer experience psychiatric problems. In fact, such symptoms may be the only indication of cancer's presence for weeks, months, or even years. This is especially true when cancerous tumors are located in the brain or spine or in some part of the endocrine system—the bodily system that secretes hormones into the blood.

The symptoms that cancer and mood disorders share include reduced appetite and weight loss, decreased interest or pleasure in life, and insomnia.

Brain and Spinal Cord Tumors

Brain and spinal cord tumors are abnormal growths of tissue found inside the skull or the spinal column. Although benign tumors are not particularly harmful in most parts of the body, this is not the case in the brain and spinal cord. Because a rigid, bony skull and spinal column protect your **central nervous system (CNS)**, any abnormal growth within it can exert pressure on sensitive tissues and impair their function. A tumor that forms on or near your spinal cord can therefore disrupt communication between your brain and your nerves elsewhere. Tumors near vital brain structures or sensitive spinal cord nerves are a serious threat to your health.

A BRIEF TUTORIAL ON TUMOR TERMS

DOCTORS USE the word *tumor* to describe both abnormal new growths (*neoplasms*) and those present from birth (*congenital tumors*). No matter where they appear in the body, tumors are usually considered *benign* (noncancerous) if their cells

- are similar to normal cells,
- grow relatively slowly, and
- are confined to one location.

Tumors are considered *malignant* (cancerous) when their cells

- differ significantly from normal cells,
- grow relatively quickly, and
- spread easily to other locations.

Brain and spinal cord tumors cause many diverse symptoms, which generally develop slowly and worsen over time. Some common psychiatric symptoms of a brain tumor include memory problems, altered thinking, personality changes, and psychotic episodes. Common symptoms that result from spinal cord tumors include altered thinking, muscle weakness, and motor problems.

Endocrine Disorders

The **endocrine system** consists of several ductless glands that secrete hormones directly into the blood. Through these secretions, the endocrine system communicates with organs and tissues throughout the body and controls their functioning. Although it responds slower than the nervous system, the endocrine system functions much like it. The effects of hormones, however, generally last much longer than the effects of neurotransmitters.

The endocrine system is the one bodily system most commonly associated with psychiatric symptoms.

Thyroid Disorders

The thyroid wraps around the front of the neck and regulates metabolic functions and energy levels. Disorders of the thyroid that relate to mood include hyperthyroidism (high thyroid) and hypothyroidism (low thyroid).

HYPERTHYROIDISM AND HYPOTHYROIDISM

In *hyperthyroidism,* the thyroid secretes too much thyroid hormone, speeding up the metabolism and producing hyperactivity. People with hyperthyroidism tend to lose weight, sweat heavily, and become intolerant to heat. They may be fatigued but have difficulty sleeping. They may also be irritable and easily upset.

In *hypothyroidism,* the thyroid secretes less and less thyroid hormone, slowing the body's metabolism. People with hypothyroidism tend to be lethargic, gain weight, or have difficulty losing it.

It's tempting to attribute symptoms of hypothyroidism, such as fatigue and weakness, to overwork, stress, or aging, but the person with hypothyroidism may also experience other depressive symptoms, such as constipation, memory loss, and disinterest in normally pleasurable activities. According to Dr. Mark Gold, Division Chief of Addictions Medicine at the McKnight Brain Institute of the University of Florida in Gainesville and author of *The Good News About Depression*, when your thyroid hormone drops too low, your brain becomes "deaf" to positive messages.

In my late twenties, I saw a doctor at the University of Texas Student Health Center because I was so inexplicably exhausted. He informed me that I had a low thyroid and prescribed some pills. After taking the full prescription and noticing no difference, I abandoned treatment. I had no idea at the time how important the thyroid was. Because the thyroid affects so many different bodily functions, its malfunction should be taken seriously.

Many years later, I started taking antidepressants but they barely helped. After a couple of years, an internist I was seeing for another matter discovered part of the reason. After one quick look at my neck she said, "You've got a goiter. I'm pretty sure you have a thyroid problem." My lab tests confirmed it, and I began taking synthetic thyroid medication to supply the hormone my thyroid no longer could. My depressions improved dramatically. I've been on thyroid medication ever since. Perhaps my brain wasn't open to what my antidepressants had to offer because of my low thyroid.

Thyroid disease is especially common in women, affecting as many as six to seven percent. Nearly three times more people with hypothyroidism experience depression than in the general population. And those with rapid-cycling bipolar disorder often have low thyroid levels in the brain even though adequate levels are present in their blood.

Although the proper amount of thyroid hormone varies with each individual, hypothyroidism and hyperthyroidism are relatively easy to find and treat.

Other Endocrine Disorders

Other endocrine conditions that may mimic or accompany mood disorders include Addison's disease, Cushing's syndrome, and diabetes.

ADDISON'S DISEASE

Also called *hypocortisolism* or *chronic adrenal insufficiency*, *Addison's disease* is a rare endocrine disorder in which the **adrenal glands** (two glands that produce stress hormones) produce insufficient **cortisol**. In some cases, it also results in too little **aldosterone**—a hormone that helps regulate water and salt balance to maintain blood pressure and kidney function.

Both high and low cortisol can impact mood. With too little cortisol, depression often results. Other symptoms may include apathy, fatigue, lack of motivation, appetite and weight loss, diarrhea, insomnia, restlessness, irritability, and even severe psychosis.

CUSHING'S SYNDROME

Essentially the opposite of Addison's disease is *Cushing's syndrome* or *hypercortisolism*. In Cushing's syndrome, the pituitary gland produces too much **adrenocorticotropic hormone (ACTH)**, prompting the adrenal glands to produce too much cortisol. Symptoms range from depression and anxiety to euphoria, irritability, and psychosis. Women may experience menstrual changes, and men may have less or even no interest in sex. Their fertility may also decrease. Of all these symptoms, depression is the most common.

DIABETES

In people with *diabetes*, the **insulin** versus **glucose** level is out of balance. Normally, when we eat, our bodies convert much of our food into glucose. This increases blood glucose levels and signals the pancreas to make insulin.

In *type 1 diabetes* (previously known as *juvenile diabetes* because it often develops early in life), the immune system kills the insulin-producing cells of the pancreas. Without enough of these cells, the pancreas can't do its job. Type 1 diabetes is both an autoimmune disorder and an endocrine disorder.

The other type of diabetes is called *type 2 diabetes* (previously known as *adult-onset diabetes* because it used to be seen more often in adulthood). Type 2 diabetes is an endocrine disorder rather than an autoimmune disorder and is often associated with excess weight. Two possible culprits may cause type 2 diabetes: 1) *insulin resistance,* in which cells can't use insulin efficiently, or 2) *insulin deficiency,* in which the pancreas makes too little insulin for the body's needs.

A CLARIFICATION OF DIABETES TERMS

BLOOD SUGAR LEVEL, or **BLOOD GLUCOSE LEVEL:** a measurement of the amount of glucose in the blood

GLUCOSE: a form of sugar that circulates in the body and provides energy for the cells

INSULIN: a hormone that helps the body move glucose from the blood and into the cells, where it's used for energy. Insulin also helps produce proteins and form and store lipids

PANCREAS: an endocrine-system organ near the liver that produces insulin

Some symptoms that diabetes and mood disorders have in common include extreme fatigue and lethargy, most likely because of low **serotonin** levels.

Like people with diabetes, those of us with bipolar disorder tend to be extremely sensitive to blood sugar changes.

Infectious Diseases

Some infectious diseases sometimes mimic or co-occur with bipolar disorder and are contracted in a variety of ways.

Hepatitis C

Hepatitis C is a liver disease caused by the *hepatitis C virus (HCV).* HCV is found in the blood of people with the disease and is spread when others are exposed to their infected blood.

In the early stages, symptoms include a loss of appetite and general malaise. Other symptoms may include depression, lethargy, anxiety, and delusional mania.

Lyme disease

A serious tick-borne infection called *Lyme disease* is caused by the *Borrelia burgdorferi* bacterium. Because it affects nerve signal transmission, Lyme disease can produce many psychiatric symptoms:

- Fatigue and sleep disturbances
- Appetite changes
- Sexual dysfunction or loss of libido
- Concentration and memory problems
- Confusion
- Obsessive behavior
- Panic attacks
- Extreme agitation
- Hallucinations
- Paranoia

Neurosyphilis

In contrast with AIDS, *syphilis,* a sexually transmitted disease caused by the *Treponema pallidum* bacterium, may not produce psychological symptoms for decades. In later stages of the illness, when the bacterium reaches the brain, the illness is called *neurosyphilis.* Its symptoms include concentration difficulties, confusion, irritability, and personality changes. Thanks to antibiotics and early detection of syphilis, few cases are seen these days.

Neurological Disorders

Epilepsy

Some people with bipolar disorder (as well as some with unipolar disorder) share symptoms common to *epilepsy* (a seizure disorder). These include memory loss, confused thinking, feelings of detachment, and auditory hallucinations.

Given that anticonvulsant medications often ease bipolar symptoms, some scientists believe that epilepsy and bipolar disorder are related.

Huntington's Disease

In *Huntington's disease,* also called *Huntington's chorea,* slowly degenerating nerve cells in the brain can cause both depressive and manic symptoms. These may include confusion and memory loss, moodiness, restlessness, irritability, and poor judgment. Because Huntington's is an inherited disease with a clear genetic marker (one faulty gene on chromosome #4), doctors can identify it more easily than many mimicking or co-occurring disorders.

Multiple Sclerosis

Multiple sclerosis (MS) results from the inflammation and breakdown of **myelin**, which insulates nerve cells in the brain and spinal cord. When myelin is destroyed, scars of hardened or *sclerotic* tissue take its place and interfere with nerve signal transmission.

While many symptoms of MS involve muscle weakness, balance, and coordination, others include fatigue, forgetfulness, difficulty concentrating, sexual problems, mood swings, and tremors. Like symptoms of bipolar disorder, symptoms of MS may occur sporadically, and be mild, moderate, or severe.

Parkinson's Disease

Parkinson's disease results from insufficient amounts of the neurotransmitter **dopamine**—a neurotransmitter related to pleasurable sensations. People with this disease therefore become unable to control their movements normally. They also display symptoms of mood disorders, particularly depression, which may appear before other symptoms are noticeable.

People with Parkinson's may experience sleep disturbances, memory loss, or a loss of motivation. Some become irritable or uncharacteristically pessimistic. Because they may also speak too rapidly or repeat their words, their speech may be mistaken as a sign of mania.

Other Psychiatric Disorders

Other psychiatric disorders can either mimic or co-occur with bipolar disorder. The most common co-occurring conditions in adults are obsessive-compulsive disorder, panic disorder, and substance abuse disorders. And particularly in children and adolescents, attention deficit hyperactivity disorder may mimic or accompany bipolar disorder. Eating disorders, premenstrual disorders, and personality disorders can co-occur with bipolar disorder too.

Anxiety Disorders

Psychiatrists divide *anxiety disorders,* which bring long-term, overwhelming anxiety and fear, into the following primary categories:

- Obsessive-compulsive disorder
- Panic disorder
- Social anxiety disorder
- Generalized anxiety disorder
- Post-traumatic stress disorder

OBSESSIVE-COMPULSIVE DISORDER

People with *obsessive-compulsive disorder (OCD)* are plagued by unwanted thoughts or images (**obsessions**) or by an urgency to perform certain rituals to stop their obsessions (**compulsions**).

People who have obsessions often feel the need to check and recheck situations. Repugnant sexual thoughts may consume them. Or they may fear that they'll become violent. People who have compulsions fear the consequences of not performing their obsessive rituals, but they derive only temporary relief from their anxiety by completing them.

Although most adults with OCD realize that such actions are illogical, they are powerless to prevent them.

PANIC DISORDER

Both adults and children with bipolar disorder also show high rates of recurrent panic attacks. People with *panic disorders* are plagued by sudden and repeated attacks of terror that can strike at any time, even during sleep. The symptoms include a sense of unreality, a fear of impending doom or even death, and a fear of losing control or losing your mind.

SOCIAL ANXIETY DISORDER

People with *social anxiety disorder,* also called *social phobia,* become extremely self-conscious in everyday social situations and experience overwhelming anxiety. The anxiety may be limited to a particular type of situation, such as using a public rest room, or be so broad-based that the person with the illness can't leave home at all.

GENERALIZED ANXIETY DISORDER

People with *generalized anxiety disorder* experience tremendous anxiety virtually every day. They may worry constantly and anticipate disasters about their health, family, money, or job. Often these worries have little basis in reality. This disorder may become so overwhelming that those affected are unable to relax at all.

POST-TRAUMATIC STRESS DISORDER

After a traumatic event such as a wreck, mugging, rape, natural disaster, or war, people may develop *post-traumatic stress disorder (PTSD).* People with PTSD relive the traumatic experience repeatedly through flashbacks in nightmares or even during the day. They often become easily startled and irritable, and sometimes even aggressive or violent.

Substance Abuse

People with mood disorders are much more likely than the general public to abuse alcohol and drugs or have relatives who do so. One out of four people with unipolar disorder and over half of those with bipolar disorder are also challenged by some form of substance abuse.

The symptoms of mood disorders and substance abuse disorders frequently intertwine. For instance, the rapid downward crash after an alcoholic high closely mimics depression. And the symptoms of cocaine abuse—euphoria, grandiosity, hypersexuality, poor judgment, irritability, hallucinations, and staying up all night—closely mimic mania.

Some of the same chemical mechanisms in the brain appear to malfunction in both mood and substance abuse disorders. In both disorders, insufficient dopamine may be involved.

So, does bipolar disorder cause substance abuse, or is it the other way around? Apparently, at least with drug abuse, bipolar disorder seems to come first. Doctors believe that many people use drugs and alcohol for self-medication. If you're agitated, a drink or two can help relax you. And if you're depressed, stimulants can make you high—at least initially. However, many people with bipolar disorder seem to use drugs and alcohol to intensify or prolong their mania or hypomania.

When you have both bipolar disorder (or another form of mental illness) and a substance abuse disorder, you're said to have a **dual diagnosis**. According to the National Mental Health Association, when you have such a combination, it would be ideal to treat both disorders at once. However, life isn't always ideal. Because of the difficulties and dangers that detoxification can present, many doctors believe in addressing the substance abuse first.

Attention Deficit Hyperactivity Disorder

Although this disorder most commonly surfaces during childhood or adolescence, some adults display *attention deficit hyperactivity disorder (ADHD)* too. In adults, however, hyperactivity may be less of a problem or take a slightly different form than in children and adolescents. ADHD can mimic or accompany bipolar disorder.

ADHD symptoms tend to relate primarily to inattention or primarily to hyperactivity. Those symptoms shared with bipolar disorder include

- difficulty concentrating;
- distractibility and forgetfulness;
- overcommitment or inability to complete activities;
- difficulty organizing things;
- excessive fidgeting and restlessness;
- extreme difficulty working or playing quietly;
- excessive interruptions, intrusions, or inappropriate comments; and
- repeated acts of impulsive risk-taking without considering the consequences.

When ADHD and bipolar disorder co-occur, these symptoms may intensify.

Eating Disorders

Sometimes depression leads to eating disorders—and for some, eating disorders trigger depression. There are three major eating disorders: anorexia nervosa, bulimia nervosa, and binge-eating disorder. The underlying factor in all of these disorders is a disturbed body image. Women are particularly prone to eating disorders because our cultural definitions of beauty so strongly emphasize being thin.

While the symptoms of each type of eating disorder differ, people who experience them generally also suffer from stress, social pressure, and other mental health problems. Each is treatable but can cause serious physical and emotional problems if left untreated.

ANOREXIA NERVOSA

The core symptom of *anorexia nervosa* is an intense, unreasonable fear of becoming fat, which doesn't ease even with severe weight loss and extremely reduced food intake. Untreated anorexia has severe physical consequences: malnutrition, disrupted menstrual periods in women, and sometimes even death.

BULIMIA NERVOSA

Bulimia involves ongoing *bingeing* (eating large quantities of food) and *purging* (vomiting, using laxatives, or exercising excessively to lose weight). Stress, intense fear of gaining weight, and depression usually trigger this disorder. People with bulimia eat to ease their stresses, and purge to relieve their guilt about overeating. Long-term purging causes many additional problems, including dental problems and electrolyte imbalances that impair nerve function.

BINGE-EATING DISORDER

Binge eating is compulsive overeating throughout the day. People with this disorder often eat quickly, feel out of control while eating, and hoard or hide food from others.

They are often depressed and isolated, and filled with guilt and self-disgust. Like anorexia and bulimia, binge eating is harmful to your health. It can trigger high blood pressure, heart problems, joint pain, and fatigue.

Premenstrual Syndrome and Premenstrual Dysphoric Disorder

Many women face *premenstrual syndrome (PMS)* and *premenstrual dysphoric disorder (PMDD),* possibly because of a shift in the balance between the brain's neurotransmitters and the female hormones estrogen and progesterone.

Common PMS symptoms include irritability, food cravings, and fatigue. Symptoms associated with PMDD are similar but usually more severe. Additional symptoms of PMDD include insomnia or sleeping too much, binge eating, confusion, difficulty concentrating, aggression, rage, and feeling overwhelmed, out of control, or even suicidal.

Occasionally, premenstrual tension gets so severe that a woman becomes psychotic for a few days nearly every month. Postmenstrually, however, the same woman may be upbeat and talkative, and much more energetic.

It isn't clear whether changes in hormone levels cause mood disorders, or whether it's the other way around. Some studies have found that bipolar symptoms worsen in relation to the menstrual cycle, but others have found no such relationship. Here's what doctors *do* know:

- Premenstrually, women's suicide attempts and threats increase, and they're more likely to be admitted then to psychiatric hospitals.
- Over two-thirds of women with unipolar disorder experience premenstrual lows.
- Women who suffer from premenstrual mood changes frequently have family histories of depression.

While my husband and I were dating, he observed that my moods shifted radically right before my periods. I'd show up at his apartment in tears, my hysterics always out of proportion to whatever was going on. When he concluded that I must have PMS, I dismissed him. I was an independent young professional woman and wanted no part of such a diagnosis.

But after tracking my moods for a couple of years, I had to admit there was a distinct pattern. Eventually, I became so aware of my symptoms that I could nearly pinpoint the moment I began sinking into a premenstrual depression. It felt as if a giant needle were injecting poison into my brain. I'd suddenly become depressed or feel uncharacteristic anger.

Because PMS and PMDD can produce severe mood swings, doctors frequently mistake them for bipolar disorder, in particular, bipolar II.

Schizophrenia

While bipolar disorder is primarily a disorder of mood, *schizophrenia* is primarily a disorder of thought. People with schizophrenia may

- display sudden behavioral changes;
- have delusions, such as believing that others can read their minds or thinking that others are trying to harm them;

- have hallucinations involving any of the senses, most commonly, hearing voices others can't hear;
- speak in a disorganized and incomprehensible manner; and
- become socially withdrawn.

Like bipolar disorder, schizophrenia may come and go, and there may be relatively stable periods in between episodes.

Unexplained Conditions

One condition that frequently mimics or co-occurs with bipolar disorder is *migraine headaches,* the cause of which is not yet confirmed. Migraine attacks create incapacitating headaches that can last for days. Some symptoms of migraines that overlap with mood disorders include

- achiness
- fatigue
- diarrhea
- confusion and mental fuzziness
- mood changes
- sensitivity to light or noise

Current theory holds that changes in blood flow to the brain may create migraines. Blood vessel constriction may stimulate the release of serotonin, leading to further constriction and reducing the amount of oxygen that reaches the brain. Then, the pain worsens as vessels dilate and tissues surrounding the brain become inflamed.

Are Co-Occurring Conditions Related?

When two conditions co-occur, the old chicken-or-egg dilemma surfaces. Which one caused what? Or was it just coincidence that you got both? Substantial evidence indicates that mood disorders, particularly depression, weaken the immune system and open the door to other illnesses.

My Medical History

My own medical history, and much of my research, strongly suggests that other illnesses and stresses can activate mood disorders in those who are predisposed to them.

Our family doctor theorized that having pneumonia around the age of one weakened my immune system. Along with harsh Kansas winters and my father's heavy smoking, this led to regular bouts of chronic bronchitis, strep throat, and tonsillitis. To treat my respiratory problems, I took a sugary codeine and benylin cough syrup my parents called "cherry pop" every year I lived in Kansas. I therefore consumed a fair amount of codeine and benylin annually until shortly after turning twenty-two and moving to Texas. My sister Jo thinks these medications might have caused my disorder, but the ties to hypothyroidism, PMS, and lupus seem too coincidental for that to be the sole cause.

I think my mood disorder must have preceded most of my other medical problems, and that my other conditions must be co-occurring rather than mimicking illnesses for two reasons:

- I have relatives diagnosed with mood disorders, and
- I've experienced significant relief after finding the right combination of psychotropic medications.

SEVEN

Uncovering Root Causes: Biochemistry and Genetics

For YEARS THERE'S been an ongoing debate about the cause of mental illness. Some people blamed personality and environment (nurture) and saw mental illness only as a product of bad parenting, negative thinking, or overemotional reactions. Others blamed genetics and biochemistry (nature) and saw mental illness only as a product of imbalanced chemicals. Both sides hold merit, but neither tells the whole story. Life—and especially brain function—is significantly more complex. People who blame only nature or only nurture overlook important factors that can help us cope.

Currently, most experts (and many of us with brain disorders) believe that mental illness involves multiple causes. It's evident that some people have a genetic predisposition. And, yes, biochemistry certainly is involved. But, as with many other physical disorders, having a genetic predisposition for an illness doesn't necessarily mean you will contract it. Whether or not a mental illness surfaces depends on many other factors, including personality, upbringing, stress, trauma, and much more. Despite all the heartache it's brought, my

illness has greatly expanded my appreciation for the interconnectedness of our minds, bodies, and spirits.

This chapter examines the nature side of bipolar disorder.

Basic Brain Structure

To understand what's happening with this illness, it helps to know a
bit about brain structure and how it relates to chemical imbalances
in the brain. Although the brain is the most complex structure in the
body, I won't be discussing it in great detail. For purposes of this
book, I'll focus on the aspects most relevant to mood disorders.

The Big Picture

The **central nervous system (CNS)** consists of two major
components:

1. the *spinal cord,* enclosed within the spinal canal, which runs
   through the vertebrae in the back
2. the *brain,* which rests atop the spinal column

The nerves in the spinal canal branch throughout the body and
constantly communicate with the brain. The human brain is about
the size of a grapefruit and weighs about three pounds.

Eight Important Brain Structures

All the parts of the brain are important, but this discussion will
concentrate on the larger areas and the areas most important to emotional functioning. Traveling more or less clockwise from the top
right to the bottom of the following figure, they are as follows:

1. The **cerebrum**—the folded, wrinkly part—is the largest part
   of the brain. A deep rift divides the cerebrum into the right
   and left **hemispheres**.
2. A thin outer layer of tissue called the **cerebral cortex** (not
   labeled in the figure) covers the cerebrum. About one-eighth

IMPORTANT BRAIN STRUCTURES AND
THE LIMBIC SYSTEM

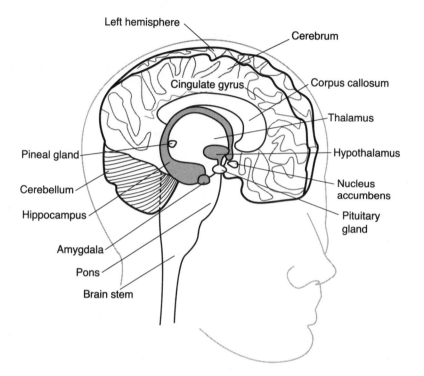

of an inch thick, the cerebral cortex is the thinking, learning, proactive portion of the brain.

3. The front third of the brain (not labeled in the figure) is the **prefrontal cortex**. It affects attention span, judgment, and impulse control, as well as organizing and problem-solving skills.

4. Within the prefrontal cortex, the **cingulate gyrus** provides the flexibility to move from one idea to another and to see multiple options.

5. The **brain stem** (at the bottom of the figure) extends deep within the brain. It is the "animal," instinctive, or reactive portion of the brain.

6. The **pons,** or bridge, above the brain stem connects the spinal cord with the cerebrum and cerebellum (the lower back part of the brain). The pons inhibits muscle activity during *REM*

(*rapid eye movement*) sleep—that part of the sleep cycle during which we dream.

7. A switching mechanism called the **reticular activating system (RAS)** in the center of the spinal cord runs from the upper brain stem into the lower cerebral cortex. It toggles between the reactive and proactive portions of the brain. When you're emotionally charged, the RAS shuts down your cerebral cortex, and instincts and training take over. When you're relaxed and don't feel threatened, the RAS switches your cerebral cortex back on and allows creativity and logic to flow.

8. The **cerebellum**, at the lower back of the brain, coordinates movement with thinking and emotions.

THE LIMBIC SYSTEM

Beneath the cerebral cortex is the **limbic system**—often called the emotional brain. It influences your emotions, thinking, memory, and motivation—including basic drives.

The limbic system includes several different structures—the shaded portions of the previous figure—three of which are especially crucial: the amygdala, the hippocampus, and the hypothalamus.

THREE PRIMARY LIMBIC STRUCTURES

The **amygdala**, located near the pons, keeps on the lookout for both threats and opportunities. Acting reflexively, it assigns emotional meaning to events and objects, and incites a quick response. This can lead to anything from showering someone with kisses to mounting a full-scale attack. But the amygdala is also sophisticated enough to interpret and relay subtler emotions, such as amusement and curiosity or skepticism and envy.

The **hippocampus** serves as a go-between, relaying information back and forth between other parts of the limbic system and the cerebral cortex. This helps link emotions to images, memory, and learning. Together, the amygdala and hippocampus help you assess the environment, tap into your senses, and generate and encode emotions. A properly functioning hippocampus helps you maintain emotional equilibrium by regulating extreme arousal states. It also influences motivation.

The **hypothalamus** is the "main switch" for the **autonomic nervous system**—the part of the nervous system that controls body temperature, breathing, heart rate, hormonal secretions, and other involuntary bodily functions. This organ, near the base of the brain, helps regulate sleep, hunger, thirst, and sex drive, as well as two extremely important glands: the pituitary gland and the pineal gland.

PRIMARY LIMBIC SYSTEM STRUCTURES

- Amygdala "lookout"
- Hippocampus "go-between"
- Hypothalamus "autonomic main switch"

SIX NEARBY BRAIN STRUCTURES

Other structures and glands in or near the limbic system also influence emotions, thinking, memory, and motivation. Again, starting near the top right moving clockwise, these include

- the **corpus callosum**, which sends nerve signals between the right and left brain hemispheres;
- the **thalamus**, which transmits sensory information to the cerebral cortex and translates nerve signals into conscious sensations;
- the **nucleus accumbens**, or "center of gratification," which helps modulate hunger, thirst, and sexual desire; and
- the **substantia nigra** (not visible in the figure), a group of dark-colored neurons in the midbrain above the pons, which along with the nucleus accumbens appears to play a major role in addictive behaviors.

Besides its role in emotion, memory, thinking, and motivation, the limbic system controls the release of hormonal secretions. Two important glands within this system are the pituitary and pineal glands.

The **pituitary gland** is often called the master gland because its hormones activate secretions in other glands. Some pituitary hormones regulate growth, maturation, and metabolism.

Although buried deep within the brain, the light-sensitive **pineal gland** serves as an internal clock and controls your body's timing system by receiving light/dark signals from the environment. Some scientists speculate that this gland may be involved in seasonal affective disorder.

The limbic system is present in other animals but is more highly developed in humans.

Moving Closer In

Although brain structure plays a part in bipolar disorder, even more important is what's happening in and between cells.

BRAIN CELLS

We have an estimated 100 billion nerve cells (or **neurons**) in our brain, each of which may be in contact with 10,000 other neurons. Neurons communicate with one another and with other parts of the body by transmitting signals through massive networks or pathways. A single neuron may participate in several different pathways.

The other 90 percent of the cells, called **glia**, appear to "hold the brain together." Glia nourish and protect neurons and tidy them up. But glia may be more important in mood disorders than previously thought. Through autopsies, researchers have learned that people with a family history of depression have significantly fewer glia cells than other people do.

NEURONAL STRUCTURE

Although different types of neurons vary in size, shape, chemistry, and connections, all neurons contain some similarities. A typical neuron consists of three major structures: a cell body, some dendrites, and at least one axon.

The **cell body** contains a **nucleus** with genetic information—or

DNA—that programs the cell to be a neuron rather than some other sort of cell—like a bone cell, a hair cell, or an organ cell.

Extending from the cell body are multiple branchlike **dendrites**, which contain large protein molecules called **receptors**. The receptors contain hollow tubes classified as two primary groups: **ion channels** and **G-protein channels**.

One or more threadlike fibers called **axons** also protrude from the cell body. An axon may be microscopically short or as long as a meter (just over 39 inches). Each axon can branch into as many as 1,000 terminals. Nerve signals travel down the axon and through the terminals on to other cells.

A material called **myelin** insulates and protects the axon. The following figure shows the parts of a neuron.

A SINGLE NEURON

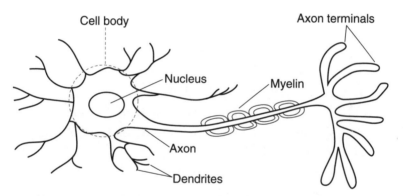

One simple way to remember the parts of a neuron is to compare the neuron to a fat extension cord. The cord itself would represent the axon. The "male" ends (prongs or protrusions) would represent the axonal terminals, and the "female" ends (sockets or outlets) would represent the receptors on the dendrites. Bet you never knew your brain cells were so sexy.

When an axon on one neuron transmits a signal, the receptors on the next neuron can pick it up and send it on. These messages consist of electrical waves of varying intensities, whose measurements determine its **action potential**. A neuron won't fire until stimulated beyond a certain threshold, apparently determined by heredity, physical condition, and environmental factors. The higher the action potential, the more likely the message will be sent on.

CROSSING THE GAP

Unlike electrical prongs and sockets, however, neurons don't physically connect, as scientists once thought. An axonal terminal doesn't plug directly into a dendritic receptor. Neuronal transmission is close but strictly hands-off. My current therapist compares it to Victorian sex.

So how the dickens do messages get to the other side? Does the electricity simply leap between them? No, biochemistry takes over.

Chemical messengers called **neurotransmitters** are produced within neuronal cell bodies and stored in little bulblike sacs called **vesicles** until they're needed. A single neuron may produce one or more different types of neurotransmitters.

The point at which two neurons nearly touch is called a **synapse** and consists of three components. The first two components are the sending and receiving neurons; the third is an infinitesimal gap between them called the **synaptic cleft**.

The first neuron is the **presynaptic neuron** (because it comes before the gap), and the second neuron is the **postsynaptic neuron** (because it comes after).

Once in the cleft, the neurotransmitters relay the message on to an adjacent cell. Because the postsynaptic receptors are "programmed" to respond only to specific neurotransmitters, a message bonds only with a suitable receptor on the postsynaptic neuron. Much like a key and lock, if the neurotransmitter doesn't match the receptor, the receptor blocks its entry. Then electricity takes over again, and that neuron passes the message on to the next neuron in the pathway, or not.

Biochemistry

Chemically speaking, when a neurotransmitter fits or "binds" with a postsynaptic receptor, channels in the receptor open or close to allow or deny access. Positively charged **sodium** ions flow through

THE SYNAPSE

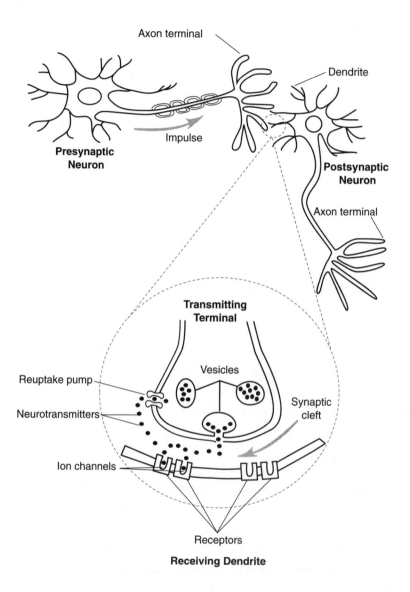

the open receptors and flood the neuron, which fires when they reach a sufficient level. The neuron's vesicles then release the neurotransmitters, which burst into the synaptic cleft. A postsynaptic neuron may receive input from hundreds of receptors, but it won't fire until that input reaches a certain level. Some neurotransmitters always *excite* (turn on) other neurons, some always *inhibit* (turn off) other neurons, and some can perform both functions.

The synaptic cleft is where many **psychotropic medications** act. And that offers tremendous hope because it opens the door for new and more effective medical solutions.

Once the postsynaptic neurons have allowed or rejected entry, one of two things may happen:

1. An **enzyme** (or protein that produces a chemical change or acts as a **catalyst**) called **monoamine oxidase** inactivates or breaks down neurotransmitters through oxidation, or
2. A "pump" on the presynaptic neuron sucks up the remaining neurotransmitters. This process is called **reuptake**.

You may have heard the terms **monoamine oxidase inhibitor (MAOI)** or **selective serotonin reuptake inhibitors (SSRI)** used in relation to two classes of antidepressants. MAOIs prevent the monoamine oxidase enzyme from inactivating neurotransmitters. SSRIs and similar medications prevent the presynaptic pump from rapidly removing and recycling them. In both cases, more neurotransmitters are available to neurons longer.

Now let's explore the roles of neurotransmitters.

Neurotransmitters

Why are neurotransmitters important? Because different medications act on different transmitters and affect the sensitivity of different receptors. Knowing as much as possible about these interactions and observing your own reactions to them will help you and your doctor find the best medical regimen for you. And I can't overemphasize the importance of fine-tuning medications and dosages until you find the best combination for *your own* biochemical makeup.

A number of neurotransmitters affect anxiety, memory, mood, stress, movement, and even regulation of the menstrual cycle. These are neither precisely excitatory nor inhibitory, but produce complex biochemical changes in the receiving cell. These can include

- **amino acids** (the building blocks of proteins),
- **neuropeptides** (compounds of amino acids found in nerve tissue),
- **first messengers** (neurotransmitters that work *between* neurons), and
- **second messengers** (molecules and compounds that work *inside* neurons).

For now, I'll limit the discussion to first messengers and second messengers because of their important role in mood disorders.

FIRST MESSENGERS

Acetylcholine—Present throughout the central nervous system, acetylcholine is especially concentrated in the brain. This neurotransmitter is more important to motor movements and thinking than mood, but it plays an essential role in learning and memory, maintaining neuronal membranes, and activating REM sleep.

Dopamine—This neurotransmitter appears to underlie addictive behaviors that often accompany mood disorders, such as alcohol and drug abuse and bingeing. Chronically low dopamine levels lead to difficulty experiencing emotional or physical satisfaction.

Like acetylcholine, dopamine affects motor movements, learning, thinking, and memory, but it also affects attention span, motivation, and sexual impulses.

Norepinephrine—This neurotransmitter provides our "get-up-and-go" and alertness. Also known as *noradrenaline,* norepinephrine arouses the *fight-or-flight response* when we're under stress, just as adrenaline does (and the name nor*adrenaline* implies). Although adrenaline is a neurotransmitter, it travels only through the nerves outside the brain, while norepinephrine travels within it.

SYMPTOMS OF THE
FIGHT-OR-FLIGHT RESPONSE

- Constriction of blood vessels to skin, causing paleness
- Chest expansion to increase air volume
- Pupil dilation
- Hair standing on end
- Increased pulse and heart rate
- Muscle contraction in preparation to fight or flee
- Release of glucose in liver to provide fast fuel
- Emptying of bladder when fear becomes extreme

Norepinephrine helps form long-term memories and lay down new pathways. When we're stressed or traumatized, the sudden jolt of norepinephrine we get may explain why our recall of stressful situations is so vivid.

Too much dopamine and norepinephrine can lead to mania and psychosis; too little can produce depressive symptoms and negativity, and muddy your thinking.

Serotonin—The neurotransmitter that got the most media coverage with the release of Prozac in the late 1980s, **serotonin** affects both mood and impulse regulation. In a sense, serotonin puts on the brakes in your brain and helps you maintain control.

Serotonin plays an important role in the sleep–wake cycle. Moderate levels are associated with rest, sleep, and relaxation. But low serotonin levels cause all sorts of problems: agitation, attention difficulties, irritability, sleep disturbances, lethargy, worrying, hopelessness, and suicidal behavior. High levels are associated with insufficient REM sleep and aggression. And extremely high serotonin levels interfere with the reticular activating system, limiting your ability to switch flexibly between excitement and inhibition.

> PSYCHIATRISTS ASSOCIATE the term **agitation** with extreme repetitious, nonproductive, tension-driven movements, such as fidgeting, hair pulling, hand wringing, and pacing.

SECOND MESSENGERS

Although mood disorders clearly involve neurotransmitter imbalances and their actions in the synaptic gap, that's not the whole story. If antidepressants simply adjusted neurotransmitters, depressive symptoms would start to improve within hours rather than weeks after starting them. Many neuroscientists now believe that antidepressants actually *alter* receptor molecules, which would explain why improvement takes more time.

In addition, mood-stabilizing agents, such as lithium, appear to work within the neuron itself. Scientists now use the terms **first messengers** (brain neurotransmitters) and **second messengers** (other molecules and compounds inside neurons) to contrast the molecules that communicate inside versus outside a cell. While first messengers communicate *between* neurons, second messengers communicate *inside* them.

Considerable evidence shows that lithium affects **G proteins**, which communicate information that leads to fine-tuning or reprogramming within a cell. Besides G proteins, some other second messengers include **choline, cyclic adenosine monophosphate, myoinositol, phosphomonoesterase**, and **protein kinase C**. These terms are in the Glossary. If you find it hard to relate to chemical terms, however, just think of second messengers as cell remodelers.

Scientists now believe that moods involve the interaction of many chemicals and pathways in the brain. In those of us with mood disorders, this interaction appears to be disrupted. Clearly, our chemical makeup is quite complex.

Neurotransmitter and Hormone Interactions

Neurotransmitters also interact with hormones, and some chemicals are both hormones *and* neurotransmitters. One example is norepinephrine. **Hormones** control growth and development, sexual activity and reproduction, blood pressure, heart rate, body temperature, appetite, energy level, and stress response.

There's a strong association between *hypothyroidism* (in which the thyroid has too little thyroid hormone) and rapid-cycling bipolar disorder. Similarly, the sudden drop in the estrogen and progesterone hormones after childbirth can create a dopamine imbalance that brings on mania.

While hormonal activity affects neurotransmitter activity, the reverse is true as well. For normal functioning, both your neurotransmitters and your hormones must be properly balanced, especially when you're subjected to stress. When they aren't, your moods will be unstable.

The Endocrine System

The **endocrine system**, which regulates hormonal activity, includes the thyroid gland, adrenal glands, sex glands, and the pituitary and pineal glands in the brain.

A diseased endocrine gland will malfunction in one of the following ways:

- It will secrete either too much or too little hormone,
- It will stop secreting the hormone altogether, or
- It will stop responding to other hormonal commands.

The Endocrine Glands

Because of the close relationship between the brain and the endocrine system, even small hormonal shifts can upset the brain's delicate chemical balance. It therefore seems logical that people with endocrine disorders display many depressive and manic symptoms. And the psychiatric symptoms of endocrine disorders occur far earlier than physical symptoms.

The **thyroid** is a butterfly-shaped gland in the neck that straddles the windpipe. The thyroid secretes two major hormones, which I'll discuss shortly.

One **adrenal gland** rests atop each of the body's two kidneys and plays an important part in the functioning of the immune system. As part of the endocrine system, the adrenal glands produce and release two stress hormones—adrenaline and cortisol. They also produce steroid hormones that help control growth, cellular repair, and sugar consumption.

And the pituitary and pineal glands mentioned in the section on the limbic system are also endocrine glands.

Hormones

The types of hormones that affect mood disorders the most are stress hormones, thyroid hormones, and sex hormones.

HORMONES THAT AFFECT MOODS

- *Stress hormones*—adrenaline and cortisol
- *Thyroid hormones*—thyroxine and triiodothyronine
- *Sex hormones*—estrogen, progesterone, and testosterone

STRESS HORMONES

Adrenaline—a neurotransmitter that travels only through the nerves outside the brain. It helps prepare the body for fight or flight.

Cortisol—the most important job of this hormone is to prepare the body to respond to stress. But it also helps

- maintain blood pressure and cardiovascular function;
- slow the immune system's inflammatory response;
- balance the effects of insulin in breaking down sugar for energy; and
- regulate the metabolism of proteins, carbohydrates, and fats.

Cortisol also affects your general sense of well-being.

THYROID HORMONES

The thyroid hormones, *thyroxine (T4)* and *triiodothyronine (T3),* help control the body's **metabolism**—the rate at which it converts nutrients into energy. They also act in concert with the hypothalamus and pituitary gland and with the stress hormones to regulate the release of cortisol.

First, the hypothalamus sends **thyroid releasing hormone (TRH)** to the thyroid and **corticotropin releasing hormone (CRH)** to the pituitary gland. This causes the thyroid to release its thyroid hormones, and for the pituitary to secrete **adrenocorticotropic hormone (ACTH).** ACTH in turn stimulates the adrenal glands to release cortisol into the blood. Finally, the cortisol signals the pituitary to reduce ACTH secretions.

But when your brain's neurotransmitters are imbalanced, this cycle gets out of control, leaving you in a state of chronic stress.

SEX HORMONES

Rampaging sex hormones may explain why bipolar disorder often surfaces during adolescence. Research has found that in both men and women, mood disorders fluctuate when hormonal levels change; however, very little research has addressed the effect of this fluctuation on bipolar disorder.

Estrogen in particular is important because it affects the firing rates of neurotransmitters like acetylcholine, dopamine, norepinephrine, and serotonin. It also enhances **glutamate** activity to accelerate neuronal communication and to promote the growth of neurons that contain acetylcholine.

If all of this information on biochemistry makes you feel completely at the mercy of chemicals, take heart. There's much that you can do to keep your neurotransmitters and hormones in better balance.

The Flexible Brain

We lose roughly 100,000 neurons a day and even more when we ingest alcohol or drugs or experience prolonged stress or chronic illness. This thought used to terrify some people because scientists once claimed that we're born with all the neurons we'd ever have. But recently, researchers have learned that even adult brains change constantly.

Because the protein molecules that form most bodily components are always being replaced, about 90 percent of the proteins in our brains change around every two weeks, and neural pathways change with experience and learning. And recent studies indicate that the mood stabilizer lithium actually *stimulates* neuron production. In response to learning, new experiences, and environmental stimuli, we're also forming new neuronal pathways.

Still, it's not the number of neurons available that's most important, it's the number of synapses that work properly. Your brain may contain as many as 100 trillion to a quadrillion synapses in all. On the average, each neuron shares over 1,000 synaptic connections with other neurons. Some share considerably more. Given this complexity, it's miraculous that our brains work at all.

Genetics

The 1999 U.S. Surgeon General's report on mental health states that multiple genes appear to cause many mental disorders, though no specific genes have been conclusively identified. Yet, bipolar disorder is clearly one of the most genetically related brain disorders. By studying family histories, twins, and special populations, researchers have found significant connections between genetics and both bipolar and unipolar disorders.

Family Ties

Families have a hard time dealing with bipolar disorder. If symptoms aren't too severe, they can often be hidden from others, particularly those the patient doesn't live with. Some families live in denial about a relative with a mental illness. Others won't discuss the problem because they view it as shameful or extremely private.

My family was one of those in which shame and denial ruled. We rarely discussed psychological problems outside the tight inner circle of my parents' home. When I first began seeing a psychiatrist for clinical depression, I knew that my sister Barbara, my niece, and a nephew had been diagnosed with psychiatric problems. But I wasn't sure what other relatives might be affected.

During my childhood, a second cousin was hospitalized for a "nervous breakdown." When my family visited her parents and siblings, my mother and aunt spoke of her only in hushed tones.

Even in childhood it was clear to me that Mother suffered from depressive symptoms. When she neared menopause, she was hospitalized briefly for a nervous breakdown, but I believe that was the only time. Although she was always easily brought to tears and clearly struggled to contain her emotions, she usually seemed "normal."

If any other relative's behavior suggested mental illness, it had to have been my father's. Daddy was a good provider who held a steady job and loved his family. But he was often extraordinarily moody and easily annoyed. His irritability frightened me, but at the time, I just assumed that's how most fathers were.

Daddy never had a formal diagnosis because he scorned psychiatry. But, based on what I now know, it's possible he may have had some form of bipolar disorder too.

What Are the Risks?

You may be concerned that if a relative has bipolar disorder you'll get it too, or that if you have it you'll pass it on to your children. Such concerns are certainly valid, but you don't necessarily contract a mood disorder just because you inherited the genes for one. Like other inherited conditions, such as diabetes, epilepsy, or heart disease, not everyone who inherits the gene (or genes) will be affected.

In roughly one out of four people with a mood disorder, no other family members have been diagnosed with one. But 80 to 90 percent of people with bipolar disorder have one or more family members with a mood disorder.

Sometimes bipolar disorder even skips a generation. Your level of risk increases with the number of genes you have in common with family members who have mood disorders. Because the diagnostic criteria and methods that investigators use in various studies differ widely, it's best to consider all risk figures as approximates.

The following table shows the approximate genetic risk of developing bipolar disorder when another relative has it. Variations in research methodology account for the statistical variations. This chart does *not* reflect the impact of alcoholism, which substantially increases the risk of developing bipolar disorder. Nor does it reflect the risk of developing unipolar disorder, which more than doubles if one or both parents are bipolar.

TABLE 6

Approximate Risk of Developing Bipolar Disorder

Relative(s) with Bipolar Disorder	Risk of Bipolar Disorder
Mother or father	about 15–30 in 100
Both mother and father	about 50–75 in 100
One sibling (other than a twin)	about 15–30 in 100
Second-degree relative	about 3–7 in 100

You're also more susceptible to anxiety and substance abuse if a first-degree relative has a mood disorder.

RELATIVELY SPEAKING

First-degree relative—one who shares half of your genes (a parent, sibling, or child)

Second-degree relative—one who shares one-quarter of your genes (a grandparent, aunt, uncle, niece, or nephew)

But when family members live together, how do we know if genetics rather than upbringing is at play? After all, they're probably exposed to the same values and traditions, many of the same experiences, and many of the same frustrations. Couldn't the whole family be "crazy"?

One way that researchers weigh the effect of nature versus nurture is by studying twins.

TWINS

Theoretically, if a trait is solely hereditary, when one identical twin has the trait, the other will as well. In other words, the trait should be present 100 percent of the time. And if one same-sex fraternal twin has the trait, the other will have it 50 percent of the time.

Studies of identical twins who grew up in different households found that when one twin had a mood disorder, the other was more likely to have one as well. In fact, the rate of concordance in twins is much higher than it is in many other genetically based illnesses (in the range of 31 to 80 percent).

> RATE OF CONCORDANCE: the rate at which a particular gene or illness is present in two different individuals or populations

But because the rate of concordance is under 100 percent, particularly in twins separated through adoption, researchers believe that more than genetics is involved.

SPECIAL POPULATIONS

One problem researchers of mood disorders face is the difficulty that co-occurring substance abuse or sociopathic disorders present.

How do scientists tease out core causes when other disorders accompany or mask bipolar disorder? One way is by studying populations in which such problems are rare.

THE AMISH STUDY

Since the 1970s, researchers for the Amish Affective Disorders Project, led by Dr. Janice Egeland, a University of Miami School of Medicine psychiatry and epidemiology professor, have studied members of the extremely conservative Amish sect in Pennsylvania. The Amish provide a unique view of bipolar disorder because drugs, alcohol, and violence are extremely rare in their culture.

In their horse-and-buggy world, manic or hypomanic behaviors tend to be noticed and recorded because they truly stand out. Because the Amish keep extensive genealogical and medical records, their researchers can access data going back more than thirty generations. Although the rates of mood disorders among the Amish are somewhat lower than the United States average, the difference seems attributable to the lack of alcoholism and sociopathy in Amish males.

The Amish study reinforces the conclusion that substance abuse and environmental factors are less important predictors of mood disorders than genetics. In short, *you don't develop bipolar disorder unless you're genetically predisposed.*

No single gene seems to predetermine whether you're likely to get bipolar disorder; rather, a composite of genes appears to be involved. Researchers have identified a number of potential suspects, but the jury's still out on the culprits.

Although mood disorders clearly involve biochemistry and genetics, there's also lots of evidence that something else is going on.

EIGHT

Delving Deep Inside: Personality

PERSONALITY, UPBRINGING, STRESS, and trauma can *affect* a mental illness even if they're not the direct cause. For instance, certain personality characteristics can mimic or co-occur with mood disorders. Upbringing, stress, and trauma can also trigger or worsen mood episodes. This chapter focuses on the relationships between personality and bipolar disorder.

The field of psychology uses many different terms to describe the personal characteristics that distinguish us as individuals. A few include *character, personality, temperament,* and *traits.* But rather than explain the tiny differences, about which many psychologists disagree, I'll describe two "umbrella" terms—temperament and personality—and use the others interchangeably.

Temperament

The ancient term *temperament* (meaning habit of mind) relates to a person's characteristic emotional reactions to the world. Researchers sometimes describe temperament with such terms as *reactivity* and *self-regulation*, or—especially in adults—*approach* and *avoidance*. Temperament appears to be genetically determined and, as most parents would confirm, is apparent from early infancy on.

When parents are aware of the signs and symptoms of mood disorders and can observe a child's behavior over time, the predisposing temperaments become fairly recognizable. They can prevent these illnesses from worsening by getting their child into early treatment.

Personality

According to the *Diagnostic and Statistical Manual of Mental Disorders,* *personality* relates the characteristic ways in which you perceive, relate to, and think about your environment and yourself. Personality emerges during childhood and changes very little over a lifetime.

Personality Theories

Researchers, psychiatrists, and psychologists use a variety of classification systems to describe personality and temperament. A few examples follow.

The Greek physician Hippocrates identified four personality types:

1. phlegmatic (calm and passive),
2. sanguine (active and cheerful),
3. choleric (angry and violent), and
4. melancholic (sad and gloomy).

In 1963, Warren Norman popularized a personality theory originally published in 1961 by Air Force personnel researchers Ernest Tupes and Raymond Christal. This theory, often called the "big five," views personality through five major dimensions:

1. neuroticism (emotional instability),
2. extroversion,

3. agreeableness,
4. conscientiousness, and
5. openness to experience.

In 1965, German-born behavioral psychologist Hans Eysenck boiled personality types down to two dimensions:

1. emotional stability versus instability, and
2. extroversion versus introversion.

Around 1990, Dr. Eysenck added a third dimension—psychoticism, which encompassed multiple factors, including achievement orientation, arousability, aggression, anger, assertiveness, egocentricism, tough-mindedness, creativity, and genius.

The parallels between these terms and bipolar symptoms are striking.

Genetic Contributions to Personality and Temperament

Quite a bit of evidence, based on studies of identical twins reared from birth in different environments, indicates that we can attribute roughly 40 percent of our personality to genetics. Some researchers tie the term temperament to the genetic factors, and personality to what develops out of them in early childhood.

Even animals display species-specific temperaments. My husband and I learned a lot about this when we adopted our calico cat, Sylvia. We'd both lived with cats for years and found their behaviors pretty predictable. But Sylvia's took us by surprise. She'd allow us to pet her, purring like other cats, then suddenly turn and attack us.

We suffered many bites and clawings, and occasionally considered giving her up. Our vet told us her behavior wasn't that unusual for a calico. She's calmed down only slightly with age, and with the introduction of a tabby named Simon. This gave her another target for her aggression, but Simon is laid-back enough to shrug off most of her attacks. He's also nearly twice her size, but she still reminds him regularly who's boss.

Although temperament doesn't determine personality directly, it interacts with our emotions, environment, experiences, and thoughts to *shape* our personality.

How Personality and Temperament Relate to Bipolar Disorder

Although everyone's personality has contradictions and inconsistencies, "normal" people feel like a person with one single identity. They may experience bouts of the blues or times when they're ecstatic, but their moods settle more quickly into their characteristic range. In contrast, if you have a mood disorder, you may feel like a completely different person during and between episodes. People in severe manic states sometimes sense that they're outside themselves, observing their behaviors as being carried out by someone else.

In *Shadow Syndromes,* Drs. John Ratey and Catherine Johnson state that even those of us with less blatant bipolar disorder live our lives as two—or even three—people:

1. a depressed self,
2. a euphoric self, and
3. a balanced self.

For many years, my mood shifts made me feel as if I had multiple personalities. But I knew that wasn't the problem. People with *dissociative identity disorder* (formerly called *multiple personality disorder*) have such vastly differing and fully developed personalities that they essentially *become* different people. They may use different names when each personality takes over, speak with different voices, or even believe they're a different sex. They forget extensive personal information when the other personality takes control.

Personality Disorders

Personality disorders can also mimic or co-occur with mood disorders. Particularly if a mood disorder goes untreated for many years, you may develop a personality disorder. *DSM-IV* lists four types of personality disorders characterized by symptoms that overlap those of mood disorders:

Antisocial Personality Disorder

People who have *antisocial personality disorder* (previously known as *psychopathic* or *sociopathic personality disorder*) tend to feel no guilt or remorse for immoral or exploitive actions. People with this disorder may

- find it hard to stay in school or keep a job,
- deceive or manipulate others for their own gain,
- become irritable and aggressive,
- start fights or torture people or animals,
- disregard their own or others' safety,
- get in trouble with the law,
- find it hard to maintain relationships, and
- be incapable of love.

The diagnostic criteria of this disorder include at least three forms of misconduct before the age fifteen.

Borderline Personality Disorder

People with *borderline personality disorder* display general emotional instability. They often

- have short-term mood changes lasting from a few hours to a few days;
- are uncertain about their goals and values, their self-image, or their sexual orientation;
- feel chronically bored or empty;

- display inappropriate or intense or uncontrolled anger;
- have unstable relationships that often alternate between intense love and intense hatred;
- fear abandonment and go to great extremes to prevent it;
- indulge in risky behaviors; and
- practice self-mutilating behavior or make repeated suicide attempts.

Sometimes people with rapid-cycling bipolar II disorder are misdiagnosed as having borderline personality disorder. This happens most often with adolescents, teenagers, and women.

In the past, some researchers thought borderline personality disorder should be classified as a mood disorder.

Histrionic Personality Disorder

People with *histrionic personality disorder* are extremely emotional and crave drama and attention. While they may be charismatic and gregarious, they may also be demanding and manipulative. They may

- constantly seek approval, praise, or reassurance;
- need to be the center of attention in every situation;
- be overly concerned about their physical attractiveness;
- dress or act in an inappropriately sexy or seductive manner;
- develop superficial impressions and are unable to describe details;
- demand immediate satisfaction and have no tolerance for delayed gratification;
- express their emotions in an overly dramatic or exaggerated way; and
- struggle to commit to meaningful relationships.

Narcissistic Personality Disorder

People with *narcissistic personality disorder* tend to be totally self-absorbed. They may

- have an overblown sense of their importance;
- require constant attention and admiration;
- exaggerate their achievements and talents;
- expect special treatment;
- exploit other people;
- lack empathy for others;
- believe their problems are unique; and
- become enraged or humiliated when others criticize them or evaluate their actions.

One of my first therapists labeled my father a "narcissistic rageaholic" and claimed he was responsible for my problems. But I defended him adamantly. Despite the difficulties we'd had, I couldn't blame Daddy for all my problems. I felt the need to take some responsibility myself, as I knew some of them had sprung from my own thoughts and behaviors. I always sensed that something else was going on.

Perhaps because my father was somewhat narcissistic, I became extra sensitive to any self-absorption. After hypomanic episodes, I was especially concerned about dominating conversations, hogging the limelight, and stepping on others' feelings. When depressed, I felt guilty about withdrawing and letting other people down.

Five Important Personality Concepts

At least five important personality concepts are significant in bipolar disorder. Those I find most meaningful include explanatory style, learned helplessness, perfectionism, unrealistic expectations, and rigid beliefs.

Explanatory Style

Closely tied to optimism and pessimism is a psychological concept called explanatory style. *Explanatory style* (formerly called *attributional style*) relates to the way we typically explain our experiences. Explanatory style more or less parallels another concept called *locus of control,* which relates to whether we feel control *over* our lives or feel controlled *by* them.

EXTERNAL EXPLANATORY STYLE

Optimists usually attribute their problems to factors outside themselves, see troubles as temporary, and shrug off disappointments. When good things occur, they're more likely to take credit for their part in making them happen. And typically, they expect more good experiences to come. During mania or hypomania, an external explanatory style can intensify, or an internal explanatory style may suddenly become more external.

INTERNAL EXPLANATORY STYLE

Pessimists usually blame themselves for their problems, see troubles as unremitting, and dwell on disappointments. When good things occur, they often consider them serendipitous. And typically, they expect more bad experiences to come. They may feel inadequate—often in every way—and think of themselves as failures. This often leads to the negative self-talk associated with depression.

Learned Helplessness

Early in life, I noticed one common symptom associated with depression: a sense of helplessness, "overwhelmedness," and feeling out of control. Years later, I learned the psychological term for it: *learned helplessness.*

In 1965, a psychologist named Dr. Martin Seligman introduced the concept of learned helplessness, which he firmly believed could lead to depression. A graduate student in experimental psychology at the University of Pennsylvania at the time, Dr. Seligman teamed up with fellow student Steven Maier and designed a study involving three groups of dogs.

In the first phase of their experiment they gave the first group of dogs small electric shocks the dogs could stop only by pushing a panel with their noses. The first group of dogs therefore retained some control. Seligman and Maier then yoked the first set of dogs to the second group of dogs. They placed the shock-producing device for the second group of dogs in such a way that it would shock the second group but not the first group. Dogs in the second group could escape only when dogs from the first group stopped the shocks by pushing the panels with their noses. The second group of dogs therefore had no control, regardless of their actions. The third group of dogs received no shocks at all.

In the second phase of the experiment, Seligman and Maier placed one group of dogs at a time in a box with two compartments. To avoid an electric shock, the dogs had to learn to jump over a low barrier from one compartment to the other. The first and third groups quickly learned to do so. But when Seligman and Maier placed the second group of dogs in the box, they passively lay down and whimpered. They didn't even try to jump to the other compartment to escape the shock because they had learned their efforts would be fruitless.

Seligman's theory of learned helplessness challenged behavioral psychology—a dominate theory in the United States for sixty years. Behavioral psychology focused only on reacting to stimuli in a person's environment. Many behaviorists initially challenged Seligman's theory, but learned helplessness has been a major tenet of psychology since 1975.

Perfectionism

The seeds for perfectionism were sown in my early childhood. Both my parents were perfectionists who had chosen exacting careers. Daddy was an engineer who designed custom tools used to manufacture aircraft, and Mother was a grade-school teacher. After our evening meal, Mother and I would sit at the dining room table, and she'd grade papers while I did my homework.

Mother often broke the silence with little eruptions punctuated with forceful jabs of her grading pencil: "Why did you miss that question, Susie! [jab] [jab] You know better than that!" or "Good for you, Jeremy! You got every [jab] answer [jab] right [jab]!" Then she'd scrawl a bright red "100" at the top of the paper and apply multicolored stars.

I followed my parents' example and became a perfectionist too. I usually earned high grades in school, but not all the time. In most subjects I found anything lower than an A extremely disappointing, though I made B's and even C's from time to time. I'm the first to admit I'm not perfect, but I *aspired* and still aspire to perfection, though I'm slowly learning to lower my expectations.

In time, people began feeding me platitudes like "Nobody's perfect," "Don't be so hard on yourself," and "Don't take yourself so seriously." They even quipped, "You're perfect just the way you are." To me, that claim was *absolutely ludicrous*. Like everyone, I had flaws and imperfections. If I didn't excel all the time, *how could I be perfect?* Although I believed—at least on some level—that *no* human being could achieve perfection, that didn't stop me from beating myself up for not doing so.

A turning point came when I bought a copy of *The Tunnel and the Light,* written by the Swiss-born doctor Elisabeth Kübler-Ross. I'd expected the book to focus on the afterlife, given the author's work and reputation. But, instead, I found it full of insights on living.

Dr. Kübler-Ross views everything in life as a circle, including human beings. She says all people have four "quadrants": their physical, intellectual, emotional, and spiritual sides.

- The *physical quadrant* contains our need for human contact.
- The *intellectual quadrant* contains intellect and thinking.
- The *emotional quadrant* contains our attitudes.
- And the *spiritual quadrant* contains our intuition.

She also claims that each of us is perfect, no matter how large or small each quadrant is. This truly struck a chord with me. My original concept of perfection resembled only the top circle in the following figure, but Kübler-Ross's statement seemed to imply that all three circles represent perfect human beings.

These quadrants vary in different people with different experiences and interests, and in different stages of life. Engineers might have large intellectual quadrants and display little emotion (like the circle on the left), while artists—and many of us with mood disorders—might have larger emotional quadrants (like the circle on the right).

OUR FOUR QUADRANTS

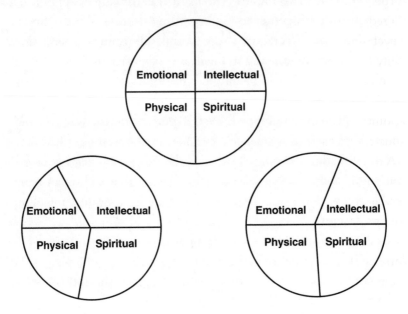

Kübler-Ross's quadrants can also apply to people who are blind but compensate for their loss of sight with an acute sense of hearing, or people with *Down syndrome* (who have reduced cognitive capabilities) being especially loving. But our society tends not to consider such people perfect. We're too conditioned to see "flaws" and "imperfections." The same holds true for those of us with mental illness.

To me, Kübler-Ross's view of perfection was quite a revelation. Sure, perfection may be a noble goal. It's even crucial in certain professions (such as engineering, teaching, and my own field—communications). But achieving perfection in *all* areas of our lives simultaneously is unachievable, even undesirable. Wouldn't life be easier if we could recognize and appreciate each other's strongest quadrants and build on others when we feel ready to do so?

Unrealistic Expectations

If you expect someone to be or act a certain way, you'll often be disappointed. You'll always want something other than what you have.

This may lead to being critical, judgmental, and rejecting. The same is true when you have unrealistic expectations of yourself.

Frequent episodes of hypomania or mania may create unrealistic expectations when you're "up." Then, when your mood levels out, reality may drop you into deep depression. You may discount or minimize every positive experience you've had, even when in a stable mood. This can create a continual state of mourning, grieving disappointments and losses. You may become so difficult to please that others will reject you, leaving you isolated and self-pitying.

A depressive episode following a manic or hypomanic episode can leave you suffering from "impostor syndrome." For years, I desperately anticipated the next high, when I could make up for a depressive episode. But if you allow such a pattern to continue and don't manage your disorder consistently, the mood cycles will most likely worsen, and your episodes will get even worse.

One further trap to beware of is comparing yourself to other people. Watch out when you have thoughts like So-and-so is doing so much better than I am. Although those of us with mood disorders share many commonalities, *no one has the exact same biochemistry, background, or experiences as you.* In a seminar given at a local psychiatric hospital, psychologist Dr. Jan Ford Mustin said when you compare yourself with others, you set yourself up to lose. Someone else will *always* be better off or worse off than you.

Rigid Beliefs

When you become too loyal to your own beliefs, they become your enemy and stand in the way of common sense. You hold fast to your beliefs, thinking that a change would indicate a lack of backbone or somehow threaten your survival. Rigid beliefs block creative thinking and cooperation with others. They lead to inflexibility, coldness, prejudice, isolation, and pain.

Some particularly helpful ways to adjust explanatory style, learned helplessness, unrealistic expectations, perfectionism, and rigid beliefs are through cognitive therapy or cognitive-behavioral therapy and through group therapy or self-help groups. *Cognitive therapy* addresses feelings you may have confused with facts. *Cognitive-behavioral therapy* does the same thing, plus it helps you change self-defeating habits.

Remember, people often equate personality and temperament with the individual. But neither is the total sum of you. Likewise, people may equate the symptoms of mental illness with those who suffer from them. But mood episodes are nothing more than *symptoms* of a brain disorder. You are not your illness. *You're a person with inherent value,* and you deserve treatment as much as any other person with a medical condition.

NINE

Reflecting on Childhood: Upbringing

IN ADDITION TO getting our physiological needs met (food, sleep, shelter, and so on), we all need to feel safe, secure, and free from fear. To build or maintain self-esteem, we need to feel loved, respected, and wanted. It's crucial we believe that we belong.

People living in healthful home environments affirm each other's feelings, reinforce each other's confidence, and celebrate each other's achievements. When children grow up in healthy families, they receive the support they need to learn and grow into independent and capable adults.

The "Bad-Parenting" Myth

Many people blame mental illness entirely on bad parenting. They think that if you develop a mood disorder that it's your parents' fault. We now know that people can be born with a genetic predisposition for a mental illness just as they can be born with a genetic predisposition for many other diseases. Whether or not they develop that disease depends on numerous factors.

While bad parenting doesn't cause mental illness, sometimes family dynamics are a contributing factor. Children with a genetic predisposition for a mental illness who are raised in dysfunctional families run a higher risk of developing one.

Researchers at the National Institute of Mental Health have identified some family behavior patterns that may contribute to mental illness. These include

- using denial to manage anger and anxiety,
- having unrealistic expectations and standards,
- finding it difficult to form intimate external relationships, and
- passing low self-esteem from parent to child.

What Makes a Family "Functional"?

A *functional*, healthy family works smoothly and supports its members. To clarify the term *support*, in this context I mean emotional support, which may or may not involve financial assistance. All family members can get both individual and group needs met and can communicate and cooperate effectively. The family helps each individual mature and reach their potential, and the relationships between all family members are open, honest, independent, and caring.

Functional families

- supply both social and sexual training,
- provide an environment conducive to *every* family member's survival and growth,
- value each individual equally,
- reinforce each member's self-esteem and sense of belonging,
- allow members to express their own thoughts and emotions in healthy ways,
- balance independence versus dependence,
- have clear but negotiable rules and expect accountability,
- view mistakes as occasions for growth,

- reduce anxiety and promote a spontaneous atmosphere of laughter and fun,
- promote maturity and clear ego boundaries,
- adjust flexibly to changing needs and stressful situations, and
- allow family members to choose their roles rather than follow traditional expectations.

People who come from functional families carry their functionality into work, school, and other environments. People who come from dysfunctional families carry their dysfunctionality into other environments as well.

What Makes a Family "Dysfunctional"?

A dysfunctional family may fulfill some of the roles of a functional family, but certainly not all. It might, for instance

- teach sexual training but reject family members with different sexual inclinations,
- value every individual but give one special treatment,
- allow family members to express thoughts and emotions but then belittle or criticize what they say,
- view mistakes as intentional attacks or carelessness, or
- deal with changes and stressful situations by depending exclusively on one or two family members rather than sharing the load more equitably.

Types of Dysfunctional Families

Although genes rather than dysfunctional families clearly seem to trigger mood disorders, unhealthful family dynamics can contribute to them as well. Five types of dysfunctional families, one or more of which are often combined, include the following:

1. The "perfect" family
2. The overprotective family

3. The distant family
4. The chaotic family
5. The abusive family

In many cases, families display more than one type of dysfunction.

The "Perfect" Family

"Perfect" families look good on the surface, but their members must submerge their true feelings for one reason or another. In these families, members are overly concerned with appearances and keeping up with the Joneses.

The Overprotective Family

Overprotective families smother family members rather than support them to mature naturally. Maturity requires that individuals have the emotional freedom to make choices without angering other family members or feeling guilty about those choices.

The Distant Family

In distant families, members display little warmth and little communication. Parents may withhold affection that children need desperately if they're to thrive. During critical stages of a child's development, an emotionally distant or absent parent presents an additional risk for mental illness.

The Chaotic Family

In chaotic families, the parents are unavailable, and rules are inconsistent or nonexistent. When both parents work long, inflexible hours, or they separate or divorce, chaotic families tend to result.

The Abusive Family

In abusive families, violence and anger rule. The children experience any one or any combination of physical, sexual, or verbal abuse. Usually, only one person in the family—one parent—is allowed to express anger, while the other parent lives in denial.

Analyzing My Own Family

For quite some time, I examined my own upbringing for clues as to what might have led to my emotional difficulties. My family had some conflicts and communication problems, but I never considered it truly dysfunctional. I associated the term only with alcoholism, drugs, and physical or sexual abuse. I could more readily identify factors in my sister Barbara's upbringing and my niece's that might have caused mental illness to emerge.

Barbara's Upbringing

When Mother and her first husband divorced, Barbara was five years old, and Mother's ex got custody of Barbara. But because his job required so much travel, he sometimes left her in foster homes. She didn't live with him regularly until her teens, when he remarried, and her new stepmother didn't much care for her.

Being only five when she lost her mother and having such an unstable upbringing caused Barbara lots of grief. She turned to alcohol for solace. Barbara's daughter and one of her former husbands have both acknowledged the profound sense of abandonment she felt. I believe that Barbara's childhood experiences triggered the bipolar disorder that emerged later on.

Because Barbara was so young and barely even saw Mother during the majority of her childhood, I don't see how my family's values, expectations, and traditions could have influenced her that much.

My Niece's Upbringing

My other two sisters and I grew up in the same household, so we *were* exposed to more of the same values, expectations, and traditions. Because her mother didn't work outside the home, however, my niece received much more love and mothering when she was young than Barbara did. However, my niece faced additional challenges my sisters and I didn't. While my father was a good provider who rarely took a drink, my niece's father had alcoholism and frequently couldn't keep a job.

When my sister divorced my niece's father, she and her children, who were in their teens, were left homeless. For a year they lived in their church's basement while my sister attended secretarial school. Several years of moving from one apartment to another followed. My niece had her first psychotic break when she was sixteen. So she, too, faced significant trauma while growing up.

My Upbringing

My parents rarely drank and didn't take illicit drugs. They didn't beat me or sexually abuse me. I thought my upbringing was fairly normal and healthy for a middle-class urban family in the 1950s and 1960s.

We ate meals together, rarely in front of a TV. We attended church and celebrated holidays as a family. We played cards and board games, completed jigsaw puzzles, and interacted with neighbors and family friends.

My parents provided many rich opportunities that other children never got. I had dance and piano lessons and was active in drama. Both my parents came to my recitals and plays. Mother drove me to these activities and to my many doctor and orthodontist appointments. From the age of nine, I was active in Camp Fire Girls and went to summer camp each year.

Like children tend to do, I took these things for granted. But it wasn't as if my parents handed me everything. To earn my allowance and these special privileges, I helped with the housework and yardwork, held the flashlight when my father worked on the car, and helped build the backyard patio.

My parents encouraged my sense of independence too. I sold greeting cards to earn a bicycle, and candy to help pay for summer camp. My family taught me how to manage a budget, cook, be considerate of others, and act responsibly. For the most part, my family seemed as functional as they come.

Although my relationship with Daddy was often difficult, I could find little evidence to blame my disorder on my upbringing. I do believe, however, that two dysfunctional patterns in my family lowered my self-esteem and compounded my illness. These were some unhealthy communication problems and my parents' use of corporal punishment.

Family Communication

One common problem in dysfunctional families is poor communication skills. Often problems arise from making assumptions about what a person thinks or means. When we assume rather than communicate more directly, havoc tends to result.

The Ladder of Inference

In 1990, a Harvard Business School professor, Dr. Chris Argyris, introduced a concept called the *ladder of inference* to explain direct versus indirect communications. Argyris's ladder consists of four levels or rungs.

- The first rung represents an observable action or statement. An example might be kissing a child good night or saying "I love you."
- The second rung represents a culturally understood meaning. In Western cultures, a kiss or saying "I love you" means someone cares for you.
- The third rung represents a meaning we attribute to the action or statement. If, for instance, you don't kiss your

child or say "I love you," the child may conclude that you don't care.

- The fourth rung represents the theories we use to make third-rung conclusions. For this example, the child might theorize that parents who care always kiss their children and say "I love you."

Operating from the ladder of inference rather than checking out your theories or assumptions makes it difficult to get your needs met.

Communicating Specifically

When I became a stepmother, I had a few problems with my stepchildren. Although I had some problems being a stepmother, they had much more to do with myself and my poor self-concept than with the wonderful children I was blessed to raise. Still, a few conflicts did arise. While I didn't label Tom or Joy and tried my best not to judge them, the differences in our standards for a "clean" household led to a few conflicts.

After discovering Adele Faber and Elaine Mazlish's *How to Talk So Kids Will Listen and Listen So Kids Will Talk,* I had a small breakthrough with Joy. I'd always asked the kids to rinse their dishes before placing them in the dishwasher because it didn't clean off sticky residue. One evening after eating spaghetti, I scolded Joy for not rinsing her plate before placing it in the dishwasher.

"But I did!" she said. "Though it's pointless anyway." When I asked her to rinse her plate again, she ran some water over it, but the residue still stuck. I then saw she wasn't being lazy or uncooperative: *I just wasn't being specific enough.* In Joy's head, "rinse" meant running water over a dish, but in mine, it meant doing so *while scrubbing off the residue.*

Most any form of talk therapy can help you learn and practice to communicate more specifically and directly.

Fair Fighting

Every family has its problems. It's human nature for individuals to sometimes disagree. Functional families are committed to working out their problems, and when they disagree, they're more inclined to fight fair. Fighting fair involves

- self-assertion rather than aggression or trying to get back at the other person,
- staying in the present and not bringing up past conflicts,
- sticking with concrete details about the problem,
- avoiding judgment,
- being honest and accurate,
- not arguing over little details,
- not blaming the other person,
- listening actively and confirming what you hear,
- focusing on one issue at a time, and
- aiming to solve the problem rather than trying to prove who's "right."

When things get too emotional, one useful technique to try is the "whisper rule." It involves

- agreeing to whisper,
- listening carefully and clarifying the other person's message,
- acknowledging what's working and what's not working, and
- requesting specific behavior changes.

Unfair fighting, on the other hand, tends to be the norm in dysfunctional families.

Family Discipline

Many parents equate discipline with punishment, but experts say there's a significant difference. *Punishment* involves chastising, penalizing, retaliating, treating roughly or harshly, and creating hurt and pain. Those who punish children often do so to control or subordinate them.

Discipline is a more loving form of correction that involves teaching and training and helping children learn self-control. Discipline helps build character and strengthen morality. It reinforces rules and acceptable behaviors.

The psychoanalyst and researcher Dr. Alice Miller says that adults who humiliate and harshly punish children lose their true authority. Rather than becoming responsible adults, such children often become vengeful and violent. Discipline involves respecting and protecting children. It involves truly listening to them and talking with them.

Corporal Punishment and Self-Esteem

When parents make children "behave" through force, fear, or punishment, they imply that adults are superior and dis-empower their children. For many children, spanking is degrading and humiliating. It leaves them feeling afraid, angry, and rejected by the very people they most need to love and trust. It conveys the idea that it's okay to solve conflicts with physical violence rather than with open communication and peaceful negotiation. It creates a sense of frustration that many children bottle up for years, then unleash when they're big enough to fight back.

"Problem behaviors" are sometimes merely attempts to communicate the child's unmet needs:

- Hunger, thirst, sleep, fresh air, and exercise;
- Safety, security, and freedom from fear; and
- Love, affection, and connection with others—including times during which the child has a parent's undivided attention.

Infants and young children often lack the developmental skills to communicate their needs to parents effectively. Parents who don't understand child development often wrongly assume the child is acting up, and consequently spank or hit them.

No Big Deal

I grew up in a neighborhood in which spanking was commonplace. Many children claimed their punishment was "no big deal," but I sensed hurt or shame in their eyes. My parents spanked us on the buttocks with their hands. Other children's parents used hairbrushes, wooden paddles, or switches. The child across the street was beaten every day, and I often rushed by her house to avoid hearing her cries.

When I witness a parent scolding a child in public with threats like "You're going to get it when we get home" or "I'll whip your butt if you do that again," I become highly distressed. Seeing someone actually strike a child makes me want to grab the parent and scream "What are you doing? Don't you realize you may be destroying your child's self-esteem?"

Still, before my second marriage, I found it hard to believe my husband when he said he and his ex-wife didn't spank the children. I thought, What am I getting into? These kids may be holy terrors when company's not around! Having grown up in a period when corporal punishment was commonplace and children regularly got spankings at school, the idea that a child "just needs a good spanking" was part of my everyday experience. I never realized there was any other choice. I always hated spanking and the way it made me feel, but I'd considered it a distasteful necessity of parenting. After marrying Ralph, I saw that he truly could deal with Tom and Joy without spanking, hitting, or even yelling at them.

When Tom was thirty, he shared his views about discipline with us. He said he didn't know until sixth grade, when staying overnight with a friend, that other parents beat their children and shouted at them constantly. Tom's friend was terrified of his father and cried himself to sleep each night.

I'm convinced that many societal problems result from the way such family interactions shatter self-esteem.

Spare the Rod

Study after study has shown the negative effects that spanking has on children's self-esteem. Some researchers believe that any time an adult physically abuses a child, the child bears an emotional scar forever. My father's spankings were humiliating and increased my fear of him.

Although many parents quote the Bible to justify their use of corporal punishment, Jesus urged us to love our children, and there are far more effective ways to show our love than spanking them. The organization End Violence Against the Next Generation (EVAN-G) associates using "the rod" for punishment with the Book of Proverbs written by Solomon, who applied harsh, punitive methods. But biblical scholars know that King Solomon's son became a cruel, oppressive, tyrannical dictator. Do we really want to follow such advice?

More and more people now see corporal punishment as unnecessary and consider it a form of physical abuse, but some still hold fast to the belief that spanking is a necessity.

VERBAL ABUSE

The experts say that verbal abuse can be just as damaging—or more so—than physical or sexual abuse.

The physical punishment my sisters and I received in our family wasn't that severe, but our father's verbal abuse was quite damaging. It affected even Mother, who had great difficulty standing up to him.

Daddy was difficult to live with (and from comments made at his memorial after he died from cancer, difficult to work with as well). He was extraordinarily stubborn, often irritable and angry, and occasionally depressed. The aura in our family transformed from calm and relaxed to watchful and anxious the moment he got home. At quite an early age, I learned that there'd be hell to pay if I upset Daddy.

In Daddy's view, most of the time he was perfectly fine. If you dared to disagree with him, you were *flat-out wrong. You* were the one who had the problem. He'd accuse my mother, my sisters, and me of ganging up on him on the rare occasions when we had the nerve to disagree with him or to confront him about his behavior.

Kay and Jo had more optimistic personalities than I did from the start, and they were better equipped than I was to deal with Daddy's difficult behaviors. And because they were just two years apart, they reinforced each other's emotional resolve. But being the youngest, the shyest, and the least self-confident, I witnessed the results when my sisters or Mother stood up to Daddy, and in my fear of any confrontation, I learned to keep my mouth shut and do what it took to keep from being disowned.

For me, Daddy became a "negative wizard"—a controlling person you may respect or even love but are terrified to confront. And a number of authority figures, including my most difficult boss, later affected me the same way.

COMMUNICATING WITHOUT LABELING

When I first moved to Austin, I worked in the Orthopedics and Physical Therapy Department at the University of Texas Student Health Center. One day, one of the nurses pulled me aside and confronted me about the mess on my desk. She said that it depressed her when she got to work and that she'd appreciate it if I'd tidy up before leaving each day. She didn't call me a slob or judge me for being disorganized or lazy. She simply told me how she felt.

It was one of the first times I remember having been confronted about my behavior without being belittled, scolded, or being spanked. That was so foreign to me. Years later, I finally understood that she was communicating from a *feeling* level. Talk therapy and self-help groups can help you learn and practice communication from a feeling level.

ADOPTING FALSE PERSONAS

As the last child and eight years younger than my closest sibling, Jo, I spent half of my childhood with my siblings and the other half essentially as an only child. Kay, ten years older than me, joined a sorority and moved out when she started college. Then she dropped out and married toward the end of her first year. Jo left for college two years later, when I was only nine. This left me with no buffer but Mother between Daddy and me.

To protect myself and prevent losing my mother's love because I feared she might side with Daddy, I withheld my feelings and opinions and hid many of my problems from my family. I was frequently depressed, but I hid my symptoms because I was convinced my parents would think I was weak, immature, or even evil.

I hated the way I felt I must bury my true self to be accepted by my father. At one point, shortly after I married Ralph, I went alone to my parents' home for some holiday. When he called to check in and I picked up the phone, he said, "You're talking funny. What's going on?" I asked him what he meant, though I knew perfectly well what he was observing. "Why are you talking in a cartoon voice?" I replied that we'd discuss it later and hung up.

At the age of fifty-one, I'm still learning who I am.

It would be easy to conclude that my upbringing led to my illness. And you could argue that mood disorders run in families only because they share the same values, expectations, and traditions, but at least in Barbara's case, that argument doesn't seem to hold.

After Barbara's suicide, the fact that she, my niece, and I all had bipolar diagnoses but grew up in separate households helped further convince me that genetics and biochemistry played a larger part.

TEN

Encountering Snarls:
Stress and Trauma

SOME PEOPLE BELIEVE that stressful or traumatic events are the sole cause of mental illness. Others think that those of us with mental illness are oversensitive and simply overreact to everything. The current thinking of mental health professionals implies that while stress and trauma don't *cause* mood disorders, they can certainly *trigger* episodes or *intensify* those in progress.

Perhaps those of us with mood disorders *are* more sensitive than others, but is sensitivity inherently "bad"? I think there's some value in it. Perhaps if others were more sensitive, the world would be a better place.

This chapter defines stress and trauma, describes how they affect our bodies, and how stress relates to mood disorders.

Stress

Most definitions of *stress* focus on anxiety and tension. They equate stress with extreme difficulty, emotional upset, pressure, strain, and the inability to keep up. Stress is not only mental but physical. It takes a toll on many bodily systems. We'll examine the physical effects of stress later in this chapter.

We speak of being "stressed out" in all kinds of situations, such as when we're

- pressured to meet tight deadlines,
- dealing with critical people,
- disciplining children or pets,
- trying to recover from a cold or a virus,
- entering new situations, or
- changing the nature of existing relationships.

Obviously, this list could consume many pages. *Life itself is stressful*—for everybody—especially in the twenty-first century. The pace keeps going faster and faster, and it becomes more and more difficult to keep up.

Because of our illness, those of us with mood disorders often face other *stressors* (stress-producing situations), which may compound our episodes even more. For example:

- Difficulty meeting basic physiological needs, such as having a place to live or enough food to survive;
- Unemployment or job instability;
- Financial problems due to hypomanic or manic overspending;
- Relationship problems at home or at work;
- Chronic or recurrent physical illnesses; and
- Heavy reliance on medical professionals, family members, and friends for treatment and support.

Just reading about stress may stress you out. (Sorry, I must include this topic, but you *do* need to know.)

"Bad" Stress and "Good" Stress

While most people associate stress with "negative" experiences, "positive" experiences produce stress as well. Starting a new job, entering a new relationship, getting married, buying a home, or going on vacation are all examples of potentially positive stressors.

Sometimes what feels like negative stress to one person may feel merely stimulating to another. One example might be public speaking—the number-one fear of most people in this country. Statistics show that the fear of speaking before an audience frightens most people more than death.

But other people actually enjoy and thrive on public speaking— including me, thanks to the training and practice I've received through Toastmasters. An experienced public speaker may have a touch of stage fright or a slight case of "butterflies in the stomach," but such feelings can actually enhance a speech when the speaker can channel it effectively.

TOASTMASTERS INTERNATIONAL

TOASTMASTERS NOT only helps you learn and practice public speaking skills but can be an excellent source of emotional and social support.

I originally joined Toastmasters to practice speaking about my work and mental illness more effectively and to help ease my social anxiety.

I first "came out" about my illness in my Toastmasters group, through which I've received much support and made many friends.

Another woman I know with severe unipolar disorder is a long-term Toastmaster. She says she's gained more from Toastmasters than she has from years of talk therapy.

The Resources section has more information about Toastmasters.

Whether negative or positive, stress always disrupts life in some way. And those of us with mood disorders are particularly sensitive to stress. It's therefore important to be aware of potential stressors and to prepare yourself to deal with them whenever possible.

Common High-Stress Experiences

Experts agree that certain life experiences produce stress in nearly everyone. These stressors go hand in hand with pain and conflict, novelty and uncertainty, or some mixture of these factors.

In 1967, Drs. Thomas Holmes and Richard Rahe, psychiatrists at the University of Washington Medical School, created a tool called the Social Readjustment Rating Scale to predict how stress might lead to physical illness. You've probably seen this scale or similar ones in magazine or newspaper articles.

Holmes and Rahe's participants rated stressors from most stressful (100) to least stressful (1), based on how much they changed or might change their lives. For instance, the death of a spouse rated 100, divorce rated 73, marriage rated 50, a change in living conditions rated 25, a vacation rated 13, and a minor legal violation rated 11.

Based on the total number of stressors each participant had experienced in the past twelve months, Holmes and Rahe predicted the likelihood that participant would experience an illness. Then they followed up on their subjects' health the next year. These were their conclusions:

- If you score 150 to 199, you have a 37 percent chance of getting sick within the next year.
- If you score 200 to 299, the chance increases to 51 percent.
- If you score above 300, the chance increases to 79 percent.

An associate professor of management at the Indiana University Northwest School of Business, Dr. Charles Hobson, with a few other researchers, conducted a similar survey in the late 1990s. The top twenty stressors among United States employees were more reflective of current concerns than Holmes and Rahe's scale and had overlapping themes:

- **Death and dying**—A spouse or mate's death rated only 87 (as opposed to 100), but a close friend's death rated 61 (as opposed to 37).

- **Crime and the criminal justice system**—A jail term rated 76 (as opposed to 63), and being a victim of a crime (70) was added.
- **Financial and economic concerns**—Foreclosure on a loan or mortgage rated 71 (as opposed to 30), and getting fired rated 64 (as opposed to 47).
- **Family-related issues**—Infidelity (69), and becoming a single parent (59) were added.
- **Health care**—A major reduction or loss of health insurance, and assuming responsibility for a sick loved one were added (both rating 56).

I'd like to see a similar study done for those of us with mental illness that would account for the stresses involved with changing doctors or therapists, trying different medications, or attempting to get treated when your insurance imposes limitations or you have little financial or emotional support. Your ability to cope with change, along with the amount of support you receive from others, also affects the likelihood that you'll get sick.

Stress Is Not All Bad

However, not all stress is bad for you. In fact, some degree of stress actually *helps* your body function properly. The stress hormones **adrenaline** and **cortisol** help the body respond to stress. Cortisol helps

- maintain blood pressure and cardiovascular function;
- slow the immune system's inflammatory response;
- balance the effects of insulin, affecting energy; and
- regulate protein, carbohydrate, and fat metabolism.

And if your adrenal gland chronically produces insufficient cortisol, you may develop the disorder called Addison's disease.

Healthy levels of cortisol vary during a twenty-four-hour day. In normal people, cortisol levels usually rise shortly before their standard wake-up time, peak about midday, and then gradually fall to the lowest level near bedtime. However, chronically high cortisol levels can overload your brain.

The Physical Nature of Stress

Although we experience stress cognitively and emotionally, it mostly affects our endocrine system, which operates as a stress feedback loop. When you encounter, or even *anticipate,* a stressor, your limbic system and cerebral cortex register your reaction. This sets off the following series of events:

- Your **hypothalamus** sends **thyroid releasing hormone (TRH)** to the **thyroid**, signaling it to quickly convert nutrients into energy.
- Your hypothalamus also sends **corticotropin releasing hormone (CRH)** to the **pituitary gland**, signaling it to secrete **adrenocorticotropic hormone (ACTH)**.
- The ACTH stimulates the **adrenal glands** to release **cortisol** into your blood to prepare you to deal with stress or crisis by fleeing or fighting.
- Your bloodstream cycles the cortisol back to the hypothalamus, which can send out more CRH if needed, or stop releasing it if your stress has decreased.

If your hypothalamus doesn't stop releasing CRH, your brain will stay locked in the stress response, possibly for days. Eventually, other mechanisms in your **endocrine system** usually help reset cortisol to normal levels.

SHORT-TERM STRESS

Short-term stress tends not to cause problems; in fact, it actually can enhance immunity. Some examples of short-term stressors include close calls, such as nearly rear-ending a car in front of you or having lightning strike nearby. But chronic stress can suppress the immune system, increase blood **cholesterol** (the sticky form of fat that impairs circulation), and even cause calcium loss from your bones.

CHRONIC STRESS

When you're depressed, you may produce high levels of cortisol all day, which can make it harder for your cerebral cortex to process crises and stressful events. Even an *anticipated* stressor, such as a potential job transfer, an upcoming move, or the anniversary of a trauma can increase stress levels.

When you worry about potential stressors, whether your concerns are warranted or not, your cortisol remains elevated and can eventually alter your brain's biochemistry. The cortisol may remain chronically high despite what's happening in your environment. Your body may circulate too much cortisol whether stressors are present or absent, when you're sitting quietly, or even when you're asleep. While chronic stress can trigger or worsen depression, the reverse is also true.

Kindling

A stressor may trigger an initial mood episode and increase the likelihood that additional stressors will trigger further episodes over time. When a disorder goes untreated or undertreated, later episodes may involve no readily identifiable stressor. A theoretical process called **kindling** (sensitization) may explain why. Just like fire-starting materials called kindling prime branches and logs for fires, kindling in the body makes it prone to further injury. For instance, a severe ankle sprain will make you susceptible to additional ankle injuries. The same process seems to hold true with the brain. Chronic stress can lead to "brain strain," and vulnerability to further stress.

Some researchers think that mood stabilizers and anticonvulsant medications work partially by reducing kindling. Lithium appears to block the early stages of kindling, and mood-stabilizing anticonvulsants (like carbamazepine, valproate, or valproic acid) appear to affect kindling somewhat later.

Consistently high cortisol levels can lead to visible long-term damage. Through MRI studies, Rockefeller University professor and head of its Laboratory of Neuroendocrinology Dr. Bruce McEwen found that long-term chronic stress actually *shrinks* the hippocampus in the brain.

All this talk about the effects of stress may make you think that stress alone causes mood disorders. But, according to the experts, this isn't true. If it were, the entire population would probably have mood disorders.

> CURRENT SCIENTIFIC knowledge indicates that *you don't develop bipolar disorder unless you're genetically predisposed.*

Currently, most scientists believe that a genetic predisposition combined with sufficient stress creates a **pathological** state (or illness), which in turn produces signs and symptoms. This also appears to be the case for other stress-related illnesses, like cancer, diabetes, heart disease, hypertension, and thyroid disease.

Signs and Symptoms of Stress

Stress can lead to changes in thinking, emotions, and behavior, and to physical changes as well. Some of the signs and symptoms include

- Anxiety and nervousness
- Appetite and weight changes
- Avoidance and procrastination
- Cold, sweaty hands
- Concentration and memory problems
- Constipation or diarrhea
- Crying or feeling all choked up
- Dizziness, faintness, and weakness
- Feeling overwhelmed and panicked
- Fidgeting and restlessness
- Headaches
- Increased use of alcohol or drugs, including nicotine
- Indigestion, nausea, and vomiting
- Irritability

- Jaw clenching or tooth grinding
- Knotted stomach or stomachaches
- Loss of libido
- Muscle pain or tension
- Pounding heart and rising blood pressure
- Seeking more social contact or withdrawing from others
- Shakiness or trembling
- Sweating
- Tiredness, often accompanied by insomnia
- Changes in urinary frequency and urgency
- Worrying and being unable to relax

Note the many parallels between the signs and symptoms of stress and those of mood disorders. Stress can certainly help cloud diagnosis. No wonder people often blame our problems on stress. Another potential problem stems from traumatic experiences.

Trauma

Although stress and trauma share similarities, they aren't quite the same. *Trauma* is or feels more

- physically violating or life-threatening,
- sudden and shocking,
- extreme and frightening, and
- short-term (though it may have long-term consequences).

Traumatic experiences might include accidents, layoffs, robberies, muggings, fires, rapes, kidnappings, torture, wars, and natural disasters.

Post-Traumatic Stress Disorder

If you've experienced particularly intense trauma, you may be diagnosed with *post-traumatic stress disorder (PTSD)*. Sometimes mood disorders are mistaken for PTSD, and sometimes these disorders co-occur.

PTSD is particularly common in military veterans, prisoners of war, victims of rape, and victims of abuse. A serious accident or a surgical procedure will sometimes produce PTSD. Much depends on what the person hears and how he or she is handled when semiconscious or anesthetized. Even a person who *witnesses* a traumatic event, such as a fatal accident or a violent act, can develop PTSD. A serious illness or the sudden death of a loved one can lead to PTSD too.

Although some psychiatrists consider post-traumatic stress disorder a memory disorder, the *DSM-IV* classifies PTSD as an anxiety disorder. Those who suffer from it essentially "relive" the traumatic event repeatedly.

People with this disorder may

- be plagued by recurrent nightmares or insomnia;
- feel intense anxiety when exposed to any stimuli they associate with the event;
- avoid people, places, or activities they associate with the event;
- become extremely startled by any unexpected stimuli, such as loud noises, certain smells, or the sudden presence of another person;
- experience hallucinations and flashbacks, and in extreme cases physically reenact the trauma as if in the midst of it;
- have outbursts of irritability or anger;
- become detached or estranged from others, or feel incapable of love;
- have difficulty concentrating and functioning at school or work, and in other social situations; and
- develop a sense of helplessness and doubt about the future.

Some people with PTSD block details about the trauma from their memories. Initially, denial may help a person get through a crisis, but the unconscious will deeply engrave the memory of trauma, which the person must eventually face in order to recover.

My Experiences of Stress and Trauma

I'd been through so many stressful and traumatic events that sometimes I felt like a professional victim. In addition to living with multiple chronic illnesses, I've been through one divorce, a sudden unexpected layoff, several minor thefts and eight break-ins, and two rapes.

During my twenties and part of my early thirties, I thought that some of these events—particularly the rapes and burglaries—might have caused my depressive episodes.

The first time I was raped was as a college sophomore. A group of theater students piled into someone's car and braved a Kansas blizzard to attend a graduate student's party. He had a large two-story house and several roommates.

When we reached the party, there were quite a few people I didn't know. Feeling a bit awkward among so many strangers, I took a seat next to a young man playing a guitar. In my late teens I'd started teaching myself to play the guitar. Later, as a summer camp counselor, I knew enough to play all the standard camp songs and several popular folk tunes. Consequently, I felt relatively comfortable sitting by a stranger plucking a guitar.

I sat and listened to him play and, when I could, sang along. When he took a break, he handed me the guitar and offered to refill my drink. That's where things went wrong. I'd had only one glass of wine at the party and was accustomed to drinking much more with little problem. But after the second glass I became semiconscious. The last thing I recall about the party was being toted over someone's shoulder to a room off the kitchen.

When I awoke the next day, I was lying naked in bed with a stranger. I'm not even certain it was the guitar player, as my "partner" was sound asleep on his stomach, and I was frantic to leave as soon as possible. I retrieved my clothing from a pool of vomit, dressed as quickly as I could, and went to the bathroom to clean up.

There was vomit in my hair, which at the time was long, and semen dripped onto my underpants. When I left the bathroom, the rest of the house seemed deserted. Everyone else must have still been sleeping or must have left much earlier. I put my coat on and trudged through deep snow the full two miles back to my dorm. Because my father had warned me of the dangers of boys slipping drugs into girls' drinks in order to take advantage of them, I concluded the rape was all my fault.

The rape that took place during my junior year of college was decidedly more traumatic. I lived off campus in a three-story house converted into several apartments. My roommates and I lived on the top floor across from a Vietnam vet and his roommate. The vet was a wiry guy, about five foot five, but still quite strong. His roommate was around six and a half feet tall and must have weighed well over 300 pounds.

I didn't interact much with the guys across the hall, but they often came over to visit with my roommates. Occasionally, I'd join in their conversations, but to me, they were mere acquaintances rather than friends. My roommate became involved with the large guy, who at one point revealed that the vet's behavior sometimes frightened him.

One day when they were over, I'd been complaining about not having a boyfriend and feeling unloved. The vet offered to "fix" things, and I turned him down. But he became insistent, picked me up, and headed for the door. I kicked and screamed, but my roommates, thinking I was playing hard to get, helped him get me out the door. I felt like a human sacrifice.

We entered his place through the kitchen. On the way to the curtained area where he slept, he nodded to a huge butcher knife. Then he said, "Better not give me any trouble." I was terrified. Small as he was, he'd already overpowered me, and the fact that he'd intimidated his roommate sprang to mind.

In junior high or high school, a local policeman had presented a rape prevention seminar. He instructed us girls to *not* resist rapists, as we stood little chance of overpowering them. He said screaming or crying would only make things worse. "You know how sometimes you want to smash an alarm clock when it's ringing? If you scream, the rapist may get angry and kill you."

I followed his advice and stopped struggling. I felt not only violated but betrayed by this experience, and had difficulty trusting others for several years.

Studies have linked the ability to cope with stress and trauma to emotional support. A supportive family, friends, and community, as well as a good therapist or a support group, can greatly aid your recovery. Even a loving pet can help.

PART THREE

Maintaining Balance

ELEVEN

Building a Foundation: First Things First

To BALANCE MOODS and emotions and stay as healthy as possible, you must first meet some basic needs. This is true for everyone but becomes especially important when you have a mood disorder. This chapter addresses the primary needs that people must usually satisfy to support good mental and physical health.

Maslow's Hierarchy of Needs

The humanist psychologist Dr. Abraham Maslow created a theory based on a hierarchy of human needs. At the lower levels are basic or *deficiency needs*—those we're driven to meet when they're lacking. At the higher levels are *growth needs*—those that help us feel fulfilled as human beings. Although needs at different levels interrelate and sometimes clamor to be filled simultaneously, we must generally fulfill lower-level needs before we can fulfill higher-level needs. As one need gets met, another invariably pops up behind it. Put another way, the higher the need on the hierarchy, the less likely it's been fully satisfied. The following figure illustrates Maslow's ideas.

MASLOW'S HIERARCHY OF NEEDS

Deficiency Needs

At the most basic level of the hierarchy (the pyramid's foundation) are *physiological needs*—those that could kill us if left unmet: oxygen, water, food, sleep, shelter, and sex. Some might argue that the lack of sex won't kill you, but if *everyone* abstained from sex, it would kill off our species. Our need for *safety*, security, and freedom from fear comes next and relates more to environment than to physicality.

Then comes our need for love, affection, and connection with others—a need that Maslow called *belongingness.* The last level of deficiency needs relates to our need for *esteem*—both self-esteem and acknowledgment from other people. This level includes the need for confidence, achievement, and independence, as well as for acceptance, recognition, and respect.

Growth Needs

Growth needs include our needs for *knowledge* and understanding, for *aesthetics* and order, for *self-fulfillment,* or following our calling, and our need to help others. Maslow called this need to make a contribution beyond ourselves *transcendence*. Some scholars group all growth needs together and call them *self-actualization needs*.

How do these needs apply to bipolar disorder? To a large extent, Maslow's hierarchy implies that to make significant progress on growth needs you must first meet deficiency needs. It implies you're not likely to make much progress in talk therapy when you're malnourished or homeless or being abused.

The same is true when biochemistry is out of balance; to successfully address other problems, you must first adjust your biochemistry. Some of us must even adjust our biochemistry in order to eat properly or get adequate sleep. The founders of the Hestia Institute in Wellesley, Massachusetts, Dr. Deborah Sichel and Jeanne Watson Driscoll, M.S., R.N., C.S., call this "getting the biology out of the way." This is one reason I'm a proponent of medication. It's generally the fastest way to balance biochemistry. And although brain chemistry is not built specifically into Maslow's model (perhaps because we knew so little about it during his lifetime), he does acknowledge that vitamins, minerals, hormones, and so on affect **homeostasis** (the body's state of stability and balance). I therefore believe he would agree that balanced brain chemistry qualifies as a deficiency need.

Let's take a closer look at some deficiency needs as they relate to bipolar disorder.

Sleep and Biorhythms

One of the most important things you can do to manage bipolar disorder is to get the right amount of sleep. When depressed, some people sleep excessively; others sleep fitfully or wake up early and can't get back to sleep. In a manic phase, you may have trouble getting to sleep or staying asleep. You may not sleep at all or get as few as three or four hours of sleep a night for days on end. Then finally you crash. In fact, sleep deprivation is such a problem that before modern treatments became available, roughly 15 percent of manic patients lost their lives to physical exhaustion.

Disrupted sleep patterns appear to cause chemical changes in the body that can trigger mood episodes. Those of us with bipolar disorder seem to have delicate "internal clocks" and losing even a single night's sleep can disrupt our *biorhythms* (natural or habitual biological rhythms, such as sleep-wake patterns) and lead to hypomania or mania.

One way doctors sometimes diagnose bipolar disorder is by observing the effects of intentional sleep deprivation. Your doctor may ask you to go without sleep for a night to see if it brings on a manic state. You may be asked to try to sleep at a lab while technicians run an **electroencephalogram (EEG)**. For an EEG, which is similar to an *electrocardiogram (EKG)* for testing the heart, electrodes run from your scalp to a machine. Your brain's electrical signals produce brain-wave patterns on the EEG machine.

TIPS FOR GETTING A GOOD NIGHT'S SLEEP

Establish a regular bedtime and stick to it as much as possible. Avoid naps, but if you find them necessary, limit them to about twenty minutes. Continuous sleep is much more restful.

If you use caffeine, limit your consumption to early in the day. If you smoke or drink alcohol, stop doing so within a few hours of bedtime.

Let yourself unwind an hour or so before bedtime. Read a book or magazine, listen to music, meditate, play with a pet, or take a bubble bath. Avoid violent TV shows, and skip upsetting news reports.

Save the bedroom for sleeping and sex. Although light reading may be okay, don't bring work to bed. And save discussions for another place and time. This includes conversations about sexual problems.

Don't try to force yourself to sleep. Just enjoy resting and feeling your muscles. Or use a relaxation technique. Some people find listening to tapes or peaceful sounds helpful.

Adjust your sleep in advance when traveling to a different time zone. For very short trips, this may not be necessary, but for longer ones adjust your sleep, meals, and medication dosage time to match the target time zone over several days.

Block out annoying distractions. If light or noise keeps you awake and you can't block them out in other ways, cover your eyes with a black sleeping mask and wear earplugs.

It's generally best to maintain a stable sleep pattern. Try to go to bed about the same time each night and get up about the same time each morning. The timing of your sleep is also important. The more restful sleep for most of us is consecutive nighttime sleep. If you tend to have insomnia, avoid taking naps, or limit them to only twenty minutes. You may require more hours of sleep to function than you did before your disorder surfaced. Some doctors recommend as much as ten hours of sleep a night for those with mood disorders. If you have trouble sleeping or are sleeping too much, by all means inform your doctor.

If you take a trip that requires changing time zones, ask your doctor for advice before you go. Jet lag can have serious consequences when you have bipolar disorder. Also consider the effects of a different environment. Do whatever you can to ensure that your accommodations will make it easy to sleep. After one night in a noisy hotel bumped me into a hypomanic state, I started traveling with earplugs.

Pay special attention to your personal biorhythms and sleep-wake patterns. I've found that the last half hour or so of sleep makes a world of difference for me. If that time gets disrupted, I don't function well all day. When do you feel the most alert? Does your energy tend to drop at any particular time of the day? I'm not much of a morning person. My energy doesn't kick in until 9 or 10 A.M., then it drops again around 3:30 or 4 P.M. A brief walk, a piece of fruit, or some caffeinated tea often perks me up, but sometimes I need a nap.

Because biorhythms also affect blood sugar levels and bowel functions, people with bipolar disorder often display symptoms of *hypoglycemia* (low blood sugar), constipation, or diarrhea.

Sometimes other cycles play a part. For instance, in some people severe depression is more prevalent in the winter, and mania in the late summer. This may relate to our need for sunshine, which people require particularly at dawn and dusk, to maintain a twenty-four-hour sleep-wake cycle. People who have **seasonal affective disorder (SAD)** may need considerably more. The use of artificial lights late into the night, say some authorities, may have extended our sleep-wake cycle beyond healthy limits.

Many women with bipolar disorder also experience *premenstrual syndrome (PMS)* and find themselves bottoming out right before their periods. This was certainly the case for me before I reached *perimenopause* (the state directly preceding *menopause*—the time when a woman's periods stop permanently).

Nutrition

It's no secret: The average U.S. diet is far from healthful. Although "proper" nutrition varies for each individual, some nutritional guidelines apply to almost everyone. Most of us consume too much sugar, caffeine, and processed foods and skimp on whole grains, fruit, and vegetables. In addition, those of us with bipolar disorder tend to either starve ourselves or eat compulsively. In the midst of a depressive or manic episode, you may lose your appetite or simply forget to eat.

Regular Mealtimes

Eating regularly scheduled healthful meals helps us maintain an adequate level of blood sugar. Although some sugar is stored in our livers for emergencies, we get most of what we need from consuming carbohydrates. These carbohydrates convert into **glucose**—the simple form of sugar found in our bloodstream. **Insulin** then helps move the glucose out of our bloodstream and into our cells.

Because glucose fuels our brains and bodies, we need a steady level to function properly. Sudden drops or spikes in blood sugar can trigger dramatic shifts in mood. Carbohydrate metabolism clearly changes during episodes. We develop insulin resistance during depression, and possibly become sensitive to insulin during mania.

I maintain my blood sugar level by eating six times a day. Although I slip up from time to time, I feel best when I closely follow the "exchange diet" recommended by the American Diabetes Association and limit my consumption of saturated fats.

Regular mealtimes can also help you remember to take your medications. Because medications are often hard on the stomach, many of them should be taken with food. Right when I get up, I take my thyroid medication because the body absorbs it best on an empty stomach. Then I do a brief set of exercises, shower, dress, and eat a decent breakfast afterward. In the late morning I eat a homemade muffin with my next batch of medication. I eat a late lunch, then have a piece of fruit, some caffeinated tea, or—on very rare occasions—a caffeinated diet soda when my energy drops around 3:30 or 4 P.M. Around 5:30 I take any mineral supplements or allergy medication I may be on with only water. I take another batch of medication at dinnertime and my last doses of the day with a bedtime snack. Not everyone with bipolar disorder takes that many doses of medicine. But because I'm managing several other health concerns— a low thyroid, systemic arthritis, menopause, irritable bowel syndrome, and allergies—it just works out that way. Follow the regimen that works best for you.

Natural Foods

I was raised on a typical American diet with lots of processed foods, quite a bit of fast food, and a fair amount of sugar. In graduate school I lived in a series of health-conscious co-ops and began eating much healthier.

My current therapist encourages her clients to eat what she calls "God foods"—natural, unprocessed foods like raw fruits and vegetables, nuts and seeds, whole grains, and chicken and fish, and to avoid additives and dyes. Upon her recommendation, I also limit my use of artificial sweeteners and white-flour products (which was minimal to begin with), and I've found these changes helpful.

Adjusting Your Diet

Sugar and Other Natural Sweeteners

Bipolar disorder and blood sugar problems can either go hand in hand or be mistaken for each other. For example, you may be anxious, confused, hungry, irritable, nervous, or have difficulty concentrating in a depressive, manic, or *hypoglycemic* (low sugar) state. In sugar-sensitive people, moods tend to peak and dip dramatically with sugar consumption.

Sugar—A sugary treat may provide a brief energy boost, but it will soon send your blood sugar plummeting. This sets up a cyclical craving for yet another sweet treat. Those of us with low serotonin and low **beta-endorphin** levels are prone to compulsive eating as well as drug and alcohol abuse.

Staying away from sugar often makes it easier to manage dietary problems. I have little difficulty avoiding most forms of sugar when I do so across the board. But if I give in and have "just one bite of birthday cake," it invariably triggers an orgy of discontrol. Before I know it, I'm smuggling candy bars and cookies and going on a major binge.

Fructose—Unless you're completely sugar-intolerant, you need not give up all forms of sugar. For instance, don't give up fruit simply because it contains fructose. Although a simple sugar, *fructose* affects blood glucose and insulin levels less than many other sugars. Just eat sweeter fruits, like apples, applesauce, bananas, dried apricots, dates, figs, grapes, pineapples, raisins, and such, in smaller portions. Fruits and vegetables also supply valuable vitamins, minerals, and fiber.

The types of sugars most important to avoid or limit are the refined sugars present in candy and gum, baked goods, ice cream, presweetened drinks, jams, jellies, many breakfast cereals, and processed and snack foods. Experts disagree about the use of natural sugars like honey, molasses, and syrups. I use them occasionally, but only in limited amounts.

Also limit simple carbohydrates that quickly convert to sugar, such as potatoes, and breads and pasta not made from whole grains or vegetables. Watch out for products labeled as "wheat" or "multi-grain," which often contain white flour or processed wheat flour. Read labels and choose 100 percent whole-wheat products or those made from other whole-grain flours. Flour made from spelt, a member of the same grain family as oats and wheat but an entirely different species, is particularly good. If you're allergic to wheat gluten, as many people with clinical depression are, use spelt-based products or skip bread and pasta altogether.

Read food labels and look for hidden sugars, like *acesulfame potassium, cane juice, dextrose, glucose, lactose, maltose, malts, saccharides, sorghum, sucrose,* and artificial sweeteners. Sugars are simple carbohydrates and therefore lead to a rapid rise in blood sugar (which makes you feel better temporarily), followed by a rapid drop (which leaves you feeling lousy). I was appalled, when I first started reading food labels, to discover how much sugar was in canned soups, fruits, and vegetables, and in "nonsugary" cereals.

NATURAL SWEETENERS

MANY GROCERY and health food stores carry processed natural substitutes for "tabletop," or plain white sugar.

FRUCTOSE—Although a simple sugar, fructose affects blood glucose and insulin levels less than many other sugars. However, avoid high-fructose corn syrup.

STEVIA—This sweetener, from the South American *Stevia rebaudiana* shrub, is considerably sweeter than sugar. But it doesn't cause sudden spikes and drops in blood sugar.

Stevia—Another, but still unproven, potential alternative to sugar is the natural sweetener stevia.

People in other countries have used *small amounts* of stevia extracts to sweeten beverages and foods for centuries without ill effects. Stevia is currently sold in many U.S. health food stores as a dietary supplement.

ARTIFICIAL SWEETENERS

Artificial sweeteners offer little advantage over sugar, though some of us tolerate them better. However, artificial sweeteners may present health risks. Researchers, scientists, consumer groups like the Center for Science in the Public Interest, the U.S. Department of Health and Human Services, the U.S. Food and Drug Administration, and food manufacturers tend to disagree about their safety.

BRAND NAMES ASSOCIATED WITH ARTIFICIAL SWEETENERS

SACCHARIN—Sweet 'n Low

ASPARTAME—Equal, NutraSweet, NutraTaste, Spoonful

SUCRALOSE—SPLENDA No Calorie Sweetener

Saccharin—United States law used to a place a warning notice on all products containing saccharin because it was considered a potential *carcinogen* (cancer-causing agent). Then, in 2000, the U.S. Department of Health and Human Services dropped it from its list of carcinogens, and Congress passed a law that allowed manufacturers to drop the warning. A study conducted by the National Cancer Institute, however, found a high incidence of bladder cancer with saccharin use.

Aspartame—After the FDA approved aspartame in 1981, it became the replacement of choice for saccharin. The FDA has received complaints about such symptoms as dizziness, hallucinations, and headaches from consumers of aspartame. Some people believe that aspartame could be carcinogenic, but we need more research for adequate proof. Those of us with mood disorders should be aware of a potential interaction between the amino acids in aspartame and neurotransmitters in the brain. Some research suggests that aspartame can block serotonin formation and can lead to depression or insomnia, but the facts are inconclusive.

Sucralose—Approved as a food additive by the U.S. Food and Drug Administration in 1998, sucralose appears to be considerably safer than saccharin and aspartame. In 1999, the FDA approved its use as a general-purpose sweetener, and it's one of the few artificial sweeteners on which most authorities agree. Even though SPLENDA comes from cane sugar, its joint manufacturers, McNeil Specialty Products Company and Tate & Lyle, PLC, say it passes through the body without affecting blood glucose levels, carbohydrate metabolism, or insulin secretion.

However, the U.S. Food and Drug Administration has not approved stevia as a food additive, partly out of concern that United States consumers would ingest theoretically toxic amounts. Some toxicologists are concerned that overconsumption may lead to cancer, reproductive problems, and changes in carbohydrate metabolism.

TAMING YOUR SWEET TOOTH

> SWEETNESS, REGARDLESS of its source, leads to cravings for more sweets in many people because it sets off a beta-endorphin response. (*Beta-endorphin* is a stimulating brain chemical.) This in turn leads to cravings and compulsive eating.
>
> Try not to eat sweets that make you crave more.

The bottom line on sweeteners is to use them in moderation, regardless of which type you use.

CHOCOLATE

Included in the list of foods to limit or avoid is the universal favorite—chocolate—because it packs a double whammy: sugar and caffeine. Chocolate cravings are especially prevalent in women who have PMS. Eating chocolate appears to lead to increased serotonin production, so those with chocolate cravings may be using it to "self-medicate."

While this may improve your mood initially, your blood glucose will soon drop and may produce symptoms of hypoglycemia. This leaves you feeling even worse. A better option is to eat small amounts of protein throughout the day. Protein helps increase energy and alertness.

CAFFEINE

When my depression was nearing its worst point, I was consuming three pots of coffee and several caffeinated diet sodas a day. Then I wondered why I had the shakes. If you can, stop consuming caffeine altogether because it tends to interfere with sleep. As stated previously, sleep is extraordinarily important when you have a mood disorder. Some people with bipolar disorder can tolerate a small amount of caffeine; others can't use it at all. If you do consume caffeine, try not to do so late in the day; otherwise, you may have difficulty falling asleep at bedtime. I limit myself to one cup of coffee in the morning and one glass of caffeinated herbal tea or soda in the afternoon. I've tried a time or two to give caffeine up entirely, but I just can't seem to do it. I feel considerably better, though, now that I consume less caffeine than I used to.

FIBER

You may also need to pay attention to your fiber consumption. Formerly called roughage, fiber consists of complex carbohydrates that our digestive systems can't break down. There are two different types of fiber: soluble and insoluble.

SOLUBLE AND INSOLUBLE FIBER

SOLUBLE FIBER *lowers blood* **cholesterol** *slightly and helps prevent heart disease. When mixed with water, it forms a gel-like substance.*

INSOLUBLE FIBER *assists with bowel functioning and helps prevent colon cancer because it passes through the digestive system virtually intact.*

Both types of fiber are important for their nutrients and for maintaining a healthy digestive system. Many foods contain both types.

Nutrition experts recommend a minimum intake of 20 to 40 grams of fiber per day. According to the American Dietetic Association, at least one-fourth of this amount should be soluble fiber to lower the risk of heart disease. If you're constipated, you may require even more. When you're in a depressive state, many of your bodily functions slow down, including elimination, and constipation is a side effect of many medications. On the other hand, some medications cause diarrhea. Adjust your fiber intake accordingly.

Good sources of fiber include whole grains and cereals (bran, whole wheat, oatmeal, brown rice), beans (black beans, kidney beans, lentils), and seeds and nuts. Others include fruits and vegetables (apples, pears, strawberries, broccoli, carrots, corn). The fiber in the skins of these foods helps slow their conversion to sugar, so be sure to eat the skins. Dairy products, fats, and meats do *not* contain fiber.

FATS

Saturated fats increase **cholesterol**, which impairs circulation (especially to your brain) and leads to heart attacks and strokes. Such fats also slow your thinking and make you feel sluggish and fatigued.

But our brains need fat to function well, including some cholesterol. Too little can cause significant problems when you have a mood disorder. Because cholesterol enhances serotonin, it acts as a natural antidepressant. Blood cholesterol levels under 160 can therefore lead to depression, accidents, or even suicide.

That presents a bit of a dilemma if you have both a mood disorder and are at high risk for heart disease. Make certain your doctor is aware of this information if you go on a cholesterol-reducing diet.

A healthy diet should provide at least 5 grams a day of *essential fatty acids*—the special fats our bodies need as much as they need vitamins. *Omega-3 fatty acids* are one type of essential fatty acid; *omega-6 fatty acids* are the other. Research has shown a correlation between a low level of omega-3 fatty acids and both depression and mania. Omega-3 fatty acids appear to inhibit nerve signal transmissions in a manner similar to that of mood-stabilizing medications.

We can obtain omega-3 fatty acids by eating fish (particularly salmon, albacore tuna, crab, halibut, herring, mackerel, anchovies, and sardines). Farm-raised corn-fed fish, however, is not a good source. The recommended amount is 1 to 5 grams of omega-3 fatty acids a day. That amounts to quite a lot of fish. A 3-ounce can of tuna, for instance, contains roughly 675 milligrams (.675 grams).

If you don't like fish or you can't consume enough, you can use fish oil supplements. Although cod liver oil was once used for medicinal purposes, an excess can lead to Vitamin A toxicity. To protect supplements from oxygen damage, such supplements should contain Vitamin E. Taking these supplements with orange juice can reduce their fishy aftertaste.

Although you can obtain some omega-3 fatty acids from plant-based sources, such as flaxseeds, pumpkinseeds, walnuts, wheat germ, and dark green leafy vegetables, so far only fish oil has been proven effective to prevent mania.

Dietary Recommendations

A good starting place for adjusting your overall diet is the U.S. Department of Agriculture's Food Guide Pyramid. It recommends

- 6 to 11 servings daily of bread, cereal, rice, or pasta,
- 3 to 5 servings daily of vegetables,
- 2 to 4 servings daily of fruit,
- 2 to 3 servings daily of milk, yogurt, and cheese,
- 2 to 3 servings daily of meat, poultry, fish, dried beans, eggs, and nuts, and
- limited use of fats, oils, and sweets.

The number of servings varies with your sex and age. These recommendations may not fit for everyone, especially if you have another condition, so check with your doctor before adjusting your diet. Nutrition is very individualized.

Both complex carbohydrates and proteins are particularly important. Carbohydrates not only convert to glucose to fuel your body but increase your serotonin level. The complex carbohydrates in raw fruits and vegetables, nuts and seeds, whole grains, beans, and soy products are important not only for their fiber and nutritional content but because they affect your serotonin level. They help reduce moodiness, inflexibility, irritability, and the tendency to worry.

Be sure you get adequate protein as well. Either too much or too little can affect the amount of serotonin in your brain. Inadequate protein also lowers dopamine and norepinephrine levels, which can contribute to depression.

If you're a vegetarian, you can obtain protein by eating beans, nuts, whole grains, and soy products. Your calcium can come from nuts and seeds, vegetables, calcium-fortified orange juice, and soy products. However, if you take an MAOI, note the following instructions.

MAOI Diet Restrictions

One class of antidepressants, the **MAOIs (monoamine oxidase inhibitors)**, brings additional dietary restrictions. MAOIs lead to a buildup of an **amino acid** called **tyramine**, which is present in certain foods and medications. When mixed with MAOIs, substances containing tyramine cause headaches, extremely high blood pressure, strokes, and in some cases, *even death.*

CAUTION FOR THOSE ON MAOIS

IF YOUR doctor prescribes an MAOI, *always* follow the dietary and medication restrictions. With MAOIs, *noncompliance can be fatal.*

When taking MAOIs, you *must* avoid:

- aged cheese, sour cream, and yogurt,
- overripe fruits (particularly bananas and plums),
- avocados, tomatoes, eggplant,
- canned or dried meats,
- sausage, liver, sauerkraut,
- some beans and legumes,
- soy products,
- caffeine and chocolate,
- beer and wine, and
- anything containing yeast.

If your doctor prescribes an MAOI, *make certain you understand all of the dietary restrictions.*

Making Dietary Changes

I know it takes a good deal of time to read labels and learn about nutrition. And it may leave you feeling like there's nothing you can eat in the entire grocery store. But you can make dietary changes a little at a time. Start by eating regular meals if you aren't already doing so. Then reduce your sugar and caffeine intake, and move on from there. Making little adjustments as you feel able not only helps reduce the stress that change brings but helps you identify what foods affect you most.

Drugs, Alcohol, and Nicotine

It's especially important for those of us with bipolar disorder to avoid drugs and alcohol. By "drugs" I mean illicit drugs, not medications prescribed or recommended by an M.D. Even over-the-counter allergy medications, cold remedies, and pain relievers can affect moods and sleeping patterns, and some compete with other medications. Check with your doctor or pharmacist before using any over-the-counter medications.

Both drugs and alcohol can imbalance brain chemistry, trigger mood episodes, and interfere with prescribed medications. Despite the temporary lift it may supply, alcohol is actually a depressant—the last thing you need when you have a mood disorder. Some doctors approve of a single glass of wine per day; others prefer you stay away from alcohol entirely.

You may not think of tobacco as a drug, but *it's as addictive as cocaine.* In addition to the well-known dangers of smoking, nicotine acts as a stimulant and affects the brain chemicals dopamine, norepinephrine, serotonin, and beta-endorphin.

Needless to say, giving up these substances isn't easy. More than half of people with bipolar disorder have substance abuse problems as well. Often, we use drugs or alcohol to dampen or intensify our fluctuating moods. Experts call this behavior "self-medicating."

Perhaps my drinking binges and experiments with drugs in college related more to attempts to self-medicate or to prolong an elevated state than to a desire to be part of the "in crowd." If you use drugs or alcohol, you may need to address substance abuse issues before anything else.

Exercise

Our ancestors got plenty of exercise to meet their bodies' physical needs, but modern technology has created a nation of couch potatoes. Countless studies have revealed the benefits of exercise and the fact that it produces **endorphins**—opiate-like hormones that make us feel good.

Exercise can be tremendously beneficial and can produce results almost immediately. (Always check with your doctor before starting any new exercise program.) Regular exercise reduces anxiety and improves concentration and energy. Even a single workout can increase your serotonin, norepinephrine, and dopamine levels. Imaging studies have shown that exercise helps activate the left prefrontal cortex, which becomes sluggish during depression.

What Type of Exercise is Best?

Aerobic exercise is the best choice for improving a depressed mood or for burning off excess manic energy. Aim for a moderate aerobic workout for thirty to sixty minutes three times a week. But build up slowly, and don't overdo it. Too much exercise can make you tired and sluggish. Even though it can tire you, it can also energize you. It's therefore best to finish exercising three or more hours before going to bed. On other days, you may benefit from nonaerobic or toning exercises.

AEROBIC VERSUS NONAEROBIC EXERCISE

AEROBIC EXERCISE (like brisk walking, bicycling, running, and swimming) increases your heart rate and oxygen flow.

NONAEROBIC EXERCISE (like lifting weights, taking a slow stroll, stretching, or doing yoga) helps build self-esteem and reduces tension.

What About Those Who Hate to Exercise?

Exercise never came naturally to me—at least since early childhood. I never gravitated toward sports and wasn't that drawn toward physical activity. What initially spurred me toward regular exercise was my miserly mind-set. I invested in a gym membership for which I paid a year in advance. Once I'd put down the money, it was fairly easy to guilt myself into going. Then, after a while, I found that each time I exercised I felt a little better and I actually missed it when I didn't go.

Over the years I've participated in aerobics, Jazzercise, and salsa classes, all of which I enjoyed because we used music, and it was more like dancing than exercise. I've also bicycled and swum laps.

BREAKING INTO EXERCISE

- Find an activity—or preferably several—that you enjoy.
- Make a commitment. Plan regular workouts with a friend, join a gym, or take a class.
- Keep your exercise gear packed and ready to go. When you return from a workout, immediately repack your bag with clean exercise clothes.
- Buy exercise videos or equipment (a standing bicycle, treadmill, rowing machine, or weight set) if you prefer to exercise at home. You can often find bargains at garage sales.

When I developed arthritis, I gained an added incentive to exercise: My knees and ankles would begin to swell if I skipped too many exercise sessions. I began attending aquatics (water aerobics), which is easier on the joints because the water cushions them. I also work out with weight machines and walk outside or on a treadmill. I've made many friends in the process.

Do whatever aerobic exercise makes you feel the best: martial arts and sports offer other possibilities (though not all sports are aerobic activities). An inexpensive option is walking—outdoors when the weather permits, or in a public building or shopping mall when it doesn't. (If you tend to spend extravagantly when you're up, leave your checkbook and credit cards at home.)

Some people find it easier to keep a commitment to exercise when they do so with other people; others prefer to exercise alone. I tend to do best when I participate in classes because I'm less likely to procrastinate or blow a session off when I have a set time for exercising. Plus, classes offer an opportunity to socialize, which can help when you're isolated from others most of the time.

Making Changes Gradually

I know the changes I'm suggesting may seem overwhelming. After all, they probably mean establishing some radically different habits. But if you take it slowly and change your lifestyle gradually, it may not be nearly as traumatic as it seems. I made many of these changes over a period of several years. But since I've been paying closer attention to them, I've experienced a number of benefits. Not only have my moods evened out, but my overall health has improved. And most of the cravings I used to experience have virtually disappeared.

STRATEGIES FOR TAKING SMALL STEPS

- Establish a regular bedtime and do your best to obtain adequate sleep. Make it a top priority.
- Eat regular meals and a balanced diet. Unless you're taking MAOIs, you can make dietary changes gradually. Cut back on sugar and caffeine first, and make other changes as you feel ready.
- Build in some regular exercise. You can start with something as simple as a ten-minute walk.

- If you're not used to taking medication, and your doctor prescribes it, set up a way to help you manage it.
- If you self-medicate with alcohol or drugs, get treated for substance abuse or join a self-help program such as Alcoholics Anonymous, Cocaine Anonymous, or Narcotics Anonymous.
- Aim to reduce the stress in your life.

Almost invariably, since my husband and I began monitoring my illness more closely, we found that an unmet need at a lower level of the hierarchy set off an episode. I'd missed a meal or eaten it extremely late, I hadn't gotten my usual amount of sleep for a few days, or I'd missed a dose or two of medication.

I consider medication one of the basic needs—primarily because the right combinations have helped me so much. But, because most people see it as part of medical treatment, I introduce common medications for mood disorders in chapter 12 and provide additional details in the Medications Appendix.

TWELVE

Seeking Medical Treatment: Medications and Procedures

BESIDES FULFILLING THE basic needs described in chapter 11, most people with bipolar disorder need some other type of treatment. This often includes medication or sometimes other medical procedures, like **electroconvulsive therapy**, **transcranial magnetic stimulation**, or **vagal nerve stimulation**. In some cases, you may need to be hospitalized for a time. Dealing with bipolar disorder is rarely an easy fix. But seeking effective treatment can enhance—or even save—your life.

Medications aren't the only options. As Dr. Stuart Yudofsky, Chairman of the Department of Psychiatry and Behavioral Sciences at the Baylor College of Medicine in Houston, says, "We're dealing with a *person,* not a sack of chemicals."

Many of us who have bipolar disorder also benefit from "talk therapy," which may consist of psychotherapy, counseling, or support groups. As a rule, medical interventions produce faster results, but psychotherapy more effectively prevents relapses. Chapter 13 discusses talk therapy, and chapter 14 covers other therapeutic alternatives and supplementary treatments.

This chapter focuses on those options that require you to see an M.D. Depending on the state in which you live, you may be able to obtain prescriptions from an advanced psychiatric nurse.

Finding the Right Doctor

Unless you're in an immediate crisis, you need not go with the first psychiatrist or other qualified practitioner you meet. If you're happy with the first doctor you talk to, great. But it may take more than one try to find the best doctor for you.

WHO'S WHO IN PSYCHIATRY

PSYCHIATRISTS are medical doctors who specialize in psychiatry. In addition to "regular" medical school, psychiatrists have four additional years of psychiatric training.

PSYCHOPHARMACOLOGISTS are medical doctors (M.D.s) or osteopathic doctors (D.O.s) with special knowledge of psychotropic medications (those that affect the mind). Osteopaths apply a holistic approach to medicine, taking both physical and mental needs into consideration.

ADVANCED PSYCHIATRIC NURSES are registered nurses who have also been trained in psychiatry and hold a master's degree. In some states, they are also licensed to prescribe medication.

Getting Referrals

Here are some starting points for locating a good doctor. Ask one or more of the following for recommendations:

- Family, friends, coworkers, or neighbors, if you're comfortable doing so
- Your therapist or counselor, if you're seeing one
- Your primary care provider
- A mental health support group
- A hospital or clinic

- A university medical school
- A nonprofit mental health organization
- A medical association or licensing board
- An *employee assistance program (EAP),* if you have access to one and are comfortable using it
- Your insurance carrier, if you have health insurance

I suggest that you *not* rely on yellow page listings or Web-based doctors. Direct referrals tend to be much more reliable. If at all possible, choose a doctor who specializes in (or at least expresses strong interest in) mood disorders.

Checking the "Fit"

When you have some referrals, request a brief interview—either by phone or in person. Ask the doctor

- What are your payment policies, and what insurance plans do you accept?
- What is your training and experience, including your knowledge about mood disorders and co-occurring conditions?
- How long is a typical appointment, and how frequently should I expect to see you?
- How flexible is your schedule, and how accessible are you between appointments?
- What hospitals are you affiliated with, in case I need to be admitted at some point?
- What should I do if an emergency arises? Do you have associates who fill in when you're unavailable?
- What is your treatment philosophy? Is it conservative or more open to new or experimental treatments?
- How do you feel about therapeutic alternatives or supplements to medication?
- What is your attitude toward psychotherapy, and what types of therapies do you recommend?

- Are you willing to communicate with my therapist and with my family and friends, if needed?

When you set your first appointment, allow some extra time for completing paperwork and bring any pertinent medical records you might have.

Changing Doctors

Make certain your doctor's treatment approach is aggressive or conservative enough for your needs. There's much more to life than just not feeling suicidal or riding constantly on the edge of mania. For well over a decade, I defined "a good day" as one during which I didn't feel suicidal or my hypomania didn't upset anyone. I settled for too little, and after switching to a less conservative psychiatrist, I found my life could be much better than I'd ever imagined. Don't make the same mistake; go for all of the quality of life you can.

Remember, *you're* the customer here. But the doctor isn't responsible for "fixing" you. Currently, bipolar disorder is a long-term condition that has no cure. Like diabetes, epilepsy, or hypertension, it can only be managed. Managing your illness requires working closely with your doctor, therapists, and other support systems. Consider your doctor a part of your treatment team, the most responsible member of which must be *you*. If you're unhappy with the first doctor, find another as soon as possible.

Medication

Many people resist taking medication—for long- or short-term use. Also, people with bipolar disorder may not be convinced they need medication, or they may be unwilling to give up their highs. When you're manic or hypomanic, it's easy to convince yourself you're cured or that you were misdiagnosed and don't need medication. Do your best to comply with your treatment plan and not give in to such thoughts. Typically, they'll only get you into trouble.

Medication Myths and Questions

Some may fear that taking psychotropic medications will

- mean they're weak,
- change their personality,
- lead to addiction,
- produce unbearable side effects or some other illness, or
- be ineffective because they've tried one or two in the past without success.

THE "WEAKNESS" MYTH

Initially, I was hesitant to take psychotropic medications because I didn't want others to perceive me as a weak person (even though some already had). And I was initially afraid to try **lithium**—a naturally occurring salt used as a mood stabilizer—because it seemed like such a serious move.

I didn't want to take medication for the rest of my life. Few people want to, for any physical disorder. But many must take insulin to control diabetes, anticonvulsants to control epilepsy, or synthetic thyroid to control a thyroid disorder. Psychotropic medications treat physical disorders too: *Bipolar and unipolar disorders are brain disorders.*

Taking psychotropic medication doesn't mean you're weak; it means you're taking responsibility to manage your illness. When you consider that you may be unable to work without medication, that you may lose your most important relationships, or there's a higher risk you'll take your life, medication becomes a lot more attractive.

THE "PERSONALITY CHANGE" MYTH

Psychotropic medications don't change your basic personality either; they just help shift your moods into a more normal range. These small shifts are usually for the good. If you're depressed, you may become a bit more outgoing. If you're manic or hypomanic, you'll be less likely to do something risky, and others will find you easier to be around. And I've found, when on the right medications, that my thoughts are less destructive.

The "Addiction" Question

Many psychotropic medications have no potential for addiction because addictive agents must work very rapidly and be associated with a quick fix. And it takes days or weeks for most mood-stabilizing agents and antidepressants to produce significant effects. However, some psychotropic medications can be addictive, particularly **benzodiazepines,** a class of medications that may be either **anti-anxiety agents** (tranquilizers), *hypnotics* (sedatives), or both.

I developed an addiction to Xanax (an antianxiety benzodiazepine) after nearly fifteen years of use. I simply couldn't get to sleep without it. Near bedtime, I'd get this tension in my stomach that I came to call my "Xanax knot." Although Xanax works quickly and effectively, it's really meant only for short-term use. My doctor had suggested several times that I get off it; he hadn't insisted because I was taking a relatively low dose.

My doctor prescribed a nonbenzodiazepine replacement a few weeks before I was to discontinue Xanax—during a vacation, when my stress level would be low. Even though I'd whittled my dose down to rarely more than one a day, I experienced pronounced withdrawal symptoms the first night off Xanax. My intense sweating, nausea, and stomach cramps resembled food poisoning. Several more days of discomfort followed, then I was fine.

The "Side Effect" Question

Practically every medication comes with side effects, and the same is true for psychotropic medications. Most are unpleasant, but many are either temporary or fairly manageable. Part of your concern may be based on the side effects of older preparations, which often led to muscle stiffness and **tardive dyskinesia** (a disorder that causes involuntary repetitive movements, such as muscle spasms, writhing or twisting, and odd facial expressions). However, newer medications present fewer severe problems.

The first side effects I experienced when I started psychotropic medications were having an extremely dry mouth and needing to urinate more frequently. Perhaps these were related: Since I was constantly drinking something to keep my mouth moist, having to pee a lot was a natural outcome.

Weight gain and sexual dysfunction are the two side effects people complain about the most. I've experienced both of these problems to a limited extent but have dealt with them by changing medications and/or adjusting dosage levels in cooperation with my psychiatrist.

Other side effects that are common with psychotropic medications include

- Anxiety or nervousness
- Appetite and/or weight changes
- Blurred or altered vision
- Confusion and/or memory problems
- Constipation or diarrhea, sometimes flatulence
- Dizziness or lightheadedness
- Drowsiness, fatigue, or sedation
- Gastrointestinal problems
- Headaches
- Increased or decreased sweating
- Increased sensitivity to light or the sun
- Insomnia
- Itchy skin or rash
- Muscle weakness
- Nausea or vomiting
- Restlessness
- Shakiness or trembling
- Slurred speech

By now you're probably thinking, "No way am I taking those meds!" But remember, no single medication brings all of these side effects. And just because a side effect appears on a list doesn't mean you will experience it. Most likely, though, you'll face one or more of these problems.

Individual Differences—Both your response to medications and the side effects you experience will depend on individual biochemistry and other factors. One of my bipolar friends was switching to the same combination I was discontinuing. The combination that didn't work for me worked for her, and the combination that didn't work for her worked for me.

Some people are extraordinarily sensitive to medication. Adults who rarely take more than a single aspirin, for instance, may require pediatric levels of medications. Others may require extremely high levels to control their disease.

Sometimes side effects are dose related. The same antidepressant can sedate me at a low dose, trigger hypomania at a higher dose, but work just fine at a dose between.

Switching Medications—You can usually accommodate most side effects. If not, you can often try a different medication. And more and better medications are being developed all the time.

If you switch medications, avoid doing so near a holiday or when your doctor is about to leave on vacation. It's likely that you'll need to stay in closer contact during such a transition.

CAUTION

WHEN STARTING any new medication, monitor your symptoms carefully. Tell your doctor immediately if symptoms get significantly worse, particularly if you have suicidal thoughts.

THE "INEFFECTIVENESS" MYTH

If you've tried medication without success in the past, believe me, there are plenty more to try. One glance at the Medications Appendix in this book will show you what I mean. And more and better medications are coming out all the time.

Some of us try one medication after another without ever finding relief. Some simply can't tolerate the side effects. Others prefer to use natural remedies, such as those discussed in chapters 11 and 14. For many of us, though, medications are a vital tool for managing our illness.

Although some people disagree, I've found enough evidence in my life and in my research to indicate that most people with bipolar disorder must correct their brain's chemical imbalance before they can expect significant recovery. I'll admit, I lean toward using medications because it's been integral to my own recovery. Had I not discovered the ease with which I could lose my life nor experienced the loss of my sister, I might have tried to make it some other way. But with effective medication, I've seen dramatic results.

CLASSES OF MEDICATIONS

The major classes of **psychotropic medicines** (those that affect the mind) used to treat bipolar disorder include *mood-stabilizing agents, mood-stabilizing anticonvulsants, antipsychotics, antidepressants, anti-anxiety agents* (tranquilizers), and *hypnotics* (sedatives). Not all of these medications have equivalent effects on bipolar disorder, but in some people may reduce certain symptoms.

This chapter presents a general description of these classes. The Medications Appendix lists the chemical and trade names for medicines commonly used to treat bipolar disorder in the United States. It also briefly describes their actions.

Doctors use a *treatment algorithm*—or flowchart—to help determine which type of medication or medications might help you most. To assist with this effort, it's important that you follow your doctor's instructions and keep in close communication about the way each new medication makes you feel. Does it improve your symptoms partially or completely? Does it cause problematic side effects? This information helps your doctor adjust the dosage or find a different medication that will help you more.

Whenever possible, it's best to change only one medication at a time. That way, it's easier to determine which medication helps relieve certain symptoms or produces certain side effects.

MOOD-STABILIZING AGENTS

These medications help both to relieve and to prevent mania and depression by keeping your moods in a more normal range. At the proper dosage, mood-stabilizing agents shouldn't cause a switch from one extreme mood to another, nor should they cause your moods to switch more rapidly.

Some people with bipolar disorder find a mood-stabilizing agent alone to be sufficient; others must use additional medications in conjunction with it. On average, those of us with bipolar disorder take three or four different medications to manage all of our symptoms.

Mood Stabilizers. Currently, **lithium,** a natural element similar to the sodium in table salt, is the only pure mood stabilizer available.

In addition to interacting with neurotransmitter receptors and presynaptic reuptake pumps on nerve cell surfaces, as many psychotropic medications do, lithium (and possibly other mood-stabilizing agents) appears to work *inside* neurons themselves, essentially reprogramming them. And some scientists believe that lithium blocks the early stages of **kindling** (the process that sets you up for further mood episodes). Kindling is like falling into a rut and traveling the same neural pathway in your brain repeatedly. (See chapter 7 for more information about neuron structure and biochemical reactions.)

Mood-Stabilizing Anticonvulsants. Doctors generally prescribe these medications, often called *antiepileptics* or *antiseizure agents*, to control convulsions and seizures. However, some anticonvulsants have mood-stabilizing properties and can be used in place of—or occasionally along with—other mood-stabilizing agents. Anticonvulsants also appear to desensitize kindling but take longer to stabilize moods than lithium does.

Calcium Channel Blockers. On rare occasions, when other mood-stabilizing agents don't help, doctors prescribe medications that are normally used to treat high blood pressure and heart problems. The Medications Appendix lists calcium channel blockers under mood-stabilizing agents.

ANTIPSYCHOTICS

Also called **neuroleptics**, classic (or typical) **antipsychotics** help relieve the delusions and hallucinations that sometimes accompany acute mania. The older, typical antipsychotics are most appropriate for short-term management of manic symptoms, but because typical antipsychotics can cause more severe side effects, the newer "atypical" antipsychotics are generally preferable. Some antipsychotics can even help treat anxiety, agitation, and insomnia in people not displaying psychosis.

ANTIDEPRESSANTS

Just as their name implies, **antidepressants** help relieve depressive symptoms. To prevent the mood swings of bipolar disorder, doctors often prescribe both a mood stabilizer and an antidepressant. Which your doctor prescribes first depends on your signs and symptoms. Psychotropic medications require careful monitoring because they can induce switches of mood from depression to mania or vice versa.

Classes of Antidepressants. There are several different classes of antidepressants with different chemical structures that work on different neurotransmitters in the brain. But even medications within the same class and with the same chemical structure may behave in slightly different ways and affect different types of receptors.

TCAs (tricyclic antidepressants), named for their three-ring chemical structure, have been around since the 1950s. They work by blocking the reuptake of neurotransmitters into nerve cells.

Tetracyclic antidepressants are a fairly new class of medication. They work similarly to TCAs and some references classify them as such, but they actually have a four-ring chemical structure. The size difference means that tricycle and tetracyclic compounds act on transport proteins in a somewhat different manner.

Many reference books list a majority of the following antidepressants simply as SSRIs or as uncategorized antidepressants, but an awareness of which neurotransmitters each category affects can help you and your doctor find the most effective medication more quickly. Briefly, these include

- **NaSSAs (noradrenergic and specific serotonergic antidepressants),**
- **NDRIs (norepinephrine and dopamine reuptake inhibitors),**

- **SARIs (serotonin antagonist and reuptake inhibitors),**
- **SNRIs (serotonin and norepinephrine reuptake inhibitors), and**
- **SSRIs (selective serotonin reuptake inhibitors).**

The Medications Appendix briefly explains which neurotransmitters they affect and how. For more detailed information, check *Goodman and Gilman's Pharmacological Basis of Therapeutics,* the *Physician's Desk Reference,* or the insert that comes with your prescription.

MAOIs (monoamine oxidase inhibitors), which first appeared in the 1960s, increase the concentration of neurotransmitters by preventing the monoamine oxidase enzyme from breaking down or metabolizing neurotransmitters *inside the nerve endings* of presynaptic neurons. Although MAOIs are very effective, doctors prescribe them less often than other antidepressants. MAOIs can increase blood pressure and prevent the safe use of certain over-the-counter medications. They also require strict dietary limitations, most of which are listed in chapter 11.

CAUTION

IF YOUR doctor prescribes an MAOI, make certain you understand what foods, beverages, and medications you *must not* ingest.

ANTIANXIETY AGENTS AND HYPNOTICS

Because anxiety and sleep disturbances often accompany bipolar disorder, many doctors also prescribe **antianxiety agents** (tranquilizers) and **hypnotics** (sedatives). These medications help relieve nervous tension and produce sedation by reducing central nervous system activity and nerve signal transmissions. This is one reason it's often unadvisable to drive or operate dangerous equipment when taking them.

Many such medications should be used only on a limited basis because they have a high potential for addiction. Some produce different effects when given repeatedly versus given just once.

- MAOIs require many dietary restrictions, and some other medications do as well. *Always check with your doctor about dietary restrictions for any medications prescribed.*
- Mood-stabilizing agents often require monitoring to ensure that they're not damaging your thyroid, kidneys, or liver. *Make certain to get blood tests regularly when taking medications such as lithium and valproic acid.*
- Many psychotropic medications can cause birth defects or pass on chemicals through breast milk. *If there's any chance you might be pregnant or breastfeeding soon, inform your doctor.*

Half-Lives

The *half-life* of a medication relates to how long it takes to metabolize or to leave your system. However, this term is misleading because most medications require *five times their half-lives* to be fully eliminated from the body. Half-lives become significant when you need to try a different medication and your system needs to be clear of the original medication first. *Always make such adjustments in cooperation with your doctor.*

And never stop a medication without first consulting your doctor, even if you feel so much better that you doubt you were ill in the first place. During hypomanic and manic episodes, people frequently doubt their need for medication and stop taking it at all. Besides increasing the chance of a relapse, doing so can lead to other serious problems. When you discontinue some psychotropic medications too quickly, hallucinations, tremors, seizures, or delirium can result. And many medications must be tapered gradually to prevent or reduce even milder withdrawal symptoms.

Welcome to "Titration World"

Dealing with medication is an ongoing task. You rarely get just one prescription that handles your illness forever. Particularly to handle PMS and fluctuations in my libido, I've had to frequently titrate my doses up and down. That's what doctors call dosage adjustments—**titrating** (TIE-traiting). You may need to titrate when introducing a new medication or abandoning an old one, to deal with side effects, or to better handle stressful situations. Psychiatrists often give you some leeway in the amount of medication to take, based on day-to-day changes and stresses in your life.

Before drifting into menopause, I had PMS management down to a fine art. Thanks to having very predictable periods, I could just increase my medication five days before they started and I'd be fine. Just 10 milligrams more a day of my antidepressant made a significant difference. I could tell within half a day's time if I'd forgotten to up the dosage.

We always kept my lithium level relatively low, partially to keep my weight down, to reduce drowsiness, and to avoid memory problems. Because of my history of losing control of sexual impulses during hypomanic episodes, we increased my lithium or decreased my antidepressant numerous times when I found myself fantasizing extensively and becoming embarrassingly flirtatious.

Practicing Patience

Most medications take a while to work. Don't expect instant changes. It's often a long process of trial and error. When you find the right medication or combination for you, it will make a world of difference. Try to be patient.

Many people who take medication abandon the effort when they don't get instant results or don't take it long enough for it to reach a therapeutic level. Some medications work dramatically, but most work subtly. You may experience gradual improvement versus instant life-altering change.

It typically takes several weeks to start getting results when you begin taking a psychotropic medication. Your doctor may also need to adjust your dosage several times to find the optimal level for you. Finding a combination and level of medication that won't overstimulate you or make you too complacent to move forward with your life requires a lot of patience.

Over the years during which I've been in steady treatment, I've tried lithium and two different mood-stabilizing anticonvulsants, *at least* seven different antidepressants, four antianxiety agents, and one antipsychotic agent. I have no records for the medications I'd tried before my thirties. Finding the most effective medication or combination of medications is often no picnic, but once you do, it's like getting a whole new life.

Some people luck out, however, and find the "magic pill" that works right away. In *A Brilliant Madness,* Anna Pearce (Patty Duke) raves about the "little beige pill" (lithium) that turned her life around and finally gave her some sense of normality.

CONSIDERING GENETIC PARALLELS

One further point worth mentioning is that if you have relatives who take medication for mood disorders, it's quite possible you'll benefit from the same ones. After multiple trials with different antidepressants, my psychiatrist and I found that the one that currently works best for me is the same one my mother responds to the best.

Shortly after my success with this antidepressant, my psychiatrist suggested trying a different mood-stabilizing anticonvulsant to boost my energy level and make me more productive. My previous mood stabilizer had pretty well controlled my hypomania, and I was initially concerned about making the switch. But an energy boost had much appeal. Knowing that my niece had had excellent results from the same medication my doctor was suggesting made me willing to try it. I'm glad I took the chance, because the difference was remarkably positive. Within four days of switching medications, I felt better than I had in decades. We had to tinker with the dosage some to find a level that wouldn't pop me into hypomania, but the process was comparatively painless.

Combining Medications

Sometimes you must combine psychotropic medications or pair them with other medications to achieve the best effect. I was taking antidepressants for two years with only minimal improvement before

I began taking thyroid medication regularly. The combination improved my depression significantly. Although I tried short-term thyroid hormone replacement for a few months in my late twenties, I had discontinued it because I didn't see a positive change.

When I entered early menopause, I began having concentration and memory problems in addition to shifting moods. I'd work on a client's project one day, then be unable to recall what I'd accomplished the next.

Because estrogen affects acetylcholine, which in turn affects thinking and memory, decreasing estrogen levels decreases acetylcholine too. Likewise, because estrogen increases serotonin in the synaptic cleft, estrogen may act as a natural antidepressant and mood stabilizer.

Normal menopause-related hormonal fluctuations can cause many problems for women with bipolar disorder even if they've been stabilized for years. *Hormone replacement therapy (HRT)* can also cause trouble, such as worsening depression or producing rapid cycling. To better manage HRT, some doctors suggest starting estrogen and progesterone at different times. That way, if HRT causes problems, it's easier to determine which medication is the culprit.

Managing Medications

Even if you've taken medication for other conditions before, managing new ones can be challenging. You may need some time to get into the habit of taking multiple doses of one or more medications a day.

Clarifying Medication Information with Your Doctor

Each time your psychiatrist or any other medical doctor prescribes a new medication, be sure to ask

- What are the potential side effects of this medication?
- What warning signs might indicate potential problems?
- Do I need to take this medication with or without food?

- Can I consume any alcohol while taking this medicine?
- Does it matter what time of day or night I take this medication?
- What should I do if I miss a dose?
- What does the medication look like? Your doctor may provide you with samples or show you a picture from the *Physician's Desk Reference* or a comparable prescription guide.
- How long might I expect to be taking this dose?
- Do you expect to increase or decrease it later?

Some sources of information about medications other than your doctor include

- pharmacists,
- package inserts that come with prescriptions, and
- sources listed in the Medications Appendix.

Checking What Your Pharmacist Provides

When you get your medication from the pharmacy, make certain immediately that it's what you expected. Pharmacies sometimes substitute a generic form or another brand, which may look different from what you were anticipating. For instance, it may be a different color, size, or shape. Sometimes this will be okay, but sometimes it will be an error. When I began taking one new antidepressant, the pharmacy mistakenly supplied a five-sided scored tablet rather than the extended release capsule my psychiatrist had prescribed.

And, occasionally, you'll find illogical preparations. When I was taking another antidepressant, the pharmacy began using a different manufacturer than the one they'd used for years. For some reason, the new manufacturer's 25-milligram capsules were *smaller* than their 10-milligram capsules. I verified with several sources that my meds were labeled correctly, but I still don't know why the smaller size contained more milligrams.

Managing Medication Costs

If your income is especially low or your illness is so severe that you can't work, you may qualify for some form of public assistance. If that's your situation, the Resources section at the back of this book lists some starting points for finding help.

Very few psychotropic medications are inexpensive. And even if you have insurance, just making copayments can be a strain. Here are a few ways you can sometimes reduce the cost of your medications:

- Ask your doctor to prescribe generic medications whenever possible.
- Obtain free samples from your doctor, particularly when you're trying out a new medication.
- Fill only a small portion of a new prescription until you learn whether the medication is effective for you.
- When you're stabilized on a medication and expect to take it for some time, ask your doctor to prescribe it for a longer period.

Through my health insurance plan, I can pay a smaller copayment when ordering "maintenance" medications as a three-month supply. However, this approach is risky until both you and your doctor are well assured that you're not at risk for abuse or suicide.

Communicating Your Medical Information to Other Doctors

Make certain to inform *all* of your doctors about *every* medication you're using, including prescriptions, over-the-counter medications, illicit drugs and alcohol, and substances like herbal remedies. Some combinations lead to side effects, and some compete with one another in your body.

Keep a list on a card in your purse, wallet, or a notebook and have the doctor update your records during each visit. Include the name of each prescription, the dosage amount, and the time or times of day you take it. Keeping your own records of how you respond to each medication and what others you were taking at the time makes it easier to find the optimal treatment. It also helps you communicate exactly what you're taking when you see other doctors or get lab work done. Date each card and store the older copies in case you need to refer to them in the future.

Remembering What to Take and When to Take It

A big challenge, particularly when you're not accustomed to medication and you're in the midst of an episode, is remembering what to take and when to take it. Besides the card I just described, I've found it helpful to store my medications in a plastic holder purchased at a local drugstore. Mine has snap-out containers for each day of the week with compartments for morning, noon, evening, and bedtime. This allows me to drop my meds for one day in my purse and leave the rest behind. I fill the containers each Sunday, which not only helps me track my medications for the week but also alerts me when I need to place refill orders.

Electroconvulsive Therapy

Shock therapy, or **electroconvulsive therapy (ECT),** has a bad reputation it probably no longer deserves. The very mention of ECT alarms a lot of people, as it did me before I really investigated it. Movies about mental hospitals often make ECT look like cruel and unusual punishment, and in its early days, ECT was often administered in less than ideal situations.

But things have changed tremendously. Improvements in equipment, anesthesia, and dosage levels have reduced the occurrence of side effects. The major remaining drawback is short-term memory loss, usually centered on the time of the ECT treatments. I have, however, spoken with people who had ECT and experience continued memory loss long after their treatment.

When you receive ECT, you're anesthetized and given muscle relaxers so that the procedure is painless and less stressful on your muscles and bones. Then electrodes are applied to your scalp, and small amounts of electricity pass through your head for 1/2 to 1 1/2 seconds. This produces a seizure lasting 25 to 120 seconds. Although the exact mechanism of ECT is still unknown, it appears to reset the brain to more normal functioning. Typically, treatments are given three times a week for six to twelve weeks.

Proponents point out that the treatment is both quick and highly effective. Because of this, it can be a better solution than medication when you're severely suicidal. Psychologist Dr. Martha Manning, author of *Undercurrents,* found ECT quite beneficial for treating her debilitating depression. Although one doctor wanted to give me ECT, I never tried it. Perhaps I should have, but I wasn't open to the idea then.

ECT can be a godsend for those whose depression medication can't seem to crack, and the treatment helps control mania as well. It's also a viable alternative for pregnant women and nursing mothers who must be off medication temporarily. And it's a safe option for elderly patients.

However, ECT tends to be less effective in the long term. Once you've completed a course of ECT, you may require medication to maintain the benefits you gained from it.

Transcranial Magnetic Stimulation

Similar to ECT but simpler to administer is a promising technique called **transcranial magnetic stimulation (TMS)** and a related form called **rapid (or repetitive) transcranial magnetic stimulation (rTMS)**. Unlike ECT, this technique does not produce a seizure and can take place while you are fully awake. A coil in which a magnetic field develops is placed against your scalp, and then a small electrical current flows into the brain tissue directly under the coil. This causes multiple neurons to fire simultaneously.

A shorter-term treatment than ECT, TMS is applied daily for about 20 minutes for five to ten days. It appears to be a good option for medication-resistant depression and mania. The only side effects appear to be mild headaches and slight muscular soreness.

Vagal Nerve Stimulation

This technique was originally developed to control epilepsy by sending electrical pulses to the brain. In **vagal nerve stimulation (VNS)**, a device similar to a pacemaker is surgically implanted under the left side of your collarbone. Then an electrode is attached to the vagus nerve in your neck. The VNS device is programmed to stimulate the vagus nerve for 30 seconds in five-minute intervals. About one-third of people with mood disorders who participated in initial VNS studies showed significant improvement. VNS appears to change norepinephrine and serotonin levels, as well as GABA and glutamate levels. Its effectiveness for both bipolar and unipolar disorders is currently under study, but it looks as promising as ECT. The only side effect appears to be some hoarseness when the device is on.

Hospitalization

For most of us with mental illness, the horror of being put away forever is a vision of the past. Now all but the most severe mood episodes can be treated successfully without hospitalization. In fact, most people with mood disorders don't require hospitalization, *provided they're treated appropriately and in time.* And even when hospitalization is necessary, the goal is to get you stabilized and back home as quickly as possible.

Hospitalization can provide a crucial "safety net" for us "tightrope walkers" and should be considered under the following circumstances:

- When suicidal, homicidal, or aggressive impulses or actions threaten your or others' safety
- When you're severely and dangerously agitated or psychotic
- When you have another dangerous medical condition, such as diabetes, and are no longer managing it properly
- When your distress or dysfunction is so severe that it requires round-the-clock care your loved ones can't provide
- When you're so apathetic that you won't eat
- When you have an ongoing substance abuse problem

- When doctors need to closely observe your reactions to medications

When you have strong support from friends and family familiar with your illness, an effective medical regimen, and regular talk therapy, hospitalization rarely becomes necessary.

Obviously, I'm a proponent of medical treatment—as frustrating and expensive as it can sometimes be. I'm convinced I wouldn't be here without it. But not everyone agrees. Talk therapy and other non-medical treatments can both enhance, and in some cases even substitute for, medical intervention.

THIRTEEN

Expressing Your Emotions: "Talk Therapy"

ALTHOUGH THE SEEDS of bipolar disorder appear to be faulty genes and biochemistry, and stress and lifestyle often play a part, other factors may be involved. As indicated in chapters 8 and 9, personality and upbringing could also be contributing factors. But even more important may be the interactions between feelings and biochemistry. Even when your brain chemistry is corrected, you need to address your feelings. Otherwise, they may rapidly tip your biochemistry back into turmoil. Psychotherapy, counseling, and support groups are good places to start.

Repressed emotions tend to fester and intensify during depressive episodes and bubble up and explode during manic ones. While traversing my "tightrope," I've had bouts of inexplicable grief that sent me into sobbing states that lasted several hours. I've felt turned inside out and wrung dry after these intense sessions. At other times I've had a driving urge to cry but have been unable to release a single tear. Sometimes I've laughed myself into extended hysterics, behind which sharp, biting anger waited in the wings.

A crucial aspect of coping with bipolar disorder is learning to express your feelings regularly and appropriately. While our feelings are unavoidable, we must learn to express them in a healthy way and not act out in doing so. Learning how to do this is a primary goal of psychotherapy.

What's Involved in Psychotherapy?

Talking about concerns and challenges on a regular basis—either one-on-one or in a group—can bring both relief and enlightenment. Many of us who have mood disorders tend to spend too much time living inside our heads. Expressing what's going on inside your head can both reduce the stress created by ruminating over worries and unwanted thoughts and offer you perspective.

But you must feel heard and safe in the therapeutic setting and trust its level of confidentiality. You should also feel respected as a person. Your therapy might consist of talking with a psychologist or a social worker. Or you might attend a therapy group run by a professional or participate in a support group run by peers.

Other options are creative therapies that use art, music, dance, drama, or writing. Although this may involve simple appreciation of the arts, most often they involve your own creativity and self-expression. I'll get into these options in chapter 17.

Studies have confirmed that psychotherapy helps stabilize moods and reduces the need for hospitalization. In addition, psychotherapy can improve your relationships and help you function better in many areas of your life.

This chapter explains common types of talk therapy.

Individual Therapy

Individual therapy—or what many people call counseling—helps you deal with the emotions that usually accompany this illness: anger, confusion, embarrassment, frustration, guilt, and resentment. Such therapy also helps you handle common fallout bipolar disorder brings: lost jobs, ruined relationships, financial and even legal difficulties. Therapy can help change unhealthy behavior patterns and distorted thoughts that have complicated your life for years. Studies show that therapy helps people adjust to being on medication and supports compliance with treatment plans.

Contrary to popular belief, most psychiatrists do little counseling. Partially because of managed care and insurance limitations, psychiatric visits are usually too brief to allow much more than giving a quick update on how you're doing and discussing any medication changes you might need.

Types of Therapists or Counselors

The person who provides your therapy will more often be another clinician, such as a psychologist, psychiatric nurse, or social worker who works in partnership with your doctor.

WHO'S WHO IN PSYCHOTHERAPY

- **PSYCHIATRISTS** are M.D.s who specialize in psychiatry. These days, most psychiatrists provide limited talk therapy.

- **PSYCHOLOGISTS** hold advance degrees (usually a master's or doctorate in psychology or clinical psychology). After completing their degree, they go through a supervised two-year internship. Psychologists provide talk therapy, but currently, can't prescribe medication. However, many have extensive knowledge about medications, and there's a chance they may be licensed to prescribe medication in the near future.

- **PSYCHIATRIC NURSES** are R.N.s who have also been trained in psychiatry. They often provide talk therapy in mental health facilities and hospitals.

- **ADVANCED PSYCHIATRIC NURSES** hold master's degrees and may provide psychotherapy. In some states, they are also licensed to prescribe medication.

- **CLINICAL SOCIAL WORKERS** hold master's (and sometimes doctorate) degrees. Most states license clinical social workers to conduct therapy only after they've been through supervised training.

■ **COUNSELORS** may or may not be formally trained in psychology. They may therefore lack the knowledge and credentials to treat a serious mood disorder. In many states, almost anyone can offer counseling services. Although counselors can help with many problems, people with severe mental illnesses usually benefit more from seeing someone with advanced knowledge.

Licensing requirements vary from state to state. Except for counselors, most of the psychiatric professionals described above must be licensed. Some therapists have specialties, such as marriage and family therapy or creative therapies.

Other Psychotherapy Options

Some people prefer to see a minister, pastor, priest, rabbi, or other religious leader rather than someone outside their faith community. Prayer and spirituality are beneficial adjuncts to medication and/or other therapeutic options. But if you have a serious mood disorder, it's not wise to rely on pastoral counseling exclusively.

Telephone counseling, radio counseling, telemedicine, and Internet-based options are other possibilities, particularly if you live in an isolated region where little else is available. If you choose to use them, however, do your best to carefully check the credentials of those you interact with.

Types of Talk Therapy or Psychotherapy

Several different techniques are useful in treating bipolar disorder:

PSYCHOEDUCATION focuses on teaching you (and possibly your family) about your illness and emphasizes recognition of early warning signs that may precede manic or depressive episodes. Chapter 5 lists some of these early warning signs.

INTERPERSONAL THERAPY aims to reduce the strain that mood disorders place on relationships. The focus is on tackling specific interpersonal problems that may be compounding your symptoms.

SOCIAL RHYTHMS THERAPY focuses on adjusting your daily routines to stabilize biorhythms, especially your sleep-wake cycle. You may learn this type of therapy in a hospital setting, as it's crucial to regularly monitor and adjust your routine to prevent further episodes.

BEHAVIORAL THERAPY focuses on modifying specific, observable behaviors or self-defeating habits, on the assumption that all behaviors consist of learned—but often maladaptive—responses to the environment. *Assertiveness training* and *social skills training* are two types of behavioral therapy that use role playing to practice more effective ways of interacting with others.

COGNITIVE THERAPY explores how thoughts and self-talk influence moods and behaviors. It identifies distortions in thinking that confuse feelings with facts. For instance, one such distortion is this dichotomous thought: If you don't love me, you hate me, and there's nothing in between. Another example is that if you're not perfect, you're a total failure. In this approach, the therapist often assigns written homework. Self-help books and some support groups help you practice cognitive therapy as well.

A further approach called *cognitive-behavioral therapy (CBT)* combines aspects of cognitive and behavioral therapy. CBT can particularly help those of us who've had mood disorders for many years and therefore have deeply ingrained distorted thoughts.

Another kind of psychotherapy, *psychodynamic therapy* (or *analysis*), uses the more classic long-term "couch and analyst" approach and involves seeing a therapist several times a week. It focuses on subjective meanings of your experiences and views unconscious motivations and unresolved conflicts as a primary cause of problems. Although this approach has value for some types of depression, it's probably less effective for treating serious brain disorders.

FAMILY THERAPY emphasizes reducing the stress within your family that results from or compounds your symptoms. You and your family members attend each session together. The sessions focus on relationship patterns rather than individuals' problems. The goal of family therapy is to change dysfunctional patterns of communication and interaction.

CAUTION

THERAPIES THAT focus too much on the past keep you stuck and disempowered. It's not your fault—nor your family's faulty—that you got sick, but *you are responsible for your own recovery*. Others can help, but even the best treatment team can't cure you or force you to recover.

For those of us with mood disorders, psychodynamic therapy probably *isn't* the best option.

The Therapeutic Relationship

Finding the right therapist is a bit like finding the right marriage or business partner. Your therapist should be someone you trust and respect and who makes you feel comfortable. But not *too* comfortable. Unless your therapist is assertive (but not pushy) and can challenge unrealistic expectations and distorted thoughts, you may not be adequately motivated to make positive changes.

To gain the most benefit from therapy, you need a therapist with whom you can be completely open. The best therapists are empathetic and genuinely concerned about your physical as well as mental well-being.

The Therapist's Role

People often enter therapy expecting the therapist to fix them as soon as possible. But the quick fix does not exist. Some courses of therapy are short-term, designed to work on specific goals; others are ongoing relationships that may last for years or even decades. Some therapists are more directive than others and may even assign "homework" for you to complete between sessions. Others prefer that you free-associate during your sessions. However, the therapist's primarily role is to help you reclaim your life on your own. Your therapist should be supportive and make occasional suggestions but should not do your thinking for you.

When you don't realize this and your therapist doesn't explain it, it can be enormously frustrating. When I first began therapy, I expected my therapist to supply all the answers. That's not the way it works.

"How Did That Make You Feel?"

If you're not used to communicating on a "feeling" level, you may feel as if you're learning a whole new language when you begin therapy.

When I first began long-term therapy, nearly every other comment out of my therapist's mouth seemed to be "How did that make you feel?" If I said I felt depressed or frustrated, she'd say I really felt angry. As far as I was concerned, anger had nothing to do with my depression or frustration (though I learned later that it actually did).

I spent many maddening sessions during which I'd say something, and she'd reply with nothing more than "And how did *that* make you feel?" My standard answer was "I'm depressed. That's why I'm here!" But that didn't cut it with her. "No," she'd reply, "you're angry." I replied that I wasn't. When she insisted I was, I felt provoked.

I was depressed. I was in a major depressive episode. I just didn't know how to talk about my feelings. I'd buried my emotions for so long, I couldn't access them. When I tried to share how I was feeling, my therapist would tell me I was "intellectualizing." I felt she was just nitpicking and playing around with words. It took me quite some time to see that she was trying to access deeper feelings. What I'd interpreted as criticism was her attempt to get me to get to the heart of my emotions. I just had no idea where to start.

The Nature of Feelings and Emotions

Those of us with mood disorders experience emotional overload at both the high and low ends of the spectrum. We may feel that our emotional intensity alone is the cause of all our problems. It may seem easier to have *no* feelings at all. But our feelings serve a purpose and are essential to our humanity. They are crucial to our survival and drive us to fulfill our unmet needs.

PRIMARY AND SECONDARY EMOTIONS

Mental health professionals often describe feelings on two levels: 1) primary and 2) secondary emotions. To examine your feelings, it can help to determine their true core. One way to think of *primary* (basic or pure) *emotions* is as feelings all infants display. Primary emotions can't be broken down into combinations of purer feelings. *Secondary emotions*, which we acquire as toddlers, can because they overlay primary emotions. Secondary emotions are more self-conscious and involve moral judgments or cognitive analysis.

PRIMARY EMOTIONS

Different experts list slightly different feelings as primary emotions. For instance:

- Both clinical psychologist and classic learning theorist Dr. O. H. Mowrer and the first radio talk-show psychiatrist David Viscott limited primary feelings to only pain and pleasure.
- Dr. Elisabeth Kübler-Ross says our five primary emotions are anger, fear, guilt, jealousy, and love.
- Psychology professor and director of the Langley Porter Psychiatric Institute at the University of California–San Francisco's School of Medicine Dr. Paul Ekman lists anger, fear, sadness, disgust, contempt, and surprise.

SECONDARY EMOTIONS

Secondary emotions include feelings such as embarrassment, envy, guilt, shame, and pride, and polar opposites such as ambivalence or decisiveness, hopelessness or hopefulness, and distrust or trust.

Dr. Viscott pointed out the importance of timing as it relates to feelings, stating that

- *resentment* is anger over past hurts,
- *guilt* is anger turned on yourself,
- *excitement* is expectation of future pleasure, and
- *contentment* is the remembrance of pleasure in the past.

Dr. Bernard Weiner, professor and Vice Chairman of UCLA's Department of Psychology, says which emotion you feel depends on your perception of the circumstances that arouse it. For instance, if you can't control a situation, you'll experience anger (a primary emotion). If you could control the situation or thought you should have but didn't, you'll experience guilt or self-pity (both secondary emotions that arise from anger).

Intellectualizing feelings removes you a step or two from your underlying emotions. Therapists who keep challenging you about the way you feel are trying to get you to dig deeper into your emotional core to help you live in the present.

Finding the Right Therapist

Particularly if you expect to be in long-term therapy, you need a therapist with whom you really "click." To get the most out of therapy, you'll be discussing your deepest, darkest fears and secrets and your fondest hopes and dreams. Finding someone you feel you can trust and feel comfortable enough to open up with is essential. In most cases, it will take more than one try to find the therapist that's right for you.

GETTING REFERRALS

Here are some starting points for locating a good therapist. In addition to the sources suggested in chapter 12 for locating a doctor, ask your psychiatrist or primary care provider for referrals to a therapist, and the clergy at your place of worship, if you have one. I suggest that you avoid yellow page listings, newspaper or magazine ads, or Internet counselors. I believe that personal referrals are best.

Speaking of places of worship, keep in mind that although many clergy are well trained for general counseling, they may have limited knowledge of serious brain disorders like bipolar disorder. Although spirituality and the power of prayer can work miracles, watch out for people who suggest you treat your illness with religion alone. No matter how well intended, they may be unintentionally risking your life.

CHECKING THE "FIT"

When you have some referrals, request a brief interview—either by phone or in person. You can learn a lot through this first conversation. Ask the therapist

- What are your payment policies, and what insurance plans do you accept?
- What is your training and experience, including your knowledge about mood disorders and co-occurring conditions?
- Do you specialize in any particular type of therapy?
- Do you focus on short-term therapy or do you more often see people on a long-term, ongoing basis?
- How do you feel about therapeutic alternatives or supplements to medication?
- How long is a typical appointment, and how frequently should I expect to see you?
- How flexible is your schedule, and how accessible are you between appointments?
- What should I do if an emergency arises? Do you have associates who fill in when you're unavailable?
- Are you willing to communicate with my doctor and with my family and friends, if needed?

Set up your first appointment and see how well you fit with one another. If you're immediately turned off, seek another therapist. If you're not certain, come back a time or two more to help with your decision. It's draining to retell your story to one professional after another, but a therapist you can't truly connect with won't do you that much good.

Working with Your Therapist

Before your first or second session, making a list or chart to talk from can both help you prepare for therapy and help your therapist assist you more effectively. List or chart

- your symptoms (see chapters 1 through 5);
- co-occurring conditions if you have them (see chapter 6);
- medications you have taken or are now taking (see chapter 12 and the Medications Appendix); and
- significant life events (See chapters 8 through 10).

List the concerns you wish to discuss with your therapist and prioritize them carefully. Bring up what's troubling you most early in the session so it won't go unaddressed. Make notes either during the session or as soon as possible afterward about any advice or insights you gained from it.

Group Therapy

The members of your group may or may not have the same diagnosis, but they'll most likely be facing similar symptoms and problems. Theoretically, the interactions in group mirror the interactions in the rest of your life. Therefore, they increase your awareness of behaviors that may be getting in your way.

Group also serves as a "lab" for practicing personal interactions. Many of us with mood disorders find it hard to form and keep relationships. During depressive episodes, we may isolate ourselves from others or drain friends and family by droning on about our pain. During euphoric hypomanic and manic episodes, our energy and excitement may overwhelm friends and family. During agitated

hypomanic and manic episodes, our impatience or obnoxiousness·
may alienate friends and family, or our anger and risky behaviors may
push them away.

Support Groups

The primary benefit of support groups is interacting with people
who know where you're coming from and can better identify with
what you're going through than most people. Support groups share
information about psychiatric disorders, treatment options, coping
techniques, and resources. Support groups often offer some or all of
the following activities:

- Newsletters, educational pamphlets, handouts, and Web
  sites
- Telephone or e-mail support between meetings
- Lending libraries for books, audiotapes, and videos
- Speaker meetings with medical experts
- Social events
- Training and opportunities for legislative advocacy

Although some support groups meet over the Internet rather than
in person, I hesitate to recommend them as a primary support unless
you live in an isolated region where little else is available. As a supplement, however, Internet groups may be just fine.

Support Groups Sponsored by Nonprofits

Many support groups for mental illness are sponsored by nonprofit
associations. Some groups limit membership to those with the mental illness the association deals with; others include or focus on families and friends concerned about loved ones with mental illness. The
following nationally based nonprofits sponsor support groups
throughout the country that can *supplement, but not replace,* competent medical treatment:

DBSA (Depression and Bipolar Support Alliance)

DBSA helps form and assist chapters that sponsor support groups for both bipolar and unipolar disorder. Most members emphasize that unipolar and bipolar disorder are disorders of the brain and recommend medication, therapy, and support groups as a first-line defense.

NAMI (National Alliance for the Mentally Ill)

Some of NAMI's state and local chapters offer support groups for those with severe mental illnesses, including bipolar disorder, and for their families and friends. Some chapters have slightly more direct support for families and friends than for people living with these illnesses.

NMHA (National Mental Health Association)

Some state and local chapters affiliated with NMHA offer support groups for those with severe mental illnesses, including mood disorders, and for their families and friends.

Recovery, Inc.

Recovery's support groups use techniques similar to cognitive therapy. Founded by Abraham Low, these groups focus on retraining the will by examining beliefs and judgments. This organization's method involves simple yet practical coping techniques that help members change their reactions to people and situations they can't control. Recovery groups help members replace "dysfunctional language" with healthier terms. Two target areas include "symptomatic idioms" (beliefs that have no basis in reality) and "tempers" (judging situations in terms of "right" and "wrong").

12-Step Programs

The support groups offered through 12-step programs, formed primarily to address addictions, focus on relying on God (or a higher power) to manage addictive disorders and emotional problems. Because many 12-step groups discourage the use of all forms of alcohol and drugs, including prescription medication, they can present a risk for those of us with mood disorders. *People with unipolar or bipolar disorder should keep taking their medications no matter what their 12-step group says.*

CAUTIONS ABOUT SUPPORT GROUPS

- Remember, few support group members are medical professionals. Group members who share their experiences with medications may inadvertently pass on misinformation.
- Nonprofessionals lack the knowledge necessary to make sound medical recommendations. *Always check with your doctor before following medical advice discussed in such a group.*
- Also, *individual chemistry varies significantly.* What someone else takes may prove disastrous for you.

The Resources section provides contact information for most of these self-help groups.

CO-COUNSELING

If you can't bring yourself to discuss problems in a group setting, another readily available and affordable option is co-counseling. *Co-counseling* (or *peer counseling*) involves a "group" of two, who divide their talking and listening time equally. They provide a confidential sounding board for each other and agree not to judge, criticize, or give advice.

Most any type of support group can help you better accept your illness and at least partially meet your needs for belongingness, esteem, and knowledge.

FINDING THE RIGHT SUPPORT GROUP

Just as with a psychiatrist or therapist, though, it's not a bad idea to shop around for a support group. These groups are as varied as the individuals who attend them, and group dynamics change as members come and go. When you're shopping for a support group, I recommend that you attend at least three meetings before moving on. Because not all group members attend each session, going several times gives you a better idea of the group overall.

However, if your first visit is particularly upsetting or the group just doesn't seem right for you at all, go ahead and look for an alternative right away.

First-Time Support Group Visits

Going to any type of group for the first time can produce anxiety. You may fear that you'll "break down" when you discuss your problems. I've been to groups where I or some other member cried constantly or felt too uncomfortable to say a word. *That's not unusual or abnormal.* Other group members have usually experienced similar feelings or behaved the same way at first. Some group members are at least a little anxious each time a new person comes.

Sometimes support groups allow attendees to bring friends or relatives along. If that would make you more comfortable, that's one option. Some people feel better joining a group if they already know someone who's in it. But if those ideas aren't good options for you, at least consider co-counseling.

I've had my frustrations with psychotherapy and support groups over the years, and at times have discontinued them for a year or more, but I've always felt a need to return. Overall, psychotherapy and support groups have helped me a great deal.

Over the past twenty-five years or so, I've been in individual talk therapy with two different social workers and two different psychologists, and I've received some psychotherapy from three different psychiatrists. I've attended groups led by therapists or counselors and several different kinds of support groups—some sponsored by nonprofit organizations and some informal community groups. On the whole, I've gained—and am still gaining—much support, friendship, and knowledge from these options.

FOURTEEN

Exploring Nonmedical Options: Alternatives and Complements

IN ADDITION TO—or in very rare cases, in place of—conventional medical treatments and therapy, many other options may help you manage a mood disorder. With the exceptions of omega-3 fish oils and phototherapy, which have solid evidence of scientific validity, few Western medical professionals have widely accepted the options in this chapter. However, some of these options are being actively explored.

Until the last few decades, Western medicine has downplayed the importance of nutrition, dietary supplements, and other approaches to healing. Medical doctors have focused more on individual diseases rather on than the person as a whole.

That's beginning to change, and some medical doctors are now acknowledging that healing techniques of other cultures may be of value. Some health insurance plans now cover such options as acupuncture, biofeedback, phototherapy, and nutritional counseling.

Although most of us who take psychotropic medications tolerate their side effects fairly well, some people find the side effects worse than the disease. A minority of people with mood disorders try virtually every medication and conventional treatment and still experience no relief. And a few people have severe side effects even on pediatric doses. Individual biochemistry and physical makeup vary significantly.

To stop seeing medical doctors or use these options in place of prescribed medications could prove disastrous. However, you may wish to ask your doctor whether one of more of these options might enhance your current treatment plan.

Carefully research any options you might wish to try, and verify that the resources and practitioners you consult are reputable. The most reliable information about alternative therapies generally comes from

- government agencies;
- professional medical or nonprofit health associations;
- Web sites sponsored by university medical schools and medical clinics,
- medical journals, books, or Web sites written and/or reviewed by scientific experts;
- recently published or posted information on the Web; and
- testimony from people you know well.

Be cautious about individuals and companies offering information as well as products. Their primary motivation may be to sell those products, and the information may be biased toward that end.

To help you evaluate alternative options, the Resources section of this book lists related organizations and Web sites, and the bibliography lists publications.

This chapter addresses some dietary supplements, bodywork options, and special devices that may help you manage your mood disorder.

Dietary Supplements

The Dietary Supplement Health and Education Act (DSHEA), which became effective in 1994, defines a *dietary supplement* as "any product intended for ingestion as a supplement to the diet." This includes vitamins; minerals; herbs, botanicals, and other plant-derived substances; and **amino acids** (the individual building blocks of protein) and concentrates, metabolites, constituents, and extracts of these substances.

CAUTION

> THE U.S. Food and Drug Administration (FDA) monitors the safety of medications, but only the manufacturer monitors the safety of its dietary supplements. The FDA does not require manufacturers to provide evidence that their products are safe unless they contain a new, unusual ingredient.

You're most likely aware of the National Academy of Sciences' *reference daily intakes (RDIs)* for vitamins, minerals, and other nutrients that most people need to stay healthy. (Until 1994, these were called *RDAs—recommended daily allowances*.) RDIs represent *average* needs that *most* people can fulfill by eating a healthful diet or by combining a less-than-ideal diet with supplements. However, those of us with mood disorders may require more or less of certain nutrients.

All vitamins and minerals, which work closely together and are intricately related, serve one or more functions to ensure good health.

CAUTIONS ABOUT DIETARY SUPPLEMENTS

- Nutritional needs vary for each individual.
- Some vitamins and minerals are *toxic* if you ingest too much.
- Some supplements conflict with certain prescriptions or over-the-counter medications.
- Some of these options may be difficult to deal with early in your treatment or during severe mood episodes.
- *Always ask your doctor which supplements are safest for you and best fit in with your treatment regimen.* If you need supplements but your doctor doesn't deal with them, see a registered dietician or a certified nutritionist.

The following sections focus on the vitamins and minerals most closely linked to the brain and nervous system.

Vitamins

The vitamins most important for mood regulation include several forms of vitamin B, vitamins C, D, and E, choline, folic acid, and inositol.

B-COMPLEX VITAMINS

The B vitamins, which work as a team, help maintain brain and nerve function in a variety of ways. Often, if you have a deficiency of one B vitamin, you'll have a deficiency of another.

- **B_1 (thiamine)** affects circulation, cognition, digestion, and energy, and has a positive effect on your nerves and attitude. Excessive use of caffeine or alcohol can decrease B_1 levels, as can a high-carbohydrate diet. Large amounts are nontoxic but may imbalance other B-complex vitamins.
- **B_2 (riboflavin)** is essential for your body to metabolize the amino acid tryptophan and produce niacin (vitamin B3). Vitamin B_2 also helps regulate certain hormones. Stress, alcohol use, antibiotics, oral contraceptives, and other medications may increase your need for vitamin B_2.
- **B_3 (niacin)** affects your circulation, memory, and nervous system function. Provided all other B-complex vitamins are balanced, your body can produce niacin with the help of the amino acid tryptophan. In some people, excess levels may cause depression and other complications.
- **B_5 (pantothenic acid)** plays an important role in antibody formation, hormone and neurotransmitter production, and the conversion of carbohydrates, fats, and proteins into energy. When you're ill, using antibiotics, or experiencing increased stress, you require more vitamin B_5.
- **B_6 (pyridoxine)** affects a wealth of bodily functions, including antibody formation, brain and nervous system function,

cell reproduction, fat and protein absorption, and hydrochloric acid production. Vitamin B_6 influences your sodium-potassium balance, helps prevent nerve disorders, and raises serotonin levels. If you're taking an antidepressant, or you're taking oral contraceptives or you're on hormone replacement therapy, you may require more vitamin B_6.

B_{12} **(cyanocobalamin),** the only vitamin also containing essential minerals, assists with the production of the neurotransmitter acetylcholine. Vitamin B_{12} affects cell formation, learning, and sleep; increases energy; lessens irritability; and prevents nerve damage.

B-Complex Related Substances

Three other substances closely related to the B-complex vitamins are choline, folic acid, and inositol. Some researchers classify these substances as vitamins and some don't. In any case, they act like vitamins.

Choline is particularly important to brain function because it helps produce the neurotransmitter acetylcholine. Without it, nerve impulses can't transmit properly from the brain to other cells in the central nervous system.

Folic acid (folate) helps form blood cells, produce energy, metabolize protein, and maintain the nervous system. Illness, stress, and the use of alcohol or oral contraceptives may increase the need for folic acid. Because of its crucial role in fetal nerve cell formation, women planning to have children should be taking adequate folate well before they conceive.

Inositol produces calmness and affects cholesterol and fat metabolism. Recent studies have shown that inositol can help decrease moodiness and depression. Excessive caffeine consumption can decrease inositol levels.

Vitamin C

Also known as ascorbic acid, vitamin C is often called the "anti-stress vitamin." Vitamin C is crucial for numerous metabolic functions, including adrenal-gland and immune-system functions, toxin elimination, and tissue growth and repair. Antidepressants, oral contraceptives, and smoking, in particular, can reduce vitamin C levels. The same is true of stress. The body can't produce vitamin C, so you must obtain it through your diet or by taking a supplement. Although it's essentially nontoxic, *vitamin C can lead to diarrhea and other side effects when taken in high doses.*

FAT-SOLUBLE VERSUS WATER-SOLUBLE VITAMINS

- Vitamins A, D, E, and K are **fat-soluble vitamins** that are stored in body fat. If you take excessive amounts, *fat-soluble vitamins can easily build up to toxic levels.* Unless you have a confirmed deficiency, don't take high levels of these supplements.
- When your body doesn't use fragile **water-soluble** vitamins such as the B-complex group and vitamin C fairly quickly, it excretes them in urine and perspiration, so you may need to supplement these vitamins every day.

VITAMIN D

This vitamin functions both like a vitamin and like a hormone. It helps keep the nervous system healthy, and assists in the absorption of vitamin C and the mineral phosphorus. People often call vitamin D the "sunshine vitamin" because it's activated when the skin is exposed to ultraviolet rays. Just fifteen minutes' worth of sunshine three times a week will ensure you have an adequate supply.

VITAMIN E

Vitamin E helps improve circulation, oxygenate the body, maintain nerves, and prevent cell damage. Although vitamin E deficiencies are rare, they can damage red blood cells and destroy nerves.

TABLE 7

Symptoms Common to Mood Disorders and Vitamin Deficiencies

Symptoms	Vitamins											
	B₁	B₂	B₃	B₅	B₆	B₁₂	Choline	Folate	Inositol	C	D	E
agitation						•						
anxiety	•		•	•						•	•	
apathy						•						
appetite loss	•		•									•
concentration problems	•					•						
confusion	•											
constipation	•					•				•		
depressed mood	•	•	•	•	•	•		•	•			
diarrhea			•									•
fatigue	•		•	•	•	•		•		•		
hallucinations						•						
headaches			•	•	•	•						
insomnia	•	•	•			•			•			
irritability	•	•		•	•							
learning problems					•	•						
memory problems	•			•	•	•	•	•				
moodiness		•				•				•		
nervousness	•	•				•						
neuromuscular problems												•
obsessive-compulsiveness									•			
restlessness					•							
visual problems											•	
weight loss											•	

CAUTIONS AND NOTES ABOUT VITAMIN SUPPLEMENTS

- Caffeine interferes with vitamin absorption, so *don't* take vitamins along with beverages that contain caffeine, such as coffee, tea, or soft drinks.
- Excess use of alcohol also depletes many vitamins.
- To best absorb vitamin supplements, take them *with food*.
- *Always consult a health care professional before taking a vitamin supplement.*

Minerals

Some of the most important minerals for mood regulation include calcium, chromium, copper, iron, magnesium, manganese, phosphorus, potassium, selenium, sodium, and zinc. Most people require large amounts of calcium, magnesium, and phosphorus, but both shortages and excesses of any of these three minerals will cause problems. In contrast, most people need only tiny amounts of chromium, copper, iron, manganese, potassium, selenium, sodium, and zinc.

CALCIUM (CA)

Nerve signal transmissions and cell membrane permeability require adequate levels of calcium. However, excess calcium can lead to *both* depressive and manic episodes. Lithium and other mood-stabilizing medications appear to regulate calcium ion hyperactivity.

CAUTION ABOUT CALCIUM AND CHOLESTEROL LEVELS

BECAUSE CALCIUM lowers cholesterol, and cholesterol levels under 160 can produce depression or *even make you suicidal,* you need to monitor both calcium *and* cholesterol.

CHROMIUM (CR)

This mineral helps us metabolize glucose; synthesize cholesterol, fats, and proteins; and produce energy. Chromium also improves serotonin function. Experts estimate that only one-tenth of those living in the United States obtain enough chromium through their diet.

CAUTION FOR THOSE WITH INSULIN-DEPENDENT DIABETES

BECAUSE CHROMIUM lowers insulin, it's especially important to consult your doctor before taking chromium supplements if you have insulin-dependent diabetes.

COPPER (CU)

This mineral promotes healthy nerves and helps ensure proper serotonin function. One important role of copper is to maintain adequate levels of **myelin**, the fatty substance that insulates nerves. Because copper and zinc closely interact, excess zinc may interfere with copper absorption.

IRON (FE)

The most prevalent mineral in the blood is iron. In addition to helping oxygenate the blood, iron helps maintain a healthy immune system and produce energy. It also plays a role in serotonin function. The body requires only a small amount of iron, but children, teens, and menstruating women sometimes need iron supplements to prevent **anemia** (a condition in which a person has too little **hemoglobin,** an important blood–oxygen transporter). If you don't fall into one of these categories, it's usually best to use a multivitamin supplement without iron—or with very little.

MAGNESIUM (MG)

This is one of the most important minerals, as insufficient amounts worsen nearly every disease. Magnesium plays a large role in enzyme activity, nerve signal transmission, calcium and potassium uptake, and proper serotonin function. Stress, alcohol abuse, and oral contraceptives can deplete magnesium levels.

MANGANESE (MN)

Although manganese deficiencies are rare, you still require a small amount to regulate blood sugar, to metabolize fat and protein, and to keep your nerves and immune system healthy. Manganese is also important to proper serotonin function.

PHOSPHORUS (P)

Along with calcium and magnesium, phosphorus assists in cell growth, hormone secretion, energy production, and nerve signal transmission. In the blood, it combines with fats to form **phospho-**

lipids, which transport nutrients between cell walls. But because of typical diets in Western societies, particularly those in which soft drink consumption is high, excess phosphorus is more prevalent than phosphorus deficiency.

POTASSIUM (K)

Potassium plays a particularly important role in our brains. Working in balance with sodium, potassium helps deliver nourishment to cells, transmit signals between them, and influence chemical reactions within them.

SELENIUM (SE)

Selenium is best known for its role in preventing cancer and heart and liver disease. It interacts with vitamin E to produce antibodies. Selenium also influences the thyroid hormone's role in fat metabolism. Selenium deficiencies have been associated with high cholesterol.

SODIUM (NA)

A component of table salt, sodium has been linked to high blood pressure, heart attacks, kidney failure, and strokes. Although excess sodium is much more common in Western diets, sodium deficiencies occur occasionally. One well-known effect of low sodium levels is dehydration. Strenuous exercise leads to sodium loss through perspiration.

Because sodium and potassium work together to maintain water balance, you may need a potassium supplement if you consume a lot of salt.

ZINC (ZN)

This mineral helps us synthesize proteins and the nucleic acids that carry genetic information: DNA and RNA. Research studies indicate that zinc also protects the immune system, eliminates toxins, and helps prevent many illnesses, including cancer. Several studies have also shown that during depressive episodes, people have significantly lower zinc levels than those not suffering from depression.

TABLE 8

Symptoms Common to Mood Disorders and Mineral Deficiencies

KEY: **Ca** = calcium, **Cr** = chromium, **Cu** = copper, **Fe** = iron, **Mg** = magnesium, **Mn** = manganese, **P** = phosphorus, **K** = potassium, **Se** = selenium, **Na** = sodium, **Zn** = zinc

Symptoms	Ca	Cr	Cu	Fe	Mg	Mn	P	K	Se	Na	Zn
anxiety		•					•		•		
cognitive problems	•							•			
confusion					•	•			•		
constipation							•				
delusions	•										
depressed mood	•				•				•	•	•
diarrhea			•								
fatigue		•		•	•		•	•	•	•	•
hallucinations					•				•		
headaches					•			•	•		
hyperactivity	•										
insomnia	•						•				
irritability					•	•	•		•		
lethargy									•		
memory problems					•					•	•
nervousness	•		•	•				•			
suicide attempts					•						
tremors/trembling					•	•					
weight change					•					•	

TWO CAUTIONS AND A NOTE ABOUT MINERAL SUPPLEMENTS

- Excessive amounts of many minerals can worsen mood symptoms, cause other health problems, or *even lead to toxicity*. Get medical advice before taking any mineral supplement.
- *Always consult a health care professional before taking a mineral supplement.*
- To best absorb mineral supplements, take them *between* meals.

While in graduate school, one of the options I tried for treating depression was to consult a nutritionist, who after receiving my lab results prescribed a combination of multivitamins and supplements. Shortly after I began taking them, a roommate who had been gone for a week or so instantly noticed the change. She said, "Well, who opened your coffin! You look great!"

I stayed on the prescribed regimen for several years. Then the expense caught up with me. I began whittling down the number of supplements I took and relying more on prescriptions because my health insurance covered them but not the supplements. Now I rely on my diet and only two basic supplements for most of my nutritional needs.

Amino Acids

The largest part of the body weight consists of water. The second largest consists of protein. **Amino acids** are crucial to brain signal transmission. They help build bodily protein, and proteins help build brain neurotransmitters. Some amino acids even act as neurotransmitters themselves.

Amino acids aid in the absorption of vitamins and minerals and assist with many other metabolic functions. The liver manufactures roughly 80 percent of the amino acids you need, but the remainder must come from protein you ingest. These 20 percent are called *essential amino acids.*

Even if you consume a healthful diet, age, drug use, stress, trauma, or other nutritional deficiencies can lead to amino acid deficiencies. This doesn't mean you must consume large portions of protein. In fact, too much protein overstresses your kidneys and liver. However, in some circumstances (for instance, if you eat a vegetarian or *vegan* diet—an entirely plant-based diet)—you may require amino acid supplement. *Because amino acids work together, you're more likely to need a combination supplement rather than one single amino acid.*

The amino acids most important for mood regulation include carnitine, gamma-aminobutyric acid, glutamic acid, glutamine, glycine, histidine, lysine, phenylalanine, taurine, tryptophan, and tyrosine.

CARNITINE

Although not a true amino acid, carnitine is chemically structured like one. It helps regulate the nervous system, increase attention span, address cognitive problems, and slow memory deterioration. Carnitine can be useful for depression.

GAMMA-AMINOBUTYRIC ACID (GABA)

This amino acid is essential to maintain brain function. **GABA**, formed from an amino acid called glutamic acid, acts as an inhibitory neurotransmitter in the central nervous system. In the right amount, and in concert with inositol and *niacinamide* (a form of vitamin B_3), GABA reduces anxiety and stress. But too much can increase anxiety and produce other symptoms.

GLUTAMIC ACID

This amino acid and excitatory neurotransmitter can convert to either GABA or glutamine in the body. Glutamic acid helps potassium cross the **blood–brain barrier** and, through its role in creating glutamine, helps detoxify the brain.

CAUTION FOR PEOPLE ALLERGIC TO MSG

IF YOU'RE allergic to monosodium glutamate (MSG), *do not* take glutamic acid supplements.

GLUTAMINE

Glutamine crosses the blood–brain barrier so readily that it's often known as "brain fuel." It helps maintain the body's acid/alkaline balance and produce both DNA and RNA. One of glutamine's unique roles is to help sweep toxic ammonia from the brain. Glutamine can reduce cravings, depression, fatigue, and impotence, and improve cognitive functions.

GLYCINE

Acting as an inhibitory neurotransmitter, glycine helps treat hyperactivity. The right amount produces energy by assisting glucose release; too much produces fatigue.

HISTADINE

This amino acid helps maintain the myelin sheaths that insulate nerve cells. Histadine converts to *histamine,* a compound that dilates blood vessels and protects the immune system. (Histamine is also involved in allergic reactions.) Although you need some histadine, excessive levels can produce anxiety and stress.

CAUTION ABOUT HISTADINE

DO NOT take a histadine supplement unless you have a confirmed deficiency.

LYSINE

A crucial building block for protein, lysine helps absorb calcium; balance nitrogen; produce antibodies, enzymes, and hormones; and repair tissues. Lysine deficiencies can lead to concentration problems, irritability, reduced appetite, and weight loss.

PHENYLALANINE

Phenylalanine converts into tyrosine, which converts to dopamine and norepinephrine. If you're irritable and moody, a phenylalanine supplement can sometimes help.

CAUTIONS ABOUT PHENYLALANINE

- If you suffer from frequent panic attacks, do *not* take a phenylalanine supplement.
- If you have allergies, avoid phenylalanine. It contains the highly allergenic chemical *phenol.*
- Phenylalanine is a major component of the sweetener aspartame. Avoid aspartame if you have one of these problems. If you need to supplement multiple amino acids, use a product that contains no phenylalanine.

TAURINE

This amino acid plays a large role in protecting the brain, particularly during dehydration. It's helpful in the treatment of anxiety, hyperactivity, and impaired brain function. A taurine deficiency may result from alcohol abuse or excessive stress, or may indicate a zinc deficiency.

TRYPTOPHAN

Without adequate tryptophan, the brain can't get enough serotonin. Although proteins contain small amounts of tryptophan, they also contain other similarly shaped, but larger, amino acids that compete with tryptophan to enter the brain. Insulin helps reduce the amount of competing amino acids in the blood to clear the way for tryptophan to reach the brain.

Tryptophan helps improve sleep and reduce moodiness. Studies have also shown that tryptophan can lower aggression, which can relate to a lack of serotonin. In addition, tryptophan lacks the side effects that antidepressants produce. But tryptophan supplements alone can do little to improve depressive symptoms. They're most helpful when used in conjunction with certain antidepressants.

A counselor I saw in my mid-twenties suggested taking tryptophan to help me better deal with my erratic sleep. Although I took tryptophan supplements for several months, I saw no improvement. Now I know why: I wasn't taking an antidepressant at the time.

In 1989, synthetic tryptophan was taken off the market after a Japanese manufacturer produced a contaminated batch that caused a rare disease called *eosinophiliamyalgia syndrome* and a number of deaths. After the U.S. Food and Drug Administration's investigation determined the source, tryptophan supplements were reapproved and are now widely available.

A form of tryptophan called *5-hydroxy-L-tryptophan (5-HTP),* a naturally derived amino acid, appears useful for the treatment of mild to severe depression. This amino acid converts to tryptophan in the body and can be used to produce serotonin. Research studies indicate that 5-HTP produces fewer side effects and that they're milder than the side effects of antidepressants.

TYROSINE

Tyrosine converts into dopamine and norepinephrine. It can improve your concentration and help you better control impulsive urges. A tyrosine deficiency can reduce the number of neuronal norepinephrine sites, which may cause depression. Tyrosine supplements are useful to prevent or reverse the effects of stress.

CAUTION FOR THOSE ON MAOIS

IF YOU take an MAOI antidepressant, *you must avoid all forms of tyrosine.* Tyrosine supplements, and foods and beverages containing tyrosine, can raise your blood pressure to *potentially fatal levels.* Ask your doctor about other MAOI-related limitations.

NOTE AND CAUTION ABOUT AMINO ACID SUPPLEMENTS

- A *D*, an *L*, or a combination, which may appear in either upper- or lowercase, often precedes the name of an amino acid supplement. Some of these letters relate to structural configurations of carbon atoms the supplements contain, or to the supplements' polarity (magnetic orientation).
- Always consult a health care professional before taking an amino acid supplement and verify what form you need to take.

Essential Fatty Acids

The brain needs fat in order to operate properly. Try to consume at least 5 grams a day of *essential fatty acids*—the special fats the body needs as much as vitamins and minerals. Essential fatty acids help the body produce *prostaglandins*—hormonelike substances of three different varieties: 1-, 2- and 3-series prostaglandins. While 1- and 3-series help prevent inflammation, 2-series tend to produce it. Research studies have shown high 2-series levels and inflammatory symptoms accompany depression. High levels of *prostaglandin E1 (PGE1)*, a 1-series form, often accompany euphoria and mania.

You can obtain omega-3 fatty acids by eating large quantities of fish or taking fish oil supplements. Fish oil contains a substance called *eicosapentaenoic acid (EPA)*, which is necessary to 3-series prostaglandin production.

NOTE AND CAUTION ABOUT ESSENTIAL OIL SUPPLEMENTS

- Essential oil supplements are available in health food stores and some grocery stores.
- *Always consult a health care professional before taking an essential oil supplement.*

Herbs

I'm open to herbal treatments, though I haven't yet tried much more than herbal teas. I've primarily used conventional medications because my health insurance covers them but doesn't cover herbs. However, I do know people who have found SAM-e or St. John's wort helpful for depression.

GINKGO

This popular herb increases the oxygen supply to every part of the body by dilating tiny blood vessels. It's particularly well known for improving memory, reducing impotence, easing muscular pain, improving blood pressure, and slowing the effects of aging. It also appears to increase concentration, improve disturbed moods, and adjust sleep patterns. Low doses are more effective than high doses.

CAUTIONS ABOUT GINKGO

- Although oral ginkgo supplements appear to be safe when used appropriately, avoid crude ginkgo plant parts, which can cause severe allergic reactions or even toxicity.
- Ginkgo can cause problems when combined with some herbs, dietary supplements, and medications, particularly certain psychotropics.
- *Always consult with your doctor before taking ginkgo.*

KAVA

This herb grows in several different varieties, and is known by several other names. Some include: ava, kava kava, kava root, kew, and *Piper methysticum*. Through its effects on the amygdala in the brain's limbic system, kava can reduce anxiety, fear, and stress. It's also helpful for insomnia.

CAUTIONS ABOUT KAVA

- Do not use kava if you are pregnant or nursing, or if you're taking antidepressants.
- Because of reports of rare but serious forms of liver damage, the FDA recently advised consumers to *discontinue or reduce taking any form of kava*. The problems reported were cirrhosis, hepatitis, and liver failure.

SAM-e (S-adenosylmethionine)

S-adenosylmethionine is a naturally occurring substance present in every cell of the body. Formed from the amino acid *methionine,* which comes from protein, S-adenosylmethionine helps build neurotransmitters and DNA. Most healthy people who consume adequate protein have all of the S-adenosylmethionine they need. However, several studies have shown that SAM-e supplements can decrease symptoms of moderate depression as well as several antidepressant medications can and with fewer side effects.

The down side is that SAM-e supplements are expensive, and because they are unregulated, you have a fifty-fifty chance of buying an effective batch. A study in 2000 reported in *Consumer Reports* found that only eleven of the twenty-three products tested contained the amounts of SAM-e shown on their labels. And only three other brands contained as much as 90 percent of their labeled amounts.

ST. JOHN'S WORT (HYPERICUM PERFORATUM)

This herb acts in the same way as MAOI antidepressants do but has milder side effects. European studies found St. John's wort helpful in about half of those who took it for mild or moderate depression—

about the same number many prescription antidepressants help. However, the first major United States study showed less positive results. St. John's wort also seems to be ineffective when depressive states are more severe.

CAUTIONS ABOUT ST. JOHN'S WORT

- *Do not* use St. John's wort if you take an antidepressant or any other medication that interacts with an MAOI.
- Because it stimulates liver enzymes to remove medications more quickly from the body, St. John's wort can interfere with other medications.

Although St. John's wort is less expensive than SAM-e, it's still unregulated, and many manufacturers sell products that don't contain enough hypericum perforatum for an effective dose.

CAUTIONS ABOUT HERBAL SUPPLEMENTS

- Excessive amounts of many herbal supplements can worsen mood symptoms, cause other health problems, or *even become toxic*.
- Herbal preparations are unregulated substances, so you can't be certain what you're getting.
- *Always consult a health care professional before taking an herbal supplement.*

NEW SUPPLEMENT MIX MAY HOLD POTENTIAL

A Canadian study reported in the December 2001 issue of the *Journal of Clinical Psychiatry* reported a 50 to 66 percent improvement of bipolar symptoms in those taking a specially formulated supplement mixture. The thirty-six-ingredient supplement administered by Dr. Bonnie Kaplan and her University of Calgary team included no lithium but did contain other minerals, vitamins, amino acids, and antioxidants.

The subjects continued taking their regular prescription medications, and experienced only mild nausea when taking the supplements without food or at slightly higher doses. Some were able to discontinue prescription medications and rely on the supplements alone.

Although the sample population involved only fourteen subjects, and three dropped out before the study's conclusion, the results offer much hope for less expensive treatment options. However, much more research is needed.

Homeopathic Medicine

The underlying principle of *homeopathy* is similar to that of immunizations: The same substances that cause toxicity and overdoses can stimulate the immune system to develop antibodies when used in highly diluted doses. Therefore, the same substances that produce symptoms can desensitize the body's reactions to them.

Homeopathic medicine has been used for centuries in other cultures, and in some countries is the treatment of choice over conventional medical approaches to healing. Some homeopaths believe that their preparations may be more effective because micro-doses may flow more readily across the blood-brain barrier. Even some medications have opposite effects when taken in extremely small doses. Just as with many prescription medications, though, we don't yet know the exact reasons why many homeopathic preparations work.

Because the United States doesn't require that homeopathic practitioners be certified, it's wise to ask about a practitioner's training and success rate in working with people who have mood disorders. Also see the Resources section.

Bodywork Options

Acupuncture

The Chinese practice of acupuncture is based on inserting needles into the body at specific points to manipulate the body's flow of energy. Theoretically, acupuncture helps balance the endocrine system and helps regulate heart rate, body temperature, and respiration, as well as sleep patterns and emotional changes. Acupuncture has been used in clinics to assist people with substance abuse disorders through detoxification; to relieve stress and anxiety; to treat attention deficit and hyperactivity disorder in children; to reduce symptoms of depression; and to help people with physical ailments.

A University of Arizona study reported in the September 1998 issue of *Psychological Science* explored the use of acupuncture for treating major depressive disorder. About two-thirds of the participants experienced a rate of clinical remission comparable to that produced by medication or psychotherapy.

Acupressure

A less invasive technique that's similar to acupuncture is *acupressure,* which you can perform on yourself. Instead of needles, acupressure uses finger pressure at the same healing points that acupuncture needles get inserted.

My stepson, Tom, a great enthusiast of natural treatments, introduced me to the art of acupressure, which involves both finger pressure and deep breathing. Although I was initially skeptical, I finally tried it when I could no longer bear the neck and back pain created from working too long at my computer. Some exercises from Michael Reed Gach's *Acupressure's Potent Points: A Guide to Self-Care for Common Ailments* produced significant relief.

Breathwork

Speaking of breathing, it's something I must often remind myself to do, especially when I'm exercising. By getting more oxygen, you can strengthen your immune system, increase your energy level, and reduce your anxiety. Breathwork can help you learn to reprogram your responses to stressful situations.

The best way to breathe is to allow your diaphragm to drop and let your stomach bulge out so your lungs have plenty of room to expand. Most of us breathe shallowly and don't allow the oxygen to reach our lower lungs.

Force yourself to stop a few times every day and do some deep breathing. But to keep from inhaling carbon dioxide rather than oxygen, avoid deep breathing in highly polluted settings.

Massage

One of the best ways I've found to manage stress is through massage. For a time, a friend studying massage gave me half-price rates, so I could have one every other week. (I was devastated when she moved to California.) I've had a couple of gift massages since but no longer get regular treatments.

In addition to relaxing tense muscles and reducing stress, massage helps release buried emotions. It's helpful for treating depression and trauma-related disorders. As with many forms of alternative therapy, laws about massage therapy vary widely. Some states require strict certification, but others states require no certification at all.

CAUTIONS ABOUT MASSAGE

- Massage can release powerful pent-up emotions that you may not be ready to deal with.
- If a massage therapist uses essential oils, you'll absorb them through your skin. Ensure that the oils used won't worsen your condition.
- *Tell any massage therapist you see about your diagnosis.*

Special Devices and Other Treatments

Aromatherapy

Another noninvasive alternative is *aromatherapy,* which involves inhaling the odors of special herbs, spices, and botanicals. The same brain system that so deeply affects moods—the **limbic system**—also processes smells because the olfactory nerves protrude deeply into it.

Although many cultures have used aromatherapy since at least that time of Hippocrates, few Western scientists take it seriously. The British journal *The Lancet,* however, has reported that the aroma of lavender oil has helped reduce depression and stress in some people.

The following chart lists a few aromas that are calming, stimulating, or either—depending on the amount used. The more you use, the more the aroma stimulates you.

TABLE 9

Calming and Stimulating Aromas

Calming	Sedating *and* Stimulating	Stimulating
■ Cinnamon leaf	■ Geranium	■ Basil
■ Frankincense	■ Jasmine	■ Lemongrass
■ Marjoram	■ Lavender	■ Peppermint
■ Nutmeg	■ Lemon	■ Rosemary
■ Orange blossom	■ Patchouli	■ Sage
■ Sandalwood	■ Rose	■ Thyme

I think aromatherapy is worth a try. You can use aromas by burning incense or scented candles, in potpourris, in your bath, on your pillow, or in a steam machine. Some useful aromas are also available as fresh flowers.

Biofeedback

Clearly, the brain interacts with the rest of the body and impacts our overall health. A field of study called **psychoneuroimmunology**, which explores the connections between cognitive processes and the autonomic, immune, and nervous systems, is now providing a new perspective on the healing process and producing some dramatic results.

Because thoughts, emotions, and bodily changes occur almost simultaneously, it's often hard to say which occur first. *Biofeedback* takes the stance that thoughts and emotions precede physiological processes. This technique involves learning how to consciously control the stress response to cope better with your illness. Before you can benefit much from biofeedback, however, your mood disorder must be under reasonably good control. Otherwise, "brain strain" will get in the way, and your efforts may be futile.

When you participate in biofeedback, the biofeedback therapist will connect you to a monitoring instrument (often an **EEG**, or **electroencephalogram**, machine) and attach electrodes to the area being monitored (usually your head). The electrodes will feed information to the monitoring instrument, which will record changes in your brain waves.

The therapist will tell you what's happening in your brain and lead you through mental exercises to help you learn to control your bodily responses. Through trial and error, you can learn to adjust your brain wave activity. The ultimate goal of biofeedback is to train you how to regulate mental and bodily processes when no machine is present.

One reason many people like biofeedback is that it provides a sense of personal mastery over their disorder. Biofeedback can decrease the sense of helplessness that often accompanies depression and can leave you feeling more optimistic.

CAUTION: BIOFEEDBACK AND VNS OR CARDIAC PACEMAKERS

IF YOU have a vagal nerve stimulation (VNS) device or cardiac pacemaker implanted, ask your doctor about the safety of using biofeedback therapy.

The Resources section provides contact information for locating qualified biofeedback therapists. Like breathwork, biofeedback can help you learn to reprogram your responses to stressful situations.

Phototherapy (Light Therapy)

Some people with bipolar disorder are especially sensitive to changes in light, seasons, temperature, and weather. Those affected find sunlight or simulated sunlight particularly important for maintaining their biological clocks. Many, but not all, of these people may have a mood disorder called **seasonal affective disorder (SAD)**, which some psychiatrists believe is another form of bipolar disorder.

This syndrome, originally identified by Dr. Norman Rosenthal and colleagues at the National Institute of Mental Health brings on depression during dark, dreary, rainy weather in many people.

Those affected begin to display depression, irritability, and sluggishness as days grow shorter. They binge on carbohydrates, sleep excessively, and withdraw from social life. Then, when spring and summer come, and light becomes more prevalent, their moods pick up, and become considerably more elevated.

Light helps regulate the body's "biological clock," which is associated with the pineal gland, which is buried deep in the brain and releases a sedating hormone called *melatonin*. Even fifteen to forty minutes of sunlight, particularly bright morning sunlight, will suppress melatonin release.

Dr. Rosenthal and his colleagues found that exposure to high-intensity light can reduce depressive symptoms. When they can't get adequate sunlight, many people find significant relief by using a high-intensity light box daily.

Light boxes are commercially available but somewhat expensive; however, some insurance plans cover them. And those who benefit from phototherapy often see dramatic differences within just a few days. Even if you must pay for your own, the quick relief can help you become productive sooner and be well worth the expense.

A few sources for light boxes follow:

- Amjo Corporation 1-877-282-2956 (1-877-BUY-AMJO) *www.sadlight.com*
- BioBrite, Inc. 1-800-621-5483 (1-800-621-LITE) *www.biobrite.com*
- SunBox Company 1-800-548-3968 (1-800-LITE-YOU) *www.sunbox.com*

In *Living Without Depression and Manic Depression,* Mary Ellen Copeland explains the proper use of a light box. It involves

1. Sitting three feet in front of the box for about two consecutive hours;
2. Keeping your eyes open (though don't stare directly at the lights);
3. Using the light box daily, preferably around the same time of day (because evening use may make getting to sleep more difficult, daytime use is generally best);
4. Tapering off as possible when days lengthen and even stopping during the summer except on cloudy or rainy days;
5. Monitoring the changes you experience and sharing them with your doctor.

It's important to replace the bulbs regularly to maintain the proper intensity of light.

Negative Ion Generators

The air we breathe contains both positive and negative ions. An **ion** is an electrically charged atom or group of atoms. As contrary as it may seem, high energy and positive moods relate to high concentrations of *negative* ions rather than the other way around.

Stuffy enclosed spaces, such as windowless rooms, tend to have low amounts of negative ions. Outdoor spaces, particularly near moving water, have the highest concentrations of negative ions. This is one reason it's important to get fresh air.

Although air purifiers and air conditioners emit negative ions, those ions attach to airborne dirt and impurities and sink to the floor; therefore, those ions can no longer circulate. If you can't get out much for fresh air or leave a window open, run a room-sized ion generator where you spend the most time. Combination air purifiers and negative ion generators are also available and reasonably priced. A few sources follow:

- Comtech Research 1-866-466-4937, *www.comtech-pcs.com*
- IPS Air Purifier Products 1-888-812-1516, *www.indoorpurifiers.com*
- Sharper Image 1-800-344-5555, *www.sharperimage.com*

Another opinion is to shower more frequently—if you have access to a shower—because the water will contain negative ions.

Negative ion treatment is especially useful for people who have seasonal affective disorder (SAD) and are especially sensitive to weather changes.

Before trying any option mentioned in this chapter, discuss it with your doctor and, if possible, get referrals to qualified practitioners. Also, learn all you can about it by reading books and articles, visiting health food stores, or talking with people at holistic health care facilities. The Resources section also contains information about alternative treatments.

FIFTEEN

Finding Firmer Footing: Lifestyle Adjustments

ANY TYPE OF mood episode tends to change your life while it's occurring and later call for some lifestyle change. Both depressive and manic or hypomanic episodes can lead to joblessness, broken relationships, a major move or homelessness, and massive financial problems.

You may feel as if you're starting life over and over again and again. I certainly have. Such problems can be overwhelming and increase the feelings of helplessness and hopelessness you may already have. But I'll bet you're neither helpless nor hopeless. Most of us are capable of managing our illness pretty well by getting effective treatment.

Those of us with mood disorders tend to either blame others or attribute everything that goes wrong in our lives to the illness. This is both self-defeating and dis-empowering. *You must accept that you have this illness, and it's up to you to manage your recovery.* This doesn't mean coping with the illness all on your own. Advice, assistance, and support from others are crucial for recovery. But no one can truly save you but yourself.

Taking good care of yourself when you have a mood disorder requires a *huge* commitment. Your health often must become your top priority; otherwise, everything else may fall apart. Especially during and shortly after a mood episode, maintaining your health may consume much of your time.

It may be a struggle to find a routine that works well for you, particularly at first. This chapter addresses some potential adjustments to make and suggests some ways to deal with them.

Where Do I Start?

A good place to start is to ask yourself "What do I need for optimal health?" I suggest you first address your deficiency needs, as described in chapter 11. This means handling your physiological needs, such as obtaining adequate sleep, nutrition, and exercise, and balancing your brain chemistry. You'll also need to fulfill your safety, belongingness, and esteem needs—either after meeting your physiological needs or while still trying to meet them.

Aim to make all the positive changes you can, but don't try to change everything at once. Take baby steps. Do what you can when you can. Preventing future episodes may require

- adjusting your sleep schedule (avoiding shift work if at all possible);
- changing your diet (including time to shop for groceries and to prepare and eat nutritious meals);
- taking dietary supplements, if necessary;
- starting to exercise, or changing or increasing what exercise you already get (unless you're overexercising);
- breaking away from abusive relationships;
- finding a job or seeking financial support (if employed, you may need to adjust your workload or job schedule);
- seeing a psychiatrist if you aren't already, or seeing a different one;
- beginning, switching, or adjusting medications;

- entering therapy, trying a different kind, or switching therapists;
- attending a support group for people whose symptoms are similar to yours;
- seeking more emotional support from family and friends;
- changing your activities or activity level;
- learning how to better deal with stress and worries; and
- keeping on top of your moods and related information.

This chapter explores the type of shelter and environment you need for optimal health at home and at work.

Living and Working in Safe Environments

Feeling safe and secure deeply affects a person's sense of well-being. It's important that your home and workplace, and any other environment where you regularly spend time, be supportive rather than stressful. A chaotic environment can lead to or compound chaotic emotions. Doing your best to keep your surroundings reasonably clean and tidy—as challenging as that often becomes during mood episodes—will help reduce your stress level and likely ease some symptoms.

Your Home Environment

You may need to move after an episode for many different reasons. For instance:

- You may no longer be able to afford to live where you did before.
- You may need to escape an abusive or difficult situation.
- You may need to find a safer neighborhood.
- You may need more emotional support from a roommate or a family member.
- You may need your own personal space.

- You may be forced to move because others can no longer cope with the consequences of your disorder.

EXAMINE YOUR SURROUNDINGS

Even the decor of your home or workplace can affect your moods, thoughts, and behaviors. Colors, for instance, can relax, depress, or energize us. For years, architects and designers have known about the effects of different colors. Colors are even an aspect of *feng shui,* an ancient Chinese design philosophy.

Scientists have found that energy from wavelengths affects our pituitary and pineal glands and stimulates them to produce certain hormones. "Cool colors," like blues, indigos, and violets, have short wavelengths. "Warm colors," like reds, oranges, and yellows, have long wavelengths.

Cool colors calm us and help us slow down, but overexposure to cool colors can contribute to depression. Warm colors stimulate and energize us, but overexposure—particularly to yellow—can lead to agitation. Most shades of green fall in between and are easy on our eyes.

Attention to our environment can help fulfill our need for aesthetics—a growth need of Maslow's Hierarchy of Needs. If you're stuck with wall or carpet colors that distress you, use curtains, bedspreads, rugs, furniture, and accessories that help block them from view. Even the color of your clothing and transportation can affect you. Do all you can to choose colors that produce positive changes.

SURROUND YOURSELF WITH SUPPORTIVE PEOPLE

It's important to have supportive people around you, whether they live with you or simply next door. Living with someone who abuses you physically or emotionally or who terrorizes you with violent or erratic behavior can scar your psyche tremendously. It's nearly impossible to keep your moods and emotions level when you feel threatened.

CAUTION

PARTICULARLY IF you have suicidal tendencies, *you can't afford to stay in a situation where you lack emotional support*—at home or at work.

Your Work Environment

Your first job when you have a mood disorder is to maintain your health to prevent future episodes. But it also helps to have some activity that takes you outside of your head. Having some type of work can increase your productivity and enhance every other aspect of your life.

Your "work" may involve a conventional paying job, looking or training for a job, or working for yourself. It may involve staying at home and caring for your family or going to school.

If your illness is particularly severe, your work may consist of trying to obtain some type of financial support or doing a volunteer job. In any case, you need something that helps you interact with others in the community.

CONVENTIONAL EMPLOYMENT

After leaving a demanding full-time conventional job and falling into deep depression, I was nervous about going back to work, even part-time. But my psychiatrist pointed out the benefit of having some structure in my life, not to mention the income. With great trepidation, I approached a former colleague about a three-quarter-time job. She offered me a full-time position, which I wasn't certain I could manage. But it had enough flexibility to allow me to continue with daytime individual and group therapy and regular psychiatrist visits, so after a few days of agonizing about it, I began the job.

At first the job felt demeaning because it didn't take full advantage of my skills and talents and my salary was considerably lower than I'd been earning in my previous job. But the regular routine kept me from dwelling on my problems day and night and helped me feel more productive.

Discussing Your Illness—Whether or not to inform an employer of your illness presents a real dilemma. The standard advice many people with mental illness offer is "No! Don't do it!" They're often terrified of being fired if their employers learn they have a mental illness. Unfortunately, sometimes that is the case.

One friend with bipolar disorder who loved her job and was doing well found her coworkers treated her differently after her return from a hospitalization. She eventually quit her job and moved on. However, I also know some people who have discussed their disorder with employers and coworkers and things have worked out fine.

Some people will empathize and work with you to help meet your needs. Others simply won't understand and may use your disorder against you at some point. You must decide for yourself what feels best for you.

I went into the position I just mentioned without telling my boss about my illness, but this secrecy eventually caught up with me. Finally, I revealed my illness in a letter. Although I don't necessarily recommend writing such a letter, I've included it to give you some idea about ways you might reveal your illness to employers.

THE LETTER TO MY BOSS

I'VE BEEN receiving treatment for a mood disorder for nearly a year and a half. My psychiatrist believes I probably have cyclothymia, a mild form of manic depression. I've been responding well to medication and therapy the last several months.

However, much of my life, I've swung from wonderful, energetic highs down into lengthy depressions. When I'm really "up," I'm highly creative and inspired and get very absorbed in my work. I tend to believe I can do virtually anything. At such times, I'm self-confident and cheerful, much more talkative and friendly, and find it extremely difficult to slow down. If this continues for more than a few days, it usually takes a dangerous turn. I begin putting in extra hours, trying to accomplish more than I realistically can. I ignore my physical needs and become disorganized, indecisive, compulsive, and ineffective. This state usually ends when I become physically ill or drop into severe depression.

I've experienced very few periods of living on an even keel. Until about a week ago, I was doing pretty well, but when my stress builds up too high, my medication and therapy just don't cut it.

> The way all this affects my work and career mainly relates to my not yet having a realistic concept of what a manageable workload is for me. Many times, I have a strong intuition that a project or deadline will be unmanageable or overstress me, but it's hard to know if that's coming from reality or temporary bouts of self-doubt.
>
> Having been the "lone ranger" in virtually every professional position I've held increases my difficulty of obtaining a clearer perspective. I hope that your knowing about my situation will help us work together more smoothly in the future.

Fortunately, my boss was sympathetic and understanding, and she kept me on. She allowed me to cut back to three-quarter-time and become a "contract worker." The arrangement worked for me for quite some time. Cutting back to a thirty-hour week not only lowered my stress but made me more productive.

If you reveal your illness, some employers will understand and work with you, but some won't. In many cases, though, you have alternatives if an employer has a problem with your staying.

Protecting Your Employment Rights—If your mood disorder, whether bipolar or unipolar, "substantially limits" your ability to work, compared to other employees, the Americans with Disabilities Act (ADA) may protect you from work discrimination and protect other employment rights. The ADA applies in workplaces with at least fifteen employees.

Whether or not you disclose your disability during a job interview is up to you. The ADA does not require that you do so. However, if you need special accommodations, such as a modified schedule, time away for therapy, or an unpaid leave of absence during a hospitalization, it's probably best to disclose your disorder. This involves informing a supervisor, human resources person, or other representative of your employer. You need not tell everyone you work with, and because this involves personal medical information, your employer can reveal the information only to supervisors or managers who must know about the accommodations you require.

Here are some actions you can take to protect your rights:

- Request the accommodations you need in writing.
- Suggest alternatives.
- Request a meeting be scheduled to discuss them.
- Provide these numbers to your employer: Job Accommodation Network (1-800-526-7234), Disability and Business Technical Assistance Centers (1-800-949-4232).
- Also direct your employer to the Disability Rights Section of the Civil Rights Division of the U.S. Department of Justice Web site: *www.usdoj.gov/crt/ada/adahom1.htm*.

Be forewarned, however, that any employer who wants to fire someone—disabled or not—can usually find some way to do so. Defending your rights may ultimately be more draining than looking for another job. The Resources section offers contact information that will help you learn more about the Americans with Disabilities Act.

WORKING PART-TIME

Part-time jobs may involve conventional employment, working on contract, freelancing, or working on your own. Some part-time and contract jobs come with benefits, usually if you work a certain number of hours.

I didn't realize it at the time, but accepting a contract job can set you up to be among the first that are "let go" when a company's workload becomes sparse. When this first happened to me, I decided to start a freelance editing service because decent-paying part-time jobs were difficult to find.

After trying awhile to earn my income completely through freelance work, which almost always leads to feast or famine, I found a more secure combination. I began working about eighteen hours a week for a local textbook publisher to have a base income, which I supplemented with freelance projects. This arrangement worked well for about four years; then I left to work with a friend who'd been my supervisor at another company many years before.

WORKING FOR YOURSELF

This option can be both exhilarating and terribly stress-provoking. Unless you have another source of income or your illness is extremely well controlled, I hesitate to recommend it. As ideal as working for yourself sounds, all of the expense and responsibility falls on your back. Sometimes you won't know where the next job will come from or when it will come. Sometimes you won't know precisely when you will get paid. Or you may have trouble collecting what you've earned. The stress and insecurities that surface in such situations can consume you.

I made a conscious choice to work from home rather than to take a conventional job primarily for the flexibility it provides to manage the needs my illness brings.

RETURNING TO SCHOOL

During my childhood, adults who returned to school usually did so because they didn't finish high school or college. After that point, they were "grown up," and, for many, new learning stopped. These days, more people are aware of the need for continuous learning. Reaching your potential involves an ongoing pursuit for knowledge—the first level of growth needs on Maslow's Hierarchy.

VOLUNTEERING

Contributing to other people's lives can be tremendously energizing and adds more purpose to your life. It need not cost you any money and need not involve a lot of time. You don't have to make some huge commitment to be helpful. You need not become a Mother Teresa. It can be as simple as listening carefully to the members of a therapy group or support group to which you belong. It can be as simple as bringing mail or a newspaper to a disabled or elderly neighbor's door. One of my bipolar friends gets a lot of pleasure from volunteering in her church's nursery.

Reducing Workplace Stress

Preparing to leave home and go to work can be stressful in itself. To reduce this stress, get to sleep at a reasonable time and prepare everything you need to start your workday the evening before:

- Pick out your clothes.
- Set out any toiletries or makeup you'll need in the morning.
- Ensure that you have any medications you need the next day.
- Check your schedule and "to do" list for the next day.
- Set out your briefcase, bag, or backpack.
- Locate your purse or wallet.
- Pack your lunch or ensure that you have lunch money.
- Find your keys, or if you're taking public transportation, the money, cards, or tokens you'll need.

If you feel too bad to go to work, call in as soon as possible. If you can't manage that, ask a family member or friend to tell your employer you're not feeling well, you're under a doctor's care, and you'll return to work as soon as possible. If your symptoms continue making it difficult for you to work, ask your doctor whether you should just try to hang in there or if you should take time off.

Increasing Your Sense of Belonging

It's darned near impossible to cope with a mood disorder all alone. Many people with a mental illness feel ostracized and disliked. But relationships play an important role in recovery, and *it's crucial to seek them out.* You need the support of family, friends, loved ones, and associates, in addition to that of mental health professionals.

BEWARE OF TOXIC RELATIONSHIPS

- Abusive or "toxic" relationships decrease self-esteem and only worsen mood disorders. Verbal abuse can do as much or more damage as physical or sexual abuse.
- Aim for supportive relationships with no "negative wizards." In other words, avoid people who have a powerful negative effect on you and make you tense or bring you down.

If you don't have the support you need in your current environment, it's crucial to find an environment where you can get it. This doesn't mean running away from your problems; it means surrounding yourself with people who genuinely care about you.

If you're recovering from a depressive episode, you may need to force yourself to reach out and reconnect with others. If you're recovering from a manic or hypomanic episode, you may need to make amends with alienated family or friends. However, you should also realize that it's not easy to live, work, or even be friends with someone who has severe mood swings. Particularly if others haven't "walked the tightrope," they may have trouble relating to you. Try not to get angry about their lack of understanding. Just do the best you can.

Discussing Your Illness with Others

When I first began talking openly about my illness, people responded in many different ways. One colleague I've known for several years and occasionally see at the grocery store backed several feet away from me as if I might attack him. Some people nodded as if they'd suspected it all along. Others took the news with total silence. But most expressed genuine concern. Many opened up and shared that they had friends or family members with mood disorders, or had been diagnosed themselves, and wanted to know more.

A CAUTION ABOUT OPENING UP

OPENING UP about my illness brought much relief and helped in my recovery, but it took more than a dozen years of treatment before I was strong enough to do so. Before you open up, consider who you need or want to know about your disorder and carefully think the decision through. There's less stigma about mental illness these days, but unfortunately, it's still out there.

If you and your friends and family learn as much as possible about your disorder, you'll all be better armed to reduce the inevitable stress and criticisms the disorder can bring. Even the calmest friends and family will sometimes need outside help to deal with the stresses your symptoms produce. Ask your doctor or therapist to help educate both you and your family about your disorder. Family therapy can be helpful, but joining a support group may help you even more. You can gain quite a bit of comfort from talking with others who have experienced similar situations. Chapter 13 and the Resources section suggest some starting places for finding support.

Receiving Comfort from Pets

A pet can provide another avenue for increasing your sense of belonging. Several of my friends with mood disorders and I receive a lot of comfort and emotional support from cats, dogs, guinea pigs, or even hamsters. If you get a pet, make certain someone can care for it if you become too ill or have to be hospitalized for a while.

If you can't have a pet where you live or feel like it's too much responsibility, you may still be able to interact with other people's. You might run a pet-sitting or dog-walking service for people in your neighborhood.

Developing a New Routine

Maintaining a regular pattern of activity helps meet security needs and increases self-esteem even if your activities are relatively limited. A routine that includes adequate sleep, regular meals, exercise, work, socializing, and relaxation will help you build a more stable foundation. One friend with debilitating unipolar depression credits the state hospital for getting her on a reasonable schedule and helping her become productive again.

With my illness, finding a balanced routine I can maintain on a regular basis has been a constant challenge. When depressed, I withdraw from most everything and must force myself into activity. When hypomanic, I feel desperate to make up for lost time. I can easily determine what my mood states were like by reviewing my calendar and "to do" lists. When I'm depressed, my calendar is nearly blank—or riddled with canceled appointments. When I'm hypomanic, my schedule shows back-to-back activities and even overlapping commitments.

My experience with the illness has made me much more cautious about commiting, as I've learned how easily I can become overinvolved. I'm a "joiner" and often take on leadership roles. I participate in a variety of organizations (for a while, I was active in more than a dozen at once). My enthusiasm about my interests is hard to quell.

Because I feel strongly about keeping my word and being responsive to others' needs, I often have difficulty taking care of my own. Eventually, overactivity brings on depressive episodes and leaves me feeling terrible about not keeping all my commitments. The hypomanic part of me still hangs on to the idea that I can do it all, although I've learned through bitter experience that I can't.

Changing Your Activities or Activity Level

When recovering from depression, you may find it helpful to add activities to your schedule slowly and carefully, allowing time to adjust to each new addition. When recovering from mania, you may need to carefully prioritize your activities and build in time to unwind and take breaks.

While activity is important, be careful not to overextend. Don't be frenetic or drive yourself impossibly hard. My manicky nature drives me to take on many different projects and pursue many different interests at a time. I stubbornly refuse to let them go. Choosing between them becomes excruciating. But prioritizing is necessary. Monitor yourself as you add each new activity.

LEARN TO SAY NO

IF YOU have a tendency to take on too much, learn how to say no—both to others and to *yourself*. Remember, no one can do it all or have it all, especially not all at once. Learning to put the brakes on is crucial for managing a mood disorder.

Building in Some "Downtime"

Let me clarify what I mean by "downtime." I'm not referring to depression or the blues. I'm talking about unpressured time to relax, wind down, and enjoy life. Because those of us with bipolar disorder tend to be impulsive, we also need to build in downtime to reflect and plan.

This is one of my biggest downfalls. I often feel as if I can't afford to relax, enjoy life, or be at peace because I think I must make up for lost time and work constantly. This sets me up for more depressive episodes.

But it's extremely important to take time out to pamper yourself a little, get some distance and perspective, and celebrate each small step you make toward recovery.

Reducing Stress

While stress alone does not *cause* bipolar disorder, it can clearly *trigger* both manic and depressive episodes and worsen your illness.

To cope with your disorder, you must therefore learn to reduce stress. Exercise alone can relieve a lot of stress, but you may also need to use other stress–reduction techniques.

- Realize you can't change your disorder but you can learn to manage it.
- Don't allow your illness to victimize you. Do whatever is needed to better manage it.
- Identify the common stressors in your life.
- Share your thoughts and feelings about them.
- Do what you can to simplify your life.
- Manage your time to conserve your energy.
- Don't rely on drugs or alcohol to solve your problems.
- Learn as much as possible about your disorder.
- Use all support and information services available to you.
- Take short relaxation breaks whenever and wherever you can.
- Build in time for fun.

- Develop and maintain a sense of humor—even about your illness.
- Learn to recognize the warning signs of impending mood episodes.

THE HEALING POWER OF HUMOR

Humor may seem an odd topic to include in such a serious book, but if we can't find some humor in our circumstances on occasion, we'll all be forced to cry.

Norman Cousins's Miraculous Recovery—Longtime editor of the *Saturday Review,* Cousins discovered the healing power of humor while recovering from a severe illness in 1964. After many tests, his doctors diagnosed his ailment as *ankylosing spondylitis,* a painful degenerative disease of the spine's connective tissues. Doctors considered his condition irreversible. One specialist said his chance for a full recovery was one in five hundred.

Cousins had learned about the negative effects of stress on the adrenal glands from reading *The Stress of Life* by Hans Selye. Because Selye explained how negative emotions could impair body chemistry, Cousins began wondering what effect positive emotions might have. With the support of his doctor, Cousins moved out of the hospital and, accompanied by a nurse, into a hotel room. He spent his time watching funny movies and reading humorous books. He also started taking large doses of vitamin C intravenously. He improved enough to return to work and even to hold a camera steadily while riding a horse "flat out." His hospitalization occurred when he was fifty-two, but he lived on to the age of seventy-eight. Cousins described this experience in *Anatomy of an Illness as Perceived by the Patient.*

Therapeutic Humor—Psychologist and former president of the American Association for Therapeutic Humor Dr. Steven Sultanoff, who describes himself as a "mirthologist," stresses the importance of humor in

- altering biochemistry,
- changing distressing thoughts and feelings,
- addressing negative behaviors,

- improving communication, and
- building positive relationships.

Sultanoff maintains a Web site that explains therapeutic humor and provides a wealth of amusing information at *www.humormatters.com*.

Laughter Clubs—A growing movement is laughter clubs, whose purpose is to improve both physical and mental health through laughter. These clubs don't rely on humor, which is subjective, but use methods that *resemble* laughter to produce real belly laughs. The leading United States "joyologist," psychologist Dr. Steve Wilson, cofounded the World Laughter Tour with Karyn Buxman, M.S.N., C.S.P., C.P.A.E., in July 1998. Hundreds of laughter clubs now exist in the U.S. and Canada.

I've not joined a laughter club yet, but I do laugh quite a bit at meetings and events held by two other organizations. One is Toastmasters, which sponsors annual humorous speech contests. The other is my Depression and Bipolar Support Alliance (DBSA) support group, where we share cartoons, puns, and funny stories in addition to discussing our problems and treatments. We do, however, try to be sensitive about the timing. If a member is deeply depressed or a newcomer is present, we soft-pedal our humor or save it for another time.

The Resources section contains contact information for all of these organizations.

REDUCING YOUR WORRIES

If you tend to worry too much (a common problem in people with mood disorders), learn how to set worries aside and not dwell on them. This is easier said than done. I'm one of several individuals, including my niece who has bipolar disorder, that other family members label "worrywarts." My great-aunt Jeannette was infamous for "fretting."

Some experts suggest reserving a time or two each week to deal with your worries rather than worry constantly. You might create a "worry box" to store cards or slips of paper with your problems written on them. Then during your official "worry session," remove each problem from the box. Ask yourself, "Is this something I can control?" If you can't change the problem, set it aside, talk it over with someone, or pray about it. If it's something you *can* change, use a written problem-solving process to help you solve it.

Problem-Solving Tips

It's generally more powerful to go through problem-solving processes in writing than to merely discuss the problems with someone. It's even more helpful to do both.

1. Describe the problem and explain why it bothers you.
2. Decide what part of the problem is real.
3. Decide what part of the problem is simply dwelling on the past or worrying about future problems.
4. Restate the problem in a way that helps you see potential solutions. Then list your options without judging them as "good" or "bad."
5. Rate the good and bad aspects of each potential option.
6. Decide which solution seems best.
7. See if you have all the information you need to apply it.
8. Act on your decision or set a time to do so.

Learning Your Warning Signs

One important part of coping with bipolar disorder is becoming conscious about every aspect of your illness. For many years, I had *no clue* when I was heading into depression or hypomania. I'd just suddenly find myself in the midst of it. I often felt as if someone had suddenly jerked my "tightrope" out from beneath me.

Once I learned what to look for and began to pay more attention to my moods, I started to recognize patterns and pick up on clues of impending changes. I was then better able to work with my doctors to adjust my medications or to alter my lifestyle to accommodate my illness.

When your routine is established, unplanned changes in it can also signal a budding mood episode. A couple of weeks after slightly reducing the dose of one antidepressant, I found myself sleeping an average of three extra hours a day, being careless about my diet, and having no interest in exercise. No stressors in my life could explain these changes. After a week of feeling like I had the flu, I returned to my previous dose (with my psychiatrist's approval), and the changes cleared virtually overnight.

Missing regularly scheduled activities can signal impending mood episodes. When I miss an exercise session—which I hold as a top priority—it usually means I'm slipping into a depression or feeling overwhelmed. When I miss a doctor's appointment, it usually means I'm so caught up in hypomanic activity that I can't keep track of my commitments.

You may have different reasons that relate to different warning signs. For instance, in a depressive episode, you may miss a doctor's appointment because you're having memory problems or because you feel too depressed to leave home. And in a manic episode you may miss a doctor's appointment because you've headed off on some unplanned adventure or you're convinced that you don't need a doctor since you're perfectly well. Warning signs differ with the individual, and you need to learn what yours are.

Monitoring Your Moods

It's helpful to chart your moods and medications (and anything else you might need to monitor). Charting can help you remember to take your medications, which can be truly challenging, especially when you're taking several different kinds or doses more than once a day. It also helps you remember and communicate important information to your doctor and therapist.

I track medications and dosage amounts, the number of hours I sleep at night, any daytime naps, diet changes, exercise sessions, sexual activity, menses, and bowel movements, as well as major events that might be affecting my moods. Then I rate my moods each day. I fill out my chart when I get up each morning or the last thing at night. This may sound like a lot of work, but it actually takes very little time.

You can obtain a free six-month personal calendar from the DBSA that comes as a 4-by-9-inch booklet. It helps you track your medications and side effects, symptoms (like panic attacks or substance abuse), hours of nighttime sleep, and your moods and their severity. There's also space to record significant life events that might affect your mood, like arguments or auto accidents. This can help you remember to watch for the warning signs that tend to precede your own mood disorders.

A WORD OF WARNING

DON'T GET *too* caught up in monitoring your illness. If you do, your entire life may consist of constant worrying, doctors' appointments, medications, lab tests, therapy sessions, and support group meetings. You'll have no time left to enjoy yourself.

After using several of these calendars, I ran into a storage problem, so I created my own customized one-page 8 1/2-by-11-inch form. I store a form for each month in a three-ring binder that includes other medical information, and I take my binder to every type of medical appointment. You can download a free copy from my Web site: *www.bipolar-tightrope.com* and duplicate it as often as you wish. Or, you may request a free copy if you enclose a self-addressed envelope with a single first-class stamp and address it as follows:

Free Daily Tracking Form
Castle Communications
PMB 358 P.O. Box 200255
Austin, TX 78720

As you're setting up a new routine and learning to better manage your illness, avoid making too many changes at once. That will only set you up for failure. Don't rush yourself. It takes an average of twenty-one days to fully adopt most new habits. Work on only one to three changes at a time. Tackle further changes only when you have the others well in hand.

SIXTEEN

Shifting Your Perspective: From Wishes to Reality

NCE YOU'VE ADEQUATELY met most of the deficiency needs of Maslow's Hierarchy of Needs, described on page 168, and have better balance of your brain chemistry, you'll be more able to work on growth needs.

In the midst of a depressive episode, positive thinking is virtually impossible. You're too far down to believe there's any hope. You may be too overwhelmed or unfocused to concentrate on such ideas. Or you may feel so flat and empty that you're not motivated to even try.

During deep depression, you can't force yourself to believe you can accomplish anything. Your "tightrope" will have fallen so low that all you see is darkness. You may discount everything you've ever accomplished and see no hope for a brighter future.

If you're in a hypomanic or manic state, you may be already thinking *way* too positively. What you're more likely to need is a reality check about grandiose new schemes.

During childhood and throughout most of my adulthood, people have nagged me about the need to change my attitude when in the midst of depressive states. They'd shower me with sayings such as

"Stop viewing the glass as half empty rather than half full." My parents, friends, and teachers encouraged me to think more positively, but I simply couldn't. My brain chemistry was too upset.

New Age enthusiasts said I could "create my own reality" by simply believing in myself, using positive affirmations, and visualizing myself achieving my goals. I know there's great value in these ideas. I participated in several New Age programs in the attempt to dig out of my depressions. But I could access their power only I was when hypomanic. Such concepts are nearly impossible to apply when you're challenged by an untreated or undertreated mood disorder. I strongly believe this because the right combination of medications helped me so dramatically.

It wasn't as if my attitude changed entirely overnight. I had years of bad programming that my brain needed to reset—and to some extent still do. But my medications significantly dampened the severity of my mood shifts and helped me start to tap my power to make positive changes. Of course, I still must monitor my illness carefully, stick to a healthful routine, and watch my stress level. But I've accomplished much more than I'd ever thought possible (at least when I wasn't hypomanic).

This chapter shares the most helpful tips I've learned about setting realistic goals, creating and using affirmations, and visualizing positive results.

Setting Goals

During depressive states, setting goals may seem fruitless. In particularly severe states of depression, you may believe you can't do anything at all. If that's the case, start with very small goals, such as getting out of bed, bathing, or getting dressed, or eating at least one well-balanced meal a day. Then celebrate each goal you accomplish.

Hypomanic or manic states tend to produce opposite goal-setting problems: You may be so overenthusiastic that you develop completely unrealistic expectations. One way to deal with this, at least in hypomanic states, is to discuss your goals with others. Carefully consider their opinions, as other people are more likely to recognize what's realistic and what's not. During manic states, you may find this impossible. Learning the warning signs of hypomania, which often escalates into mania, can help you address potential problems before they get out of hand.

Why Set Goals?

One reason to set goals is that they help you move toward recovery and better manage your illness. Goals can also increase your self-confidence and give you some sense of control (though my therapist says people can't *control* anything; they can only plan things and manage their reactions to what happens). Goal setting also helps you focus and positively channel your energy.

Guidelines for Goal Setting

Experts generally suggest that people use the following criteria when setting goals:

- **Base goals on your values**—Don't set goals based on someone else's expectations. Set goals *you* find meaningful.
- **Make goals specific**—For example, rather than setting a goal of having lots of friends, decide what kinds of friends you want. Then get involved in activities where you'll be most likely to meet those kinds of people.
- **Make goals measurable**—For example, rather than saying you want to get more sleep, set the specific number of hours you want to get each night.
- **Make goals realistic**—For example, rather than setting a goal of repainting your entire home in a weekend, set a goal of repainting one room each weekend or each month.
- **Make goals you have the power to meet**—For example, rather than setting a goal of getting a promotion, set a goal that increases your chances of being promoted.
- **Don't make your goals overly complex**—Use the KISS principle, which most people state as "Keep it sim-

ple, stupid." Given that most of us are hard enough on ourselves already, I prefer: Keep it simple, *sweetheart*.

Areas for Goal Setting

Experts on goal setting suggest creating goals for many different aspects of life. Some possibilities follow:

- Home environment, including interior and exterior
- Health, sleep, nutrition, exercise, and weight control
- Relationships with family, friends, and associates
- Income, work, career, and job skills
- Leisure, play, hobbies, sports, and recreation
- Spirituality, religion, and appreciation of life
- Appreciation of nature, plants, and animals
- Knowledge, learning, and exploring new information
- Self-expression and creativity
- Community involvement and contributing to society

Clearly, this list could go on and on and become quite overwhelming. Or this list may not include every area you value. What's important is to form goals that address *your* needs and interests. I can't prescribe precisely what areas to address; however, one good place to start is with goals that address the deficiency needs listed in Maslow's hierarchy—physiological, safety, belongingness, and esteem.

Because goals are personal, much depends on your personal values—what matters most to you.

Value-Based Goals

Setting priorities has never been my strong point. I've always responded to others' priorities better than my own. Other than my desires to be thoughtful and empathetic, to appreciate and protect nature, to contribute to society, and to be nonviolent, I found my values difficult to sort out.

An impaired limbic system, which controls your moods, also limits your ability to set and prioritize goals. Attempting to be logical during extreme anxiety, says author Tracy Thompson, is like reasoning with a swarm of bees.

EXERCISE 1

If you have trouble setting goals based on your values, you might try this exercise:

1. Around the same time on the same day each week, list the goals most on your mind.
2. Do this for three consecutive weeks.
3. Put the list away each week without looking at it until the fourth week.
4. On the fourth week, compare all of your lists. Most likely, you'll find some differences.
5. Make a master list and prioritize your goals.

EXERCISE 2

If you find it hard to prioritize your goals, try this exercise:

1. Put each goal on a slip of paper and compare two slips at a time.
2. Set the "losing" goal aside.
3. Compare a third goal to the "winner" from the first two goals, and set the "losing" goal aside.
4. Keep comparing your goals until you find your top priority.
5. Write down that goal, and then repeat this process with all the slips you've set aside until you have a prioritized list.

Especially when setting goals for shorter periods, such as a week to three months, keep the number limited. You can always set more goals later. You need not set every goal you wish to achieve over your entire life.

Reward Yourself for Your Progress

Reward yourself when you meet or make progress toward a goal. This *doesn't* mean celebrate by downing a triple-size banana split or buying an entire new wardrobe. It means acknowledging your progress and rewarding yourself in a healthful way. Some examples of healthful rewards include

- trying a new food at a restaurant or from the grocery store;
- going for a walk or drive;
- spending quality time with a loved one, friend, or pet;
- viewing a sunrise, sunset, or the moon;
- relaxing with a book or magazine;
- working on a hobby;
- pampering yourself with a massage or bubble bath; and
- giving yourself a hug or a pat on the back.

Because mood disorders often challenge self-esteem, you may be inclined to discount your accomplishments. Learn to acknowledge yourself for your achievements and to accept compliments when others praise anything you've done. Rather than responding with a comment like "It was no big deal" or "I didn't do anything special," just say "Thanks!" Remember, it takes a lot of strength to cope with a mood disorder. Give yourself a break.

Don't Punish Yourself for Falling Short

Don't punish yourself if you don't complete a goal. If you make progress, acknowledge what you've done. If you don't make progress, vow to take a small step toward it tomorrow. Some psychologists and behavior therapists suggest applying a punishment technique, such as snapping your inner wrist with a rubber band, the moment you notice you've performed a self-defeating habit. I think that's a bit harsh. I suggest refocusing on your goal rather than beating yourself up. If you're depressed, you tend to punish yourself already.

Dr. Phillip McGraw, who through seminars has taught thousands of people to apply better life skills, describes four essential questions that help you evaluate your beliefs and self-talk to separate truth from false perceptions. I've adapted McGraw's questions to help you evaluate goals and "failures," and to work through many other challenges related to mood disorders. McGraw's four criteria appear in bold, and my adaptations follow:

1. **Is it inarguably factual?** Would others agree that this goal is reasonable and achievable in the time frame you have in mind?
2. **Does the thought or attitude support your interests?** Does this goal come from your own values and interests, and lead you toward recovery?
3. **Does the thought or attitude advance and protect your health?** Does this goal consider the challenges of maintaining your health and staying on top of a disorder?
4. **Does the thought or belief help you obtain what you need, want, and deserve?** Would others agree with your answer?

You may wish to discuss your goals with your doctor or therapist, with a support group member, or with a relative or friend. Weigh the other person's perception carefully. Sometimes, others may over- or underestimate your capabilities, but many times, others can offer a more realistic perspective.

Affirmations

While an *acknowledgment* takes place after the fact, an *affirmation* applies to the present or the future. It either confirms a current state of being or reinforces your commitment to a future action. New Age thinkers use affirmative statements to reprogram the subconscious. Affirmations for future goals work powerfully *if you believe you can accomplish them.* This can lead to problems when you're suffering from a mood disorder because your mind may be packed full of negative self-talk.

Negative self-talk often contains phrases such as "I should," "I must," "I'd better," "I need to," "I have to," and so on. In the mid 1940s and early 1950s, Karen Horney addressed the tyranny of "shoulds." And Dr. Albert Ellis coined the term "*mus*turbation" to describe the severe anxiety and panic you can create by believing that you "must" complete certain actions to get others to accept you.

I fought depression so much of my life that negative self-talk became second nature. I picked up much of the vocabulary from Mother, whose conversation was filled with self-recriminations for as long as I can remember.

Dr. Ellis describes three basic *musts* that often lead to emotional problems:

1. Believing you must perform well and/or win others' approval to prove your adequacy as a person.
2. Believing others must treat you fairly and considerately, and that those who frustrate you are rotten people.
3. Believing your life conditions must provide what you want and must keep you from harm or else your life will be unbearable, and you'll have no chance for happiness.

My husband kept saying things like "cancel, cancel" when I criticized myself (which really pissed me off at times). *But I simply couldn't reset my negativity.* Cognitively, I could accept an affirmation like "Everyone is worthy of love; therefore, I am worthy of love." But *emotionally*, it got twisted into "Everyone is worthy of love *except me.*"

The first affirmation I managed to buy into when depressed was—quite literally—"I am not a piece of shit." That, at least was *factually* inarguable, no matter how bad I felt.

A JOURNAL ENTRY
RELATED TO THIS REALIZATION

I'VE FELT a shift in my emotional patterns over the last three days. Somehow, I had the sudden, clear realization that *I am not a piece of*

> *shit*! I may make mistakes, have a hard time keeping all my commit-
> ments, lack self-discipline, lack some skills and knowledge to be "per-
> fect" at what I do, sell myself short, settle for being a victim, get
> manipulated, be a doormat, withhold my feelings, let others tell me
> how to lead my life or determine what I do, and sometimes act irre-
> sponsibly or immaturely, but that doesn't prove I'm unworthy, worth-
> less, or a piece of shit!

From there, I went on to talk myself into other affirmations. For me, this was an incredible breakthrough.

Guidelines for Creating Affirmations

The words we choose and the ways in which we communicate are some of the most powerful tools available to us as human beings. It's therefore wise to be careful about the way we "language" goals and affirmations. Experts suggest creating affirmations in the present or present progressive tense, as if they've already been achieved or are in the process of being achieved. For example, rather than saying "I'm going to find a job that really interests me," use "I'm finding a job that really interests me." This word emphasizes the present rather than the future.

Some people—including my husband—even go so far as to write goals, affirmations, and "to do" lists in the *past tense*: "I found a job that interests me," as if they've already been achieved. Ralph creates lists with items such as

- mowed lawn,
- answered and cleared e-mails,
- prepared agenda for Monday's meeting,
- called Tom,
- e-mailed Joy,
- paid bills.

I haven't yet reached a point where I write items on my "to do" list as if I've already completed them until they're really done. I'm too concerned that would befuddle my overchallenged memory and that I'll think I've finished something I haven't actually done. I therefore use present progressive statements instead. Choose the tense and wording that makes the most sense to you.

So, what do you do with your affirmations once you've created them? Some suggestions appear in the following section.

How to Use Affirmations

To gain any value from affirmations, you must read, say, or listen to them repeatedly. You can access your affirmations by

- listing them on a tablet or compiling them in a notebook;
- placing them on cards small enough to carry in your wallet, purse, or pocket;
- posting them on signs and sticky notes on the bathroom mirror, the refrigerator, a desk lamp, or some other surface you'll see daily;
- calling your answering machine and leaving them as messages to yourself;
- using a computerized reminder program or a text-to-speech program;
- transferring them to audiotape;
- subscribing to an automated service, such as Mr. Wakeup (at *www.ipingsecure.com/mrwakeup_menu.asp*); or
- any other technique you find convenient.

Experts recommend that you use your affirmations at least twice a day because repetition will more deeply imprint them in your brain.

My Preferred Approach

The technique that's worked best for me is to tape my affirmations and listen to the tape regularly. The first year I did this, I trimmed down a list of goals I'd made for the year to eighteen—the exact number I could fit on a one-minute audiotape. I wrote a script and read it aloud, timing myself until it was about the right length. Then I recorded it on a sixty-second answering machine tape so it would repeat continuously. (It took several tries to get the timing right.) That whole year, each time I walked around the neighborhood, I listened to the tape in my Walkman.

Perhaps this approach worked best for me because it combined my affirmations with physical action, a combination author Tracy Thompson also found useful. Although others emphasize that belief in an affirmation is more important, Thompson found rote repetition helpful. My approach used a combination.

You need not set as many goals as I did nor use a sixty-second tape. My goals were *terribly* aggressive, and shorter tapes are readily available. (In fact, I was a little hypomanic when I made that tape.) About a third of my goals were unreasonable. But I achieved or still am achieving another third. The other third represent ongoing challenges that I work on when I can. Some examples follow:

My Most Reasonable and Helpful Affirmations
- I have the power for positive change.
- I am erasing self-defeating habits and behaviors.
- I limit TV viewing and use my time consciously.

Affirmations I Made and Am Making Significant Progress On
- I really *can* do what I want to do.
- I freely and honestly express who I am.
- I eat only what I need to keep healthy.

Unrealistic and Potentially Hypomanic Affirmations
- I exercise aerobically at least three times a week *and* for strength and flexibility at least three times a week.
  (To accomplish what I had in mind would have required *at least nine hours a week*. That was unreasonable due to other commitments.)
- I *always* achieve great results!
  (This affirmation signals perfectionism, an unreasonable goal for *any* human being.)

- I believe in myself—*no matter what!*
  (This is unrealistic, considering my diagnosis and the number of years I went untreated or undertreated.)

Another technique to help shift your perspective and develop healthier thoughts and behaviors is visualization.

Visualization

Also called *guided imagery, visualization* involves going into a state of deep relaxation and creating a mental image of recovery and wellness, or some goal you want to achieve. You may already associate visualization with optimal athletic performance, because athletes use the technique a lot. If you watch a basketball player aiming for a free throw or a golfer getting into position for the next swing, you can see visualization at work.

The Use of Visualization in Health Care

Healthcare professionals also use visualization sometimes to treat substance abuse, depression, panic disorders, phobias, stress, and a number of other conditions. One of the most fascinating applications I'm aware of is the work of Dr. Carl Simonton and Stephanie Matthews-Simonton, who since the 1970s have used visualization successfully to supplement cancer treatment.

The Simontons ask their patients to first enter a state of relaxation (chapter 18 suggests some techniques). Then the patients visualize their bodies healing, using the following steps. I've generalized these somewhat to apply them to all sorts of illnesses.

1. Create a mental image of your illness or symptoms, visualizing it or them in a way that makes sense to you.
2. Picture your treatment eliminating the source of your illness and symptoms or strengthening your body's self-healing powers.
3. Watch your body's natural defenses and natural processes eliminating the source of your illness and symptoms.

4. Imagine yourself healthy and free of your illness and symptoms.
5. Use this technique fifteen to twenty minutes, three times a day.

One of the Simontons' cancer patients visualized troops of tiny knights killing off his cancer cells, which he envisioned as furry little animals. He assigned each knight a quota of animals to spear each day and saw his chemotherapy as a way to make the cancer cells puff up like popcorn and explode. After one session late in his treatment, he became concerned because he couldn't "see" any knights. Medical tests confirmed the reason: His cancer was in remission.

The Use of Visualization for Mood Disorders

For a mood disorder, you might visualize a mood-stabilizing medication working within your neurons, reprogramming them to produce more stable moods. You might visualize an antidepressant circulating longer in neuronal synapses and stimulating the growth of new receptors. As you learn more about troubling or distorted thoughts that recur during your mood episodes, you might visualize the growth of healthier neural pathways to replace them.

What If I Have Trouble Visualizing Things?

The Simontons say you need not be concerned if you can't "see" the image you're trying to visualize, provided you can sense or imagine it. Also, if your mind drifts during the visualization process, guide it gently back to the image. Don't be harsh on yourself. If you noticed you couldn't complete some of the instructions during the visualization process, it may indicate that you don't yet believe or accept them. In such a case, it's time to confront your attitude about recovery.

Another technique is to use physical representations of your goals. Some professionals suggest creating an *image book*. Although you can include anything you find meaningful to your goals in an image book, a few ideas include brochures, photos or pictures from magazines, inspiring quotations, and lists of your goals and affirmations.

A woman in my Toastmasters club and her husband plan to own

a motor yacht within the next three years. They want a boat they can live on at least three months of the year. Their extensive image book contains

- yacht brokers and pricing information,
- maps showing locations of marinas and fuel stops,
- a boater's log,
- a free-departure checklist,
- navigation information,
- water safety rules,
- instructions for repairing diesel engines, and
- notes from a U.S. Coast Guard Power Squadron Course.

They've posted pictures of yachts they like all over their house to remind them of their goal. Owning a motor yacht has become a major commitment they're working toward constantly.

If affirmations and visualizations sound a bit like brainwashing, it's because they are. But I see nothing wrong with that, provided *you're* the one washing your brain, *and you're in a stable state.*

I also want to reemphasize that when you have a mood disorder, it takes much more than positive thinking to set realistic goals, create and use affirmations, and visualize positive results. In my own experience, I was unable to accept these techniques in any meaningful way before getting my biochemistry rebalanced.

When in hypomanic states, I've created so many new goals and turned over so many "new leaves" that I could have been entirely "reforested." But, inevitably, I got too wound up and tried to accomplish too much at a time. I'd push myself too hard and fall from my "tightrope" into a depressive pit.

Whether you're depressed, hypomanic, or manic, pattern yourself after the tortoise who won the race by moving slowly forward rather than the hare who sprinted and then, confident that he would win, laid back to rest.

SEVENTEEN

Being All That You Can Be: Creativity and Self-Fulfillment

IF YOU DON'T consider yourself creative or artistic, please don't just dismiss this chapter and move on. Chances are, you're more creative than you think. We're all born with some creativity; as children, we demonstrate it through play all the time. As adults, we're often discouraged from activities most people consider creative. But you may draw more on creativity than you think. Creativity isn't exclusive to "artistic" people. Carpenters, computer programmers, engineers, hairdressers, and teachers all apply creative skills. So do business entrepreneurs, politicians, and religious leaders.

Creativity involves not only the ability to use your imagination, but to be resourceful. If you've ever fashioned a substitute for something you didn't have on hand, you applied creativity.

This chapter discusses both creativity and self-fulfillment, but I don't mean to imply that only artistic types can experience self-fulfillment. Creative endeavors can be highly fulfilling, and it's hard to separate the two. One important aspect of coping with a mood disorder is nurturing your creative side, and creative activities are therapeutic.

Creativity and Madness

Since at least the time of Greek philosopher and scientist Aristotle, societies have associated creative and imaginative individuals with madness. Terms like "divine madness," "creative genius," and "mad genius" have been used to describe artists of all sorts, as well as inventors, philosophers, scientists, and political leaders. Many people, including some artists, consider suffering a necessity for good art. I don't recall thinking that myself, although depression and chaos have accompanied many of my creative efforts. But as many artists do, I sometimes used creativity to pull myself out of despair.

Although I'd heard that most artists were eccentric, drank too much, and sometimes committed suicide, I didn't associate these behaviors with mental illness for many years. To me, creativity just meant "marching to a different drummer," overdrinking meant drowning your sorrows, and having suicidal thoughts was so second nature that I assumed anyone with poor self-esteem had them from time to time.

My introduction to the link between creativity and madness came through a traveling exhibit that the Mental Health Association in Texas brought to Austin. The display contained information both about the historical mistreatment of those with mental illness and about famous artists whose mental illness drove them to suicide.

Touched with Fire

The link between creativity and mood disorders has been widely publicized in recent years, perhaps in part because of the work of Johns Hopkins University School of Medicine psychiatry professor Kay Redfield Jamison. Dr. Jamison made an extensive study of artists and mood disorders, which she reported in her book *Touched with Fire*. This book examines the mood swings, productivity cycles, suicide attempts, and deaths of well-known musicians, painters, poets, and writers from the past. Applying genealogy, Dr. Jamison traces the incidence of mood episodes and suicide in several artists' families. Among the many famous individuals included are

TABLE 11

Some Public Figures with Acknowledged Mood Episodes or Disorders

Hypomania, Mania, or Bipolar Disorder	Depression or Unipolar Disorder
Actors/Entertainers	**Actors/Entertainers**
Robert Downey Jr., Anna Pearce (Patty Duke), Carrie Fisher, Margot Kidder, Ben Stiller, Jean-Claude van Damme	Halle Berry, Marlon Brando, Tony Dow, Sir Anthony Hopkins, Harrison Ford, James Garner, Mariette Hartley, Ashley Judd, Jessica Lange, Joan Rivers, Winona Ryder
Actor/comedian/humorists	**Actor/comedian/humorists**
Shecky Greene, Kevin McDonald, Spike Milligan, Jonathan Winters	Drew Carey, Jim Carrey, John Cleese, Rodney Dangerfield, Ellen DeGeneres, Daman Wayans
Advocates/Politicians	**Advocates/Politicians**
Kitty Dukakis, Thomas Eagleton	Tipper Gore, Barbara Bush, James Farmer
Astronaut	**Athletes (Olympic Medalists)**
"Buzz" Aldrin	Greg Louganis, Oksana Baiul
Media personalities/TV journalists	**Media personalities/TV journalists**
Dick Cavett, Jay Marvin	Dick Clark, Mike Douglas, Deborah Norville, Mike Wallace
Musicians	**Musicians**
Peter Gabriel, Kristin Hersh, Charley Pride	Ray Charles, Eric Clapton, Leonard Cohen
Screenwriters/movie directors	**Physicist/writer**
Tim Burton, Francis Ford Coppola	Stephen Hawking
Poets/Writers	**Poets/Writers**
Patricia Cornwell, Kaye Gibbons, Peter Nolan Lawrence, Kate Millett, Robert Munsch, Frances Sherwood	Art Buchwald, Sandra Cisneros, Michael Crichton, Meri Ana-Ama Danquah, John Kenneth Galbraith, Kurt Vonnegut, Tom Wolfe, Rod McKuen
Singers/songwriters	**Singers/songwriters**
Adam Ant, Connie Francis, Jeannie C. Riley, Axl Rose, Gordon Sumner (Sting), Tom Waits, Brian Wilson	Sheryl Crow, Billy Joel, Elton John, Janet Jackson, Courtney Love, Ozzy Osbourne, Donny Osmond, Marie Osmond, Dolly Parton, Bonnie Raitt, James Taylor

- musicians Irving Berlin and Robert Schumann,
- painters Georgia O'Keeffe and Vincent van Gogh,
- poets Sylvia Plath and Percy Shelley, and
- writers Ernest Hemingway and Virginia Woolf.

Many well-known contemporaries have been "touched with fire" as well. Table 11 lists some public figures who've been open about their struggles with depression or bipolar disorder.

Do All "Creative Types" Suffer from Mood Disorders?

Does this mean that everyone with a mood disorder is artistic or a leader? Certainly not. But even if you don't think you're creative, you may find some comfort in knowing you're in famous company.

From a study of forty-seven award-winning British writers, painters, and sculptors, Dr. Jamison learned that 89 percent had experienced "intensely creative" one- to four-week periods with symptoms that resembled hypomania. Of the writers, more novelists, playwrights, and poets had such episodes than 8 percent of the biographers she studied.

Of Dr. Jamison's subjects, more than 50 percent reported pronounced changes, as summarized below.

SIMPLY CREATIVE OR MENTALLY ILL?

- *Mood changes:* enthusiasm, increased self-confidence, euphoria, emotional intensity, and expansive feelings
- *Physical changes:* increased energy and decreased need for sleep
- *Cognitive changes:* quick mental associations, fluent thoughts, improved concentration, rapid thinking, and expansive ideas
- *Other changes:* increased sense of well-being and enhanced sensory awareness

Because most of these changes parallel symptoms of hypomania, it's hard to tell what's going on. With the exception of concentration, these changes tend to intensify when a person moves from hypomania to mania. Fewer of the painters and sculptors had been treated for mood disorders than had the writers, but the reason wasn't clear. Nearly all of Dr. Jamison's subjects reported that a decreased need for sleep, an urgency to work, and an elevated mood preceded their creative surges. Except when using creative endeavors to work myself out of depressive episodes, this has matched my experience as well.

Many creative people live perfectly normal lives. But artists of all sorts suffer disproportionately from mental illness. Dr. Arnold Ludwig, Emeritus Professor of Psychiatry at the University of Kentucky Medical Center in Lexington, performed a study of creative professionals and other notable professionals, based on their biographies, which spanned thirty years. He found that the creative professionals had experienced mood disorders, psychosis, or substance abuse, or had attempted suicide two to three times more often than the other professionals had.

One controversial question about these links remains to be answered. Could creativity cause mood disorders, or could it be the other way around? No one currently seems to know the answer. But I have some observations of my own.

MEDICATION AND CREATIVITY

One concern this connection raises is the resistance many creative people with mood disorders have to treatment involving psychotropic medication. They often fear that medications will mean they'll lose their creative inspirations. But sustained creative output requires enormous concentration, focus, discipline, and persistence. During mood episodes, these abilities frequently deteriorate. They are accessible to those of us with mood disorders between episodes or during early hypomania, but usually vanish as we near deeper depression or approach mania. Effective medications help many creative individuals use their talents more productively.

Before getting on a mood stabilizer, I'd frequently pop out of bed every hour or two and write frantically until Ralph tracked me down and dragged me back to bed.

I'd spill out increasingly disjointed inspirations similar to this:

JOURNAL ENTRY TWO MONTHS BEFORE A SUICIDE ATTEMPT

> SO MUCH going on, and no way to record thoughts as rapidly as they come. Or perhaps I *mean* I *recall* no way I can do so (No! I *think* I meant *want*) to record them. As fast as I'm *recalling* them. Or *creating* them? Perhaps [*sic*] it's in our childhood—after our reprogramming, or during—I don't know—at some point, we become senile—much more so than in "old age." Perhaps all of life is circular. Yes! Exactly what the circle is made of is a puzzle I don't recall.

When I began taking a mood stabilizer, my artistic inspirations still came, though rarely with the intensity I'd previously experienced. For me, this was a positive change. My creativity became more manageable—something I could harness and work with, and as my moods became more stabilized, my self-esteem improved. And I no longer sabotaged myself during depressive states by rejecting people who were interested in marketing my work.

TAPPING THE FLOW

My experience of creativity, particularly before on effective medication, was comparable to turning on a faucet for a single cup of water and being unable to stop the flow. Inspirations came with such force and speed that their power swept me away. Soon, I'd be treading desperately, trying to keep my head above the surface.

With medication, my ability to "tap the flow" without "drowning" has vastly improved. But in times of extreme stress, creative inspirations can still sweep away my focus, discipline, and productivity.

My Creative Endeavors

Ever since I can remember, people have remarked about my creativity and imagination. When I was little, I found that odd, and in many ways I still do. I don't consider myself any more creative than most people are. My interests, skills, and talents have, however, always involved some sort of creative pursuit.

As a kindergartner, I wanted to learn to play the piano, perhaps because my sister Kay did. I took piano lessons for ten years and got to be a fairly decent player, but I played more for my own and my family's enjoyment than anything else.

In early grade school, I dreamed of being a ballerina, though after two years of ballet, tap, and acrobatics, it became obvious I was too uncoordinated and awkward. (Plus, I couldn't see well enough without my thick glasses to ensure I wouldn't pirouette off the stage.) I took ballet again during graduate school, and although dancing felt wonderful, I was never cut out to be a ballerina.

During junior high and high school, I worked at a day camp, where I learned to play the guitar with the help of fellow counselors and began dabbling in songwriting. In college, I played well enough to sing and play in public a couple of times.

My interest in theater began in eighth grade, when I joined the drama club. My early acting roles included a space-age mother, a hillbilly, a nun, a dwarf, and an elderly arthritic fundamentalist. Despite my concerns about being typecast, I even played a princess "with a face so plain that it stopped clocks"—my only lead in college.

For one community theater musical, I played three roles: a sightseer, a Cuban dancer, and a Salvation Army band member—for which I learned the accordion because the other band members could play only percussion.

My theater experiences went well beyond acting and lasted more than a dozen years. I painted sets, handled props, applied stage makeup, made costumes, ran lights, and wrote a few plays myself. I loved the theater, but I lacked the confidence, self-esteem, and support to use any of these talents professionally.

My family had supported my creative efforts during childhood, but I always had the impression that they thought of them as cute and never took them seriously. My uncle Emery, a college professor who had been published, was the one exception. I'd started writing children's books in third and fourth grade, and during one visit, I grilled him for information about his publisher.

He told me his editor worked for the academic department but that the company also published children's books. Uncle Emery sent my work to his editor, who kindly wrote back. He informed me that although my work showed imagination, most children's books were written by adults who'd been writing for many years. If I wished to get published, he said I must first work very hard on grammar and spelling and show my stories to many people. I concluded I'd have to wait until I was older, but that letter offered a glimmer of hope.

THE "REAL WORLD"

When the time neared for me to start college, my parents became less enthused about my artistic interests. They wanted me to find a major that would provide a secure living "in case something happened to my husband, and I was forced to work outside the home." In those days, it was common to expect young women to finish college, marry, perhaps work a couple of years, and start a family. The question of a real career never came up.

The only major we could agree on was interior design, although I found it unfathomable that people would want or need someone else to decide how their environments should look. In my first semester, I learned that interior design majors had to take math—a subject I found enormously difficult. I got my parents' approval to switch my major to theater only after I convinced them I could teach drama after graduation, though I had little interest in doing so.

I'd been so thoroughly brainwashed about societal expectations of young women that I panicked when I wasn't engaged by my senior year. When a roommate brought home an attractive young soldier that she'd met through her waitressing job, I latched on to him immediately. Although we really had little in common, we married the day after my college graduation.

A month later, he transferred to a base in central Texas. Although we could manage on one income, I wasn't cut out to be a home-maker. I was in no rush to start a family and knew I'd go nuts without a job. But jobs were scarce in the small town of Temple, Texas, and a bachelor's degree in theater didn't get me far. The lack of a second car also limited my options.

I finally got a break when the school year started and a teacher in our apartment complex left her summer job. It was at a clothing store within walking distance. I worked there until we relocated to Austin, where I worked for three years as a receptionist, a secretary, and a waitress before entering graduate school.

I nurtured my artistic side through community theater, but I had to abandon that when I entered graduate school, because many classes met at night.

ARTISTIC "SOUL MURDER"

When I first read psychotherapist Richard Carson's book *Taming Your Gremlin: A Guide to Enjoying Yourself*, many years ago, what struck me most was his chapter "The Pleasant Person Act." Among the standard advice our society doles out—bathe regularly and keep your hair clean; listen to others carefully; make eye contact but don't stare; shake hands but not too firmly—was what I consider one particularly harmful statement: *Don't try to be something special*. Such advice can "murder" one's artist soul.

Carson warns that pleasant behaviors should come from *you* rather than from your "gremlin" and that buying in to what your "gremlin" wants can create a sense of emptiness.

Although many types of people are advised to ignore their own specialness, I believe that artists—particularly in the United States—hear this advice much more often than people with other talents and interests. A few of the messages our society regularly feeds artists are:

- There are no new ideas, and even if there were, you can't generate enough to make a living.
- There's too much competition for you to break in. Your work is good—but not good enough.

- You're too sensitive to be an artist. You'd have to be much tougher to survive such a cutthroat business.
- You have to know some big-name person or you'll never get a break.
- You have to sell your soul to make it big.

In my view, accepting such messages is what sells your soul. And I think the fact that I bought in to these messages significantly worsened my illness. I believe a good portion of my recovery has come from reclaiming my creative spirit and following the path I set on but circled away from many times because of others' comments or because of my own fears.

Many people mock artists who are trying to develop their talents and have trouble seeing the potential in their early work. A local science fiction/fantasy/horror writing critique group sponsored by the Writers' League of Texas calls this belittling practice "squashing a fairy." Wendy Wheeler, longtime leader of the group, suggests critiquing the work of novices with extra sensitivity and care.

My stepdaughter, Joy, caught the acting bug at the age of eleven during a summer visit with her California cousins. Both boys had acted in commercials, in TV shows, and films, thanks partially to their stage mom. When Joy returned to Texas with stars in her eyes and a suitcase full of headshots from Hollywood actors she met, I was a bit concerned. I feared that she'd confront the same type of discouragement I had.

But neither Ralph nor I discouraged her from pursuing her dreams. Performing was clearly in her blood. Joy became a stand-up comic during college, then headed to Los Angeles to pursue a career in comedy, acting, writing, and film production. She's getting excellent reviews, and we're proud of her determination to follow her own vision and realize her dreams.

REGAINING MY ARTISTIC SOUL

Every passion I've ever had related to the arts and self-expression. Perhaps part of this passion came from repressing childhood feelings and needing to make up for it. Although I sampled many kinds of creativity over the years, my true love has always been writing. I've begun writing, abandoned it, and returned to it repeatedly.

Other than standard English comp and the playwriting classes I took in college, I had no formal training to be a writer. I'd been excluded from high school journalism because I was home sick on the official sign-up day.

I did, however, apply writing skills in a variety of jobs with other primary focuses and talked my way into communications positions from which I learned a lot but for which I wasn't well prepared.

Shortly after my worst depression and suicide attempt, I began to learn everything I could on writing and publishing without another return to school. I joined the local writers' league and volunteered at conferences and workshops, so I could attend at a reduced rate. I joined multiple writing critique groups to hone my craft.

I believe that giving myself permission to pursue my creative visions helped enormously on my road to recovery. Perhaps creative people who don't have such outlets have a higher risk of developing or worsening a mental illness.

Creative or Expressive Therapies

One reason psychiatric treatment programs sometimes offer expressive therapies is that they help you access buried emotions and express them safely. Creative therapies work when they're noncompetitive and participants' creations aren't judged as good or bad. Usually, therapists certified in art, dance, drama, music, or writing therapy run such therapy programs.

Art Therapy

Releasing buried or disturbing feelings through art helps many individuals work through inner conflicts and enhance their self-esteem. Art therapy has proven particularly effective in the treatment of those diagnosed with depression or schizophrenia, or those who have experienced abuse or trauma.

Author Tracy Thompson hadn't felt the need to draw since childhood. Then one day, she bought some soft lead pencils and a sketch-book and began to draw each morning before work. Numbness and a lack of feeling had marked her depression, but drawing helped Tracy access her emotions and significantly aided her recovery.

Dance or Movement Therapy

Dance or movement therapy provides another useful mode of self-expression and releasing repressed feelings. Natural dancers often experience improved mood when they let their feet fly. Exercise and movement have powerful healing effects.

If you lack confidence about your dancing skills, other options are available. Some people prefer slow-moving Eastern martial arts such as aikido or tai chi. These techniques have proven especially helpful for developing a better sense of control and ease about the body, particularly in people who have suffered emotional, physical, or sexual abuse.

Even aquatics classes have helped me feel more at home in my body.

Drama Therapy

Drama therapy uses the processes and products of drama and theater to help express emotions appropriately, relieve symptoms, and promote personal growth. This active, experiential approach helps you tell your story, access inner feelings, solve problems, improve relationships, and carry out life roles more flexibly.

Such therapy may involve techniques such as pantomime, puppetry, improvisation, role-playing, and theatrical production.

Music Therapy

Music, which has been used as a therapeutic tool for centuries, appears to release naturally occurring chemicals, such as endorphins and opiates. These soothe the troubled brain. Although in therapeutic settings music therapy is currently more often used outside the United States, it has proven helpful for treating depression, grief, stress, schizophrenia, and even childhood autism.

While growing up, I released unexpressed and unacceptable emotions by playing the piano. This was therapeutic, and usually acceptable, except for the time my angry playing sent a vase atop the family piano traveling all the way across and onto the floor.

Journaling, Poetry, and Writing Therapy

Many people find writing to be a powerful way to access feelings, let go of painful experiences, and gain new insights. Journaling, poetry therapy, and writing therapy are a few therapeutic approaches. You may participate in these therapies in a therapeutic setting, a nonpsychiatric setting, or completely on your own.

Even if you don't consider yourself a writer or have no inclination to write, you can benefit from writing about your emotions. In 1992, Martha Francis and James Pennebaker of Southern Methodist University introduced therapeutic writing. They found that it can help reduce all sorts of health problems. Such a session involves

- **Preparing to Write**
  1. Set aside about 20 to 30 minutes during which you won't be disturbed.
  2. Gather paper and a pen or whatever instrument you prefer.
  3. Find a secluded, comfortable location.
  4. Before beginning, take a little time to get relaxed.
- **Writing About Your Emotions**
  1. Begin writing about whatever's on your mind *without worrying about grammar or spelling.*
  2. Aim to express your deepest emotions.
     —If depressed, you may want to explore your difficult or painful emotions regardless of when the events or comments that hurt you took place.
     —If hypomanic or manic, you may want to capture inspirations or goals or release angry or disturbing feelings.
  3. Write for 20 to 30 minutes, then set your work aside.

4. You need not share your writing with anyone unless you want to.
5. Have a writing session every day for at least five consecutive days.

WHAT IF I GET WRITER'S BLOCK?

If you can think and communicate in most any manner, you can write. Just write about whatever you're thinking. I know, you may be thinking, that's easy for a writer to say, but I'm not a writer!

If you feel stuck, which I sometimes do myself, a few warm-up exercises may be helpful. But remember, these are just unblocking exercises. Therapeutic exercises help you access emotions.

- Write about a *memory*—no matter how distant or recent.
- Write about a *belief*—whether your own or someone else's.
- Write about *something you sense*: what your surroundings look like, what the surface you're writing on feels like, what you hear or smell, what your mouth tastes like.

After a few minutes of writing, explore the feelings these topics bring up. Then move on to deeper emotions.

WHAT CAN I DO ABOUT PERSISTENT WRITER'S BLOCK?

- Remember, therapeutic writing is merely a tool to help you express your feelings. It's not about writing itself.
- Forget about grammar and spelling.
- Don't worry about someone reading your work.
- No one need grade or judge what you're writing. You can even destroy your work when you're done.
- If you *still* feel stuck, write about not knowing what to write or how difficult you find the writing process. Explain how you *feel* about writing, and explore the reasons why.

I used to worry that I wouldn't have enough ideas to write about. One thing that helped me immensely was meeting with a writing group for two hours on Saturday mornings. We met at a local restaurant, and having breakfast was a great motivator. We based our sessions on the work of Natalie Goldberg, author of *Writing Down the Bones*. Goldberg's approach is much like Pennebaker's process.

Our group would pick a topic more or less at random—sometimes a single word or phrase, sometimes a response to another piece of writing, a snapshot, or a photo from a magazine. Then everyone would write until they'd written what they wanted to say—or until it became clear that they wanted to spend much more time writing on that topic later.

For most topics, we'd write from fifteen to thirty minutes. Then we'd go around the circle and read our work aloud. If someone didn't want to share what he or she had written, we'd just move on to the next person. After finishing one topic, we'd go to another. It was fascinating to hear what different thoughts and feelings the same topic brought up.

Sometimes people suggested topics about which I felt certain I had nothing to say. Two examples were "bottles" and "garden party." Initially, nothing came to mind for either subject, but after complaining about the topics a while on paper, I produced some of my best work. For the bottles topic, I wrote a short story about a homeless woman who discovered a bottled message that brightened her day. For the garden party topic, I wrote a story about some thirsty vegetables that sang and danced to make it rain so they could get a drink.

Creative therapies may be part of a treatment program either in or out of a psychiatric hospital, or may be offered by a private therapist. To locate an art, dance, drama, music, or writing therapist, ask your therapist for a referral, check with community mental health facilities, or look under Creative Therapies in the Resources section.

Nonpsychiatric Options

If you prefer a public group not specifically designed for those with mental illness, you may benefit from

- taking an art class at a local art school or museum,
- taking a dance class or joining a dancing club,
- performing or assisting with a community theater group,
- playing in a band or orchestra, or
- participating in a writing group.

You can also pursue creative or expressive activities entirely on your own. Many people who'd never consider doing so in public benefit from using personal sketchbooks, doing needlework, dancing in their bedrooms or living rooms, becoming different characters in front of their mirrors, playing an instrument for their own pleasure, or keeping a diary or journal.

Is Everyone Who Has a Mood Disorder an Artist or a Genius?

Bipolar disorder has been called the "genius disease." Does the artist/genius link apply to everyone with a mood disorder? Certainly not. Mood disorders coexist with mental retardation as well as genius.

And if you consider yourself neither creative nor a leader, you may be wondering, what about the rest of us? Can we ever experience happiness or self-fulfillment? The short answer is yes.

Self-Fulfillment

Self-fulfillment or *self-actualization*—near the top of Maslow's Hierarchy—involves achieving your potential.

Some people see self-fulfillment as selfish; however, Maslow, who studied "self-actualizers" extensively, disagreed. He found them

- autonomous, independent, individualized, and democratic;
- accepting of both themselves and others;
- comfortable both with solitude and with social situations;
- able to sustain intimate relationships with a few individuals rather than superficial ones with many;
- ethical, moral, and value-driven;

- humble, respectful, and sympathetic;
- grounded in reality and not thinking in dichotomies;
- creative, spontaneous, appreciative of nondemeaning humor; and
- concerned more with outside problems or with their missions rather than with themselves.

To reach self-actualization or self-fulfillment can require a lifetime. Often, it entails involvement with massive social needs. But what different people find fulfilling depends on a variety of factors, including temperament, personality, interests, lifestyle, and values.

Some ways people achieve self-fulfillment include

- in their roles as loving parents,
- by gardening or preserving nature,
- in cooking unusual dishes,
- through athletic achievements,
- in their religious beliefs and practices, or
- by serving others.

Dr. Maslow said that even if all your other needs get satisfied, you may still be discontented and restless if you're not doing what you're fitted for. To be at peace with yourself, you must be what you *can* be. True self-fulfillment comes only by achieving your potential.

Achieving Your Potential

After diet and exercise, one of the best things you can do to improve brain function is to find your mission in life. Almost any activity will relieve the rumination of depression or the "brain spin" of hypomania, including work you don't especially enjoy. However, doing what truly interests you and what you have a passion for helps even more.

Our bodies function best when we pursue activities that fit us, whether or not they produce tangible rewards. Our society tends to judge the value of activities solely on the money associated with them, which Dr. Christiane Northrup says leads many of us to work for "a dying" rather than "a living." Many of us put up with lousy work environments for "benefits" while sacrificing happiness and health.

Granted, you can't ignore the cost of living, particularly when in psychiatric treatment. But if you ignore your interests and talents, you may give up all hope of happiness and healing.

Discovering Your Potential

Richard Bolles, author of the best-selling book *What Color Is Your Parachute?,* is the job-hunting guru of all time. His advice applies not only to finding employment, but also to learning more about

- your dreams,
- your passions,
- where you want to live,
- how you want to spend your time, and
- your purpose or mission in life.

Ralph and I have used Bolles's book many times for job hunting and recommend it to job seekers regularly. Ralph follows Bolles's advice systematically, but I tend to jump from one section to another.

Many communities offer workshops based on Bolles's approach. If you're uncertain about what you want to do, I encourage you to attend one or to use the book on your own. Don't just thumb through it; at least complete some of its exercises. If possible, read it cover to cover, and then use Bolles's process to improve your life. And don't let society's negative messages get in your way. Bolles also maintains an informative Web site: *www.JobHuntersBible.com.*

When I first described my plans for this book and my mission to my former psychiatrist, he concluded I must be having grandiose illusions of the literary kind and bumped my diagnosis up to bipolar I. Admittedly, I was hypomanic when we discussed it. Plus, I'd envisioned a treatment center in a natural setting where artists of all kinds who also had a mental illness could get not only psychiatric help but guidance and support for marketing their work successfully.

I think my doctor thought I planned to make this happen entirely on my own. I do tend to take too much on myself and not delegate or rely on others. And although I'd worked as a technical writer and an editor in previous jobs, I'd never written and published a book of my own at that point. To my doctor, my capabilities were totally unproven. I hope to prove him wrong.

EIGHTEEN

Taking Leaps of Faith: Spirituality and Transcendence

THE STRONG FEELINGS and opinions people often have about spirituality make it a tough topic to address. Many people equate spirituality only with religion, and many people hold firm to their own religious beliefs. Other people have turned away from organized religions because they could not relate to images of a punishing God or got turned off by male domination in places of worship.

Not all people can relate to the terms God, higher power, or supreme being. If that's true for you, substitute whatever word you wish—or ignore religious expressions of spirituality. Religious preferences vary widely, and you have the right to believe—or not believe—in whoever or whatever you wish. You can be a spiritual person without associating with any sort of religious community.

Personally, I equate spirituality with connectedness to the spiritual side of every individual, as well as to creation itself. My view includes whoever or whatever formed the universe and whatever lies beyond it.

This chapter explores some thoughts about religion, spirituality, and transcendence as they relate to mood disorders.

Over the centuries, people have associated mental illness with demon possession, evil spirits, and immorality. During or after depressive or manic episodes, many of us with mood disorders make those same associations ourselves. I don't believe that we're possessed by demons or evil spirits when our illness overtakes our thoughts and behaviors, though sometimes it *feels* as if we are. And I won't argue that we don't perform immoral actions, because we sometimes do when our symptoms become too intense to control. Whether you agree or not, I don't think this makes us immoral *people*. Quite a few friends and relatives who suffer from mental illness are some of the most moral people I know.

I'm humiliated about my history of hypersexuality and the continuing sexual obsessions that overtake my mind on those now rare occasions when I become hypomanic. My psychiatrist and psychotherapist can attest to the extent that this distresses me. However, I have managed—often with the help of increased medication—to be faithful during both of my marriages. The first marriage, in my early twenties, lasted about three years; my current marriage is in its eighteenth year and still going strong. I *do* value monogamy.

Ostracizing those with mental illness—even one's own fellow worshippers—because of religious beliefs often prevents those who desperately need help from seeking treatment.

Organized Religion

Some people say that people with mental illness need only put their faith in God and prayers and they'll be cured. Some claim we wouldn't need treatment if only we'd turn our lives over to religion. My sister Barbara strongly believed in God and prayer, but they weren't enough to save her. You need more than religion to cope with a serious brain disorder.

There's also a religious stigma against suicide. Churches have often excluded from sacred burial grounds the bodies of those who took their own lives. However, just as God doesn't judge those who die from cancer or other illnesses as sinners, says the deeply religious Dr. Elisabeth Kübler-Ross, he doesn't judge those who die from suicide as sinners.

Faith and Hope

Many people with a mental illness find great comfort in religion and prayer. Some say they could never live with their illness without a strong belief in God.

Religion offers many benefits, two of which are faith and hope. *Faith* relates to trust in the future—to the belief that life will improve at some point. To the feeling that a "safety net" lies beneath the "tightrope" upon which you walk. *Hope* relates to positive expectations. A deep sense of hopelessness is one of the highest indicators for potential suicide.

A place of worship can provide a supportive social network and increase your sense of belonging—provided it makes you feel accepted and comfortable rather than shunned. Researchers have found the faithful to be physically healthier and more optimistic overall.

Religious Beliefs and Mood Disorders

Religious beliefs sometimes present special challenges during mood episodes.

Faith and Hope During Depression

Faith and hope are often difficult to maintain during depressive episodes, or following hypomanic or manic ones. You may conclude that you're worthless and unworthy, and that God is punishing you or has abandoned you. Even fully healthy people sometimes feel this way when in crisis or under great duress. Mark (15:34) wrote that even Jesus felt deserted during his crucifixion and cried out: "My God, my God, why hast thou forsaken me?"

Faith and Hope During Mania

Some manic episodes bring confusing and terrifying hallucinations of the devil or of a vengeful God. Others bring delusions of grandeur that center on religious themes. Those who experience such grandiosity may become driven to share some religious message, believe that they're deities or prophets, or think that God has granted them the power to heal others.

Religious Approaches to Peer Support Groups

Many people with religious inclinations find 12-Step groups helpful both for treating addictions and for managing mood disorders.

"12-Step" Programs

The support groups offered through 12-Step programs focus on God, a higher power, or a supreme being to live free of addictions, disorders, and other problems.

AA (ALCOHOLICS ANONYMOUS)

One of the best-known 12-Step programs, Alcoholics Anonymous focuses on recovery from alcoholism. Its spiritual orientation emphasizes members' powerlessness over alcohol and the need to rely on a higher power to restore sanity and maintain sobriety.

AL-ANON/ALATEEN

The 12-Step groups sponsored by Al-Anon and Alateen provide support for family members and friends of those who have alcoholism.

DRUG-SPECIFIC SUPPORT GROUPS

Twelve-Step programs similar to AA but focusing on drug addictions include *CA (Cocaine Anonymous)*, *MA (Marijuana Anonymous)*, and *NA (Narcotics Anonymous)*. These groups are not necessarily limited to just one type of drug.

DUAL RECOVERY ANONYMOUS (DRA)

The groups sponsored by DRA are meant for those who have a **dual diagnosis**—a chemical dependency as well as an emotional or mental illness.

EA (EMOTIONS ANONYMOUS)

These groups focus on recovering from emotional problems and building and maintaining emotional wellness. Their members meet to support each other's recovery from a wide variety of emotional problems.

MANIC DEPRESSIVES ANONYMOUS (MDA)

The groups sponsored by MDA are similar fellowships in which members share experience, strengths, and hopes as well as insights into living. Their members address common problems and encourage others toward recovery.

The Resources section contains contact information for all of these organizations.

The Twelve Steps

With a small amount of editing to account for the variety of 12-Step programs I've listed, the twelve steps involve participants

1. Admitting their powerlessness over an addiction, disorder, or problem;
2. Believing that God can help resolve their addiction, disorder, or problem;
3. Deciding to turn their will and life over to that higher power;
4. Taking a fearless moral inventory of themselves;
5. Admitting to God, to themselves, and to another person the nature of their wrongs;
6. Being ready to have God remove their character defects;
7. Asking God to remove their shortcomings;
8. Listing all the people they have harmed and being willing to make amends to every one;
9. Making direct amends to those they've listed, except when doing so would injure those individuals or others;
10. Continuing their personal inventory and promptly admitting when they're wrong;

11. Using prayer and meditation to better connect with God, and requesting only the knowledge of what they're meant to do with their life and asking for the power to do so; and

12. Carrying the message of their spiritual awakening, achieved by following these steps and practicing 12-Step principles in all they do.

CAUTION

> PARTIALLY BECAUSE many 12-Step members struggle with alcohol and illicit-drug addictions, their support groups often disdain *any* form of medication. Remember, *illicit drugs and psychotropic medications aren't the same.*
>
> If you get involved with a 12-Step group, *don't stop taking your prescribed medications.*

You need not participate in 12-Step programs nor believe in God or a higher power to tap the wisdom of these steps. Many steps relate to seeing yourself and others realistically, telling the truth, making amends, calming the mind, and reconnecting with your soul.

Prayer

Whether ill or healthy, many people find great comfort in prayer. The widely known "Serenity Prayer," most often attributed to Reinhold Niebuhr, is the official prayer in many 12-Step groups and offers much to those of us with mood disorders as well.

Serenity Prayer

God grant me the Serenity
to accept the things I cannot change,
Courage to change the things I can,
and the Wisdom to know the difference.

Living one day at a time,
Enjoying one moment at a time;

Accepting hardships as the pathway to peace. Taking, as He did,
   this sinful world
as it is, not as I would have it.

Trusting that He will make all things right
if I surrender to His Will;
That I may be reasonably happy in this life,
and supremely happy with Him forever in the next.
Amen.

Regardless of your beliefs, this prayer provides good advice to help you better cope with the challenges of life and living with a mood or substance abuse disorder.

My Religious Upbringing

I grew up in a religious family, though we were neither fundamentalists nor fanatical about our beliefs. My mother, having grown up in a Methodist family full of ministers, Sunday school teachers, choir directors, and even the church organist, had strong ties to Christianity. Her mother even boycotted the grocery store closest to her home because it was open on Sunday afternoons.

Quite early on, I developed some resistance to religion. The people in the church I grew up attending seemed more concerned about looking good than about loving and serving others. The congregation seemed to be going through the motions, verbalizing the responses printed in the program without absorbing their messages. I'm sure there must have been true believers and generous people among them, but in our church's atmosphere, I felt excluded rather than embraced and loved.

One experience in particular reinforced those feelings. My father's mother lived about an hour from my parents' house, and once a month or so, we'd drive down to spend Sundays with her. The Sunday after one of these visits, the church's children's choir was scheduled to perform, and I was looking forward to singing in it. I dressed as instructed for the event, but when we got to church that day, the

choir director said only children who had been present for the previous week's rehearsal would be allowed to sing. I was heartbroken.
It seemed an unjust punishment for something I couldn't control.

For many years, all it took to bring up these old feelings of exclu-
sion was hearing Bill Staines's 1979 song "A Place in the Choir" on
the radio.

> *All God's critters got a place in the choir*
> *Some sing low, some sing higher,*
> *Some sing out loud on the telephone wires,*
> *And some just clap their hands, or paws, or anything they got now.*

My Evolving Religious Views

Dr. Abraham Maslow expressed his concern that when conventional
churches become too dogmatic and convinced that *their* beliefs are
the only *true* beliefs, they actually destroy the religious experience.
Congregants may limit their spiritual experiences to a single day of
a week; religious holidays; a single building; and sacred rites, music,
and foods. Blind faith, unquestioning obedience, and unwavering
loyalty to one religion can cause major problems. Intolerance of others' religious and spiritual beliefs has been—and continues to be—a
major cause of war.

In early grade school, I attended vacation Bible school for several
summers. I don't remember a great deal about sessions at our church
other than singing "Jesus Loves Me," reciting "The Lord's Prayer," listening to sermons I couldn't comprehend, doing craftwork, and
drinking Kool-Aid. However, because our church was across town,
I attended Bible school at a friend's church in our neighborhood at
least one summer. My strongest memory of that experience was the
cutthroat enthusiasm with which the children sang "Onward Christian Soldiers." I couldn't—and still can't—sort out the dichotomy
between religious messages of war versus love.

• • •

One summer as a counselor at Camp Ko-Ha-Me, a coworker introduced me to the Quaker faith. Now more frequently called the Religious Society of Friends, Quakers believe that part of God resides within every individual. That fit better with my beliefs than those of any other religion to which I'd been exposed. I also identified with the Quaker commitments to pacifism and social service.

After divorcing my first husband in my mid twenties, I began attending Friends' meetings in Austin. I felt at home among the Friends' community. Our meetings were "silent meetings," in which we sat in quiet contemplation and connected with our spiritual side. There was no preacher, no recitation, no choir. However, when moved by the spirit, people would sometimes rise and punctuate the silence with a brief observation, poem, or song. I felt embraced by this community of informal, loving, thoughtful people.

However, I stopped attending Friends' meetings when one man from the group began pursuing me relentlessly, wanting to marry. From my perspective, he was just a friend with a mutual interest in photography. I didn't want to get involved.

After living a secular life for more than two decades, I've only recently begun to reconnect with a religious group.

Connecting with Your Spiritual Side

There are many other ways of quieting the mind and reconnecting with the soul than participating in organized religion. Setting aside time to do whatever makes you feel most grounded, at peace, and connected with the world can help you reduce stress and better manage your life.

This section suggests some techniques you may find useful, regardless of your beliefs.

Communing with Nature

Although Daddy believed in God, Jesus, and the teachings of the Bible, he felt most spiritual when communing with nature. That was one of the few things we had in common. Daddy found his greatest peace when on a lake in his fishing boat. It didn't matter whether he caught a thing; just being out in nature soothed him.

While growing up, I found my greatest peace at Camp Ko-Ha-Me, where I went as a camper for seven summers and worked as a counselor-in-training and then a counselor for four more. In addition to being out in nature, many camp activities helped us slow down and appreciate our surroundings. As an adult, I've tapped that same sense when camping, hiking, or merely driving down old country roads.

The old saying "Take time to smell the roses" holds a lot of wisdom. Nature offers many healing powers. Tap as many of your senses as you can to appreciate its wonders:

- Eat something new and different, savoring its flavor on your tongue. Taste the sweat that pours from your face after an aerobic workout. Slowly sip a healthy drink, such as a fruit juice or decaffeinated tea.
- Feel the wind blow through your hair, a captured snowflake melting on your tongue, your hands in the warm soil of the earth, the strength of your muscles.
- Inhale the essence of fragrant flowers, herbs and oils, pot-pourri, incense, or scented candles.
- Listen to the wind rustling in the trees, to a bird's call, to a babbling brook, or to rain pouring on a roof.
- Watch the sunrise or sunset, or clouds rolling across the sky. Follow the changing patterns of the moon and stars. Take a stroll or drive that's off your beaten path.

Allow yourself to reconnect with nature's wonders.

Quiet Time

You can sometimes calm the racing thoughts of hypomanic or manic states, or ease the pain and anxiety of depression, by building regular quiet time into your schedule. Listen to soothing music, pour your feelings into the pages of a journal, stroke the soft coat of a pet, take a quiet stroll, go to a park, or simply sit outside for a while.

Gratitude Journals

Particularly when you're depressed, a "gratitude journal" can be a useful tool. As often as possible, record the best thing about your day: some discovery you made, a task you completed, a new insight, or anything else you're thankful for. Your entries need not be earth-shattering. They can be simple things: getting a call from a loved one, finding a bargain on some necessity, gaining an insight from therapy or a support group, learning a bad storm left you unharmed.

For a structured approach to such a journal, I recommend Caroll McKanna Shreeve's book *Life Is Good: A Guided Gratitude Journal*.

Tranquillity Corners

A friend who's a retired psychologist suggests making a "tranquillity corner," a place where you can go to calm your mind. We keep a tropical aquarium in one corner of the living room with a comfy swivel rocker nearby. Sitting there, rocking, and watching the fish for even five minutes helps me quiet my mind and get into better focus.

Others find comfort when surrounded by plants, artwork, or lit candles.

Relaxation and Meditation

In 1975, Dr. Herbert Benson, then an associate professor at Harvard Medical School and Director of the Hypertension Section of Boston's Beth Israel Hospital, described the affects of stress on the body and the benefits of stress-reduction techniques in *The Relaxation Response*. A variety of such techniques exist, but most have a common purpose: silencing the chatter of our conscious minds and freeing our awareness from our egos. Most techniques fall into one of two general categories:

1. **ACTIVE APPROACHES**—Those in which the intent is to bring the mind into sharper focus, often by focusing on an

affirmation or repeated word or sound, a contemplative thought or a favorite prayer, an object, or a symbol.

2. **PASSIVE APPROACHES**—Those in which the intent is to clear your mind of clutter and make way for new possibilities.

BASIC RELAXATION AND MEDITATION TECHNIQUES

Many forms of meditation begin with a relaxation exercise. For example:

1. Isolate yourself in a quiet, softly lit room and close the door.
2. Assume a comfortable position. Sit either in a chair with your feet flat on the floor or cross-legged on a cushion. If you prefer, lie on your back on the floor instead.
3. Breathe deeply from your diaphragm, allowing the stomach to rise and the air to reach the bottom of your lungs.
4. *For active approaches,* concentrate on:
    —an affirmation or a repeated word or sound, such as peace, relax, or om;
    —a contemplative thought, such as "Let there be peace" or a favorite prayer;
    —an object, such as a lit candle, a crystal, or a flower; or
    —a symbol, such as a cross or a totem.
5. *For passive approaches,* let all emotions, thoughts, and perceptions leave your mind. When thoughts come up, gently let them go and do your best to clear your mind.

Because of excess chatter in my brain, I've found active approaches easier to use than passive approaches. I've had the best luck with *progressive relaxation* (tensing and releasing various muscle groups), sometimes followed by *visualization* exercises. I sometimes find relaxation tapes *or* tapes of sounds in nature helpful—when I'm able to still my mind enough to concentrate on them.

MEDITATION IN MOTION

Tai chi—The ancient Chinese practice of *tai chi* strengthens the body and its immune system through a series of slow yoga- and karate-like movements, accompanied by deep breathing and positive thoughts. Tai chi is a moving form of meditation, a form of exercise, and a tool for self-healing.

By developing an understanding of *chi*—the vital life force that energizes our bodies—tai chi practitioners reconnect with nature, the universe, and other human beings. The Chinese claim that we obtain chi from the air we breathe, the food we eat, and the environment in which we live.

Tai chi's gentle exercises can

- revitalize muscles, tissues, organs, and bones;
- relieve pain; and
- reduce stress.

When you perform its movements rapidly, tai chi also becomes an effective martial art for self-protection.

Yoga—The ancient Indian practice of *yoga* employs deep breathing, careful positioning, and stretches to balance energy. Addressing the body as a unified whole, yoga helps improve physical, emotional, and mental health, and can supplement other treatments.

The Limits of Our Knowledge

The information in this book reflects only current thoughts in psychiatry and neurology, and my own experiences. Some new discovery could change our present "reality" at any time.

I don't believe that human beings can explain *anything* with full truth and confidence, and certainly not matters of spirituality. As I see it, we can only *theorize* about reality and what happens to us when we die. Regardless of what we learn or "prove," we must rely on current beliefs, "facts," and "knowledge" that may very well be proven wrong. History has shown repeatedly how much we don't know.

One interesting theory from the late 1970s significantly impacted both science and spirituality. *Chaos theory* reversed scientists' emphasis on analyzing individual parts of systems to analyzing systems as a whole. Scientists learned that they could model phenomena previously thought totally unpredictable and chaotic with geometrical equations. Some examples of such systems include weather patterns and the flow of waterfalls.

At the 1979 annual meeting of the American Association for the Advancement of Science, meteorologist Edward Lorenz delivered a paper entitled "Predictability: Does the Flap of a Butterfly's Wings in Brazil Set Off a Tornado in Texas?" Although these thoughts may sound ludicrous and were initially received as a joke, it seems Lorenz was on to the interconnectedness of everything.

Chaos theory brought scientists and religious thinkers closer together. The realization that even "chaos" and "randomness" have order supports the existence of a higher intelligence—a higher power. The "butterfly effect" became a powerful symbol for chaos theorists.

Mysteries and Miracles

When Barbara died many years ago, I felt a need to honor her spirit in the only way I knew how: communicating about the need to address mental illness openly, to seek and stick with treatment, and to take suicidal thoughts seriously. This notion gave more purpose to my life than anything I've done. Although it's taken a long time to prepare for and begin that mission, I believe it's why I'm still here.

Several times in this book, I've mentioned the work of Dr. Elisabeth Kübler-Ross. I found her book *The Tunnel and the Light* quite spiritually enlightening. It touched me much in the way that I hope this book will touch others. The ending, in which she compares our earthly bodies to cocoons from which our butterfly spirits fly when we die, struck me especially because I had imagined Barbara's spirit empowering butterflies. Only in the midst of writing this book did I notice that the publisher for *The Tunnel and the Light* is also the publisher for this book. The coincidence was one of the many I've experienced since starting my mission.

Life is full of mysteries and miracles.

Transcendence

The highest growth need in Maslow's Hierarchy of Needs is transcendence—making a contribution beyond ourselves, a goal, mission, or vision beyond our own personal interests.

Although the term is sometimes used in relation to mystical experiences, in this book I'll limit my discussion to reaching out to others.

Despite the fact that transcendence appears at the top of Maslow's Hierarchy, you need not fulfill every need that comes before it to transcend your circumstances and help others. As Maslow says, these needs don't always appear in a precise order. Sometimes they overlap or skip around.

Even those of us with serious mood disorders can experience transcendence in many ways:

- Attending a group meeting to support others
- Buying a meal for someone who's unemployed
- Calling a friend in need of help
- Giving a ride to someone who otherwise would have none
- Helping someone locate appropriate treatment
- Sharing what you've learned about your illness
- Volunteering your time
- Advocating for improved mental health services or changes in related laws

Not only will such experiences help others; they'll help you as well.

NINETEEN

Helping Others: When Someone You Know Has a Mood Disorder

WHEN SOMEONE'S IN the midst of a mood episode, it's usually challenging for everyone around. You may be confused, frustrated, angry, or frightened by the person's behavioral changes. In the attempt to straighten things out, your first urge may be to minimize or negate the person's feelings. But when a mood disorder takes the brain hostage, it's frequently impossible to change intense feelings and distorted thoughts.

Until you've observed several episodes, it's difficult to recognize early warning symptoms and know when it's time to intervene. If you notice uncharacteristic behavior early on, sometimes it helps to show your concern and to allow the person to express repressed feelings. If your relationship is too strained to do this, which is often the case when you live together, someone else may be better able to fill this role. A person affected may be more receptive to a close, trusted friend or relative.

You or another may be able to gently steer the person toward more healthful routines, such as sleeping regular hours, regularly eating healthful meals, and exercising. Suggesting that the person attend a support group meeting where he or she can talk with others who've experienced similar symptoms may help as well. Sometimes simply involving the person in pleasurable or relaxing activities can help.

Showing Concern and Support

Remember that the person's symptoms relate an *illness,* and that illness does not define the person as a whole. Helping a person through an episode takes genuine compassion, patience, and sensitivity.

Give the person your full attention. Maintain eye contact and avoid fidgeting or restraining the person, provided the person isn't being destructive. Listen without interrupting or trying to control the conversation. As you listen, summarize the person's comments when appropriate to verify that you've heard them correctly. Resist the urge to make comments merely to fill silences. Just sitting in the same room can show your support, whether the person feels like talking or not.

- Hold a hand or gently touch an arm if the person is open to physical contact.
- Offer a shoulder to cry on (and have plenty of tissues on hand).
- Offer to hug or hold the person if your relationship permits physical contact.

When you do speak, do so calmly, even if you're frustrated or angry. You need not agree with what was said, and if you don't, you need not express your disagreement. Never say that you know how the person feels. You may identify with the person's feelings or situation, but you have no way of knowing precisely how *anybody* feels. Focus on the person's moods and behaviors, not the person as a whole.

Words That Help

- I'm concerned because you haven't been yourself lately.
- Is something troubling you?

- I'm here to listen if you want to talk.
- This must be very hard for you.
- I'm sorry that you're hurting.
- Please don't give up. You mean so much to me.
- What would help you most right now?
- We can work through this together.
- You're not alone in this.
- This will pass, and we can ride it out together.
- I love you, and I'm not going to leave you (if you truly mean it).
- We're here on earth to see each other through.

Words That Hurt

- You think *you've* got problems!
- Who said life was fair?
- Quit whining and feeling sorry for yourself.
- You have no reason to be depressed. You should be glad you don't have a *real* problem.
- It's time you change your attitude.
- You're lazy and irresponsible. It's time you grew up.
- What wrong with you? You *know* better than this.
- You never think about others. You're embarrassing everyone.
- Are you on drugs or drunk?
- Control yourself, you maniac!

How to Tell When It's Time to Seek Help

Until an episode becomes extreme, you may barely notice symptoms unless you know a person really well. The following warning signs focus on behaviors you might observe in someone you interact with regularly. You may observe changes in the person like the following:

- SLEEP—sleeping longer than usual, less than usual, or not sleeping well. Individual needs vary widely, but sleeping two hours more or less than usual may indicate an oncoming episode.

- **APPETITE**—eating significantly more or less than usual or having no interest in eating. Radical changes in food choices can also signal trouble. For instance, if someone who's usually conscientious about nutrition starts bingeing on junk food, that person may be entering an episode.
- **MOOD**—becoming more depressed and negative or more elated and optimistic than usual. The person may display a marked lack of self-esteem, or believe that he or she can accomplish the impossible.
- **BEHAVIOR**—withdrawing from others or becoming argumentative, irritable, and obtrusive. The person may drop out from his or her regular routine, or begin making elaborate plans and piling on new activities.

If these symptoms persist for four or more days (without the obvious need for hospitalization), they may indicate an oncoming hypomanic or manic episode. If they persist for two weeks or more, they may indicate an oncoming depressive episode.

Helping Someone Get Treatment

Talking someone into getting treatment for a mental illness is one of the toughest tasks you can undertake. To benefit from and stick with treatment, the person must acknowledge the need. But many people lack the insight to recognize their symptoms, to realize that they're ill, or to see the benefits of treatment.

Early intervention is the best way to keep an episode from escalating into a more serious state. But few people seek treatment during the earliest stages of depression, before their energy level drops so low that they can't get out of bed. Women are more prone to seek medical help for depression because they're more in touch with their feelings. Men usually get treatment only when they become so depressed that others force them into it.

During hypomania and early mania, most of us don't feel sick; we feel fantastic. We may think you're overreacting or that *you're* the one who needs help. So you'll probably have a tougher sell on your hands, particularly if this is a first or second episode. Those of us who've experienced several episodes and understand our illness may be easier to persuade because we're more likely to recognize our early warning signs.

Because everyone's an individual, everyone responds in different ways to suggestions that it's time to seek help. The following tables display only *potential* ways to encourage someone to seek treatment on an outpatient basis. You must decide for yourself—or with the help of a mental health professional—the best way to help in each situation. If you don't have permission to contact the person's doctor or therapist, seek advice from a treatment center or from a mental health organization.

TABLE 12

Potential Ways to Help Someone in a Depressive Episode

Warning Signs	Potential Ways to Help
■ Extreme anxiety ■ Great difficulty functioning ■ Uncharacteristic disorganization and scatteredness ■ Disturbed sleep or disturbed eating patterns for two weeks or more ■ A lack of joy or enthusiasm about anything in life	■ Encourage the person to talk with a therapist or counselor. Offer to go along if possible. ■ Encourage the person to call the doctor and adjust medication as recommended. ■ Encourage the person to attend a support group meeting. Offer to go along if possible.
■ Extreme withdrawal ■ Disturbed sleep or disturbed eating patterns for two weeks or more and, possibly, a change in weight ■ An obsession with death or talk about suicide without any plan or attempt	■ Encourage the person to talk with a therapist or counselor. Offer to go along. ■ Encourage the person to see the doctor. Help make the appointment if needed and offer to go along if possible. ■ Along with a friend or relative, drive the person to a crisis center.

TABLE 13

Potential Ways to Help Someone in a Hypomanic or Early Manic Episode

Warning Signs	Potential Ways to Help
■ Sleeping two to four hours less than usual for four or more days	■ Encourage the person to call in sick to work.
■ Uncharacteristic disorganization and scatteredness	■ Encourage the person to see the doctor. Help make the appointment if needed and offer to go along if possible.
■ A lack of concern about personal safety or consequences of actions	
■ A lack of concern about others	
■ Obtrusive or inappropriate behavior	
■ Extreme overconfidence	■ Along with a friend or relative, drive the person to a crisis center.
■ Sleeping very little or not at all for four or more days (unless other symptoms call for hospitalization)	
■ Hostility and extreme anger	

When Hospitalization Becomes Necessary

Few people look forward to being hospitalized, regardless of the reason. This is especially true in the case of psychiatric hospitals. But hospitalization may be needed for a variety of reasons. Sometimes it helps pin down a more accurate diagnosis. Sometimes it's needed to monitor the effects of medications. Sometimes a person becomes so overwhelmed that it's impossible to cope. Sometimes the person loses all touch with reality and is at risk of ruining his or her life.

TABLE 14

Indicators That It's Time to Consider Hospitalization

For Depressive Episodes	For Manic Episodes
■ When the person is too worried or despondent to perform life's daily activities for an extended period	■ When the person becomes delusional but can't recognize that anything's unusual
■ When the person's thoughts and judgment are significantly impaired	
■ When the person becomes unable to meet basic needs (getting out of bed, bathing, dressing, and so on) and can barely respond to questions	■ When the person is belligerent, threatening, or out of control
■ When the person becomes physically self-abusive (cutting or bruising the body, repeatedly bashing the head against the wall, or similar acts)	■ When the person is completely incoherent, has hallucinations, or becomes paranoid
■ When the person talks about death, expresses hopelessness, or seems close to attempting suicide, particularly if he or she is using illicit drugs or alcohol	■ When the person hasn't slept for days and is at risk of total exhaustion

Voluntary Treatment

The best situation is when the person checks into the hospital voluntarily. However, voluntary commitment presents some risk because, in some cases, those who sign themselves in can leave when they want. Some states require that patients who wish to leave make a written request before the hospital can release them. To keep a person in the hospital, a doctor may have to file an application for involuntary commitment, or the family may have to get a judge's order.

Involuntary Treatment and Emergency Commitment

If a person becomes violent or seems in imminent danger of committing suicide, get professional assistance immediately. *Don't attempt to handle such a crisis on your own.* In most communities, hospitals can send a mobile crisis team to evaluate, and if necessary, drive the person to an appropriate facility. Sometimes you may have to involve the police.

Although exact criteria for involuntary commitment and emergency commitment vary from state to state, they generally require that the person's health or life be in danger, or that the person has become a threat to someone else's health or life. These laws, which patients and mental health advocates fought for for years, frustrate families who are genuinely concerned about their loved ones. The laws exist in part to keep families from hospitalizing relatives unnecessarily and to ensure that people get treatment in the least restrictive environment.

To protect patients' rights, one or more doctors (depending on state laws) must determine 1) whether the threat is imminent, and 2) whether hospitalization is the least restrictive option. The only exception is for minors with a mental illness.

If you strongly disagree with the doctor's evaluation and still feel the person requires hospitalization, you may have to get a judge's order.

A judge's options typically include

- *Discharge*—releasing the person from the hospital without requiring further treatment,
- *Protective Custody*—hospitalizing the person for a couple of weeks (in Texas, it's fourteen days),
- *Temporary Commitment*—hospitalizing the person for a few months (in Texas, it's ninety days), or
- *Outpatient Treatment*—committing the person to a day hospital or community mental health program.

Many families feel the laws prevent people from receiving treatment when they need it most. As both a patient and a family member, I have mixed feelings. I value my rights and my freedom, yet I also value my health and my life. I've talked my way out of hospitalization when it might have saved me years of pain.

The distorting thoughts that accompany severe mood disorders often make us incapable of knowing when we most need help. And because doctors and judges are human, they sometimes make the wrong decision. Unfortunately, a decision not to order treatment sometimes ends in tragedy.

Helping Someone Cope After Hospitalization

It's important to learn all you can about the person's illness, preferably before he or she leaves the hospital. Discuss your questions with mental health providers, and read all you can. The Resources section lists a number of organizations and Web sites you can turn to for information.

Before you can make any progress, you may need to regain the person's trust. Involuntary commitment often makes a person feel betrayed. If that's the case, say why you felt hospitalization was needed, empathize with what the person went through, and explain that you applied your best judgment. If the person still resents you, express regret that hospitalization was needed, but don't apologize for acting in the person's best interest. Ask for forgiveness, and explain that you'll do all you can to support the person's recovery and that you'd like to help prevent further hospitalizations.

Don't expect the person to feel fully recovered and jump right back into his or her routine after discharge. If the person has started a new medication while hospitalized, it may take several weeks to adjust. Just because the person has been discharged does not imply that he or she is well. Treatment standards call for treating patients in the least restrictive environment, and insurance limitations often dictate how long someone is hospitalized.

Allow the person to set the pace. Don't be overprotective or constantly wait on the person either. When others are oversolicitous, many of us feel guilty or become angry. Treat the person as an equal. Allow him or her to take on small responsibilities while working toward recovery. This can help the person feel useful and productive, and strengthen shattered self-esteem.

Establish a Partnership to Keep the Person Well

Explain that you're ready to do whatever you can to aid the person's recovery, to prevent future episodes, to reduce the need for hospitalization, and to keep the person in the community.

Talk through everything the person needs to support recovery, including prescribed medications and therapy. Don't dictate what the person needs to do or plan everything on your own. If possible, accompany the person to follow-up doctor visits and discuss how you can best help. Allow the person to voice his or her own opinions and to develop or assist with making treatment and recovery plans as much as possible.

Help the person set and prioritize small, reasonable, achievable goals. Expect gradual progress rather than giant leaps, and acknowledge the person's progress regularly.

Set Ground Rules

Someone you live with may need additional support to stay well. You may, for instance, need to

- support diet, mealtime, and bedtime adjustments;
- encourage the person to add, expand, or reduce exercise;
- support the person to take breaks and build in quiet time;
- address banking privileges and use of credit cards; and
- renegotiate transportation and household chores.

Agree on the ground rules as soon the person seems able, particularly for prohibited behaviors, such as limiting or disallowing alcohol consumption and stopping the use of illicit drugs. If your relationship is especially strained and full of conflicts, get a professional's help to set up the ground rules. This can reduce some of the tension and help you live together more easily.

Keep on Top of Medications

The primary reason people have recurring episodes is that they go off their medications, forget doses, or can't remember what they've taken and when. Some people resent reminders to take medications. They may view your efforts as mistrust, invasions of privacy, nagging, or attempts to control their lives. Others of us appreciate reminders. You're more likely to get a positive response if you emphasize that your reminders are only meant to support the person's recovery.

If the person doesn't already have an effective system for organizing medication, offer to help set up one. But don't do it all on your own. Suggest some ideas and ask for feedback on the person's preferences.

WORDS TO REINFORCE A PERSON'S RECOVERY

- I love you, and I'll always be here for you (provided you truly mean it).
- You're so much more than your illness.
- You seem to be feeling better. Is that true?
- You're making great progress. (Provide specific examples.)
- I'm proud of you. You're a strong person.
- I think you've made a good decision.
- You handled that well.
- I enjoyed being with you today.
- You've worked hard.
- Thanks for helping out.

Take Care of Your Own Needs

Before you can effectively help someone else, you need a chance to release your own emotions. You need to talk about your own anger, embarrassment, pain, resentment, and sorrow about the person's illness. You may need to come to terms with every upsetting incident. You might talk to a mental health professional, a member of the clergy, a close friend, or a family member. You may want to join a family support group. A number of organizations sponsor such groups. See the Resources for contact information.

Don't try to tough it out on your own. Allow friends, neighbors, and other family members to help. But choose your support team carefully, and base your openness about the situation on the person's feelings. Although we shouldn't be ashamed or embarrassed by mood disorders, we also need to "come out" only when we're ready. Respect the person's wishes and privacy as much as possible.

Discuss What to Do in the Future

Because mood disorders cause recurrent episodes, it's wise to plan for them. When the person is more stable, take some time to discuss treatment preferences, should others need to take over in a severe episode. Confirm that you understand those preferences thoroughly and write them down.

You or the person can address this informally, by writing a crisis plan, or formally, through an advance directive (a declaration for mental health treatment). Options vary from state to state. In either case, the document generally addresses issues such as the following:

- Symptoms the person recognizes as indicators for the need for treatment but may not notice during an episode
- Names of people permitted to confer with mental health providers
- Treatment facilities the person prefers and why
- Treatment facilities the person finds unacceptable and why
- Doctors the person prefers and why
- Doctors the person finds unacceptable and why
- Medications the person prefers and why
- Medications the person finds unacceptable and why
- Other treatments that might help, the circumstances in which to use them, and why
- Treatments the person finds unacceptable and why

Such plans both guide those helping a person through an episode and reassure that the person's wishes will be considered.

Thanks to treatment advances in recent years, it's unlikely you'll have to seek legal measures such as obtaining power of attorney, guardianship, or conservatorship, particularly if you help someone get treatment early on.

About 80 percent of people with unipolar disorder recover or improve significantly with treatment. About 25 percent of people with bipolar disorder essentially recover. Around 55 to 65 percent improve enough to work in less stressful situations or in less challenging positions than they might have achieved prior to becoming ill. The remaining 10 to 20 percent have continuing symptoms that show a less hopeful outcome.

Among other factors, a positive prognosis depends on compliance with medications, the absence of substance abuse, the absence of other psychiatric diagnoses, and a strong support network.

Mood disorders are the most treatable of all mental illnesses and can be treated more successfully than many other lifelong or life-threatening physical disorders.

TWENTY

Living Beyond Labels: Overcoming Stigma and Advocating for Change

ONE OF THE largest factors that prevent people from seeking treatment is the stigma of mental illness. As with many illnesses and disabilities, people with no experience or understanding of them are uneasy about and afraid of the unknown. They may envision being lobotomized and tortured, being so overmedicated that they become drooling zombies, and being locked away for life.

The thought of losing one's mind is indeed terrifying. But what many people don't realize is how *treatable* most mental illnesses are and that people who receive effective treatment, particularly early on, can lead normal lives. The vast majority of people with mental illness are capable of leading fairly normal, productive lives. With the proper treatment, we can go to school, hold down a job, raise a healthy family, pay taxes, and contribute to society.

The stigma associated with mental illness has lessened a bit since I first sought treatment in the early 1970s. But unfortunately, a significant amount still prevails. A 1996 survey conducted by the National Mental Health Association explored United States citizens' attitudes about the causes of mental illness. These were some of its findings:

- 71 percent blamed character flaws or emotional weaknesses
- 65 percent blamed bad parenting
- 35 percent blamed immoral behavior

Despite the explosion of knowledge about brain disorders that took place in the 1990s and its continuing expansion, mental illness is sorely misunderstood. This chapter discusses the challenges and results of stigma, and suggests areas for advocacy and change.

Stigma from a Historical Perspective

Over the centuries, people with mental illness have endured abuse and torture of all sorts. Particularly during the Stone Age and the Middle Ages, people thought that mental illness indicated demonic possession. They drilled holes in skulls of "the possessed" to release evil spirits, boiled them in water, or burned them at the stake.

During the eighteenth century, Europeans housed those with mental illness in filthy prisons, chained them to walls and flogged them, and treated them like criminals. In hospitals such as London's famous "Bedlam" (Bethlehem Asylum), "inmates" were on view for public entertainment like animals in zoos.

Glimmers of Dignity

During the eighteenth and nineteenth centuries, reformers such as French physician Philippe Pinel and U.S. citizens Dr. Benjamin Rush—Surgeon General of the Continental Armies, and philanthropist Dorthea Dix advocated for the dignity of people with mental illness.

During the early colonial period, those with mental illness had no place to go for treatment in the United States, so relatives cared for them in their homes. In 1751 Pennsylvania Hospital became the first institution to admit patients with mental illness. A group of Pennsylvania Quakers opened the Friends Asylum in Frankford, just outside Philadelphia, in the spring of 1817, where patients began receiving humane treatment. Dix's efforts led to the building of additional asylums in twenty U.S. states and in Canada. But treatment approaches were still limited by the lack of knowledge about the brain.

Mind Versus Body

Since at least the time of Hippocrates, physicians had viewed mental illnesses as physiological disorders. But when psychoanalysis came into vogue in the late 1800s and early 1900s, many people latched on to the idea that they were all in the mind. Psychoanalysis stressed subconscious conflicts, repressed feelings, defense mechanisms, sexual fixations, and dreams, rather than underlying disease.

By the early 1900s, physicians had reverted to the view of French philosopher René Descartes, who saw the mind and body as separate entities. This view restigmatized mental illness and to some extent continues still today.

Again, society blamed those affected for their illness and treated them like criminals. Then finally, advocacy efforts in the 1950s led to new concern. The Mental Health Bell, the official symbol of the National Mental Health Association, was cast in 1953. The metal in the 300-pound bell came from the chains that bound warehoused patients. The bell symbolizes the stigma and discrimination that still bind those of us with mental illness today.

Thanks primarily to early medications, a movement called *deinstitutionalization* took place in the 1960s. Its intent was to get people out of institutions and back into the community. In 1963, President Kennedy signed the Community Mental Health Centers Act, meant to help create about 2,000 community mental health centers. But the movement backfired. Hospitals released patients more quickly, but community-based resources were underfunded—if funded at all. Consequently, those with mental illness revolved in and out of hospitals, went entirely untreated, were jailed—frequently for minor offenses, or wound up homeless on the street.

Stigma in the Present

Sixteen percent of incarcerated people in the United States have some form of mental illness. Their total number is *four times larger* than the number of patients receiving treatment in state mental hospitals. The largest "mental health treatment facility" in the U.S. is the Los Angeles County jail.

Stigma affects not only those of us with mental illness but extends to our families as well. Having a relative or even associating with someone who has mental illness embarrasses many people. Because few people talk openly about mental illness, those affected often sense that they're alone. But mental illness strikes about one in five U.S. citizens each year and touches one in four families.

In the late 1990s, the National Institute of Mental Health estimated that one out of one hundred adults in the United States (roughly 2.3 million) experience bipolar disorder in any given year. However, at the May 2002 annual meeting of the American Psychiatric Association, Dr. Robert Hirschfeld, professor and Chair of the Department of Psychiatry and Behavioral Sciences at the University of Texas Medical Branch in Galveston, indicated that the figure may be three times higher. Dr Hirschfeld reported the results of a survey sent to 127,800 U.S. adults, whose age, gender, household income, and region matched 2000 U.S. Census data. The study, using a validated screening tool called the Mood Disorder Questionnaire, received 85,358 responses. Thirty-seven percent screened positively for bipolar I or II.

So why the continuing stigma?

Attitudes and Misconceptions

United States citizens tend to pride themselves on self-sufficiency and therefore sometimes reject and shun people who can't do as well. Rather than express empathy and acceptance, those with healthy brains dole out blame and disapproval. Many still believe that those of us with brain or substance abuse disorders are merely weak-willed. They tend to discount the physical components of our disorders.

Part of the stigma problem relates to terminology. People associate the term depression, for instance, with everyday blues, temporary loss, or short-term grief. More accurate terms for bipolar disorders, such as hypothalamic-pituitary-adrenal disorders, will probably never catch on because of their complexity.

Even mental health providers sometimes treat us with impatience and minimize or dismiss our pain. Some medical professionals don't yet acknowledge mind-body connections or recognize the similarities between brain disorders and other organ diseases. Despite revelations of **psychoneuroimmunology**, the scientific discipline that explores links between the mind and autonomic, immune, and nervous system functioning, some doctors don't take biochemical imbalances seriously.

Until I had to check my mother into a nursing home, I'd associated such attitudes with older clinicians, who might have had little exposure to information on the brain or mental illness during their training. But when I turned Mother's medications over to her nurse at the facility, this young professional saw no urgency to order refills of Mother's antidepressant or even medication to slow the progression of Alzheimer's. This nurse said, "Oh, those meds are *mental*," as if the state of one's brain is of no consequence. I was incensed. Had we not previously concluded that the facility was Mother's best option, I'd have moved her out immediately. (Incidentally, that nurse is no longer working there.)

Labels, Fear, and Misinformation

Entertainers have joked about people with illnesses and disabilities for years. They've called those with mental retardation "retards" and "dummies," those with cerebral palsy "spastics" or "spazzes," and those who must rely on canes, crutches, or wheelchairs "cripples" or "gimps." They've poked fun at blindness, deafness, and epileptic "fits." Disability advocates and a more informed public are slowly getting entertainers to be more sensitive. But people still poke fun at mental illness.

Much of the stigma about mental illness may relate to public fears that we're all homicidal maniacs. And that perception is growing worse. One study found that the U.S. public connected mental illness with violence 13 percent more often than it did in the 1950s. This was especially true among the 31 percent of respondents who equated mental illness only with extreme psychotic states.

When people commit violent crimes, newspaper, magazine, and television reports tend to stress any history of mental illness. The media often sensationalize such crimes, which adds to the public perception that we're dangerous. I won't claim that we never become violent, because when in extreme episodes, some of us do. But studies show that those of us with mental illness are no more violent than people with normal brains, that those of us who do become violent usually had such tendencies well before the illness surfaced. Outbursts in those with mental illness typically relate to feeling threatened or to alcohol or drug abuse, just as they do in normal people who become dangerous or violent.

VIOLENCE AND MENTAL ILLNESS

- The overall risk that someone with a mental illness will become violent is quite low.
- The risk increases if the person experiences a psychotic state, particularly if not on medication or noncompliant with treatment.
- The greatest risk occurs with a dual diagnosis—the co-occurrence of a mental illness plus a substance abuse disorder.
- The risk is highest for those closest to the person with the mental illness, such as family members or other people he or she knows well.
- The risk that a person with mental illness will harm a stranger is minimal.
- The contribution of mental illness to society's overall level of violence is extremely small.

When those of us with mental illness do become violent, we're far more likely to harm ourselves than to harm others. Our society tends to believe that suicide is rare. I wish that that were true. However, suicide is epidemic. But it's rarely covered in the news unless the suicide relates to a homicide or involves a unique situation or a celebrity. Most families keep such deaths private, sometimes out of shock, shame, or guilty feelings. Sometimes because it's so hard to face the awful truth.

U.S. SUICIDE VERSUS HOMICIDE RATES

A HIGHLY underpublicized fact is that the ratio of suicides to homicides in the United States approaches *3* suicides for every *2* homicides. *This figure should shock and shame us all.*

Some still equate committing suicide with committing a crime, and many fundamentalists consider it an affront to God. But as I see it, the *real* crime is the barriers people face to get effective treatment.

What Are the Results of Stigma?

Our society still tends to exclude people with mental illness from the workplace. Employers fear we won't be able to "cut it," that we'll cause trouble, or that we'll affect health insurance rates. Neighborhoods fight the presence of halfway houses. Some communities reject and harass the homeless, who often have no place to go. Society resists investing in sorely needed services that could improve and save many lives.

Unemployment

Believing that people with mental illness lack intelligence or are incapable of holding a job keeps many employers from hiring us. Sometimes our employment histories show gaps because at times we were too ill to continue in stressful positions or we required hospitalization.

When we've been unemployed at length, our workplace wardrobes may be limited. We may lack enough work outfits to last an entire week, or have to wear used or bargain clothing. Though we try to look our best, we often lack the funds to do so. Medications, therapy, and particularly hospitalization costs drain meager budgets.

Even with good insurance coverage, our finances may be pinched because of multiple copayments. Many of us are underinsured or lack health insurance altogether.

Inflexible work schedules also present challenges. Some of us can work eight-hour days or even longer without problems but find conventional starting times impossible to manage. We may have difficulty getting to sleep when we need to or require extra sleep to function well. Sometimes the medications we take to calm our brains enough to sleep lead to morning grogginess. Driving in rush-hour traffic can make us exceptionally anxious. And some of us must rely on rides from others or on public transportation, which means we have less control over exact arrival times.

But most of us are eager to work and normalize our lives. Much like women first entering a male-dominated workforce, we usually work extra diligently to prove our worth and to retain our jobs. Sometimes we scale back on doctor and therapy visits because we fear the consequences of leaving work long enough to keep appointments. This tends to further compound our problems.

Homelessness

Although exact numbers are impossible to obtain, experts estimate that approximately 750,000 people in the United States are homeless on any given night and that roughly one third of them have a severe mental illness. Alcohol or drug addiction among the homeless occurs in comparable amounts. Up to one-fifth of homeless people also have a **dual diagnosis**—a mental illness plus a substance abuse problem.

Treatment and housing programs for dual diagnoses are challenging to find. People with substance abuse disorders often don't qualify for mental health programs, and people with mental illness often don't fit well in addiction programs. Besides, many homeless people seek food and shelter rather than treatment, most likely because they're preoccupied with satisfying needs for food and shelter first. But housing programs usually require those that they assist to be in treatment.

Some people still believe that mental illness, substance abuse, unemployment, and homelessness are problems only lazy, disgraceful wretches face. Surely, people in such circumstances *must* have done something wrong. Some people believe that homelessness is merely a lifestyle choice. Rumors still persist that street-corner beggars make big bucks and see no reason to find "honest work."

If those represent your feelings, I'm tempted to suggest you drive to a thrift shop, purchase some shabby garments, make a cardboard sign, and plant yourself on a street corner.

Then try sleeping in a shelter for a while. But be prepared to pay $5 to $10 for the privilege, common rates that shelters charge for a single night. If you can't access a bed, like more than 37 percent of homeless people, you may be forced to sleep on the street.

CAUTION

DON'T ACTUALLY *try this; doing so would be foolish.* Even if you think you're street-smart, you'd be risking your life. Just *imagine* living this way day after day and having to relying on overcrowded, underfunded public services to cope.

Limitations Society Must Soon Resolve

Thanks to the efforts of high-profile advocates like former First Lady Rosalynn Carter, mental health advocate Tipper Gore, and others, legislators are finally paying more attention to these problems. We made great strides in 2002, with the federal ruling that serious brain disorders are physical illnesses and the attention both the U.S. House and Senate have given to parity legislation for serious mental illnesses.

But the battle is far from over. Opponents are working hard to discredit and block parity efforts. Some view psychiatry and medication as pampering for the "worried well" rather than medical necessity.

Managed Care and Insurance Problems

Because most people employed in conventional jobs are covered by some form of managed care, they're already aware that managed care groups are often more preoccupied with cost cutting than with providing adequate coverage.

Employers balk at the cost of parity, fearing its impact on their bottom line, and saying they can't afford to provide it. But mental health coverage has been shown to reduce absenteeism and job turnover, to increase productivity, and to improve workers' output. Because many people see primary care physicians for "purely physical" conditions that turn out to be mental health issues, overall health care costs often decrease as well.

Of course, the quality of managed care varies widely from one organization to another. Many plans may still place unreasonable restrictions on

- the types of medications the insurance covers,
- the number or length of visits with psychiatrists or psychotherapists, and
- the length or dollar limit for hospital stays.

A young friend recently sought her first psychiatrist consult for depression. Getting in for her first visit took three months. Because her insurance plan doles out only one referral at a time, if the first doctor didn't work out and she needed a second referral, she'd have to face another long wait. Three or more months is a long time to go without treatment, particularly if a depression worsens.

Privacy of medical records is another concern when we're insured by employers. Many of us worry that disclosing our brain or substance abuse disorders will set us up to be laid off or fired. I've even worried that because I'm on my husband's health insurance, the expense of my treatment may one day jeopardize his job.

A Shortage of Community-Based Services

For those who even seek treatment—now estimated at one third of those who truly need it—waiting lists are long, appointments scheduled much too far apart, and quality time with trained professionals tightly controlled. People enter the hospital when things get desperate, then often wind up on the streets within a few days. That's one reason so many homeless people display mental illness.

Lack of Treatment or Undertreatment

Stigma prevents many seriously ill people from even seeking help. By the time we begin treatment—often in the midst of a major episode—scrambled neural pathways may be so well established that our brains are much harder to stabilize. Disordered thinking may be so deeply ingrained that it takes years to turn it around.

Government programs such as Supplemental Security Income (SSI) and Social Security Disability Insurance (SSDI)—both administrated by the Social Security Administration—do provide a modest income for individuals with severe mental illness. But funds are limited, initial applications are denied half of the time, and appeals often take a year or more.

Those with SSI or SSDI may qualify for additional assistance, including food stamps, Medicaid and Medicare, housing or rental assistance programs, vocational training, and employment services. But these services barely begin to address the need. The Resources section provides information for some of these services. Contact a local treatment center or mental health organization to learn about other options in your community.

Prison-Based Treatment

Due partially to the lack of community-based services, increasing numbers of people with mental illness wind up in jail. This is particularly true of those who lack insurance, jobs, and homes. Although the exact number is unknown, experts estimate that up to 20 percent of incarcerated individuals have a severe mental illness. This figure *excludes* nonpsychotic forms of mood disorders, impulse control disorders, cognitive impairment, anxiety disorders, and substance abuse present with no other diagnosis.

Imprisonment not only criminalizes mental illness but increases the risk that detained individuals will be victimized, sexually abused, or commit suicide. Few jails or prisons have enough trained staff, if any, to meet the needs of those who are ill. Sometimes incarcerated patients don't receive crucial psychotropic medications. A punitive atmosphere, overcrowding, idleness, and isolation cause further problems. Consequently, their condition often grows more severe than it was before incarceration. And jails often release those with mental illness onto the streets with no plan for follow-up care.

Advocating for Better Treatment

Mental illnesses are real, often life-threatening physical illnesses that deserve treatment just as much as any other illness. But is our society ready to acknowledge this and to remove the barriers that prevent so many from getting effective treatment? How much longer will it take to resolve problems that have reached epidemic proportions but could be more effectively and inexpensively addressed if treated early on? How many more deaths must occur to wake us up? How much more suffering, wasted years, and lost potential will it take before we can acknowledge the value in every human life?

Learn All You Can About Your Illness

Learn all you can about the disorder you or your loved one is dealing with and about mental health in general. Then share that knowledge with others. The Resources section of this book lists many different sources of information.

When You Can, Inform Others About Your Illness

Unfortunately, even those of us with mental illness perpetuate the stigma by hiding our disorders from others and not informing our families, friends, and employers. In a 1999 online survey of National Depressive and Manic-Depressive Association members, 38 percent of respondents with mood disorders said they didn't inform others about their illness because they're too embarrassed or ashamed.

> THE STRAIN of trying to keep a lid on this illness makes our situation even worse. When I finally "came out," it brought huge relief and many positive changes to my life.
>
> Whether or not you "come out" at all is *entirely your decision*. If you do, I suggest discussing your illness with selective groups of people and not going public until you feel *thoroughly* prepared. The naysayers are ready and willing to attack and tear you down.

But please inform *someone* you trust about your mood disorder—whether diagnosed or merely suspected. *And if you're considering suicide, talk with someone immediately.*

Address the Stigma

When you notice stigmatizing information in the media, don't just ignore it. Write a letter to the editor, contact the radio station or the television network. Join the National Stigma Clearinghouse or a mental health organization such as the Depression and Bipolar Support Alliance, the National Alliance for the Mentally Ill, or the National Mental Health Association. Recruit others for an anti-stigma campaign. Then act on the stigma alerts such groups provide.

Advocate for Better Funding and Legislation

Learn about the mental health services available in your community. Ask mental health professionals about current needs. Share what you learn with local, state, and national legislators. Do so politely, but persistently.

Contribute to Mental Health and Research Organizations

Support nonprofit associations that address mental health issues and organizations that fund research on brain disorders and mental health.

The Resources section lists several worthy organizations that could use support.

While it's almost impossible to hide florid mania or especially severe depression, it's not that difficult to hide the milder episodes. I did it with fair success over decades by living out of state, away from friends and family members, hiding out during depressive episodes, and keeping quiet about the embarrassments and expenses that resulted from my hypomanic states. But I paid, and am still paying, an enormous price for not getting effective treatment earlier.

Both for your own sake and because mood disorders have a genetic basis, it's important to inform family members and be open about your illness. You may very well find another relative who is affected and who can better understand your situation. And provided you act in time, you may very well help save each other's lives.

Moving Toward Solid Ground

BY OPENLY SHARING my own experiences and drawing from extensive research, I've aimed to demystify the true nature of mood disorders and mental illnesses—as we now know them—in this book.

Mental Illness Myths Demystified

The following are some common myths about mental illness and their demystifications:

- *There's no good reason for the mentally ill to act so crazy. They just need to learn some self-control.* When experiencing breakdowns or episodes, those of us with serious brain disorders such as bipolar disorder, unipolar disorder, and schizophrenia become hostages to our imbalanced biochemistry. We may become impulsive, lose our sense of judgment, and lack the ability to maintain self-control. We can exercise that control *only* when our brain chemistry is balanced and we can recognize and respond to early warning signs quickly. That's not an easy task. A depressive episode can jerk the tightrope from beneath us and plunge us into paralyzing hopelessness in an instant. When hypomanic or manic, we often feel so good that we're convinced we're well and don't recognize that an episode has begun. We and our loved ones must often experience multiple episodes before learning all the warning signs and what steps we must take to keep an episode from worsening.

- *We all get depressed from time to time. Positive thinking should be enough to turn things around.* Clinical depression differs significantly from the blues or normal grief in intensity, duration, and greatly impacts your normal routine. While nonclinical depression slows people down, they can usually go about their normal activities and function reasonably well. People experiencing clinical depression, on the other hand, may find everything a struggle and feel no relief for months. They may neglect their basic needs and completely withdraw from life.

- *Lots of people think about suicide at times but don't actually attempt it. Those who say they want to kill themselves are just seeking sympathy.* Three-fourths of those who end their own lives communicate their intention either directly or indirectly to a friend or family member before their death. This may be a desperate call for help or an attempt to say a final good-bye. Regardless of the reason, it's best to take such statements seriously rather than expect them to pass.

- *The mentally ill are eccentrics who crave attention. They aren't sick, and many of them don't want treatment.* Mental illness can lead to eccentric behaviors, but those behaviors usually appear only during episodes. The rest of the time, most of us who monitor our illness carefully function pretty well. For a variety of reasons, some people with mental illness do refuse treatment:

　　—Many are preoccupied by their drive to meet basic needs such as finding food and shelter.

—Many avoid treatment because of stigma or fear.

—Many associate mental illness with only its extreme forms and don't know about lesser-known symptoms.

- *Psychiatric diagnoses involve a lot of guesswork. They're not made scientifically. "Shrinks" are quacks.* With each new edition of the *Diagnostic and Statistical Manual of Mental Disorders*, the criteria for various disorders have become more tightly defined. But when a psychiatrist observes only certain symptoms and the patient doesn't disclose others or isn't in the midst of a severe episode, diagnosis becomes difficult. Psychiatrists are medical doctors with extensive training. As with any profession, some individuals are less qualified or less ethical than others. In my experience, most psychiatrists are knowledgeable and genuinely concerned.

- *Lots of people with "mental illness" have some unrelated physical illness. When that gets treated, the "mental illness" should go away.* Although the symptoms of many different illnesses can mimic a mental illness, unfortunately, they can also co-occur with one. Just as having a punctured lung does not rule out having a broken leg, a mental illness can accompany one or more other illnesses.

- *Mental illness is all in your head. It has no physical basis.* There's a tiny bit of truth in the first statement, given that the brain is in the head. And it's becoming clear that the mind and body interact. But electronic and computerized technologies do show clear structural and functional irregularities in the brains of many who suffer mental illnesses. And genetics and biochemistry clearly play a part.

- *The mentally ill have warped personalities.* Some, but not all, people with mental illness also have a personality disorder. But many of us, particularly if we have milder forms of brain disorders, can hide our illness so well that family members and close friends might not realize our mental illness exists.

- *People with mental illness come from bad families.* Some forms of mental illness do run in families—most likely due to a combination of genetic abnormalities, dysfunctional relationships, environmental factors, shared stressors, or poor lifestyle choices. But that doesn't make those families "bad." "Good" and "bad" are nothing more than personal judgments.

- *The mentally ill are weak. They're just overreacting to normal stress.* Some of us are more sensitive or emotional than other people. And we may have less than ideal coping skills. But many of us have endured repeated stressors that would challenge anyone, and with each new stressor, the kindling effect can intensive further episodes.

- *The mentally ill just won't take responsibility and help themselves.* During episodes, we may not be able to control our actions, but the rest of the time, most of us are just as responsible as anyone. Many of us lack the resources or face incredibly challenging barriers to get effective help or don't know where to start.

- *If "imbalanced brain chemistry" causes mental illness, then medication should rebalance it and cure the problem.* Although the right medication can help significantly, serious mental illnesses such as bipolar disorder, unipolar disorder, and schizophrenia are usually lifelong conditions. In comparison, taking insulin for diabetes or anticonvulsants for epilepsy may slow the underlying disease, but medications don't cure either condition. Because mental illness also affects thinking and behavior, other forms of treatment may also be needed to supplement medications.

- *Talking about problems won't solve them. It only makes you dwell on them more. Instead of yammering on endlessly in therapy, these people should take action.* Taking action does help, but talking about problems and seeking a different perspective is useful as well. Many of us who participate in talk therapy have deeply buried emotions that we can't safely express in other settings. It's invaluable to talk about feelings with a trained professional who can sort them out or to share them in a support group among others who can identify with our feelings.

- *The mentally ill can do nothing to help themselves other than find good mental health professionals, take the right medications, and undergo lengthy hospitalizations.* Because supportive professionals and carefully tailored medications help, many people with mental illness never require hospitalization. Frequently, those who do remain in the hospital stay only for a few days. Other things that help those of us with mental illness better cope or even prevent future episodes include the following:

  —Learning as much as possible about our illness and recognizing our personal warning signs of impending episodes
  —Taking an active role with our treatment teams
  —Attending to basic physical needs such as sleep, diet, exercise, and relaxation
  —Finding healthy ways to identify and express our feelings
  —Having a close relationship with a family member, friend, or support group
  —Living in a supportive environment
  —Keeping our stress level low
  —Adjusting our lifestyle
  —Setting reasonable, achievable goals and celebrating each one we meet
  —Using affirmations and visualizations
  —Nurturing our talents and interests
  —Attending to our spiritual side
  —Reaching out to others

- *Once they get effective treatment, the mentally ill should be able to get right back into normal life.* After a severe episode, most of us must ease back into our lives. Sometimes we must make major changes. To move toward recovery and to prevent further episodes, we must monitor our illnesses carefully. We need to track medications, sleep, diet, exercise, and adjust to new routines. This takes quite a bit of effort and time.

- *The mentally ill just need to change their attitudes and be more realistic.* Mental illness can certainly affect one's attitude, but it can also affect the ability to be realistic. The longer an illness has gone untreated or undertreated, the more challenging such changes may become.

- *The mentally ill are immature and self-absorbed. They just need to grow up and become responsible.* I won't argue that we're never immature or self-absorbed. Sometimes we're both, but other times we're not at all. Oversimplification and labels reduce the integrity of those who suffer, promote further stigma, and ignore the very real physical components involved in mental illness.

- *Those people are sick because they have no faith in God. All they really need is religious commitment and prayer.* Faith and religion can be quite beneficial, and many people with mental illness are highly spiritual. But it takes more than prayer to manage mental illness.

- *Friends and relatives often overreact and push those who "march to a different drummer" into unnecessary treatment.* This may happen in rare cases, but a far more common problem is the extraordinary number of undiagnosed and untreated people with mental illness who suffer needlessly.

- *The mentally ill are too undependable, weird, or violent to function in society.* During an episode, we may be less dependable than others, and our behaviors may be a bit bizarre. When not in an episode, most of us blend in as well as anybody. And despite popular belief, most people with mental illness are no more violent than other people in our society.

Reasons for Hope

Having a mood disorder is no reason to give up hope. Pharmaceutical companies are constantly developing more effective psychotropic medications with fewer side effects. And as scientists and doctors learn more about the brain and mind-body connections, treatments are becoming more holistic.

Researchers are hard at work to find better ways to diagnose mood disorders and more quickly determine which treatments will work best for which people. In 2002, a research team led by Dr. Ian Cook at the University of California at Los Angeles learned that a simple one-hour EEG may have the potential to predict how a person with depression might respond to antidepressants. The changes in prefrontal cortex brain waves of subjects who responded well to antidepressant treatments showed changes within a couple of days even though clinical improvements were evident only after two to four weeks. Such a test could save patients months of tedious and frustrating trials with one antidepressant after another in the attempt to find the most effective medication for their individual biochemistry.

One of the few benefits of the World Trade Center tragedy on September 11, 2001, is that the public finally began to understand the challenge of living with the some of the anxieties that we who walk the "tightrope" experience every day. Many in the United States have become more empathetic and more concerned about other people as a result of this unfortunate loss.

As challenging as both unipolar and bipolar disorders can be, they remain the most treatable of all mental illnesses, and I'm convinced that by carefully adjusting and monitoring your lifestyle and treatment, you too can move toward more solid ground.

MEDICATIONS APPENDIX

THIS APPENDIX IS meant to give you some idea of the wealth of medications currently available in the United States for treating mood disorders. *It is not meant to substitute for your doctor's advice.* However, sometimes—out of unfamiliarity with a certain medication, concerns about side effects, or another reason—some doctors, particularly general practitioners, hesitate to prescribe a certain treatment. And sometimes that *very* treatment may be the best one for *you.* By knowing what medications are available, you'll be better prepared to work with your doctor to obtain optimal results.

Dosage Determinations

The proper dosage depends on many factors, including age, gender, exact diagnosis, diet, illicit drug and alcohol use, individual biochemistry and co-occurring conditions you might have, other medications you are taking, your sensitivity to medications, and the side effects you experience.

When you start a new medication, your doctor will usually prescribe a lower dose and then gradually increase (or "titrate") it as both of you learn how it affects you. Because individuals tolerate and metabolize medications differently, your dose may be higher or lower than that of other patients on the same medication. Don't get overly concerned if your dosage varies from that of friends or family members taking the same medication, or if it falls slightly out of the ranges listed in pharmaceutical guides.

If you're on a low dose for six weeks or so and your symptoms don't improve, ask your doctor whether a higher dose might be more helpful. If you're on a high dose for six weeks or so and you're having bad side effects, ask if you can take a lower dose or switch to another medication.

CAUTIONS

1. Always follow your doctor's instructions about the frequency and timing of doses.
2. Ask your doctor about any concerns. If you don't get satisfactory answers, seek a second opinion.
3. When starting any new medication, monitor your symptoms carefully. Tell your doctor immediately if symptoms get significantly worse, particularly if you have suicidal thoughts.
4. Don't change your dosage or medication on your own. Always check with your doctor first.
5. By all means, *don't suddenly stop taking your medication.* Doing so may cause significant, or even dangerous, side effects.

Some medications can be taken once a day or once a week, but many must be taken in divided doses during a single day.

Although some agents, such as lithium citrate, are available in liquid form, the information in these tables applies only to preparations in capsule or tablet form.

Half-Life Determinations

A **half-life** is the amount of time it takes for your body to metabolize or eliminate half of the substance you've ingested. However, most medications require *five times their half-lives* to be fully eliminated from the body. Half-lives become important when you need to try a different medication or stop one entirely.

The half-lives of psychotropic medications range from an hour to more than a week. The factors that affect dosage (age, gender, and so on) can also affect half-lives. The half-lives listed in pharmaceutical guides may not consider all of these factors. For more specific information, talk with your doctor or a pharmacist.

How to Use These Tables

The following tables are organized alphabetically, first by medication type, then by classification, listed vertically in the left-hand column. The middle and right-hand columns list chemical and brand or trade names alphabetically within each classification. To locate a medication when you know its trade name but not its chemical name, look down the right-hand column.

Trade names that duplicate chemical names don't necessarily indicate generic forms; they may merely indicate that preparations companies have named them after the chemical terms. Likewise, the lack of a duplicated name doesn't necessarily indicate that no generic form is available. If you prefer a generic medication, just ask your doctor if one exists and if he or she will prescribe it.

Pronunciations

Because, especially for nonscientists, chemical and medication names can be easily confused and difficult to pronounce, a phonetic spelling follows these terms. Some names have alternate pronunciations, but this list contains pronunciations that people commonly use.

Symbol Key

*A single asterisk follows those agents that come in multiple forms, such as controlled release, extended release, half-strength, bedtime dose, weekly dose, and so on.

**Double asterisks precede those antianxiety agents that have a significant sedating effect.

TABLE 15

Medications Table

ANTIANXIETY AGENTS (TRANQUILIZING) AND HYPNOTIC (SEDATING) AGENTS		
Classification	**Chemical Names**	**Trade Names**
Benzodiazepines Increase the actions of GABA to inhibit the actions of certain neuro-transmitters **CAUTION:** Due to their strong potential for addiction, dosages levels for these agents should be kept as low as possible. Working closely with your doctor, take benzo-diazepines *only as long as you absolutely need them!*	alprazolam al–PRAZZ–oh–lam	Alprazolam Xanax ZAN–ax
	chlordiazepoxide hydrochloride klor–dye–az–uh–PAHK–sid hy–druh–KLOH–ride	Chlordiazepoxide HCl Librium LIB–ree–uhm
	clonazepam klaw–NAZZ–uh–pam	Clonazepam Klonopin KLAW–nuh–pin
	clorazepate dipotassium klo–RAZZ–uh–pate dye–poh–TASS–ee–uhm	Clorazepate Tranxene* TRAN–zeen
	diazepam dye–AZZ–uh–pam	Diazepam Valium VAL–ee–uhm
	**estazolam es–TAZZ–oh–lam	Estazolam ProSom PRO–sohm
	**flurazepam hydrochloride flu–RAZZ–uh–pam hy–druh–KLOH–ride	Dalmane DOLL–main Flurazepam Hydrochloride
	lorazepam luh–RAZZ–uh–pam	Ativan AT–uh–van Lorazepam
	oxazepam ox–AZZ–uh–pam	Oxazepam Serax SEHR–ax
	**temazepam tuh–MAZZ–uh–pam	Restoril RES–tah–rill Temazepam
	**triazolam try–AZZ–oh–lam	Halcion HAL–see–on Triazolam
Nonbenzodiazepines Antianxiety Agents Act as partial agonists to stimulate certain serotonin receptors	buspirone hydrochloride byou–SPY–rohn hy–druh–KLOH–ride	BuSpar BYOU–spar Buspirone Hydrochloride
Nonbenzodiazepine Hypnotic Agents Act at a subset of benzodiazepine sites to increase GABA activity	zaleplon ZAH–luh–plon	Sonata so–NAH–tah
	zolpidem tartrate zole–PI–dem TAR–trait	Ambien AM–bee–ehn

Table continued on next page

ANTIDEPRESSANTS

Classification	Chemical Names	Trade Names

MAOIs
(monoamine oxidase inhibitors)
Increase serotonin, norepinephrine, and dopamine concentrations by preventing the monoamine oxidase enzyme from metabolizing neurotransmitters *inside* nerve endings of presynaptic neurons
 	
CAUTION:
If your doctor prescribes an MAOI, verify exactly what foods, beverages, and medications *you must not ingest!*
	isocarboxazid
	  eye–soh–kar–BOX–uh–sid
		Marplan
		  MAHR–plan

	phenelzine sulfate
	  FEEN–ell–zeen SUHL–fate
		Nardil
		  NAHR–dill

	tranylcypromine sulfate
	  tran–ell–SIGH–pro–meen
	  SUHL–fate
		Parnate
		  PAR–nate

NaSSAs
(noradrenergic and specific serotonergic antidepressants)
Block certain adrenergic and serotonergic receptors
	mirtazapine
	  mur–TAZ–a–peen
		Mirtazapine
		Remeron*
		  REM–eh–rohn

NDRIs
(norepinephrine and dopamine reuptake receptors)
Increase norepinephrine and dopamine concentrations
	bupropion hydrochloride
	  byou–PRO–pee–on
	  hy–druh–KLOH–ride
		Wellbutrin*
		  well–BYOU–trin

SARIs
(serotonin antagonist and reuptake inhibitors)
Increase serotonin concentration by inhibiting its reuptake and diverting it to certain nonserotonin receptors on receiving neurons
	trazodone hydrochloride
	  TRAZZ–oh–dohn
	  hy–druh–KLOH–ride
		Desyrel
		  DEHZ–uh–rell
		Trazodone
		  Hydrochloride

SNRIs
(serotonin and norepinephrine reuptake inhibitors)
Increase norepinephrine and serotonin concentrations
	venlafaxine hydrochloride
	  ven–la–FAX–een
	  hy–druh–KLOH–ride
		Effexor*
		  ehf–ECKS–or

SSRIs
(selective serotonin reuptake inhibitors)
Increase serotonin concentration. Some also increase dopamine and norepinephrine concentrations.
	citalopram hydrobromide
	  SIGH–tal–oh–pram
	  hy–druh–BRO–mide
		Celexa
		  sell–ECKS–ah

	escitalopram oxalate
	  es–SIGH–tal–oh–pram
	  AHK–suh–late
		Lexapro
		  LEX–ah–pro

Classification	Chemical Names	Trade Name

SSRIs *continued*	fluoxetine hydrochloride
	flu–OX–e–teen
	hy–druh–KLOH–ride
	(Also see Atypical
	Antipsychotics)
		Fluoxetine
		Prozac*
		  PRO–zak
		Sarafem
		  SAIR–uh–fem
		Symbyax
		  SIMM–bee–ax

	fluvoxamine maleate flu–VOX–a–meen MAY–lee–ate	Fluvoxamine Maleate Luvox LOO–vocks
	paroxetine hydrochloride pa–ROCKS–a–teen hy–druh–KLOH–ride	Paxil* PACKS–ill
	sertraline hydrochloride SER–trah–leen hy–druh–KLOH–ride	Zoloft ZOH–loft

TCAs
(tricyclic
antidepressants)
Block both serotonin
and norepinephrine
reuptake; some by
increasing norepineph-
rine more than sero-
tonin, others by
increasing serotonin
more than
norepinephrine
	amitriptyline hydrochloride
	am–uh–TRIP–tuh–leen
	hy–druh–KLOH–ride
		Amitriptyline
		  Hydrochloride
		Elavil
		  ELL–uh–vill

	amoxapine (see Tetracyclics)	
	clomipramine hydrochloride kloh–mip–RUH–meen hy–druh–KLOH–ride	Anafranil an–AF–ran–ill Clomipramine*
	desipramine hydrochloride duh–ZIP–ruh–meen hy–druh–KLOH–ride	Desipramine Norpramin nor–PRAM–in
	doxepin hydrochloride DOX–uh–pin hy–druh–KLOH–ride	Doxepin* Sinequan SIN–uh–kwan
	imipramine hydrochloride em–IP–rah–meen hy–druh–KLOH–ride	Imipramine Hydrochloride Tofranil toe–FRAY–nill

	maprotiline hydrochloride
	ma–PRO–tuh–leen
	hy–druh–KLOH–ride
		Ludiomil
		  LOO–dee–oh–mill
		Maprotiline
		  Hydrochloride

	nortriptyline hydrochloride nor–TRIP–tuh–leen hy–druh–KLOH–ride	Nortriptyline* Pamelor PAM–eh–lore
	protriptyline hydrochloride pro–TRIP–tuh–leen hy–druh–KLOH–ride	Vivactil vie–VACK–till
	trimipramine maleate try–MIP–ra–meen MAY–lee–ate	Surmontil SIR–mon–till
Tetracyclics Act similarly to TCAs; have a 4-ring structure that acts differently on transport proteins NOTE: Some sources list amoxapine as a tri- cyclic, but it has a 4-ring rather than 3-ring chemical structure.	amoxapine a–MOX–a–peen	Amoxapine

ANTIPSYCHOTICS

Classification	Chemical Names	Trade Names
Atypical Antipsychotics Inhibit neurotransmitter activity by blocking certain dopamine receptors and sometimes by also increasing serotonin or both serotonin and norepinephrine concentrations	aripiprazole ay–ruh–PIP–ray–zole	Abilify ah–BILL–i–fye
	olanzapine oh–LAN–za–peen	Zyprexa* zye–PRECKS–ah
	quetiapine fumarate kwee–TYE–uh–peen FYOU–muh–rate	Seroquel SAIR–oh–kwell
	risperidone RIS–per–i–dohn	Risperdal RIS–per–dahl
	ziprasidone hydrochloride ZIH–pray–si–dohn hy–druh–KLOH–ride	Geodon GEE–oh–dahn
Typical Antipsychotics Inhibit dopamine activity by blocking certain dopamine receptors	haloperidol hal–oh–PER–i–dole	Haldol HAL–doll Haloperidol
	thioridazine hydrochloride thi–oh–RID–a–zeen hy–druh–KLOH–ride	Mellaril MELL–uh–ril Thioridazine Hydrochloride
	trifluoperazine hydrochloride tri–flu–oh–PER–a–zeen hy–druh–KLOH–ride	Stelazine STELL–uh–zeen Trifluoperazine Hydrochloride

MOOD-STABILIZING AGENTS

Classification	Chemical Names	Trade Names
Mood Stabilizers Appear to work *inside* neurons to reprogram them; but also interact with neurotransmitter receptors and reuptake pumps on neurons	lithium carbonate LITH–ee–uhm KAR–boh–nate	Eskalith*. ES–ka–lith Lithium Carbonate Lithobid* LITH–oh–bid Lithonate LITH–oh–nate Lithotabs LITH–oh–tabs
Mood-Stabilizing Anticonvulsants Some increase GABA activity to inhibit certain neurotransmitters; others adjust glutamate activity to excite certain neurotransmitters	carbamazepine kar–bah–MAZZ–uh–peen	Carbamazepine Carbatrol* kar–BAH–troll Epitol EP–uh–tall Tegretol* TEH–greh–tall
	divalproex sodium dye–VAL–pro–ex SOH–dee–uhm (see valproate)	
	gabapentin GAB–ah–pen–tin	Neurontin NUH–rahn–tin
	lamotrigine lah–MOH–truh–jeen	Lamictal lah–MICK–tall

Classification	Chemical Names	Trade Names
Mood-Stabilizing Anticonvulsants *continued*	oxcarbazepine ox–kar–BAZE–eh–peen	Trileptal try–LEP–tall
	topiramate toe–PIE–rah–mate	Topamax TOE–pah–macks
	valproate val–PRO–ate	Depakote* DEHP–uh–coat Depakene DEHP–uh–keen Valproic Acid val–PRO–ick ASS–id
	valproate sodium or valproic acid (see valproate)	
	zonisamide zoh–NIS–uh–mide	Zonegran ZAHN–uh–gran
Mood-Stabilizing Calcium Channel Blockers Block the flow of calcium ions into neurons and produce an effect similar to that of anticonvulsants by reducing neural activity	diltiazem hydrochloride dill–TIE–a–zem hy–druh–KLOH–ride	Cardizem* KAR–di–zem Diltazem*
	nifedipine nye–FED–uh–peen	Adalat CC AD–uh–lat Nifedipine* Procardia* pro–KAR–dee–uh
	verapamil hydrochloride ver–AP–uh–mill hy–druh–KLOH–ride	Covera–HS co–VEHR–uh Verapamil* Verelan* vehr–eh–lan

Information Sources

American Psychiatric Association: *www.psych.org/public_info/
medication.cfm#mental*

Consumer Reports Complete Drug Reference. Yonkers, N.Y.: Consumer
Reports, 2001.

DiPiro, Joseph (Ed.). *Pharmacotherapy: A Pathophysiologic Approach* (5th ed.).
New York: Appleton & Lange/McGraw Hill, 2002.

Goldberg, Ivan. "Trade and Generic Names of Psychiatric Medications":
www.psycom.net/depression.central.drugnames.html

Kahn, David A., Ruth Ross, David J. Printz, and Gary S. Sachs. "Medication Treatment of Bipolar Disorder 2000." Expert Consensus Guideline
Series, a Postgraduate Medicine Special Report, April 2000.

Keltner, Norman L., and David G. Folks (Eds.). *Psychotropic Drugs* (2nd ed.)
St. Louis, Mo.: Mosby, 1997.

Maxmen, Jerrold S., and Nicholas G. Ward. *Psychotropic Drugs: Fast Facts*
(2nd ed.). New York: W.W. Norton & Company, 1995.

Medical Economics Company. *The PDR Family Guide to Prescription Drugs.*
New York: Crown, 1996.

Medscape DrugInfo: *www.medscape.com/px/drugdirectory/about-druginfo.asp*

Mondimore, Francis M. *Bipolar Disorder: A Guide for Patients and Families.*
Baltimore, Md.: Johns Hopkins University Press, 1999.

National Alliance for the Mentally Ill.: *www.nami.org/helpline/medlist.htm*

National Depressive and Manic–Depressive Association. *Finding Peace of Mind:
Medication and Treatment Strategies for Depression.* Chicago: NDMDA, 2001.

Prescription & Over–the–Counter Drugs. Pleasantville, N.Y.: Reader's Digest, 1998.

Preston, John, and James Johnson. *Clinical Psychopharmacology Made Ridicu-
lously Simple* (3rd ed). Miami: MedMaster, 1997.

Preston, John D., John H. O'Neal, and Mary C. Talaga. *Handbook of Clinical Psychopharmacology for Therapists, 3rd ed.* Oakland, CA: New Harbinger, 2002.

RxList: *www.rxlist.com*

Sachs, Gary S., David J. Printz, David A. Kahn, Daniel Carpenter, and John
P. Docherty. *Medication Treatment of Bipolar Disorder 2000.* Minneapolis,
Minn.: Healthcare Information Programs/McGraw-Hill, 2000.

Texas Department of Mental Health and Mental Retardation. *TMAP Procedural Manual: Bipolar Disorders Module: Guideline Procedures Manual.* June
1999: *www.mhmr.state.tx.us/centraloffice/medicaldirector.bpdman.pdf*

Thomson Healthcare: *www.pdrhealth.com/drug_info/index.html*

Torrey, E. Fuller, and Michael B. Knable. *Surviving Manic Depression: A Manual on Bipolar Disorder for Patients, Families, and Providers.* New York: Basic
Books/Perseus Books Group, 2002.

Whybrow, Peter C. *A Mood Apart.* New York: HarperPerennial, 1997.

Wilcox, Richard E. "Medications and the Brain: How Our Brains React to
Mental Disorders and Respond to Medications." Presentation for
NAMI–Austin, June 25, 2001.

NOTES

THIS SECTION LISTS the sources used for the statistics and technical information in this book. The bibliography provides complete citations for both these sources and for other materials I used to increase my understanding of mental illness and brain disorders. In addition, it includes citations for books I mention or recommend in the book.

Chapter 1
p. 13: Sidebar - "Violence and Mania": Swanson, 101–136.
p. 17: Sidebar - "Hypersexuality and Promiscuity During Hypomanic and Manic Episodes": Goodwin and Jamison, 37, 310–311.
pp. 19, 20: Sidebars entitled "Alcohol Abuse" and "Drug Abuse": Sloan, 2, 6.

Chapter 2
p. 25: Sidebar - "Hyposexuality and Reduced Libido During Depression": Goodwin and Jamison, 311.
p. 30: In *The Noonday Demon*: Solomon, 86.
p. 34: When depression strikes alone: Crow, 7.

Chapter 3
p. 37: Sidebar - "Teen and Adolescent Suicide": Jamison, *Night Falls Fast*, 89–90.
p. 44: Sidebar - "Substance Abuse and Suicide": Jamison, *Night Falls Fast*, 126–128; Quinnett, *Ask a Question, Save a Life*, 12.

Chapter 4
p. 51: Sidebar - "Mental Illness and Suicide": Jamison, *Night Falls Fast*, 100–102; National Institute of Mental Health. *The Numbers Count*.

p. 52: . . . people confuse the terms mood: *Bipolar Treatment*. Panel presentation. National Depression and Manic Depression Association Conference, Houston, Texas, Oct. 3, 1999; Ratey and Johnson, 150.

p. 54: People go through stages of grief: Kübler-Ross, *On Death and Dying*, viv.

p. 55: Forty-four percent of the respondents: Lewis.

p. 55: It's akin to having "walking pneumonia": Ratey and Johnson, 30.

pp. 57–58: Information about "naysayers" and Scientologists: Citizens Commission on Human Rights; Torrey and Knable, 295–297.

p. 60: Advance Directives: Advocacy, Inc. "How to Make an Advance Directive."

Chapter 5

p. 65: . . . time to seek treatment: Whybrow, 101–102.

p. 68: . . . the majority of doctors: Lewis.

p. 73: Table 1—"Depression in Unipolar or Bipolar Disorder" adapted from American Psychiatric Association. *Diagnostic and Statistical Manual of Mental Disorders: DSM-IV,* 317, 327, 349.

p. 75: Table 2—"Manic and Hypomanic Episodes in Bipolar (but Not Unipolar) Disorder" adapted from American Psychiatric Association. *DSM-IV,* 328, 329, 335.

p. 76: In children and young adolescents: Mondimore, 160.

p. 76: Older adolescents and adults: National Institute of Mental Health. *Bipolar Disorder Research at the National Institute of Mental Health*, 10.

p. 76: While unipolar disorders tend to emerge: National Depressive and Manic-Depressive Association. "Facts About Depression."

p. 76: . . . older adults with late-onset versus early-onset: National Institute of Mental Health. *Bipolar Disorder Research at the National Institute of Mental Health*, 11-12.

pp. 74, 76: Sidebars entitled "Childhood and Adolescent Depression" and "Childhood and Adolescent Mania and Hypomania" adapted from Papolos and Papolos. *The Bipolar Child*, 13–15, 19–23, 40, 41, 51, 52.

p. 74: An estimated one-third of children and adolescents: *American Academy of Child and Adolescent Psychiatry*.

p. 78: Table 3—"Basic Types of Bipolar Disorders" adapted from American Psychiatric Association. *DSM-IV,* 317, 318.

p. 78: One-third of those with cyclothymic disorder: Ratey and Johnson, 107.

p. 79: Rapid cyclying involves: National Depressive and Manic-Depressive Association. *Bipolar Disorder: Rapid Cycling and Its Treatment,* 4–5.

p. 81: People who have dysthymia in childhood: Whybrow, 110.

p. 81: . . . bipolar II disorder may be the most unrecognized: Sichel and Driscoll, p. 69.

p. 82: Table 4—"Early Warning Signs" adapted from National Depressive and Manic-Depressive Association. *Living with Manic-Depressive Illness,* 15.

Chapter 6

p. 85: . . . some psychiatric disorders may be autoimmune disorders as well: Gold, 70–71.

p. 86: People with lupus: Arthritis Foundation. *Arthritis Information: Systemic Lupus Erythematosus (Lupus),* 4–5, 7.

p. 87: One-fourth to one-half of people: National Mental Health Association. "Co-Occurrence of Depression with Medical, Psychiatric, and Substance Abuse Disorders" and "Co-occurrence of Manic Depression with Medical, Psychiatric, and Substance Abuse Disorders."

p. 89: Although it responds slower than the nervous system: Gold, 128–129.

p. 90: . . . when your thyroid hormone drops too low: Gold, 130.

p. 90: Thyroid disease is especially common in women: Cronkite, 161; National Depressive and Manic-Depressive Association. *Bipolar Disorder: Rapid Cycling and Its Treatment.*

p. 95: The most common co-occurring conditions in adults: Cronkite (quoting A. John Rush), 29; Kahn, Ross, Printz, and Sachs, 2; Papolos and Papolos. *The Bipolar Child,* 209.

p. 97: . . . drugs and alcohol to intensify: Brady and Sonne, 19–24.

p. 100: Here's what doctors *do* know: Gold, 318.

p. 101: Substantial evidence indicates: Gold, 175–176.

Chapter 7

p. 108: We have an estimated 100 billion: Hobson, 28.

p. 108: . . . glia . . . "hold the brain together": Andreasen, *The Broken Brain,* 124–125; Marano, 34; Torrey and Knable, 111-112.

p. 112: A number of factors (including heredity, physical condition, and environment): Howard, 2000, 45.

p. 114: When we're stressed or traumatized: Howard, 40.

p. 115: Second messengers: Mondimore, 80–82; Torrey and Knable, 125.

p. 116: Because of the close relationship: Papolos and Papolos. *Overcoming Depression,* 91; Gold, 131.

p. 117: Sidebar—"Hormones That Affect Moods": Andreasen, *Brave New Brain,* 77; Satcher.

p. 118: Estrogen . . . affects the firing rates of neurotransmitters: Sichel and Driscoll, 51.

p. 119: Because the protein molecules: Whybrow, 83.

p. 119: . . . lithium actually *stimulates* neuron production: Travis, 309.

p. 119: . . . multiple genes appear to cause many mental disorders: Satcher.

p. 119: The 1999 U.S. Surgeon General's report: Satcher.

p. 120: In roughly one out of four: Staff Interview with John Nurnberger, 62, 70.

p. 121: But 80 to 90 percent: National Mental Health Association. "Depression: Bipolar Disorder."

p. 121: Sometimes bipolar disorder even skips: Papolos and Papolos. *The Bipolar Child,* 167.

p. 121: Nor does it reflect the risk: Gerson, 373–401; Mondimore, 195.

p. 121: Table 6—"Approximate Risk of Developing Bipolar Disorder" adapted from Papolos and Papolos. *The Bipolar Child,* 168.

p. 122: . . . rate of concordance in twins: Ratey and Johnson, 120.

p. 122: But because the rate of concordance: Torrey and Knable, 118.

p. 122: Since the 1970s, researchers: Goodwin and Jamison, 163.

p. 123: Although the rates of mood disorders: Goodwin and Jamison, 164.

Chapter 8

p. 125: . . . personality relates: American Psychiatric Association. *Diagnostic and Statistical Manual of Mental Disorders: DSM-IV Text Revision,* 826.

p. 125: The Greek physician Hippocrates: Gleitman, Fridlund, and Reisberg, 685.

p. 125: In 1963, Warren Norman popularized: Norman, 574–583; Tupes and Christal; Howard and Mitchell Howard.

p. 126: In 1965, German-born behavioral psychologist Hans Eysenck: Eysenck and Rachman.

p. 126: Around 1990, Dr. Eysenck: Revelle. Zuckerman. *Psychobiology of Personality*; Zuckerman. "Impulsive Unsocialized Sensation Seeking: The Biological Foundations of a Basic Dimension of Personality," 219–255.

p. 126: . . . roughly 40 percent of our personality: Whybrow, 83.

p. 126: Even animals: Gleitman, Fridlund, and Reisberg, 696–697.

p. 127: In *Shadow Syndromes*: Ratey and Johnson, 141.

p. 130: Explanatory style: McGraw, 168–171.

p. 131: In 1965, a psychologist: Seligman, *Learned Optimism,* 19–28; Seligman and Maier, 1–9.

p. 133: She says all people have four "quadrants": Kübler-Ross, *The Tunnel and the Light,* 42–43.

p. 135: One further trap: Mustin.

Chapter 9

p. 138: Researchers at the National Institute of Mental Health: Duke, 98.

p. 138: A functional, healthy family: Bradshaw, 42, 54, 55.

p. 140: Maturity requires that individuals: Bradshaw, 42.

p. 143: In 1990, a Harvard Business School professor: Argyris.

p. 145: Fair fighting: Bradshaw, 54.

p. 145: . . . the "whisper rule": Otto, Reilly-Harrington, Sachs, and Knauz, eds., with Miklowitz and Frank.

p. 146: The psychoanalyst and researcher: Miller. "An Open Letter to All Responsible Politicians."

p. 147: Some researchers believe that any time: Riak.

p. 148: The organization End Violence Against the Next Generation: Hunt. Note: An earlier version appeared in Appendix D of Miller, *Breaking Down the Wall of Silence.*

Chapter 10

p. 154: These stressors go hand in hand: Papolos and Papolos, *The Bipolar Child*, 211.

p. 154: In 1967, Drs.: Holmes and Rahe, 213–219.

p. 154: An associate professor of management: Hobson, Kamen, Szostek, Nethercut, Tidemann, and Wojnarowicz, 1–23.

p. 155: Healthy levels of cortisol: Andreasen. *Brave New Brain*, 236.

p. 156: . . . stress feedback loop: Andreasen. *Brave New Brain*, 235–236; Andreasen. *The Broken Brain*, 180–181; Papolos and Papolos, *The Bipolar Child*, 211.

p. 156: If your hypothalamus doesn't stop: Sichel and Driscoll, 52–53.

p. 157: Through MRI studies: McEwen, Gould, and Sakai, 18–24.

p. 159: Post-traumatic stress disorder: Cronkite (quoting Stephen P. Hersh), 38.

Chapter 11

p. 167: Maslow's Hierarchy of Needs: Maslow, 15–25, 57.

p. 169: The founders of the Hestia Institute: Sichel and Driscoll, p. 147.

p. 170: In fact, sleep deprivation: Andreasen, *The Broken Brain*, 51.

p. 170: . . . losing even a single night's sleep: National Institute of Mental Health. *Bipolar Research at the National Institute of Health*, 1–2.

p. 170: Sidebar—"Tips for Getting a Good Night's Sleep": Otto, Reilly-Harrington, Sachs, and Knauz, eds., with Miklowitz and Frank, 24.

p. 171: Because biorhythms also affect blood sugar: Swedo and Leonard, 134; Sichel and Driscoll, 148.

p. 172: Carbohydrate metabolism clearly changes: Goodwin and Jamison, 483.

p. 174: In sugar-sensitive people: DesMaisons, *Potatoes Not Prozac*, 50.

p. 179: Cholesterol: Norden, 98; Ratey and Johnson, 352; U.S. Department of Agriculture and U.S. Department of Health and Human Services, 14–15.

p. 174: Although a simple sugar, fructose: American Diabetic Association. *Nutrition: Sweetners.*

p. 177: Sidebar—"Taming Your Sweet Tooth": DesMaisons, *Potatoes Not Prozac*, 49; DesMaisons, *The Sugar Addict's Total Recovery Program*, 22–25, 163.

p. 177: . . . the universal favorite chocolate: Cronkite (quoting Barbara Parry), 167.

p. 178: Sidebar—"Soluble and Insoluble Fiber": American Dietetic Association. *Fiber Facts: Soluble Fiber and Heart Disease.*

p. 178: Nutrition experts recommend a minimum: Note: Currently, the American Cancer Society and National Cancer Institute recommend 20–30 grams, and the U.S. Surgeon General recommends 35–40 grams.

p. 179: Blood cholesterol levels under 160: Norden, 98.

p. 180: Food Guide Pyramid: U.S. Department of Agriculture, 14.

p. 180: Both complex carbohydrates and proteins: Amen, 80–81.

p. 181: MAOI diet restrictions: Keltner and Folks, 108; Mondimore, 107; UPMC Health System.

p. 182: You may not think of tobacco: DesMaisons, 176.

p. 182: More than half of people with bipolar disorder: National Mental Health Association. *Co-Occurrence of Depression with Medical, Psychiatric, and Substance Abuse Disorders.*

p. 183: Even a single workout: Norden, 75.

p. 183: Aim for a moderate aerobic workout: Norden, 79.

Chapter 12

p. 187: "We're dealing with a person . . .": Yudofsky.

p. 195: . . . lithium (and possibly other mood-stabilizing agents): Mondimore, 81.

p. 195: Lithium appears to block: National Institute of Mental Health. *Bipolar Disorder.*

p. 199: . . . this term [half-life] is misleading: Wilcox.

p. 199: . . . when discontinued too quickly: Maxmen and Ward, 336–337.

p. 201: In *A Brilliant Madness*: Duke, 99.

p. 202: Because estrogen affects acetylcholine: Sichel and Driscoll, 51.

p. 202: Normal menopause-related hormonal fluctuations: Sichel and Driscoll, 279.

p. 205: Electroconvulsive therapy: Restak, *The Mind,* 188; Manning, 121.

p. 206: The only side effect [of TMS]: George, 1999.

p. 207: . . . one-third of people with mood disorders: Papolos and Papolos, *Overcoming Depression.*

Chapter 13

p. 210: Studies have confirmed that psychotherapy: National Institute of Mental Health, *Bipolar Disorder,* 16.

p. 216: Both clinical psychologist and classic learning theorist: Gleitman, Fridlund, and Reisberg, 481; Viscott, 70.

p. 216: . . . our five primary emotions: Kübler-Ross, *The Tunnel and the Light,* 49.

p. 216: Psychology professor and director of the Langley Porter Psychiatric Institute: Ekman, "An Argument for Basic Emotions," 169–200.

p. 217: . . . timing as it relates to feelings: Viscott, 72.

p. 217: . . . which emotion you feel depends on: Weiner, "The Emotions Consequences of Causal Attributions."

p. 221: Recovery's support groups use techniques: Recovery, Inc.

p. 222: *Co-counseling (or peer counseling):* Copeland, 160–171.

Chapter 14

p. 225: The . . . (DSHEA) . . . defines a dietary supplement: U.S. Food and Drug Administration Center for Food Safety and Applied Nutrition. *Overview of Dietary Supplements.*

p. 227: Vitamins: Amen; Balch and Balch, 16–22; Bernstein, 250–260; Netzer, 687, 695–700; National Institutes of Health Clinical Center; Swedo and Leonard, 89.

p. 230: To best absorb vitamin supplements (see sidebar—"Cautions and Notes About Vitamin Supplements"): Howard, 2000, 100.

p. 231: Minerals: Balch and Balch, 27–33, 318; Baumel, 78; Dubovsky, Murphy, Christiano, and Lee, 3–14; National Institutes of Health Clinical Center; Netzer, xv; Norden, 92–93; Swedo and Leonard, 182.

p. 231: Sidebar—"Caution for Those with Insulin-Dependent Diabetes": Balch and Balch, 28.

p. 234: To best absorb mineral supplements (see sidebar) "Two Cautions and a Note about Mineral Supplements": Howard, 2000, 100.

p. 235: Amino acids: Balch and Balch, 45, 47-50, 317; Baumel, 67–72; Wurtman and Suffes, 20–21.

p. 236: Sidebar—"Caution for People Allergic to MSG": Balch and Balch, 47.

p. 237: Sidebar—"Caution Regarding Histadine": Balch and Balch, 48.

p. 237: Sidebar—"Cautions about Phenylalanine": Balch and Balch, 50.

p. 240: Herbs: Swedo and Leonard, 182.

p. 240: Sidebar—"Cautions about Ginkgo": Balch and Balch, 99, Therapeutic Research Faculty.

p. 241: Sidebar—"Cautions about Kava": Center for Food Safety and Applied Nutrition, U.S. Food and Drug Administration. "Kava-Containing Dietary Supplements May Be Associated with Severe Liver Injury." *www.dfsan.fda.gov/~dms/addskava.html,* March 25, 2002.

p. 241:. . . you have a fifty-fifty chance: Schardt. "SAM-e SO-SO," 10–11.

p. 241: . . . only eleven of the twenty-three [SAM-e] products: *Consumer Reports,* Oct. 1999.

p. 242: Sidebar—"Cautions about St. John's Wort": Schardt. "St. John's Worts and All," 6–8.

p. 242: A Canadian study: Kaplan, et al. *Journal of Clinical Psychiatry,* Dec. 2001.

p. 243: Homeopathy: Davis; Ullman, 5–6, 14, 42.

p. 245: Sidebar—"Cautions about Massage": Center for Mental Health Services Knowledge Exchange Network (KEN). *Alternative Approaches to Mental Health Care;* Lamberton.

p. 245: Aromatherapy: Baumel, 152; Lamberton.

p. 246: Biofeedback: Center for Mental Health Services Knowledge Exchange Network (KEN). *Alternative Approaches to Mental Health Care.*

p. 247: Phototherapy: Baumel, 163; Copeland, 73; Papolos and Papolos, *The Bipolar Child,* 112–113; Wurtman and Suffes, 187.

p. 249: Negative ion generators: Howard, *The Owners Manual for the Brain,* 2000, 687.

Chapter 15

p. 257: Protecting your employment rights: Advocacy, Inc. Handout #321: "Employment Advice for Persons with Psychiatric Disabilities"; Americans with Disabilities Act.

p. 264: To cope with your disorder: Arthritis Foundation. *Coping with Stress: Making Stress Work for You,* 4.

p. 265: Therapeutic humor: Sultanoff, 1.

pp. 266–267: Reducing your worries and problem-solving tips: Otto, Reilly-Harrington, Sachs, and Knauz, eds., with Miklowitz and Frank, 25–27.

p. 269: It takes an average of twenty-one days: Milteer.

Chapter 16

p. 273: An impaired limbic system: Morrison.

p. 274: Attempting to be logical: Thompson, 234.

p. 274: Exercise #1: Adapted from Brothers, *Positive Plus.*

p. 274: Exercise #2: Adapted from Crystal and Bolles, 191.

p. 276: McGraw's four criteria: McGraw, 217.

p. 276: New Age thinkers use: Tice, FM III-4.

p. 277: In the mid 1940s and early 1950s: Horney, 6485.

p. 277: . . . the term *mus*turbation: Ellis and Harper, 203.

p. 277: . . . three basic *musts*: Ellis, 60.

p. 280: Perhaps this approach worked: Thompson, 234.

p. 281: Healthcare professionals also use visualization: Center for Mental Health Services Knowledge Exchange Network (KEN) *Alternative Approaches to Mental Health Care.*

p. 281: One of the most fascinating applications: Simonton, Matthews-Simonton, and Creighton, 135.

p. 282: One of the Simontons' cancer patients: Matthews-Simonton.

p. 282: . . . creating an *image book*: Mustin; Butler and Butler.

Chapter 17

p. 285: Since at least the time of Greek philosopher: Torrey and Knable, 267; Mondimore, 209.

p. 286: Table 11—"Some Public Figures with Acknowledged Mood Episodes or Disorders": Ikelman; National Depressive and Manic-Depressive Association. *A Guide to Depressive and Manic-Depressive Illness,* 13; National Depressive and Manic-Depressive Association. *Consumer's Guide to Depression and Manic Depression,* 12; Mood Disorders Society of Canada, Inc.; Pendulum Resources.

p. 287: From a study of forty-seven award-winning: Jamison, *Touched with Fire,* 125–124.

p. 287: Sidebar—"Simply Creative or Mentally Ill?": Jamison, *Touched with Fire,* 79.

p. 288: Nearly all of Dr. Jamison's subjects: Jamison, *Touched with Fire,* 78.

p. 288: Dr. Arnold Ludwig: Ludwig, 330–356.

p. 292: When I first read psychotherapist Richard Carson's: Carson, 106–109.

p. 294: Releasing buried or disturbing feelings: Center for Mental Health Services Knowledge Exchange Network (KEN). *Alternative Approaches to Mental Health Care.*

p. 294: Author Tracy Thompson: Thompson, 259.

p. 295: Dance or movement therapy: Center for Mental Health Services Knowledge Exchange Network (KEN). *Alternative Approaches to Mental Health Care.*

p. 295: Drama therapy: National Association for Drama Therapy. Last modified July 10, 2002. *www.nadt.org/html/About.htm*

p. 295: Music therapy: Center for Mental Health Services Knowledge Exchange Network (KEN). *Alternative Approaches to Mental Health Care.*

p. 296: Dr. James Pennebaker: Pennebaker and Francis, 280–287. Note: Dr. Pennebaker is now at the University of Texas at Austin.

p. 299: *Self-fulfillment or self-actualization:* Maslow, *Motivation and Personality,* 126.

p. 299: Some people see self-fulfillment: Maslow, *Motivation and Personality,* 127.

p. 300: After diet and exercise: Ratey and Johnson, 363.

p. 300: Our bodies function best: Northrup, 501.

p. 301: Richard Bolles: Bolles.

Chapter 18

p. 304: However, just as God: Kübler-Ross, *The Tunnel and the Light,* 141.

p. 305: Researchers have found the faithful: Newberg, D'Aquili, and Rause, 130.

p. 305: Mark (15:34): King James Version.

p. 308: Serenity Prayer: Spiritwalk.

p. 310: Dr. Abraham Maslow expressed his concern: Maslow, *Religions, Values, and Peak-Experiences,* viii, 4, 14, 24, 33–35.

p. 313: Relaxation and meditation: Newberg, D'Aquili, and Rause, 117, 120.

p. 314: Tai chi: Tom Gohring's School of T'ai chi. *www.taichitom.com/qigong(chee-kung).html*

p. 315: Yoga: Center for Mental Health Services Knowledge Exchange Network (KEN). *Alternative Approaches to Mental Health Care.*

p. 315: One interesting theory: Gleick, 5, 8, 11, 16, 20, 21.

p. 316: At the 1979 annual meeting: Lorenz.

p. 317: The highest growth need: Maslow, *Religions, Values, and Peak-Experiences,* xvi, 41–42, 59–68.

Chapter 19

p. 320: How to tell when it's time to seek treatment: Fieve, 187–193.

pp. 322–324: Tables 12–14—"Potential Ways to Help Someone in a Depressive Episode," "Potential Ways to Help Someone in a Hypomanic or Early Manic Episode," and "Indicators That It's Time to Consider Hospitalization": Adapted from "Fieve-Dunner Manic-Depressive Mood Scale." Fieve, p. 203.

p. 324: Some states require that patients: Advocacy, Inc: "Rights of People Receiving Voluntary Inpatient Mental Health Services."

p. 325: Although exact criteria for involuntary commitment: Amadore, 156–172.

p. 325: A judge's options: Advocacy, Inc: "A Consumer's Guide to the Commitment Process Under the Texas Mental Health Code: Advocating the Legal Rights of Texas with Mental Illness."

p. 329: . . . by writing a crisis plan: Advocacy, Inc: "How to Make an Advance Directive"; Copeland, 211–217, 241–248.

p. 330: About 25 percent of people with bipolar disorder: Torrey, 101.

p. 330: Around 55 to 65 percent improve enough to work: Torrey and Knable, 101.

Chapter 20

p. 331: The vast majority of people with mental illness: Carter, 17.

p. 331: A 1996 survey: National Mental Health Association. *American Attitudes About Clinical Depression and Its Treatments.*

p. 332: Stigma from a historical perspective: Andreasen, *The Broken Brain,* 1–2, 142–150; Gleitman, Fridlund, and Reisberg, 758–761; Satcher; Van Atta in collaboration with Roby and Roby, 1.

p. 333: The Mental Health Bell: National Mental Health Association, *The NMHA Bell Story.*

p. 334: Sixteen percent of incarcerated people: National Alliance for the Mentally Ill, 1999.

p. 334: The largest "mental health treatment facility": National Health Care for the Homeless Council, "Incarceration, Homelessness and Health."

p. 334: But mental illness strikes about one in five: Satcher.

p. 334: However . . . Dr. Robert Hirschfeld: Hirschfeld; National Depressive and Manic-Depressive Association, News release. "New Data Suggest Bipolar Disorder May Affect Three Times More Americans Than Believed."

p. 336: One study found: Phelan, Link, Stueve, and Pescosolido. "Public Conceptions of Mental Illness in 1950 in 1996: Has Sophistication Increased?"

p. 336: When people commit violent crimes: National Mental Health Association, *MHIC: Mental Illness and the Family: Stigma: Building Awareness and Understanding About Mental Illness.*

p. 336: Sidebar—"Violence and Mental Illness": Phelan, Link, Stueve, and Pescosolido; Swanson in Monahan and Steadman, 101–136; Eronen, Markku, Angermeyer, and Schulze, S13–S23; Steadman, Mulvey, Monahan, Robbins, Appelbaum, Grisso, Roth, and Silver, 393–401; Swartz, Swanson, and Burns, S75–S80; Mulvey and Fardella, 40.

p. 337: Sidebar—"U.S. Suicide versus Homicide Rates": Jamison. Speech delivered for St. Stephens Parent Association.

p. 338: Although exact numbers are impossible: Fazel and Danesh, 545–550.

p. 338: Up to one-fifth of homeless people: American Psychological Association.

p. 342: In a 1999 online survey: Lewis.

Epilogue

p. 346: Three-fourths of those who end their own lives: American Foundation for Suicide Prevention, "When You Suspect Suicide."

BIBLIOGRAPHY

Advocacy, Inc. "A Consumer's Guide to the Commitment Process under the Texas Mental Health Code: Advocating the Legal Rights of Texan with Mental Illness." Handout #311. Austin, TX: Advocacy, Inc., Rev. Jan. 1996.

————"Employment Advice for Persons with Psychiatric Disabilities." Handout #321: Austin, TX: Advocacy, Inc., April 1997.

————"How to Make an Advance Directive." Handout #317. Austin, TX: Advocacy, Inc., Rev. Oct. 2000.

————"Rights of People Receiving Voluntary Inpatient Mental Health Services." Handout #303. Austin, TX: Advocacy, Inc., Rev. Feb. 1995.

Allen, John J. B., and Rosa N. Schnyer. "The Efficacy of Acupuncture in the Treatment of Major Depression in Women." *Psychological Science,* Sept. 1998, Vol. 9 Issue 5, 397–401.

Amadore, Xavier. *I Am Not Sick: I Don't Need Help!: Helping the Seriously Mentally Ill Accept Treatment—A Practical Guide for Families and Therapists.* Peconic, NY: Vida Press, LLC, 2000.

Amen, Daniel G. *Change Your Brain, Change Your Life.* New York: Three Rivers, 1998.

American Diabetes Association, Inc. and The American Dietetic Association. *Exchange Lists for Weight Management.* Chicago: ADA, 1999.

————*Nutrition: Sweeteners. www.diabetes.org/80/main/ application/commercewf?origin=*.jsp&event=link(F1_2)

American Dietetic Association. *Fiber Facts: Soluble Fiber and Heart Disease.* Posted in 1999. *www.eatright.com/nfs/nfs88.html*

American Foundation for Suicide Prevention. *"Facts about Suicide."* Undated fact sheet based on 1997 rates.

American Psychiatric Association. *Diagnostic and Statistical Manual of Mental Disorders: DSM-IV.* Washington, DC: APA, 1994.

————*Diagnostic and Statistical Manual of Mental Disorders: DSM-IV Text Revision.* Washington, DC: APA, 2000.

Americans with Disabilities Act. *www.usdoj.gov/crt/ada/adahom1.htm*

Andreasen, Nancy C. *Brave New Brain: Conquering Mental Illness in the Era of the Genome.* New York: Oxford University Press, 2001.

―――*The Broken Brain: The Biological Revolution in Psychiatry.* New York: Harper and Row, 1984.

Andreasen, Nancy C., and Donald W. Black. *Introductory Textbook of Psychiatry.* Washington, DC: American Psychiatric Press, Inc., 1991.

Argyris, Chris. *Overcoming Organizational Defenses: Facilitating Organizational Learning.* Boston: Allyn and Bacon, 1990.

Artal, Michel, with Carl Sherman. "Exercise Against Depression." *The Physician and Sports Medicine,* vol. 26, no. 10, Oct. 1998.

Arthritis Foundation. *Arthritis Information: Systemic Lupus Erythematosus (Lupus),* booklet. Atlanta: Arthritis Foundation, 1990.

―――*Coping with Stress: Making Stress Work for You.* Publication No. 9326/10-90. Atlanta: Arthritis Foundation.

Balch, Phyllis A., and James F. Balch. *Prescription for Nutritional Healing. 3rd ed.* New York: Avery/Penguin Putnam Inc., 2000

Baumel, Syd. *Dealing with Depression Naturally, The Drugless Approach to the Condition that Darkens Millions of Lives.* New Canaan, CT: Keats Publishing, Inc., 1995.

Becker, Gretchen. *Type 2 Diabetes: An Essential Guide for the Newly Diagnosed.* New York: Marlowe & Company, 2001.

Benson, Herbert, with Miriam Z. Klipper. *The Relaxation Response.* New York: Avon, 1975.

Bernstein, A. L. "Vitamin B_6 in Clinical Neurology." *Annals of the New York Academy of Sciences,* 1990, 585:250–260.

Biederman, Joseph. "Further Evidence of a Bidirectional Overlap between Juvenile Mania and Conduct Disorder in Children." *Journal of the American Academy of Child and Adolescent Psychiatry,* April 1999.

Bolles, Richard N. *What Color Is Your Parachute?: A Practical Manual for Job-Hunters and Career-Changers.* Berkeley, CA: Ten Speed Press, updated annually.

Bradshaw, John. *Bradshaw On: The Family―A Revolutionary Way of Self-Discovery.* Deerfield Beach, FL: Health Communications, Inc., 1988.

Brady, Kathleen, and Susan Sonne. "The Relationship between Substance Abuse and Bipolar Disorder." *Journal of Clinical Psychiatry,* 56, Suppl. 3, 1995, 19–24.

Brothers, Joyce. *Positive Plus: The Practical Plan for Liking Yourself Better.* New York: G. P. Putnam's Sons, 1994.

Burland, Joyce. *What Hurts, What Helps: A Guide to What Families of Individuals with Serious Brain Disorders Need from Mental Health Professionals. 4th ed.* Arlington, VA: NAMI, 1997.

Butler, Melissa, and Jessie Butler. Personal communication. Austin, Texas.

Cameron, Julia. *The Artist's Way: A Spiritual Path to Higher Creativity.* New York: Jeremy P. Tarcher/G. P. Putnam's Sons, 1992.

Carson, Richard. *Taming Your Gremlin: A Guide to Enjoying Yourself.* New York: Harper Perennial, 1983.

Carter, Rosalynn. *Helping Someone with Mental Illness.* New York: Times Books/Random House, 1999.

Center for Food Safety and Applied Nutrition, U.S. Food and Drug Administration. "Consumer Advisory: Kava-Containing Dietary Supplements May be Associated with Severe Liver Injury." March 25, 2002. *www.cfsan.fda.gov/~dma/addskava.html*

Center for Mental Health Services, U.S. Department of Health and Human Services, 1996.

Center for Mental Health Services Knowledge Exchange Network (KEN). *Alternative Approaches to Mental Health Care.* Posted March 2001. *www.mentalhealth.org/publications/allpubs/ken98-0044/default.asp*

Center for Science in the Public Interest. "Chemical Cusine." *Nutrition Action Healthletter,* March 1999, 4–9.

———"SAM-e SO SO." *Nutrition Action Healthletter.*

———*Stevia: Not Ready for Prime Time.* CSPI Press Release. *www.cspinet.org/new/stevia/html,* downloaded May 2002.

Citizens Commission on Human Rights: *www.cchr.org*

Cloud, John. "Mental Health Reform: What It Would Really Take." *Time,* June 7, 1999, 54–56.

Consumer Reports "The Low Down on SAM-e." Oct. 1999.

Copeland, Mary Ellen. *Living without Depression and Manic Depression: A Workbook for Maintaining Mood Stability.* Oakland, CA: New Harbinger, 1994.

Cousins, Norman. *Anatomy of an Illness as Perceived by the Patient: Reflections on Healing and Regeneration.* New York: W. W. Norton, 1979.

Cowdry, Rex. *Commonly Prescribed Psychotropic Medications.* *www.nami.org/helpline/medlist.htm.*

Cronkite, Kathy. *On the Edge of Darkness: Conversations about Conquering Depression.* New York: Doubleday, 1994.

Crow, John, ed. *Advancing Mental Health: A Guide for Journalists.* Chicago: NDMDA, 1996.

Crystal, John C., and Richard N. Bolles. *Where Do I Go From Here with My Life?* Berkeley, CA: Ten Speed Press, 1974.

Davis, Stephen E. Personal communication and unpublished paper entitled "Mood Foods." Austin, TX.

Davidson, Jonathan R. T., and Kathryn M. Connor. *Herbs for the Mind: Depression, Stress, Memory Loss, and Insomnia.* New York: Guilford Press, 2000.

Davidson, Richard J. "Ask the Doctors." *Outreach: Newsletter of the National Depressive and Manic-Depressive Association,* summer 2002.

DesMaisons, Kathleen. *Potatoes Not Prozac.* New York: Simon and Schuster, 1998.

———*The Sugar Addict's Total Recovery Program.* New York: Ballantine, 2000.

Dowling, Colette. *You Mean I Don't Have to Feel This Way?: New Help for Depression, Anxiety, and Addiction.* New York: Charles Scribner's Sons, 1991.

Dubovsky, Steven L., James R. Murphy, John M. Christiano, and Chau-Shoun Lee. "The Calcium Second Messenger System in Bipolar Disorders: Data Supporting New Research Directions." *Journal of Neuropsychiatry and Clinical Neurosciences,* winter 1992, 4(1):3–14.

Duke, Patty. *A Brilliant Madness: Living with Manic-Depressive Illness.* New York: Bantam, 1992.

Ekman, Paul. "An Argument for Basic Emotions." *Cognition and Emotion,* 6:169–200.

Elbert, Douglas P. "The Public Mental Health System Isn't Working Well Today: Views of One Mental Health Consumer." *NAMI Texas News,* vol. 16 no. 2, April/May 2002, 8.

Ellis, Albert. *How to Stubbornly Refuse to Make Yourself Miserable about Any-thing—Yes, Anything.* New York: Carol Publishing, 1994.

Ellis, Albert, and Robert A. Harper. *A New Guide to Rational Living.* North Hollywood, CA: Wilshire, 1975.

Engler, Jack, and Daniel Goleman. *The Consumer's Guide to Psychotherapy.* New York: Simon and Schuster/Fireside, 1992.

Eronen, Markku, Matthias C. Angermeyer, and Beate Schulze. "The Psychiatric Epidemiology of Violent Behaviour." *Social Psychiatry and Psychiatric Epidemiology,* 33 (Suppl. 1) 1998, S13–S23.

Evans, Patricia. *The Verbally Abusive Relationship: How to Recognize It and How to Respond.* Holbrook, MA: Bob Adams, Inc., 1992.

———*Verbal Abuse Survivors Speak Out on Relationship and Recovery.* Holbrook, MA: Bob Adams, Inc., 1993.

Eysenck, Hans J., and Stanley Rachman. *The Causes and Cures of Neurosis.* San Diego, CA: Knapp, 1965.

Faber, Adele, and Elaine Mazlish. *How to Talk So Kids Will Listen & Listen So Kids Will Talk.* New York: Avon, 1982.

Fawcett, Jan, Bernard Golden, and Nancy Rosenfeld. *New Hope for People with Bipolar Disorder.* Roseville, CA: Prima Health, 2000.

Fazel, S., and J. Danesh. "Serious Mental Disorder in 23,000 Prisoners: A Systematic Review of 62 Surveys." *The Lancet.* 2002, 359(9306):545–550.

Fieve, Ronald R. *Moodswing.* Revised and expanded edition. New York: William Morrow, 1989.

Fitzgerald, P. B., T. L. Brown, and Z. J. Daskalakis. "The Application of Transcranial Magnetic Stimulation in Psychiatry and Neurosciences Research." *Acta Psychiatr Scand* 2002: 105: 324–340.

Gach, Michael Reed. *Acupressure's Potent Points: A Guide to Self-Care for Common Ailments.* New York: Bantam, 1990.

George, Mark. *Depression Management,* panel presentation. National Depressive and Manic-Depressive Association Annual Conference, Houston, Texas, Oct. 2, 1999.

Gerson, Elliot. "Genetics" in Goodwin, Frederick K., and Kay Redfield Jamison. *Manic-Depressive Illness*. New York: Oxford University Press, 1990, 373–401.

Gleick, James. *Chaos: Making a New Science*. New York: Viking/Penguin, 1987.

Gleitman, Henry, Alan J. Fridlund, and Daniel Reisberg. *Psychology, 5th ed*. New York: W. W. Norton, 1999.

Goble, Frank G. *The Third Force: The Psychology of Abraham Maslow*. New York: Grossman, 1970.

Gold, Mark S. *The Good News about Depression*. New York: Bantam, 1995.

Goldberg, Natalie. *Writing Down the Bones: Freeing the Writer Within*. Boston: Shambhala, 1986.

Goleman, Daniel, and Joel Gurin, eds. *Mind/Body Medicine: How to Use Your Mind for Better Health*. Yonkers, NY: Consumer Reports Books, 1993.

Goodwin, Frederick K., and Kay Redfield Jamison. *Manic-Depressive Illness*. New York: Oxford University Press, 1990.

Goor, Ron, and Nancy Goor. *Eater's Choice. 5th ed*. New York: Houghton Mifflin, 1999.

Gorenstein, Ethan E. *The Science of Mental Illness*. New York: Academic Press/Harcourt Brace Jovanovich, 1992.

Hales, Robert E., Stuart C. Yudofsky, and John A. Talbott, eds. *The American Psychiatric Press Textbook of Psychiatry*. Washington, DC: American Psychiatric Press, Inc., 1999.

Hark, Lisa. *Bulk Up on Fiber*. New Providence, NJ: Center for Cardiovascular Education, 2000.

Herman, Judith Lewis. *Trauma and Recovery*. New York: Basic, 1997.

Hirschfeld, Robert A., et al. "Lifetime Prevalence of Bipolar I and II Disorders in the United States." American Psychiatric Association Annual Meeting, May 2002.

Hobbs, Christopher. *Stress & Natural Healing*. Loveland, CO: Interweave Press, 1997.

Hobson, Charles J., J. Kamen, J. Szostek, C. M. Nethercut, J. W. Tidemann, and S. Wojnarowicz. "Stressful Life Events: A Revision and Update of the Social Readjustment Rating Scale." *International Journal of Stress Management,* 1998 5 (11):1–23.

Hobson, J. Allan. *The Chemistry of Conscious States*. Boston: Back Bay Books/Little, Brown, 1994.

Holmes, Thomas H., and Richard H. Rahe. "The Social Readjustment Rating Scale." *Journal of Psychosomatic Research*, vol. 11, no. 2:213–219.

Horney, Karen. *Neurosis and Human Growth*. New York: W. W. Norton, 1950

Howard, Pierce J. *The Owner's Manual for the Brain: Everyday Applications from Mind-Brain Research*. Austin, TX: Leornian Press/Bard Productions, 1994.

———*The Owners Manual for the Brain: Everyday Applications from Mind-Brain Research, 2nd ed*. Atlanta: Bard Productions, 2000.

Howard, Pierce J., and Jane Mitchell Howard. *The Big Five Quickstart: An Introduction to the Five-Factor Model of Personality for Human Resource Professionals*. Posted in 2000. *http://centacs.com/quikindx.htm*

Hunt, Jan. "Ten Reasons Not to Hit Your Kids." Berkeley, CA: End Violence Against the Next Generation (EVAN-G).

Huxley, N. A., S. V. Parikh, and R. J. Baldessarini. "Effectiveness of Psychosocial Treatments in Bipolar Disorder: State of the Evidence," *Harvard Review of Psychiatry,* vol. 8 no. 3, 2000, 1168–1176.

Hybels-Steer, Mariann. *Aftermath: Survive and Overcome Trauma*. New York: Fireside/Simon & Schuster, 1995.

Ikelman, Joy. *Famous (Living) People Who Have Experienced Depression or Manic-Depression*. Revised April 2, 2002. *www.frii.com/~parrot/living.html*

Jamison, Kay Redfield. *Night Falls Fast: Understanding Suicide*. New York: Knopf, 1999.

———*Touched with Fire: Manic-Depressive Illness and the Artistic Temperament*. New York: Free Press/Simon & Schuster, 1994.

———*An Unquiet Mind: A Memoir of Moods and Madness*. New York: Knopf, 1995.

———Speech delivered for St. Stephens Parent Association. Austin, TX. Nov. 29, 2001.

Jennings-Sauer, Cheryl. *Living Lean by Choosing More*. Dallas, TX: Taylor, 1989.

Kahn, David A., Ruth Ross, A. John Rush, and Susan Panico. *Expert Consensus Treatment Guidelines for Bipolar Disorder: A Guide for Patients and Families,* 1997.

Kahn, David A., Ruth Ross, David J. Printz, and Gary S. Sachs. "Treatment of Bipolar Disorder: A Guide for Patients and Families," *Expert Consensus Guideline*. Bethesda, MD: NIMH, April 2000, *www.psychguides.com/Bipolar_2000_Guide.pdf*

Kaplan, Bonnie, et al. *Journal of Clinical Psychiatry,* Dec. 2001.

Kaplan, Bonnie J., Steven A. Simpson, Richard C. Ferre, Chris P. Gorman, David M. McMullen, and Susan G. Crawford. "Effective Mood Stabilization with a Chelated Mineral Supplement: An Open-Label Trial in Bipolar Disorder." *Journal of Clinical Psychiatry,* Dec. 2001, Vol. 62, 936–944.

Katz, Jack. *How Emotions Work*. Chicago: University of Chicago Press, 1999.

Keltner, Norman L., and David G. Folks. *Psychotropic Drugs, 2nd ed.* St. Louis, MO: Mosby, 1997.

Kersey, Katharine C. *Don't Take It Out on Your Kids!: A Parent's Guide to Positive Discipline*. Revised edition. New York: Berkley Publishing, 1994.

Kramer, Peter D. *Listening to Prozac: A Psychiatrist Explores Antidepressant Drugs and the Remaking of the Self.* New York: Penguin, 1993.

Kübler-Ross, Elisabeth. *On Death and Dying*. New York: Macmillan, 1969.

———*The Tunnel and the Light*. New York: Marlowe, 1999.

Lamberton, Heather. *Aromatherapy and Its Role in Treating Depression*. Posted in 1997. *http://users.breathemail.net/elouera/articles/treatments-for-depression.lwp/003.htm*

Lewis, Lydia. *Ten Barriers to Wellness,* presentation, National Depressive and Manic-Depressive Association 2001 Annual Conference, Cleveland, Ohio, Aug. 18, 2001. Chicago: NDMDA, 2001.

Lorenz, Edward. "Predictability: Does the Flap of a Butterfly's Wings in Brazil Set Off a Tornado in Texas?" *American Association for the Advancement of Science,* 1979 Annual Meeting.

Ludwig, Arnold. "Creative Achievement and Psychopathology: Comparisons Among Professions." *American Journal of Psychotherapy,* 46 (1992): 330–356.

Manning, Martha. *Undercurrents: A Therapist's Reckoning with Her Own Depression.* New York: HarperCollins, 1994.

Marano, Hara Estroff. "Depression: Beyond Serotonin." *Psychology Today,* March/April 1992.

Maslow, Abraham H. *The Farther Reaches of Human Nature.* New York: Viking, 1971.

———*Motivation and Personality, 3rd ed.* Rev. by Robert Frager, James Fadiman, Cynthia McReynolds, and Ruth Cox. New York: Longman/Addison-Wesley, 1987.

———*Religions, Values, and Peak-Experiences.* New York: Arkana/Penguin, 1994.

Matthews-Simonton, Stephanie. "Psychological Intervention in Treatment of Cancer." Audio cassette.

Maxmen, Jerrold S., and Nicholas G. Ward. *Psychotropic Drugs: Fast Facts, 2nd ed.* New York: W. W. Norton, 1995.

McCaleb, Rob. *Stevia Leaf–Too Good to be Legal? www.holisticmed.com/sweet/stv-faq.txt*

McEwen, Bruce S., E. A. Gould, and R. R. Sakai. "The Vulnerability of the Hippocampus to Protective and Destructive Effects of Glucocorticoids in Relation to Stress." *British Journal of Psychiatry,* 160:18–24.

McGraw, Phillip C. *Self Matters: Creating Your Life from the Inside Out.* New York: Simon and Schuster, 2001.

Miller, Alice. *Breaking Down the Wall of Silence.* New York: Penguin, 1997.

———*The Drama of the Gifted Child: The Search for the True Self.* New York: Basic, 1981.

———"An Open Letter to All Responsible Politicians." London: Virago, Feb. 2000.

Milteer, Lee. "Success Self-Programming: Eight Powerful Techniques That Create Success." Audiocassette Program. Boulder, CO: CareerTrack, 1985.

Monahan, John, and Henry J. Steadman (eds.). *Violence and Mental Disorder: Developments in Risk Assessment.* Chicago: University of Chicago Press, 1994.

Mondimore, Francis Mark. *Bipolar Disorder: A Guide for Patients and Families.* Baltimore, MD: John Hopkins University Press, 1999.

Mood Disorders Society of Canada, Inc. "Something in Common." Undated handout.

Morrison, Jack, presentation delivered for Austin DMDA support group, Oct. 18, 2001.

Mulvey, Edward P., and Jess Fardella. "Are the Mentally Ill Really Violent?" *Psychology Today.* Nov./Dec. 2000, 40.

Murphey, Cecil. *Breaking the Silence: Spiritual Help When Someone You Love is Mentally Ill.* Louisville, KY: Westminster/John Knox Press, 1989.

Mustin, Jan Ford. "Putting Your Dreams Into Action." Workshop presented at Charter Lane Hospital, Austin, TX. July 11, 1990.

National Association for Drama Therapy. Last modified July 10, 2002. *www.nadt.org/html/About.htm*

National Depressive and Manic-Depressive Association. Brochure: *Bipolar Disorder: Rapid Cycling and Its Treatment.* Chicago: NDMDA, 2002.

———*Consumer's Guide to Depression and Manic Depression.* NDMDA Publication No. GB 1000. Chicago: NDMDA, 2000.

———"Facts About Depression." Chicago: NDMDA, 2001.

———*Finding Peace of Mind: Medication and Treatment Strategies for Depression.* Brochure GB 3070. Chicago: NDMDA, 2001.

———*A Guide to Depressive and Manic-Depressive Illness: Diagnosis, Treatment and Support.* NDMDA Publication No. GB 1000. Chicago: NDMDA, 1999.

———*Just a Mood . . . or Something Else?* Brochure EB 3003. Chicago: NDMDA, 1999.

———*Living with Manic-Depressive Illness: A Guidebook for Patients, Families and Friends.* Chicago: NDMDA, 1997.

———News release. "New Data Suggest Bipolar Disorder May Affect Three Times More Americans Than Believed." Chicago: NDMDA, May 21, 2002.

———*Suicide Prevention and Depressive Disorders,* Brochure EB 3007. Chicago: NDMDA, 2000.

National Health Care for the Homeless Council. Policy Statement. "Incarceration, Homelessness and Health." June 2001. *www.nhchc.org/policypapers/policypapers2001*

National Institutes of Health Clinical Center. *Facts about Dietary Supplements. www.cc.nih.gov/ccc/supplements*

National Institute of Mental Health. *Anxiety Disorders,* NIH Publication No. 00-3879. Bethesda, MD: NIMH, 1995, Reprinted 2000. *www.nimh.nih.gov/anxiety/anxiety.cfm*

———*Bipolar Disorder,* NIH Publication No. 01-3679. Bethesda, MD: NIMH, 2001.

———*Bipolar Disorder Research at the National Institute of Mental Health,* Fact Sheet, No. 00-4502. Bethesda, MD: NIMH, 2000.

———*Going to Extremes,* NIH Publication No. 01-4595. Bethesda, MD: NIMH, 2001.

———*Medications,* Publication No. 02-3929. Bethesda, MD: NIMH, 2000, revised April 2002.

————*The Numbers Count,* NIH Publication No. 01-4584, 2001.

————*Schizophrenia,* NIH Publication No. 99-3517. Bethesda, MD: NIMH, 1999.

National Mental Health Association. *American Attitudes about Clinical Depression and Its Treatments.* NMHA survey conducted April 16, 1996.

————"Co-Occurrence of Depression with Medical, Psychiatric, and Substance Abuse Disorders." Posted July 2001.

————"Co-Occurrence of Manic Depression with Medical, Psychiatric, and Substance Abuse Disorders." *www.nmha.org/infoctr/factsheets*

————"Depression: Bipolar Disorder." Fact sheet. *www.nmha.org/infoctr/factsheets/25.cfm*

————*Eating Disorders and Depression.* College Student and Depression Fact Sheet. *www.nmha.org/camh/college/eatingdisorders.pdf*

————*MHIC: Mental Illness and the Family: Stigma: Building Awareness and Understanding about Mental Illness.* Fact sheet. Downloaded Feb. 17, 2002. *www.nmha.org/infoctr/factsheets/14.cfm*

————*The NMHA Bell Story.* Downloaded July 19, 2002. *www.nmha.org/about/bellstory.cfm*

————*Stigma: Building Awareness and Understanding about Mental Illness.* NMHA MHIC Fact sheet.

————*Substance Abuse: Dual Diagnosis,* NMHA MHIC Fact sheet.

Netzer, Corinne T. *The Corinne T. Netzer Encyclopedia of Food Values.* New York: Dell, 1992.

Newberg, Andrew, Eugene G. D'Aquili, and Vince Rause. *Why God Won't Go Away: Brain Science and the Biology of Belief.* New York: Ballantine, 2001.

Norden, Michael J. *Beyond Prozac.* New York: HarperCollins, 1995.

Norman, Warren T. "Toward an Adequate Taxonomy of Personality Attributes: Replicated Factor Structure in Peer Nomination Personality Ratings." *Journal of Abnormal and Social Psychology,* 1963, #66, 574–583.

Northrup, Christiane. *Women's Bodies, Women's Wisdom: Creating Physical and Emotional Health and Healing.* New York: Bantam, 1995.

Otto, Michael W., Noreen Reilly-Harrington, Gary S. Sachs, and Robert O. Knauz, eds., with David J. Miklowitz and Ellen Frank. *Collaborative-Care Workbook: A Workbook for Individuals and Families.* Produced for the Systematic Treatment Enhancement Program (STEP) for Bipolar Disorder. Boston: Partners Bipolar Treatment Center, Aug. 1999.

Papolos, Demitri F., and Janice Papolos. *Overcoming Depression.* New York: HarperCollins, 1992.

————*The Bipolar Child.* New York: Broadway, 1999.

Pasternak, Charles A. *The Molecules Within Us: Our Body in Health and Disease.* New York: Plenum, 1998.

Pendulum Resources. "Famous People with Bipolar Disorders," 1999. *www.pendulum.org/pwbpd/famous.htm*

Pennebaker, James W., and Martha E. Francis. "Putting Stress into Words: Writing about Personal Upheavals and Health." *American Journal of Health Promotion* 6, 280–287.

Phelan, Jo C., Bruce G. Link, Ann Stueve, and Bernice A. Pescosolido. "Public Conceptions of Mental Illness in 1950 to 1996: Has Sophistication Increased?" Presentation, American Sociological Association, Toronto, Ontario, Aug. 1997.

Preston, John D. *Lift Your Mood Now: Simple Things You Can Do to Beat the Blues.* Oakland CA: New Harbinger, 2001.

Quinnett, Paul G. *Ask a Question, Save a Life.* Spokane, Washington: QPR Institute, 1995.

———*Suicide: The Forever Decision.* New York: Crossroad, 1987, 1992.

Ratey, John J., and Catherine Johnson. *Shadow Syndromes.* New York: Random House, 1997.

Restak, Richard M. *The Mind.* New York: Bantam, 1988.

———*Receptors.* New York: Bantam, 1994.

Revelle, William. *Personality Processes.* Last modified March 1, 1996. *http://pmc.psych.nwu.edu/revelle/publications/AR.html*

Riak, Jordan. *Plain Talk about Spanking.* Parents and Teachers Against Violence in Education (PTAVE), 1992, revised July 2001. *http://nospank.net/plntk.htm*

Rosen, David H. *Transforming Depression: A Jungian Approach Using the Creative Arts.* New York: Penguin, 1993.

Rush, A. John, Mark S. George, Harold A. Sackeim, Lauren B. Marangell, Mustafa M. Husain, Cole Giller, Ziad Nahas, Stephen Haines, Richard K. Simpson Jr., and Robert Goodman. "Vagus Nerve Stimulation (VNS) for Treatment-Resistant Depressions: A Multicenter Study." *Biological Psychiatry*, vol. 47, no. 4, Feb. 15, 2000, 276–286.

Sachs, Judith. *Nature's Prozac: Natural Therapies and Techniques to Rid Yourself of Anxiety, Depression, Panic Attacks and Stress.* Englewood Cliffs, NJ: Prentice Hall, 1997.

Sapolsky, Robert M. *Why Zebras Don't Get Ulcers: An Updated Guide to Stress, Stress-Related Diseases, and Coping.* New York: W. H. Freeman, 1994, 1998.

Satcher, David. *Mental Health: A Report of the Surgeon General,* 1999. *www.surgeongeneral.gov/library/mentalhealth/home.html*

Schardt, David. "SAM-e SO-SO." *Nutrition Action Healthletter*, March 2001, 10–11.

———"St. John's Worts and All." *Nutrition Action Healthletter*, Sept. 2000, 6–8.

———"Stevia: A Bittersweet Tale." *Nutrition Action Healthletter*, April 2000.

———"Stevia: Not Ready for Prime Time," Center for Science in the Public Interest. Press Release. Posted March 21, 2000, *www.cspinet.org/new/stevia/html*

School of Public Health. "A "Natural" Treatment for Depression?" *University of California, Berkeley Wellness Letter*. vol. 16, issue 4. Jan. 2000.

Seligman, Martin E. P. *Helplessness: On Depression, Development, and Death*. San Francisco: Freeman, 1975.

———*Learned Optimism*. New York: Knopf, 1991.

Seligman, Martin E.P., and Steven F. Maier. "Failure to escape traumatic shock." *Journal of Experimental Psychology*, 74, 1–9.

Selye, Hans. *The Stress of Life* (2d ed.) New York: McGraw Hill, 1978.

Shreeve, Caroll McKanna. *Life is Good: A Guided Gratitude Journal*. Cincinnati, OH: Walking Stick Press, 2001.

Sichel, Deborah, and Jeanne Watson Driscoll. *Women's Moods: What Every Woman Must Know About Hormones, the Brain, and Emotional Health*. New York: William Morrow, 1999.

Simonton, O. Carl, Stephanie Matthews-Simonton, and James Creighton. *Getting Well Again: A Step-by-Step, Self-Help Guide to Overcoming Cancer for Patients and their Families*. Los Angeles: J. P. Tarcher, 1978.

Simpson, S. G., Folstein, S. E, Meyers, D. A., et al. "Bipolar II: The Most Common Bipolar Phenotype?" *American Journal of Psychiatry*. 150:901–903.

Sloan, Kevin L. "Detecting Bipolar Disorder Among Treatment-Seeking Substance Abusers," *American Journal of Drug and Alcohol Abuse,* Feb. 2000.

Snyder, Carl H. *The Extraordinary Chemistry of Ordinary Things, 3rd ed.* New York: John Wiley & Sons, 1998.

Solomon, Andrew. *The Noonday Demon: An Atlas of Depression*. New York: Scribner, 2001.

Spiritwalk. *Readings*. Posted July 1, 2001. *www.spiritwalk.org/serenityprayer.htm*

Staff Interview with John Nurnberger. "Post Update—The Genetics of Bipolar Disorder," *Saturday Evening Post*. Jan/Feb 1999.

Steadman, Henry J., Edward P. Mulvey, John Monahan, Pamela Clark Robbins, Paul S. Appelbaum, Thomas Grisso, Loren H. Roth, and Eric Silver. "Violence by People Discharged from Acute Psychiatric Inpatient Facilities and By Others in the Same Neighborhoods." *Archives of General Psychiatry,* 55, 1998, 393–401.

Sultanoff, Steven M. "Laugh It Up," *American Association for Therapeutic Humor*. July/Aug., 1992, 1.

Suppes, Trisha, Sherwood Brown, Ellen Dennehy, and Ellen Habermacher. *Bipolar Disorders Module: Guideline Procedures Manual,* volume 1, version 2. TMAP Procedural Manual. Dallas, TX: Texas Medication Algorithm Project, June 1, 1999.

Swanson, Jeffrey W. "Mental Disorder, Substance Abuse, and Community Violence: An Epidemiological Approach." In Monahan, John, and Henry J. Steadman (eds.). *Violence and Mental Disorder: Developments in Risk Assessment*. Chicago: University of Chicago Press, 1994.

Swartz, Marvin S., Jeffrey W. Swanson, and Barbara J. Burns. "Taking the Wrong Drugs: The Role of Substance Abuse and Medication Noncompliance in Violence Among Severely Mentally Ill Individuals." *Social Psychiatry and Psychiatric Epidemiology.* 33 (Suppl. 1), 1998, S75–S80.

Swedo, Susan A., Henrietta Leonard. *It's Not All in Your Head: Now Women Can Discover the Real Causes of Their Most Commonly Misdiagnosed Health Problems.* New York: HarperCollins, 1996.

Thayer, Robert E. *The Origin of Everyday Moods: Managing Energy, Tension, and Stress.* New York: Oxford University Press, 1996.

Thompson, Tracy. *The Beast.* New York: Plume/Penguin, 1995.

Tice, Louis. *New Age Thinking for Achieving Your Potential: Facilitator Manual.* Seattle, WA: The Pacific Institute, 1981.

Torrey, E. Fuller, and Michael B. Knable. *Surviving Manic Depression: A Manual on Bipolar Disorder for Patients, Families and Providers.* New York: Basic, 2002.

Travis, J. "Lithium Increases Gray Matter in the Brain." *Science News,* vol. 158, no. 20, Nov. 11, 2000.

Tupes, Ernest C., and Raymond E. Christal. *Recurrent Personality Factors Based on Trait Ratings.* (ASD-TR-61-67). Lackland Air Force Base, TX: Aeronautical Systems Division, Personnel Laboratory, May 1961.

Ullman, Dana. *The Consumer's Guide to Homeopathy: The Definitive Resource for Understanding Homeopathic Medicine and Making It Work for You.* New York: Putnam, 1995.

Underwood, Anne. "Nourishing Your Brain." *Newsweek,* April 23, 2001. 60–61.

UPMC Health System. *"MAOI Diet Facts."* Form #5076-82190-8201. Pittsburgh, PA: University of Pittsburgh, 2001.

U.S. Department of Agriculture. *Nutrition and Your Health: Dietary Guidelines for Americans,* 2000. *www.usda.gov/cnpp/DietGd.pdf*

U.S. Department of Agriculture and U.S. Department of Health and Human Services. *Dietary Guidelines for Americans, 2000.* Washington, DC: USDA, 2000. *www.health.gov/dietaryguidelines/dga2000/dietgd.pdf*

U.S. Food and Drug Administration Center for Food Safety and Applied Nutrition. *Overview of Dietary Supplements.* Posted Jan. 2001. *www.cfsan.fda.gov/~dms/supplmnt.html*

Van Atta, Kim. In collaboration with David S. Roby and Ross Roby. *An Account of the Events Surrounding the Origin of Friends Hospital.* Frankford, PA: Friends Hospital, 1980. *www.friendshospitalonline.org/eventsaccount.htm*

Viscott, David: *Emotional Resilience: Simple Truths for Dealing with the Unfinished Business of Your Past.* New York: Harmony/Crown (Random House), 1996.

Weiner, Bernard. "The Emotions Consequences of Causal Attributions." In Clark, M. S., and S. T. Fiske, eds. *Affect and Cognition: The 17th Annual Carnegie Symposium on Cognition.* Hillsdale, NJ: Erlbaum, 1982.

Whybrow, Peter C. *A Mood Apart: The Thinker's Guide to Emotion and Its Disorders.* New York: HarperCollins, 1997.

Wilcox, Richard E. Personal communication. Austin, TX.

Wittenberg, Margaret M. *Experiencing Quality: A Shopper's Guide to Whole Foods.* Austin, TX: Whole Foods Market, Inc., 1987.

Wurtman, Judith, and Susan Suffes. *The Serotonin Solution: The Potent Substance That Can Help You Stop Bingeing, Lose Weight, and Feel Great.* New York: Ballantine/Random House, 1996.

Wurtzel, Elizabeth. *Prozac Nation: Young and Depressed in America.* New York: Houghton Mifflin, 1994.

Yudolfsky, Stuart. *Depression Management,* panel presentation. National Depressive and Manic-Depressive Association Conference, Houston, Texas, Oct. 2, 1999.

Zuckerman, Marvin. "Impulsive Unsocialized Sensation Seeking: The Biological Foundations of a Basic Dimension of Personality." In Bates, John E. and Theodore D. Wachs. *Temperament: Individual Differences at the Interface of Biology and Behavior.* Washington, DC: APA, 1994, 219–255.

——*Psychobiology of Personality.* Cambridge: Cambridge University Press, 1991.

RESOURCES

Mood Disorders

Bipolar Disorders Treatment Information
Center (BDTIC)
Madison Institute of Medicine
7617 Mineral Point Rd., Ste. 300
Madison WI 53717
Office: 1-608-827-2470 (8:30 a.m.–5 p.m.
Central Time) Fax: 1-608-827-2479
mim@miminc.org
www.miminc.org/aboutbipolarinfoctr.html
▪ Provides information on mood stabiliz-
  ers, other medications, and other forms
  of treatment

Bipolar Person's Significant Others
(BPSO)
www.bpso.org
▪ Provides information and support to the
  families, friends, and loved ones of
  those who suffer from bipolar disorder
▪ Has private, closed and unmoderated
  Internet mailing list

Depression and Bipolar Support Alliance
(DBSA)
(formerly National Depressive and Manic-
Depressive Association [NDMDA])
730 N. Franklin St., Ste. 501
Chicago IL 60610-7204
Toll-free: 1-800-826-3632,
Office: 1-312-642-0049
(M–F 8:30 a.m.–5 p.m. Central Time),
Fax: 1-312-642-7243
www.DBSAlliance.org

▪ Sponsors 6 state chapters and nearly
  1000 support groups across the country
▪ Publishes quarterly newsletter *Outreach* and extensive brochures
  regarding mood disorders

Depression and Related Affective Disor-
ders Association (DRADA)
Meyer 3-181
600 N. Wolfe St.
Baltimore MD 21287-7381
Baltimore office: 1-410-955-4647
Washington, DC office: 1-202-955-5800
www.drada.org
▪ Works to alleviate the suffering arising
  from depression and bipolar disorder by
  assisting self-help groups, providing
  education and information, and lending
  support to research programs
▪ Publishes quarterly newsletter *Smooth
  Sailing* and bimonthly newsletter
  DRADA Update

Depression: Awareness, Recognition,
and Treatment (D/ART) Program
5600 Fishers Lane, Room 10-85
Rockville, MD 20857
Toll-free: 1-800-421-4211,
Office: 1-301-443-4513
www.nimh.nih.gov
▪ Is the publications division of the
  National Institute of Mental Health

National Foundation for Depressive Illness, Inc. (NAFDI)
P.O. Box 2257
New York, NY 10116
Toll-free: 1-800-239-1265, Office: 1-212-
696-1088, Fax: 1-212-696-0563
www.depression.org
- Provides information packets and referral listings at nominal cost, or free if a
  donation can't be made
- Educates the public about depressive
  illness, its consequences, and its treata-
  bility
- Publishes quarterly newsletter *NAFDI
  News*

Recovery Inc.
802 N. Dearborn St.
Chicago, IL 60610
Office: 1-312-337-5661,
Fax: 1-312-337-5756
inquiries@recovery-inc.com
www.recovery-inc.com
- Uses a self-help approach similar to
  cognitive-behavioral therapy
- Teaches simple yet practical coping
  techniques that help members change
  their reactions to people and situations
  they can't control
- Sponsors over 700 active groups in the
  United States, Canada, England, Ire-
  land, Israel, Puerto Rico, Spain, and
  Wales

12-STEP GROUPS FOR EMOTIONAL SUPPORT

Depressed Anonymous (DA)
P.O. Box 17414
Louisville, KY 40217
Office: 1-502-569-1989
info@depressedanon.com
www.depressedanon.com

Emotions Anonymous (EA)
Emotions Anonymous International
P.O. Box 4245
St. Paul, MN 55104-0245
Office: 1-651-647-9712,
Fax: 1-651-647-1593
info@EmotionsAnonymous.org
www.emotionsanonymous.org

Manic Depressives Anonymous (MDA)
P.O. Box 212
Collingswood, NJ 08107
mda@manicdepressivesanon.org or in
California cal-mda@manicdepres-
sivesanon.org
www.manicdepressivesanon.org

FOR CHILDREN AND ADOLESCENTS

American Academy of Child and
Adolescent Psychiatry (AACAP)
3615 Wisconsin Ave. N.W.
Washington, DC 20016-3007
Office: 1-202-966-7300,
Fax: 1-202-966-2891
www.aacap.org
- Promotes mentally healthy children,
  adolescents, and families through
  research, training, advocacy, prevention,
  comprehensive diagnosis and treatment, peer support, and collaboration
- Publishes a monthly magazine *Journal
  of the American Academy of Child and
  Adolescent Psychiatry*, a bimonthly
  magazine *AACAP News*, and a series of
  fact sheets called *Facts for Families*

The Bipolar Child
www.bipolarchild.com
- Publishes quarterly online newsletter
  The Bipolar Child Newsletter
- Has suggested reading list

Child & Adolescent Bipolar Foundation
1187 Wilmette Ave. PMB #331
Wilmette, IL 60091
Hotline: 1-847-256-8525, Office: 1-847-
256-8525 (8 a.m.–5 p.m. Central TIme),
Fax: 1-847-920-9498
cabf@bpkids.org
www.bpkids.org
- Helps families manage the needs of
  bipolar children while minimizing the
  adverse impact on the family
- Educates families, professionals, and
  the public about early-onset bipolar disorders
- Publishes periodic e-bulletin (electronic
  newsletter)

Federation of Families for Children's
Mental Health (FFCMH)
1101 King St., Ste. 420
Alexandria, VA 22314
Office: 1-703-684-7710,
Fax: 1-703-836-1040
ffcmh@ffcmh.org
www.ffcmh.org
- Sponsors state, chapter, and partner
  organizations
- Provides leadership for a broad nation-
  wide network of family-run organiza-
  tions
- Has list of available publications (some
  in English and Spanish)
- Publishes quarterly newsletter *Claiming
  Children*

Focus Adolescent Services: An Internet
Clearinghouse of Information,
Resources, and Support
Toll free: 1-877-362-8727 (1-877-FOCUS-AS)
help@focusas.com
www.focusas.com
- Provides information on teen and family
  issues, including depression
- Provides a directory of family help
  pages for United States and Canada

Juvenile Bipolar Research Foundation
(JBRF)
49 S. Quaker Rd
Pawling, NY 12564
www.bpchildresearch.org
- Promotes research for the study of
  early-onset bipolar disorder
- Has professional LISTSERV for physicians who treat or supervise treatment
  of children and adolescents diagnosed
  with bipolar disorder

FOR SENIOR CITIZENS

Older Adult Consumer Mental Health
Alliance (OACMHA)
c/o Bazelon Center for Mental Health Law
1101 15th St. N.W., Ste. 1212
Washington, DC 20005
Office: 1-202-467-5730 Ext. 140
OACMHA@aol.com
- Advocates for views of older persons
  with major mental illnesses

FOR WOMEN AFTER CHILDBIRTH

Depression After Delivery, Inc. (D.A.D., Inc.)
91 E. Somerset St.
Raritan, NJ 08869
Toll-free: 1-800-944-4773 (800-994-4PPD)
www.depressionafterdelivery.com
- Sponsors 7 state/local chapters
- Promotes universal awareness of mood
  and anxiety disorders surrounding preg-
  nancy and childbirth

Postpartum Support International
The Center for Postpartum Health
20700 Ventura Blvd. #203
Woodland Hills, CA 91364
Toll-free: 1-805-967-7636, Office: 1-818-
887-1312, Fax: 1-818-887-9606
www.chss.iup.edu/postpartum
- Has East Coast and West Coast offices

SEASONAL AFFECTIVE DISORDER

National Organization for Seasonal
Affective Disorder (NOSAD)
P.O. Box 40133
Washington, DC 20016
www.nosad.org
- Helps people affected by seasonal
  affective disorder (SAD) find support
  and treatment

SUBSTANCE ABUSE

National Clearinghouse for Alcohol and
Drug Information (NCADI)
P.O. Box 2345
Rockville, MD 20847-2345
Toll-free: 1-800-729-6686, Toll-free Spanish line: 1-877-767-8432, TDD line: 1-800-
487-4889 Office: 1-301-468-2600,
Fax: 1-301-468-6433
info@health.org
www.health.org and
www.health.org/links
- Provides current information and materials concerning alcohol and substance
  abuse prevention, intervention, and
  treatment
- Offers a wide variety of mostly free
  services and publications
- Publishes a bimonthly magazine *Prevention Pipeline*

Substance Abuse and Mental Health
Information Center (SAMHSA)
National Mental Health Information
Center (CMHS)
P.O. Box 42490
Washington, DC 20015
Toll-free: 1-800-789-2647 (M–F 8:30
a.m.–5 p.m. Eastern Time) TDD line:
1-866-889-2647, Fax: 1-301-984-8796
International office: 1-301-443-1805,
International TDD line: 1-301-443-9006
ken@mentalhealth.org
www.mentalhealth.org
- Supports the Knowledge Exchange
  Network (KEN)
- Has online list of free and for-cost publi-
  cations

Dual Recovery Anonymous (DRA)
World Service Central Office
P.O. Box 218232
Nashville, TN 37221-8232
Toll-free: 1-877-883-2332,
Fax: 1-615-673-7677
www.draonline.org

SUICIDE PREVENTION

American Association of Suicidology
(AAS)
4201 N.W. Connecticut Ave., Ste. 408
Washington, DC 20008
Office: 1-202-237-2280,
Fax: 1-202-237-2282
info@suicidology.org
www.suicidology.org
- Serves as a national clearinghouse for
  information on suicide
- Promotes research, public awareness
  programs, education, and training for
  professionals and volunteers
- Publishes a quarterly newsletter *Surviving Suicide*

American Foundation for Suicide Preven-
tion (AFSP)
International Headquarters
120 Wall Street, 22nd Floor
New York, NY 10005
Toll-free: 1-888-333-2377 (1-888-333-
AFSP), Office: 1-212-363-3500 (M–F 9
a.m.–5 p.m. Eastern Time),
Fax: 1-212-363-6237

inquiry@afsp.org
www.afsp.org
- Sponsors country, state, and regional
  chapters
- Supports programs for suicide survivors
- Provides information and education
  about depression and suicide
- Publicizes information about the need
  for research, prevention, and treatment
  for depression and suicide

GENERAL MENTAL
HEALTH INFORMATION

The Carter Center
Mental Health Program
One Copenhill
453 Freedom Parkway
Atlanta, GA 30307
carterweb@emory.edu
www.cartercenter.org
- Seeks to reduce stigma and discrimination against people with mental illnesses; to achieve equity for mental
  health care comparable to other health
  care; to advance promotion, prevention,
  and early intervention services for children and their families; and to increase
  public awareness worldwide about
  mental health and mental illness and to
  stimulate local actions to address those
  issues
- Provides downloadable news and information articles online

GOVERNMENT INFORMATION
SOURCES

National Center Complementary and
Alternative Medicine (NCCAM)
NCCAM Clearinghouse
P.O. Box 7923
Gaithersburg, MD 20898
Toll-free: 1-888-644-6226, TTY toll-free
line: 1-866-464-3615, International toll-
free line: 1-301-519-3153, Fax toll-free
line: 1-866-464-3616
info@nccam.nih.gov
www.nccam.nih.gov
- Supports research and provides information on complementary and alternative medicine options

National Institute of Mental Health (NIMH)
6001 Executive Blvd., Room 8184, MSC 9663
Bethesda, MD 20892-9663
Office: 1-301-443-4513,
Fax: 1-301-443-4279
nimhinfo@nih.gov
www.nimh.nih.gov
- Focuses on diminishing the burden of mental illness through research
- Provides list of available publications

NONPROFITS AND OTHER ORGANIZATIONS

National Alliance for the Mentally Ill (NAMI)
Colonial Place Three
2107 Wilson Blvd., Ste. 300
Arlington, VA 22201-3042
Toll-free: 1-800-950-6264, Office: 1-703-524-7600, Fax: 1-703-524-9094
www.nami.org
- Sponsors affiliates in all states, the Virgin Islands, and Puerto Rico
- Publishes quarterly magazine *Advocate* and periodic electronic newsletter *NAMI E-News*

National Alliance for Research on Schizophrenia and Depression (NARSAD)
60 Cutter Mill Rd., Ste. 404
Great Neck, NY 11021
Toll-free: 1-800-829-8289 (voice mail), Office: 1-516-829-0091,
Fax: 1-516-487-6930
www.narsad.org
- Provides educational materials, including books, videos, and brochures
- Raises and distributes funds for scientific research into the causes, cures, treatments, and prevention of brain disorders, primarily schizophrenia, depression, and bipolar disorder
- Sponsors NARSAD Artworks, a program in which people with mental illness produce museum-quality products to promote public education, destigmatize mental illness, and enhance the self-esteem and income of artists with mental illness

National Empowerment Center (NEC)
599 Canal St.
Lawrence, MA 01840
Toll-free: 1-800-769-3728,
Fax: 1-978-681-6426
www.power2u.org
- Provides a message of recovery, empowerment, hope, and healing to people diagnosed with mental illness
- Has a catalogue of free publications

National Mental Health Association (NMHA)
2001 N. Beauregard St., 12th Floor
Alexandria, VA 22311
Toll-free: 1-800-969-6642 (1-800-969-NMHA), TTY: 1-800-433-5959, Office: 1-703-684-7722 (M–F 9 a.m.–5 p.m. Eastern Time), Fax: 1-703-684-5968
infoctr@nmha.org
www.nmha.org
- Sponsors over 340 affiliates in 42 states
- Provides a free public service for individuals seeking help for themselves, family members, or colleagues
- Publishes a monthly newsletter *The Bell*
- Has brochures and fact sheets on a variety of mental health topics

National Mental Health Consumers' Self-Help Clearinghouse
1211 Chestnut St., Ste. 1207
Philadelphia, PA 19107
Toll-free: 1-800-553-4539 (800-553-4KEY), Office: 1-215-751-1810,
Fax:1- 215-636-6312
info@mhselfhelp.org
www.mhselfhelp.org
- Empowers consumers by providing technical assistance information, personal consultations, and follow-ups
- Publishes a quarterly newsletter *The Key* and technical assistance guides

Treatment Resources and Referrals

CLINICAL TRIALS AND MEDICATION ASSISTANCE

CenterWatch Clinical Trials Listing Service
22 Thomson Pl. 36T1
Boston, MA 02210-1212
Toll-free: 1-800-765-9647, Office: 1-617-856-5900, Fax: 1-617-856-5901
www.centerwatch.com
- Provides consumers and their advocates with a variety of information about clinical research
- Publishes newsletters, books, and directories—both free and for sale

Stanley Bipolar Treatment Network
A Program of the Stanley Medical Research Institute
info@bipolarnetwork.org
www.bipolarnetwork.org
- Promotes understanding about the causes of bipolar disorder and schizoaffective disorder, and establishes strategies for long-term treatment
- Has several centers across the country to contact for information: California, Maryland, Ohio, Texas, and also in the Netherlands and Germany
- Participation in network is voluntary, and anyone over 18 years of age with bipolar disorder or schizoaffective disorder is eligible

Systematic Treatment Enhancement Program for Bipolar Disorder (STEP-BD)
Toll-free: 1-866-240-3250,
Office: 1-617-724-6058
stepbd@mailcity.com
www.stepbd.org
- Offers outpatient treatment for bipolar disorder and studies the effects over time through an ongoing nationwide study
- Available at 16 sites across the country, most connected with universities
- Accepting patients through October 2003 (deadline may be extended if grant receives additional funds)

Pharmaceutical Research and Manufacturers of America (PhRMA)
1100 Fifteenth Street N.W.
Washington, DC 20005
Office: 1-202-835-3400
www.phrma.org
- Represents the country's leading research-based pharmaceutical and biotechnology companies
- Publishes *Directory of Prescription Drug Patient Assistance Programs,* available at www.phrma.org/searchcures/dpdpap
- Has online publications about prescription drugs and the pharmaceutical industry

TRADITIONAL PSYCHIATRIC ORGANIZATIONS

American Association for Marriage and Family Therapy (AAMFT)
AAMFT – Central Office
112 S. Alfred St.
Alexandria, VA 22314
Office: 1-703-838-9808,
Fax: 1-703-838-9805
www.aamft.org

American Association of Geriatric Psychiatry (AAGP)
7910 Woodmont Ave., Ste. 1050
Bethesda, MD 20814-3004
Office: 1-301-654-7850 (9 a.m.–5:30 p.m. Eastern Time), Fax: 1-301-654-4137
main@aagponline.org
www.aagpgpa.org

American Psychiatric Association (APA)
1400 K St. N.W.
Washington, DC 20005
Toll-free: 1-888-357-7924,
Fax: 1-202-682-6850
apa@psych.org
www.psych.org

American Psychological Association (APA)
750 First St. N.E.
Washington, DC 20002-4242
Toll-free: 1-800-374-2721, Mental Health Professional Referral Line: 1-800-964-2000, Office: 1-202-336-5510, TDD/TTY line: 1-202-336-6123

www.apa.org (main)
www.helping.apa.org (help center)
- Publishes several free mental health brochures

ALTERNATIVE PRACTITIONER ORGANIZATIONS

American Association of Pastoral Counselors
9504-A Lee Highway
Fairfax, VA 22031-2303
Office: 1-703-385-6967,
Fax: 1-703-352-7725
info@aapc.org
www.aapc.org
- Provides and promotes theologically informed, spiritually sensitive, ethically sound, and clinically competent counseling and consultation as an extension of the ministry of faith communities

American Dietetic Association (ADA)
216 W. Jackson Blvd.
Chicago, IL 60606-6995
Toll-free: 1-800-877-1600,
Office: 1-312-899-0040
(8:30 a.m.–4:45 p.m. Central Time)
Washington, DC office:
American Dietetic Association
1120 N.W. Connecticut Ave., Ste. 480
Washington, DC 20036
Office: 1-202-775-8277
www.eatright.org
- Provides food and nutrition services, focusing on obesity and its prevention, complementary care and dietary supplements, retail food practices, genetic research, and biotechnology
- Promotes optimal nutrition and well-being for all people

Biofeedback Certification Institute of America
10200 W. 44th Ave., Ste. 310
Wheat Ridge, CO 80033
Office: 1-303-420-2902,
Fax: 1-303-422-8894
bcia@resourcenter.com
www.bcia.org

National Association of Social Workers (NASW)
750 N.E. 1st St., Ste. 700
Washington, DC 20002-4241
Toll-free: 1-800-742-4089,
Office: 1-202-408-8600
www.naswdc.org

National Center for Homeopathy (NCH)
801 N. Fairfax St., Ste. 306
Alexandria, VA 22314
Toll free: 1-877-624-0613,
Office: 1-703-548-7790,
Fax: 1-703-548-7792
info@homeopathic.org
www.homeopathic.org

National Certification Commission for Acupuncture and Oriental Medicine (NCCAOM)
11 Canal Center Plz., Ste. 300
Alexandria, VA 22314
Office: 1-703-548-9004,
Fax: 1-703-548-9079
info@nccaom.org
www.nccaom.org

CREATIVE THERAPIES

American Art Therapy Association, Inc. (AATA)
1202 Allanson Rd.
Mundelein, IL 60060-3808
Toll-free: 1-888-290-0878,
Office: 1-847-949-6064
(M–F 9 a.m.-5 p.m. Central Time)
Fax: 1-847-566-4580
info@arttherapy.org
www.arttherapy.org

American Dance Therapy Association (ADTA)
2000 Century Plz., Ste. 108
10632 Little Patuxent Pkwy
Columbia, MD 21044
(8:30 a.m.–4 p.m. Eastern Time),
Fax: 1-410-997-4048
info@adta.org
www.adta.org

American Music Therapy Association
(AMTA)
8455 Colesville Rd., Ste. 1000
Silver Spring, MD 20910
Office: 1-301-589-3300 (M–F 10 a.m.–4
p.m. Eastern Time), Fax: 1-301-589-5175
info@musictherapy.org
www.musictherapy.org

National Association for Drama Therapy
(NADT)
733 N.W. 15th Street, Ste. 330
Washington, DC 20005
Office: 1-202-966-7895,
Fax: 1-202-638-7895
info@nadt.org
www.nadt.org

Arts in Therapy (AiT)
chriss@artsintherapy.com
www.artsintherapy.com
- Provides online community for creative
  arts therapists (CATs) and those who
  are interested in the healing arts

The Arts We Need, Inc. (TAWN)
P.O. Box 2652
New York, NY 10009
Office: 1-212-420-4772,
Fax: 1-646-390-3596
info@theartsweneed.org
Web site:www.theartsweneed.org
- Promotes creative arts therapy and
  related arts programs for people with
  special needs and assists those
  attempting to start an arts program or
  improve an existing program

ASSISTANCE AND INFORMATION SOURCES

Americans with Disabilities Act (ADA)
U.S. Department of Justice
950 N.W. Pennsylvania Ave.
Civil Rights Division
Disability Rights Section—NYAVE
Washington, DC 20530
Toll-free: 1-800-514-0301 (M,W, F 10
a.m.–6 p.m., Th 1 p.m.–6 p.m. Eastern
Time), TDD/TTY Toll-free: 1-800-514-0383
www.usdoj.gov/crt/ada/adahom1.htm
- Provides information about the ADA
  statute and ADA Title II and III regula-

tions, as well as technical assistance
materials, enforcement information,
and general ADA information
- Publishes information about laws and
  accessibility for the disabled in standard
  print, large print, Braille, and on audiotape and computer disk

Center for Science in the Public Interest
(CSPI)
1875 N.W. Connecticut Ave., Ste. 300
Washington, DC 20009
Office: 1-202-332-9110,
Fax: 1-202-265-4954
cspi@cspinet.org
www.cspinet.org
- Conducts research and advocacy pro-
  grams in health and nutrition
- Provides current useful information
  about consumers' health and well-being
- Publishes monthly newsletter *Nutrition
  Action Healthletter*

Food and Nutrition Information Center
Agricultural Research Service, USDA
National Agricultural Library
10301 Baltimore Ave., Room 105
Beltsville, MD 20705-2351
Office: 1-301-504-5719,
TTY: 1-301-504-6856, Fax: 1-301-504-6409
fnic@nal.usda.gov
www.nal.usda.gov/fnic
- Provides information about food and
  human nutrition, including dietary
  guidelines, food composition, dietary
  supplements, and food safety
- Provides nutritional resources for child
  care; Women, Infants, and Children
  (WIC); healthy school meals; and food
  stamp programs

National Institute on Disability and
Rehabilitation Research (NIDRR)
400 S.W. Maryland Ave.
Washington, DC 20202-2572
Office: 1-202-205-8134,
TTY line: 1-202-205-4475
www.ed.gov/offices/OSERS/NIDRR
- Is one of three components of the U.S.
  Department of Education's Office of
  Special Education and Rehabilitative
  Services (OSERS), and operates in con-
  cert with the Rehabilitation Services
  Administration (RSA) and the Office of

Special Education Programs (OSEP)
- Generates, disseminates, and promotes new knowledge to improve the lifestyle options available to disabled individuals
- Conducts research on employment, independent living and community integration, and other associated disability research areas
- Publishes an online list of resources

FINANCIAL SUPPORT

Social Security Administration
Office of Public Inquiries
6401 Security Blvd., Windsor Park Bldg.
Baltimore, MD 21235
Toll-free: 1-800-772-1213,
TTY Toll-free: 1-800-325-0778
(7 a.m.–7 p.m. Eastern Time)
www.ssa.gov
- Offers automated information 24 hours a day through touch-tone phone
- Has two programs that pay benefits to people with disabilities: Social Security Disability Insurance (SSDI) and Supplemental Security Income (SSI)
- Provides downloadable SSA publications online

U.S. Food and Drug Administration
5600 Fishers Lane
Rockville, MD 20857
Toll-free: 1-888-INFO-FDA (888-463-6332)
www.fda.gov
- Ensures the safety and effectiveness of foods and medications and their proper labeling intended for human use

HOUSING PROGRAMS

Center for Housing and New Community Economics (CHANCE)
Institute on Disability/UCE
University of New Hampshire
7 Leavitt Lane, Ste. 101
Durham, NH 03824-3522
drv@cisunix.unh.edu
www.alliance.unh.edu
- Works to improve and increase access to integrated, affordable, accessible housing for people with mental illness
- Works in partnership with ADAPT (a national organization that focuses on promoting community services for peo-

ple with disabilities)
- Has list of publications available online

National Home of Your Own Alliance
Institute on Disability/UCE
University of New Hampshire
7 Leavitt Lane, Ste. 101
Durham, NH 03824-3522
www.alliance.unh.edu/nhoyo.html
- Promotes opportunities for people with disabilities to own and control their homes
- Operates a national information clearinghouse: National Home of Your Own Alliance Clearinghouse

U.S. Department of Housing and Urban Development (HUD)
451 S.W. 7th St.
Washington, DC 20410
Office: 1-202-708-1112,
TTY line: 1-202-708-1455
www.hud.gov
- Focuses on creating opportunities for home ownership; providing housing assistance for low-income people; working to create, rehabilitate, and maintain the nation's affordable housing; enforcing the nation's fair housing laws; and helping the homeless
- Has an online library of materials, including a page for people with disabilities that contains general information, federal resources, fair housing laws, and related links

ADVOCACY AND LEGAL INFORMATION

Bazelon Center for Mental Health Law
1101 N.W. 15th St., Ste. 1212
Washington, DC 20005-5002
Office: 1-202-467-5730, Fax: 1-202-223-0409, TDD line: 1-202-467-4232
webmaster@bazelon.org
www.bazelon.org
- Collaborates with local, regional, and national advocacy and consumer organizations to reform public systems and service programs for those with mental illness
- Publishes handbooks and manuals, and issues papers and reports on key legal and policy issues

National Stigma Clearinghouse
245 Eighth Ave., #213
New York, NY 10011
Office: 1-212-255-4411
stigmanet@webtv.net
http://community.webtv.net/stigmanet
- Focuses on correcting inaccurate images of mental illness in news, advertising, and entertainment media
- Issues periodic *Stigma Alerts* via e-mail, fax, and mail

The Treatment Advocacy Center (TAC)
3300 N. Fairfax Dr., Ste. 220
Arlington, VA 22201
Office: 1-703-294-6001,
Fax: 1-703-294-6010
info@psychlaws.org
www.psychlaws.org
- Advocates eliminating legal and clinical barriers to timely and humane treatment for brain disorders
- Publishes a bimonthly newsletter *Catalyst*

United Cerebral Palsy (UCP National)
1660 N.W. L St., Ste. 700
Washington, DC 20036
Toll-free: 1-800-872-5827, Office: 1-202-776-0406, TTY line: 1-202-973-7197,
Fax: 1-202-776-0414
www.ucpa.org
- Advances the independence, productivity, and full citizenship of people with cerebral palsy and other disabilities, including mood disorders
- Has a nationwide network of 111 affiliates in 39 states
- Of people UCP serves, 65 percent have disabilities other than cerebral palsy

OTHER HELPFUL ORGANIZATIONS

Association for Applied and Therapeutic Humor (AATH)
1951 W. Camelback Rd., Ste. 445
Phoenix, AZ 85015
Office: 1-602-995-1454,
Fax: 1-602-995-1449
office@aath.org
www.aath.org
- Promotes research into the roles that humor and laughter play in well-being

- Educates health care professionals and lay audiences about the values and therapeutic uses of humor and laughter
- Supports innovative programs that incorporate the therapeutic use of humor

Toastmasters International, Inc.
P.O. Box 9052
Mission Viejo. CA 92690
Office: 1-949-858-8255 (8 a.m.–5 p.m. Pacific Time), Fax: 1-949-858-1207
tmembers@toastmasters.org,
clubs@toastmasters.org
www.toastmasters.org
- Sponsors over 8,500 clubs in over 70 countries
- Provides a mutually supportive, positive learning environment in which every member can develop communication and leadership skills, which also foster self-confidence and personal growth
- Publishes a monthly magazine *The Toastmaster*

The World Laughter Tour, Inc.
1159 S. Creekway Ct.
Ghanna, OH 43230
Toll-free: 1-800-669-5233 (1-800-NOW-LAFF) (U.S. and Canada), Office: 1-614-855-4733, Fax: 1-614-855-4889
info@worldlaughtertour.com
www.worldlaughtertour.com
- Promotes awareness of therapeutic laughter worldwide by setting up clubs and offering training in therapeutic laughter techniques
- Publishes books, manuals, newsletters, videocassettes, CDs, and other information and products on laughter therapy

PUBLICATIONS AND WEB SITES

InteliHealth
960 Harvest Dr., Ste. C
Blue Bell, PA 19422
Comments@InteliHealth.com
www.intelihealth.com
- Provides credible health information from trusted sources
- Publishes daily and weekly health e-mails and *InteliHealth Catalog*

Internet Mental Health
editor@mentalhealth.com
www.mentalhealth.com
- Is a Web site that works to improve understanding, diagnosis, and treatment of mental illness throughout the world
- Publishes an online magazine *Mental Health Magazine*
- Has an online booklist

MayoClinic
www.mayoclinic.com
- Provides up-to-date information on all kinds of health issues
- Publishes weekly e-mail newsletter *Housecall*

McMan's Depression and Bipolar Web
McMan's Weekly
P.O. Box 331
Southington, CT 06489
jmcmanamy@snet.net
www.mcmanweb.com
- Provides articles, essays, links, and news on depression and bipolar disorder
- Publishes online newsletter *McMan's Depression and Bipolar Weekly*

MEDLINEplus Health Information
c/o U.S. National Library of Medicine
8600 Rockville Pike
Bethesda, MD 20894
custserv@nlm.nih.gov
www.medlineplus.gov
- Is a Web-based database that helps consumers locate authoritative health information
- Covers health topics, medication information, dictionaries, directories, and other resources

Medscape
WebMD Medscape Health Network
224 W. 30th St.
New York, NY 10001-5399
Office: 1-212-624-3700
www.medscape.com
- Is a Web site that provides timely clinical information and journal articles relevant to health care practice

Mental Health InfoSource
2801 McGaw Ave.
Irvine, CA 92614-5835
Toll-free: 1-800-933-2632,

Office: 1-949-250-1008
www.mhsource.com
- Is a commercial Web site that promotes mental health education
- Publishes a periodic newsletter *Psychiatric Times* and a bimonthly newsletter *Geriatric Times*
- Has an online store of products and publications

Mental Health World
c/o Independent Living Center
3108 Main St.
Buffalo, NY 14214-1384
mhw@buffnet.net
www.mentalhealthworld.org
- Is a nonprofit quarterly journal published by mental health consumers to promote hope and understanding through education

Mental Help Net (MHN)
570 Metro Place
Dublin, OH 43017
www.mentalhelp.net
- Is a Web site that offers mental health news, topic centers, a reading room, message boards, chat rooms, and in-depth book reviews

Pendulum Resources
www.pendulum.org
- Is a Web site that provides information on bipolar disorder, including articles and links to other sites

Psych Central
www.psychcentral.com
- Is a Web site that provides an index for psychology, support, and mental health issues, resources, and people on the Internet

PubMed
A service of the National Library of Medicine
www.ncbi.nih.gov/entrez/query.fcgi
- Is a Web site that provides access to over 11 million MEDLINE citations and additional life science journals via a search and retrieval system that integrates information from databases at the National Center for Biotechnology Information (NCBI)

GLOSSARY

ACETYLCHOLINE: a *neurotransmitter* present throughout the *central nervous system* but that affects the *parasympathetic nervous system* in particular. Acetylcholine is especially concentrated in the brain. It's more important to motor movements and thinking than to mood, but it plays an essential role in learning and memory, maintaining neuronal membranes, and activating REM sleep.

ACID: a sour water-soluble *compound* containing hydrogen that can react with a base to form a salt.

ACTH: see *adrenocorticotropic hormone*.

ACTION POTENTIAL: a measurement of an electrical wave that may vary in intensity. When one *neuron* transmits a signal to another, the higher its action potential, the more likely the signal will be sent on.

ADENINE: a base composed of carbon, hydrogen, and nitrogen that codes hereditary information in *DNA* and *RNA*.

ADENOSINE: a component of *RNA* composed of an *adenine* linked to the sugar *ribose*.

ADRENAL GLAND: one of two glands that rest atop the kidneys and play an important part in *immune system* functioning. The adrenal glands produce and release two stress *hormones*—*adrenaline* and *cortisol*—as well as steroid hormones that help control growth, cellular repair, and *sugar* consumption.

ADRENALINE: one of the two *hormones* (the other being *cortisol*) that help the body respond to stress. Adrenaline acts as a *neurotransmit-*

ter between nerve cells outside the brain and helps prepare the body to fight or flee from stressful situations.

ADRENERGIC: refers to *neurons* and nerve fibers of the *autonomic nervous system* that employ the activating *neurotransmitter norepinephrine,* or to medications that mimic *sympathetic nervous system* actions.

ADRENOCORTICOTROPIC HORMONE (ACTH): the *hormone* that the *pituitary gland* sends to the *adrenal glands* to stimulate them to release *cortisol* into the blood when a person is in pain.

AFFECTIVE ILLNESS: a mood disorder characterized by *depression* alone and/or *mania* or *hypomania.* Also see *mood disorder.*

AGITATION (OR PSYCHOMOTOR AGITATION): repetitious, non-productive, tension-driven movements, such as fidgeting and pacing.

AGONIST: a substance that occupies certain cell *receptors* to stimulate or mimic a biological response. Also see *antagonist.*

ALDOSTERONE: a *hormone* that helps regulate the balance of water and salt to maintain blood pressure and kidney function.

ALKALINE: refers to a caustic or corrosive substance that is soluble in alcohol or water and forms a cleaning agent when combined with oil or fat. When combined with *acids,* alkaline *compounds* (or *bases*) neutralize to form *salts.*

ALKYL: a component of some *organic molecules* that contains a chain of carbon and hydrogen *atoms,* but that has lost one hydrogen *atom.*

AMINE: a derivative of *ammonia* that affects the *aminergic system.*

AMINERGIC SYSTEM: the chemical system that oversees the brain's waking state.

AMINO ACID: an *organic molecule* consisting of an *amine radical* plus a *carboxyl* radical to form *protein* in the body.

AMMONIA: a pungent water-soluble *alkaline* gas *molecule* composed of nitrogen and hydrogen.

AMYGDALA: a brain structure located near the pons. The amygdala looks for both threats and opportunities, assigns emotional meaning to events and objects, and incites a quick response.

ANION: a negatively charged ion.

ANTAGONIST: a substance that reduces or blocks the action of another substance or of some physiological process. Also see *agonist.*

ANTIANXIETY AGENT: a medication commonly known as a tranquilizer that helps relieve nervous tension and produce sedation by reducing *central nervous system* activity and nerve signal transmissions.

ANTIBODY: a type of *protein* cell that stimulates the *immune system.*

ANTICONVULSANT: a medication used primarily to prevent or control convulsions or seizures. Some anticonvulsants also have mood-stabilizing properties and can be used successfully in place of the naturally occurring mood stabilizer *lithium.*

ANTIDEPRESSANT: a medication that specifically treats *depression* by increasing *neurotransmitter* levels in the brain and interfering with their *reuptake.*

ANTIPSYCHOTIC: a medication used to treat *psychotic* symptoms, such as *hallucinations* or *delusions,* or to help control fluctuating moods.

ATOM: the smallest part of an *element* that can exist on its own.

AUTONOMIC NERVOUS SYSTEM: the part of the nervous system that controls body temperature, breathing, heart rate, hormonal secretions, and other involuntary bodily functions. Also see *parasympathetic nervous system.*

AXON: the threadlike fiber of a *neuron* that transmits electrical signals to another neuron.

BASE: a *chemical compound* that can neutralize an *acid* to form a *salt.*

BENZODIAZEPINE: a type of potent medication that may be an *antianxiety agent* (tranquilizer), a *hypnotic* (sedative), or both. Benzodiazepines tend to be addictive and should generally be used only for brief periods.

BETA-ENDORPHIN: a pituitary *endorphin* with even greater pain-relieving powers than morphine.

BIPOLAR DISORDER (OR MANIC DEPRESSION): a brain disorder involving both *mania* and/or *hypomania* usually in addition to *depression.* Three major types of bipolar disorder are *bipolar I, bipolar II,* and *cyclothymic disorder.*

BIPOLAR I: the classic, florid form of *bipolar disorder* with the most severe symptoms. Diagnosis is based on having had one or more manic or *mixed episodes,* usually alternating with major depressive episodes, although some people experience only manic episodes. Also see *major depressive disorder, mania.*

BIPOLAR II: a milder form of *bipolar disorder* sometimes called "soft bipolar," in which *hypomania* occurs in place of *mania.* Hypomanic symptoms include euphoria that switches to anger and aggression. A hypomanic episode may *not* include *delusions* or *hallucinations* nor require hospitalization; however, a depressive episode might.

BLOOD-BRAIN BARRIER: the protective shield that prevents certain substances from reaching the brain.

BOND: see *chemical bond.*

BRAIN STEM: the "animal," instinctive, reactive part of the brain.

CAMP: see *cyclic adenosine monophosphate.*

CARBOHYDRATE: a *compound* containing carbon, hydrogen, and oxygen. Carbohydrates are often present in starchy, sugary, and high-fiber plants and foods.

CARBOXYL: an *organic radical* consisting of one carbon *atom,* one hydrogen atom, and two oxygen atoms.

CARBOXYLIC ACID: an *organic acid* containing a *carboxyl radical.* Carboxylic acids are found in fats and oils, and also in cell membranes.

CATALYST: a substance that accelerates a chemical reaction or produces it under a different condition than normal (for example, at a lower temperature).

CATECHOLAMINE: an adrenaline-like substance, such as *dopamine* or *norepinephrine,* formed from the *amino acid tyrosine.*

CATION: a positively charged *ion.*

CELL BODY: the portion of the cell that contains a *nucleus* with genetic information, which programs the cell to be a specific kind of cell.

CENTRAL NERVOUS SYSTEM (CNS): the bodily system consisting of the spinal cord and brain. The nerves from the spinal cord branch throughout the body and constantly communicate with the brain. Also see *autonomic nervous system, peripheral nervous system.*

CEREBELLUM: the lower back brain structure that coordinates movement with thinking and emotions.

CEREBRAL CORTEX: the thin outer layer of brain tissue that covers the *cerebrum*. The cerebral cortex is the thinking, learning, proactive portion of the brain.

CEREBROSPINAL FLUID: the clear liquid that bathes the brain and spinal cord.

CEREBRUM: the folded, wrinkly upper front part of the brain that consists of right and left *hemispheres*.

CHEMICAL BOND: an attractive force that holds *atoms* together in *chemical compounds*.

CHEMICAL COMPOUND: a combination of two or more different *elements* or chemicals.

CHLORIDE: a *chemical compound* comprised of *chlorine* and another substance, such as *sodium chloride,* the chemical name for table salt. Also see *sodium*.

CHLORINE: an *element* consisting of two *molecules* isolated as a heavy, pungent gas.

CHOLESTEROL: a sticky form of fat that impairs circulation, especially to the brain, and that often leads to strokes and heart attacks.

CHOLINE: a water and alcohol-based *alkaline* vitamin from which the *neurotransmitter acetylcholine* forms. Choline closely relates to B-complex vitamins and also acts as a *second messenger*.

CINGULATE GYRUS: a structure in the brain's *prefrontal cortex* that provides the flexibility to move from one idea to another and to see multiple options.

CLINICAL DEPRESSION: a biologically based form of depression, as opposed to normal grief, unhappiness about a loss, or "the blues." Clinical depression involves long-term unrelenting feelings of despair or deadness, and affects cognitive, physical, and/or social functioning.

CNS: see *central nervous system*.

COMPOUND: see *chemical compound*.

COMPULSION: an uncontrollable urge to perform a certain act or ritual repetitively to avoid an unacceptable, anxiety-producing idea or desire.

COMPUTED TOMOGRAPHY (CT): a noninvasive imaging technique that uses X rays and computer analysis to create a three-dimensional image of internal tissues and structures. CT scanners convert X-ray pictures into digital computer code to make high-resolution video images.

CORPUS CALLOSUM: the portion of the brain that sends nerve signals between the right and left brain *hemispheres*.

CORTICOTROPIN-RELEASING HORMONE (CRH): a *hormone* the *hypothalamus* secretes to stimulate the *pituitary gland* to release *ACTH hormones*. Also see *adrenocorticotropic hormone (ACTH)*.

CORTISOL: one of two important stress *hormones* (the other being *adrenaline*). Cortisol's most important job is to prepare the body to respond to stress.

CT: see *computed tomography*.

CYCLIC: related to a *chemical compound* that contains a ring of *atoms*.

CYCLIC ADENOSINE MONOPHOSPHATE (cAMP): a *molecule* that controls the rate of *DNA* transcription, affects cellular reactions, and mediates hormonal effects. It is also a type of *second messenger*.

CYCLOTHYMIC DISORDER: a very mild but chronic form of *bipolar disorder*. A diagnosis of cyclothymic disorder is based on a history of several *hypomanic* episodes and periods of depressive symptoms, without meeting the criteria for major depressive episodes. These symptoms must have been present for at least two years. Also see *clinical depression, major depressive disorder*.

DELUSION: a fixed false belief that others can't reason a person out of despite evidence that it isn't true.

DENDRITE: a branchlike part of a *neuron* that contains *receptors* for accepting messages from other neurons.

DEOXYRIBONUCLEIC ACID (DNA): the *molecule* in every cell that transmits genetic information.

DEPRESSION: see *clinical depression*.

DNA: see *deoxyribonucleic acid*.

DOPAMINE: a brain *neurotransmitter* specifically associated with some forms of *psychosis* and movement disorders. Dopamine appears to underlie addictive behaviors, such as alcohol and drug abuse and bingeing, which often accompany *mood disorders*. Dopamine also affects attention span, learning, thinking, memory, motor movements, motivation, and sexual impulses.

DUAL DIAGNOSIS: the combination of both a *mental illness* and a *substance abuse disorder.*

DYSTHYMIC DISORDER: a mild and often chronic form of *clinical depression* (or *unipolar disorder*) in which the focus is more on thoughts than on actions. A diagnosis of dysthymic disorder involves the presence of symptoms most of the day nearly every day for at least two years and having symptoms subside for no more than two months.

ECT: see *electroconvulsive therapy.*

EEG: see *electroencephalogram.*

ELECTROCONVULSIVE THERAPY (ECT): a form of treatment in which an anesthetized patient receives small amounts of electricity through electrodes attached to the scalp. This treatment produces a brief seizure that appears to "reset" the brain to more normal functioning.

ELECTROENCEPHALOGRAM (EEG): a noninvasive procedure that measures brain activity by using electrodes attached to the scalp, which graphically record brain patterns on an EEG machine.

ELEMENT: a naturally occurring fundamental substance, such as carbon, helium, hydrogen, lead, nitrogen, oxygen, phosphorus, or sodium. Elements are composed only of like *atoms.*

ENDOCRINE SYSTEM: a bodily system consisting of several ductless glands that secrete *hormones* directly into the blood. Through these secretions, this system communicates with organs and tissues and controls their functioning. The endocrine system, which regulates hormonal activity, includes the *thyroid gland,* the *adrenal glands,* the *sex glands,* and the brain's *pituitary* and *pineal glands.*

ENDOGENOUS: biologically based.

ENDORPHIN: a morphinelike *endogenous* chemical that helps relieve pain.

ENZYME: a *protein* derived from living cells. Enzymes produce chemical changes or act as catalysts but appear to remain unchanged by the process.

EPINEPHRINE: an activating *neurotransmitter* that the *adrenal glands* and *sympathetic nervous system* fibers secrete. Epinephrine helps produce the fight–or–flight syndrome.

ESTER: an often-fragrant *compound* formed by the reaction between an *acid* and an alcohol, when water is eliminated.

ESTERASE: an *enzyme* that accelerates the reaction of water with alcohol and *acid* to form an *ester.*

FAT-SOLUBLE VITAMIN: a vitamin that is *soluble* in fat solvents and relatively insoluble in water, such as vitamins A, D, E, and K.

FIRST MESSENGER: a brain *neurotransmitter,* such as *acetylcholine, dopamine, norepinephrine,* or *serotonin,* that binds to a *receptor* on a cell's surface to transmit information between cells. First messengers communicate between brain *neurons.* Also see *second messenger.*

G PROTEIN: a *protein* that extends through a cell membrane and combines with *enzymes* and other proteins to transfer genetic material and information from one cell to another. G protein is a type of *second messenger.*

GABA: see *gamma-aminobutryric acid.*

GAMMA-AMINOBUTRYRIC ACID (GABA): an *amino acid* that functions as the principal inhibitory *neurotransmitter* to reduce brain activity. GABA is made from *glucose.*

GANGLIA: a group of neuronal bodies found in the *peripheral nervous system* (the portion outside the brain and spinal cord).

GLIA: brain cells that act as cellular "glue" and that make up 90 percent of the brain.

GLUCOSE: a form of *sugar* that is the primary source of energy in the human body.

GLUTAMATE: an *amino acid* that acts as an excitatory *neurotransmitter.*

HALLUCINATION: a subjective auditory, gustatory, tactile, or visual perception that has no basis in reality. Hallucinations usually arise from a nervous system disorder or in response to use of an illicit drug (such as LSD).

HEMISPHERE: the left or right half of the cerebral portion of the brain, including the *cerebral cortex,* the *cerebrum,* its associated fiber systems, and deeper subcortical structures.

HIPPOCAMPUS: a part of the brain's *limbic system* that serves as a go-between. It relays information back and forth between other parts of the limbic system and the *cerebral cortex*. The hippocampus helps link emotions to images, memory, and learning, and also influences motivation.

HOMEOSTASIS: the bodily state of stability and balance.

HORMONE: a chemical regulator that works constantly to keep the body in a state of *homeostasis*. Hormones control growth and development, sexual activity, reproduction, blood pressure, heart rate, body temperature, appetite, energy level, and the stress response.

HYDROXYL (OR HYDROXIDE): a neutral or negatively charged *ion* or *radical* consisting of one hydrogen *atom* and one oxygen atom.

HYPNOTIC (OR SEDATIVE): a medication used primarily to induce sleep. Hypnotics help relieve nervous tension and produce sedation by reducing *central nervous system* activity and nerve signal transmissions.

HYPOMANIA: a state similar to mania, but less severe. A diagnosis of hypomania requires that symptoms be present for at least four days. Also see *mania*.

HYPOTHALAMUS: a *limbic system* organ near the base of the brain. The hypothalamus is the "main switch" for the *autonomic nervous system*. It helps regulate sleep, hunger, thirst, and the sex drive, as well as the *pituitary* and the *pineal glands*.

IMMUNE SYSTEM: the body's protective system against outside invaders, like bacteria and viruses.

INSULIN: a polypeptide *hormone* that helps the body use *glucose*, produce *proteins*, and form and store *lipids*.

INTERCELLULAR: relates to activity between cells.

INTRACELLULAR: relates to activity within a cell.

ION: an *atom* or group of atoms that has become electrically charged. Although ions can exist in gaseous or solid environments, those that exist in liquid (electrolytes) are more common.

ION CHANNEL: an entry point in a cell membrane that opens or closes to allow or deny *ions* or *neurotransmitters* to access the cell.

Ion channels are made of *proteins* and allow only the type of ion they are programmed to receive to enter the cell.

KINASE: an *enzyme* that transfers a *phosphate radical* from one *molecule* to another.

KINDLING: a sensitization of the brain that begins with an actual or anticipated initial stressor that triggers an episode. Kindling appears to increase vulnerability to further stressors and to lead to further episodes.

LIMBIC SYSTEM: an important group of brain structures near the *brain stem* that help regulate emotion, memory, and certain aspects of movement

LIPID: a greasy *organic compound* that, along with *carbohydrates* and *proteins*, is a major structural component of cells. Lipids are insoluble in water but are *soluble* in fat solvents.

LITHIUM: a naturally occurring mineral *salt* used as a *mood stabilizer*.

MAGNETIC RESONANCE IMAGING (MRI): an imaging technique that uses radio waves, magnetic fields, and computer analysis to create an image of internal tissues and structures. MRI can distinguish between the brain's white matter and watery gray matter. MRIs do not display teeth and bones.

MAJOR DEPRESSIVE DISORDER: a severe and often episodic form of *clinical depression* (or *unipolar disorder*) in which the focus is more on actions than on thoughts. A diagnosis of major depressive disorder involves the presence of symptoms most of the day nearly every day for at least two weeks.

MANIA: a condition that involves extreme changes of moods, thoughts, and feelings; appetite and sleep patterns; energy and activity levels; self-esteem and confidence; and concentration and decision-making abilities. When hospitalization is necessary to protect the person or to protect others, symptoms be may present for any length of time. When hospitalization is not necessary, a diagnosis requires that symptoms be present for at least one week. Also see *hypomania*.

MANIC DEPRESSION: see *bipolar disorder*.

MAOI: see *monoamine oxidase inhibitor*.

METABOLISM: the chemical changes in living cells that convert nutrients into energy for vital processes and activities.

MIXED EPISODE: a *bipolar* episode in which both *depression* and *hypomania* or *mania* occur simultaneously.

MOLECULE: a group of two or more *atoms* held together by a *chemical bond*.

MONOAMINE OXIDASE INHIBITOR (MAOI): a class of *antidepressants* that increase the concentration of *serotonin, norepinephrine,* and *dopamine* by preventing the *monoamine oxidase enzyme* from metabolizing *neurotransmitters* inside nerve endings of *presynaptic neurons.* See the Medications Appendix.

MONOAMINE OXIDASE: an *enzyme* that metabolizes the *neurotransmitters* through oxidation (combining them with oxygen *molecules*).

MONONUCLEOTIDE: a combination of a nitrogenous *base,* a *sugar,* and a *phosphoric acid.* Mononucleotides are the building blocks of *DNA* and *RNA.*

MOOD DISORDER (OR AFFECTIVE DISORDER): a condition whose primary feature is a disturbance of mood. Although mood disorders primarily affect moods, they also produce significant physical symptoms and affect thinking and behavior.

MOOD STABILIZER: a medication used to treat or prevent *mania* or *hypomania.* Mood stabilizers can also reduce or prevent depressive symptoms. See the Medications Appendix.

MOOD-STABILIZING ANTICONVULSANT (ALSO CALLED ANTIEPILEPTIC OR ANTISEIZURE AGENT): a medication usually prescribed to control convulsions and seizures. Some *anticonvulsants* have mood-stabilizing properties. See the Medications Appendix.

MRI: see *magnetic resonance imaging.*

MYELIN: a fatty substance that insulates and protects each *axon* of a *neuron.*

MYOINOSITOL: a *polar lipid* present in the vitamin B complex that greatly affects cell membrane function. Myoinositol is a type of *second messenger.*

NASSA: see *noradrenergic and specific serotonergic antidepressant.*

NDRI: see *norepinephrine and dopamine reuptake inhibitor.*

NEUROLEPTIC: an *antipsychotic* medication particularly used to treat *psychosis* and *schizophrenia* but also used to treat severe manic symptoms. Also see *mania*.

NEURON: a nerve cell that consists of a cell body containing a *nucleus* and one or more *axons* and *dendrites*.

NEUROPEPTIDE: a peptide (or *compound* of *amino acids*) found in nerve tissue in the brain.

NEUROTRANSMITTER: a chemical messenger that relays signals between adjacent nerve cells in the body.

NORADRENERGIC AND SPECIFIC SEROTONERGIC ANTI-DEPRESSANT (NaSSA): an *antidepressant* medication that blocks certain *adrenergic* and *serotonin receptors*. See the Medications Appendix.

NOREPINEPHRINE (OR NORADRENALINE): a *neurotransmitter* related to *epinephrine* that is found in both the *peripheral* and *central nervous systems*. Norepinephrine arouses the fight-or-flight response when the body experiences stress.

NOREPINEPHRINE AND DOPAMINE REUPTAKE INHIBITOR (NDRI): an *antidepressant* medication that increases the concentration of *norepinephrine* and *dopamine* in the brain. See the Medications Appendix.

NUCLEIC ACID: a large *molecule* composed of linked *mononucleotides*. *DNA* and *RNA* are nucleic acids.

NUCLEOSIDE: a *compound* consisting of a *sugar molecule* and a nitrogenous *base*. Nucleosides are found in *DNA* and *RNA*.

NUCLEOTIDE: see *mononucleotide*.

NUCLEUS: the part of a cell that contains hereditary information (*DNA* and *RNA*) and controls the cell's metabolism, growth, and reproduction.

NUCLEUS ACCUMBENS: the "center of gratification," which helps modulate hunger, thirst, and sexual desire.

OBSESSION: a persistent unwanted thought or image.

OPIOID: a medication or naturally occurring substance similar to opium that relieves pain and produces a sense of well-being, *or* one or more of its *alkaloid* derivatives.

ORGANIC: relates to a chemical substance that contains carbon and/or to a substance derived from a living organism.

PANCREAS: an *endocrine-system* organ near the liver that produces *insulin*.

PARASYMPATHETIC NERVOUS SYSTEM: the part of the autonomic nervous system that constricts the pupils, dilates the blood vessels, slows the heart rate, and stimulates the digestive and genitourinary systems. Also see *autonomic nervous system, sympathetic nervous system*.

PATHOLOGICAL: relates to an abnormal or disease-related response.

PERIPHERAL NERVOUS SYSTEM: a part of the body's nervous system that stimulates sensory neurons throughout the *central nervous system* and activates motor *neurons* in muscles and glands.

PET: see *positron emission tomography*.

PHOSPHATE: a *chemical compound* formed from *phosphoric acid,* or an *organic* phosphoric *compound* bound to nitrogen or a *carboxyl* group in way that permits energy release.

PHOSPHOLIPID: a phosphorus-containing *lipid* composed of small but very *polar* molecular parts. Phospholipids are extremely important in forming cell membranes.

PHOSPHOMONOESTERASE: a *phosphate* that acts on an *ester* containing a single ester group. Phosphomonoesterase is a type of *second messenger*.

PHOSPHORIC ACID: a strong acidic *compound* formed from *phosphate* groups linked together by oxygen.

PINEAL GLAND: the part of the brain that serves as the body's internal clock and controls its biorhythms (timing system) by receiving light/dark signals from the environment.

PITUITARY GLAND: a small oval-shaped structure located at the base of the brain. It is often called the "master gland" because its *hormones* activate other glandular secretions.

PKC: see *protein kinase C*.

POLAR: related to a pair of oppositely charged (positive or negative) electric or magnetic regions.

PONS: the "bridge" above the *brain stem* that connects the spinal cord with the *cerebrum* and *cerebellum*. The pons inhibits muscle activity during REM (rapid eye movement) sleep.

POSITRON EMISSION TOMOGRAPHY (PET): a noninvasive computerized imaging technique that uses radioisotopes (a radioactive isotope) injected into the bloodstream to record information. PETs show the distribution of substances in tissues and provide a visual measure of *metabolism* within the brain.

POSTSYNAPTIC NEURON: the receiving *neuron* across the *synaptic cleft* from the transmitting neuron. Also see *presynaptic neuron*.

POTASSIUM: an *ion* and also an important naturally occurring *salt* contained in fluids both inside and outside cells. Even small changes in potassium levels can cause serious medical emergencies.

PREFRONTAL CORTEX: the front third of the brain, which affects attention span, impulse control, and judgment as well as organizing and problem-solving skills.

PRESYNAPTIC NEURON: the transmitting *neuron* across the *synaptic cleft* from the receiving neuron. Also see *postsynaptic neuron*.

PROTEIN: a naturally occurring complex *compound* consisting of *amino acid* residues bound to various *elements* by carbon and nitrogen. Proteins contain other essential compounds, such as *antibodies*, *enzymes*, or *hormones*.

PROTEIN KINASE C (PKC): a calcium-activated enzyme that combines *phosphoric acid* with a *hydroxyl* group on a *protein* and is important to hormonal binding. Protein kinase C is a type of *second messenger*.

PSYCHODYNAMIC: related to the interaction of conscious and unconscious mental or emotional states, and their influence on personality and behavior.

PSYCHONEUROIMMUNOLOGY: the scientific discipline that explores mind-body links that relate to autonomic, immune, and nervous system functioning.

PSYCHOSIS: a condition in which thoughts, behaviors, and emotional responses are distorted, disorganized, or impaired, and/or the person affected can't recognize reality and interact normally with others.

PSYCHOTIC: a state characterized by *delusions* and/or prominent *hallucinations*.

PSYCHOTROPIC: a term used to describe a medication or drug that has a specific action on the mind.

RADICAL: a group of *atoms* or *elements* bound together that passes intact from one *compound* to another but rarely can exist on its own for long.

RAPID CYCLING: a bipolar state in which manic or hypomanic and depressive symptoms alternate during a single day or from day to day. A diagnosis of rapid cycling involves having four or more depressive, manic, hypomanic, and/or mixed episodes in any combination throughout a single year. Also see *clinical depression, hypomania, mania, mixed state.*

RAPID (OR REPETITIVE) TRANSCRANIAL MAGNETIC STIMULATION (RTMS): a noninvasive technique similar to *electroconvulsive therapy* that uses magnetization to "reset" the brain to normal functioning. This technique stimulates the brain more than once per second at 1 Hz. Also see *transcranial magnetic stimulation.*

RAS: see *reticular activating system.*

RECEPTOR: a hollow tube inside a *neuron's dendrite* that is programmed to receive a certain type (or types) of *neurotransmitter.*

RETICULAR ACTIVATING SYSTEM (RAS): a switching mechanism in the center of the spinal cord that runs from the upper *brain stem* into the lower *cerebral cortex.* The RAS "toggles" between the reactive and proactive portions of the brain.

REUPTAKE: a process in which a "pump" on the *presynaptic neuron* sucks up the leftover *neurotransmitters* from the *synaptic cleft* after the *postsynaptic neurons* have rejected their entry.

RIBONUCLEIC ACID (RNA): the *molecule* in every cell that controls cellular chemical activities such as *protein* production.

RIBONUCLEOSIDE: a *nucleoside* in which *ribose* is the *sugar* component.

RIBOSE: a simple *sugar* consisting of carbon, hydrogen, and oxygen that is obtained primarily from *RNA.*

RNA: see *ribonucleic acid.*

RTMS: see *rapid transcranial magnetic stimulation.*

SAD: see *seasonal affective disorder.*

SALT: an ionic crystalline *compound* that results from replacing part or all of the hydrogen in an *acid.* Also see *ion.*

SARI: see *serotonin antagonist and reuptake inhibitor.*

SCHIZOAFFECTIVE DISORDER: a combination of schizophrenia (a thought disorder in which one has false beliefs and *hallucinations*) and a *mood disorder.*

SEASONAL AFFECTIVE DISORDER (SAD): a disorder whose symptoms vary with the season, weather, and/or level of light. Some experts consider SAD a form of *bipolar disorder.*

SECOND MESSENGER: a *molecule* or *compound* other than a *neurotransmitter* that communicates inside a *neuron.* Second messengers mediate cell activity by relaying *intercellular* signals from *hormones* or neurotransmitters bound to the cell's surface. Also see *first messenger.*

SELECTIVE NORADRENERGIC REUPTAKE INHIBITOR (SNRI): an *antidepressant* medication that selectively inhibits *serotonin* and *norepinephrine reuptake.* See the Medications Appendix.

SELECTIVE SEROTONIN REUPTAKE INHIBITOR (SSRI): an *antidepressant* medication that selectively inhibits the *reuptake* of *serotonin.* See the Medications Appendix.

SEROTONIN: a *neurotransmitter* found in the *central nervous system* and peripheral *ganglia* that is implicated in *depression.*

SEROTONIN ANTAGONIST AND REUPTAKE INHIBITOR (SARI): an *antidepressant* medication that increases the concentration of *serotonin* by inhibiting serotonin *reuptake* and diverting serotonin to certain nonserotonin *receptors* on *postsynaptic neurons.* See the Medications Appendix.

SEX GLANDS: the ovaries and testes.

SINGLE PHOTON EMISSION COMPUTED TOMOGRAPHY (SPECT): a noninvasive, nonradioactive computerized technology that helps reveal functional or structural irregularities in the brain. SPECT shows blood flow by imaging trace amounts of radioisotopes.

SNRI: see *serotonin and norepinephrine reuptake inhibitor.*

SOCIOPATHIC: related to aggressive, antisocial, or unremorseful behavior.

SODIUM: a very chemically active metallic *element* that is the chief *cation* in both blood and other bodily fluids.

SOLUBLE: capable of dissolving or being dispersed.

SPECT: see *single photon-emission computed tomography*.

SSRI: see *selective serotonin reuptake inhibitor*.

SUBSTANCE ABUSE: the overuse or dependence on alcohol, prescribed or over-the-counter medications, or illicit drugs.

SUBSTANTIA NIGRA: a group of dark-colored neurons in the midbrain above the *pons,* which along with the *nucleus accumbens* appears to play a major role in addictive behaviors.

SUGAR: one of many water-*soluble carbohydrate compounds* that vary in sweetness, depending on its source.

SYMPATHETIC NERVOUS SYSTEM: the part of the autonomic nervous system that enlarges the pupils, shrinks the blood vessels, speeds the heart rate, and slows digestion and hormone secretion. The brain activates the sympathetic nervous system when a person is frightened or stressed. Also see *autonomic nervous system, parasympathetic nervous system*.

SYNAPSE: an area in the brain that includes at least one *presynaptic neuron* and one *postsynaptic neuron,* plus the *synaptic cleft* between.

SYNAPTIC CLEFT: an infinitesimal gap between two *neurons*.

TARDIVE DYSKINESIA: a disorder that causes involuntary repetitive movements, such as muscle spasms, writhing or twisting, and odd facial expressions.

TCA: see *tricyclic antidepressant*.

TERMINAL: the end of an *axon*'s branch that transmits messages to other cells.

TETRACYCLIC: an *antidepressant* medication similar to a *tricyclic antidepressant*. Tetracyclics have a four-ring chemical structure. See the Medications Appendix.

THALAMUS: the portion of the brain that transmits sensory information to the *cerebral cortex* and translates nerve signals into conscious sensations.

THYROID: a butterfly-shaped gland in the neck that straddles the windpipe and regulates metabolic functions and energy levels.

THYROID-RELEASING HORMONE (TRH): a *hormone* the *hypothalamus* releases to signal the *thyroid* to convert nutrients into energy.

THYROXINE (T4): an *amino acid* produced by the *thyroid* gland that is essential in making other thyroid *hormones*. T4 is also used in almost every bodily process, including *metabolism* and growth.

TITRATING: adjusting medication dosages.

TMS: see *transcranial magnetic stimulation*.

TRANSCRANIAL MAGNETIC STIMULATION (TMS): a noninvasive technique similar to *electroconvulsive therapy* that uses magnetization to "reset" the brain to normal functioning. Also see *rapid transcranial magnetic stimulation*.

TRH: see *thyroid-releasing hormone*.

TRICYCLIC ANTIDEPRESSANT (TCA): an *antidepressant* medication that blocks the uptake of *neurotransmitters* into nerve cells. Tricyclics have a three-ring chemical structure. See the Medications Appendix.

TRIIODOTHYRONINE (T3): the most powerful *thyroid hormone* that affects almost every process in the body, including *metabolism*, body temperature, growth, and heart rate.

TYRAMINE: an *amino acid* present in certain foods and medications.

TYROSINE: an *amino acid* that converts into the *neurotransmitters dopamine* and *norepinephrine*.

UNIPOLAR DISORDER: a brain disorder characterized by depressive episodes but no *manic* or *hypomanic* episodes. Also see *clinical depression, dysthymia, major depressive disorder*.

VAGAL NERVE STIMULATION (VNS): a technique used to control epilepsy and now being tested to treat *mood disorders*. VNS sends electrical pulses to the brain. A device similar to a cardiac pacemaker is inserted under the skin on the chest, then electrical simulation flows through the left vagus nerve in the neck. Doctors don't yet fully understand how VNS works, but current theory implies that it alters nerve pathways that lead to seizures.

VESICLE: a bulblike sac within a neuron in which *neurotransmitters* are stored.

VNS: see *vagal nerve stimulation*.

ACKNOWLEDGMENTS

$\mathbf{I}$ N ADDITION TO the contributions of Drs. Charles L. Bowden, Lauren B. Marangell, Jim Van Norman, Richard E. Wilcox, M. Theresa Valls, Carol Pierce-Davis, and Peter C. Whybrow, mentioned in the Author's Note, I am indebted to many, many others.

For her tremendous courage and inspiring work to educate others about bipolar disorder and suicide, I want to thank Dr. Kay Redfield Jamison, Professor of Psychology at Johns Hopkins University School of Medicine. I'm also indebted to teacher, writer, and lecturer Mary Ellen Copeland for her long-term efforts in helping others cope with mood disorders and for the sage advice she provided about this book's content early on.

Many other mental health professionals and advocates provided information and support for my efforts:

- John Bush, President of the Depression and Bipolar Support Alliance (formerly known as the National Depressive and Manic-Depressive Association), and Executive Director of the Texas Society of Psychiatric Physicians
- Laura Hoofnagle, Publications Manager, Depression and Bipolar Support Alliance
- Pam Brown, former President of the Austin Chapter of the National Association for the Mentally Ill

- Dian Cox, who worked with me many years ago at the Mental Health Association in Texas, and has been a friend and reliable source of information about the field ever since.

Another individual who inspired much of this book's content is my friend and client Dr. Oscar Mink, Licensed Psychologist and Full Professor at the University of Texas at Austin's College of Education. He patiently explained many psychological concepts and other philosophies integrated into this book.

Many members of my Depression and Bipolar Support Alliance support group have also assisted with this book and cheered me on. To protect their privacy and anonymity, I won't list their names, but I deeply appreciate their contributions. Many of these people have become some of my best friends.

I also appreciate the encouragement of Exchange Park Toastmasters club members, who helped me become comfortable speaking openly about my struggles with bipolar disorder, suicide, and mental illness. I want to also thank Pam Brown, Don Darling, Anita Earnest, Jesus Garcia, Glenn McIntosh, Jim Bob McMillan, Mickey Michaels, Frank Rilling, Beverly Scarborough, and the Austin Community Access Channel for assisting in my early efforts to make mood disorders a more public issue.

I'm grateful to the total strangers who shared their own experiences with this illness or those of family members and friends. Their calls, e-mails, letters, and in-person conversations reinforced the need for this book and strengthened my resolve to complete it.

Prior to the book's final submission, many friends provided generous assistance. For their astute observations, knowledge, encouragement, and multiple reviews, I'd like to thank fellow members of the Writers' League of Texas's Old Quarry writing group: Diane Barnet, Don Darling, Dyanne Fry Cortez, Marsha Edwards, Karen Enyedy, Dayna Finet, Marge Harrington, Ron Jaeger, Shalon Kearney, Kyung Kim, Michael Morgan, P. J. Pierce, Janis Russell, Terri Rector Fann, and

Judy Woodard. Many of us have critiqued one another's work for nearly fourteen years.

Other dear friends who have helped significantly include:

- Tom Doyal, who guided me through the intricacies of my first literary agency and publishing contracts;
- Mercedes Newman, who created the wonderful illustrations and patiently made multiple adjustments;
- Nancy Carroll and Steve Weikal, who gave time on very short notice to capture the perfect author photograph;
- Heather Renwick and Pamela Speciale, for research, word processing, proofreading, and general office support;
- Pam Williams, for research, preproduction adjustments, and for being one of my most enthusiastic supporters;
- Jill Bartel, who came in to make "a few last-minute adjustments" that turned into more than two months' work and put my needs above her own for much longer than she should have; and
- Rebecca Sankey, who read multiple drafts, made wonderful editorial suggestions, and reminded me how much this book is needed and of the value she saw in it whenever I was feeling overwhelmed.

I'm grateful for my agent, Carole Bidnick, who took the bold risk of working with me sight unseen and matched this project with an excellent publisher.

I especially appreciate Matthew Lore, my editor and publisher, both for his excellent editorial direction and for his flexibility, patience, and understanding when health problems led to multiple requests for extended deadlines.

Other people at Marlowe & Company also deserve acknowledgment, particularly associate editor Sue McCloskey; Johanna Tani, the book's copyeditor; Pauline Neuwirth, the book's interior designer; and Linda Kosarin, Avalon's art director, and Christine Van Bree, for their work on the cover.

Finally, I want to thank my family. My mother, sisters, nieces, and other relatives offered encouragement, supplied information, provided assistance, and rescheduled visits in the interest of getting this book out.

My husband, Ralph, and stepchildren, Tom and Joy, have been amazingly supportive despite all that they have sacrificed because of my disorder. Especially, without Ralph's unconditional love and belief in me, this book and my mission to share what I've learned from my illness would have been an impossible dream.

INDEX

A

abusive family, 141
acetylcholine, 113
aches and pains, inexplicable, 25–26
action potential, 109–10
actions, self-destructive, 33–34
activity levels, 14–15, 262–64
acupressure, 244
acupuncture, 243–44
addiction
 to medication, 191–92
 see also substance abuse
Addison's disease, 91, 155
ADHD (attention deficit hyperactivity disorder), 97–98
adolescents
 bipolar disorder in, 75–77
 depression in, 74
 suicide by, 37
adrenal glands, 91, 117, 155, 156
adrenaline, 117, 155
adrenocorticotropin hormone (ACTH), 91, 118, 156
Advance Directive for Mental Health Treatment, 60
aerobic exercise, 183
affirmations, 276–81
age of onset, 22, 34–35, 76–77
aggression, 12–13
agitation, 115
AIDS (acquired immune deficiency syndrome), 85–86

Al-Anon/Alateen, 306
alcohol, avoiding, 182–83
alcohol abuse, 19, 32–33, 96–97, 122–23
Alcoholics Anonymous (AA), 306
alternative therapies, 224–50
 acupressure, 244
 acupuncture, 243–44
 aromatherapy, 245–46
 biofeedback, 246–47
 breathwork, 244–45
 creative therapies, 294–99
 dietary supplements, 225–43
 homeopathic medicine, 243
 information about, 225
 massage, 245
 negative ion generators, 249–50
 phototherapy (light therapy), 247–49
Americans with Disabilities Act (ADA), 257
amino acids, 113, 226, 235–39
Amish Affective Disorders Project, 123
amygdala, 106
analysis, 213
anemia, 232
anger, 12–13, 31
anorexia nervosa, 98
anti-anxiety agents, 198, 355
anticonvulsant medications, 157, 358–59

antidepressants, 79, 115, 196–98, 356–57
 see also specific medications
anti-epileptics, 196
antipsychotics, 196, 358
anti-seizure agents, 196
antisocial personality disorder, 128
anxiety disorders, 95–96
appetite changes, 14, 29, 321
Argyris, Chris, 143
aromatherapy, 245–46
artificial sweeteners, 176–77
artistic people, 285–94, 299
art therapy, 295
aspartame, 176
assertiveness training, 213
attention deficit hyperactivity disorder (ADHD), 97–98
attitude, positive, 270–71
attributional style. *See* explanatory style
autoimmune disorders, 85–87
autonomic nervous system, 107
axon, 109, 111

B

bad parenting, 137–38
B-complex vitamins, 227–28
behavioral psychology, 132
behavioral therapy, 213
behaviors
 bizarre, 20–21
 warning sign, 321
belonging, sense of, 260–62
Benson, Herbert, 313

benzodiazepines, 192, 355
binge-eating disorder, 99
biochemistry, 111–16, 169
biofeedback, 246–47
biorhythms, 170, 171, 213
bipolar disorder
  accepting, 51–53
  age of onset of, 22, 34–35, 76–77
  in children and adolescents, 76, 80
  defined, 71
  diagnosing, 65–71, 77–78, 81, 347
  early warning signs, 81–83
  gender and, 77
  genetic link of, 119–23
  living with, 3–4
  number of episodes and, 71
  personality and, 124–36
  recognizing you have, 48–49
  signs and symptoms of, 75
  sleep needs and, 169–72
  suicide and, 51
  types of, 74
  see also mood disorders
bizarre thoughts/behaviors, 20–21
blood sugar level, 92, 172–77
Bolles, Richard, 301–2
borderline personality disorder, 128–29
brain
  cells, 108
  flexibility of, 119
  scans, 70
  stem, 105
  structure, 104–11
  tumors, 88–89
breathwork, 244–45
Brilliant Madness, A (Pearce), 201
bulimia nervosa, 98–99

C
caffeine, 178
calcium, 231
calcium channel blockers, 196, 359
cancer, 87–88
carbohydrates, 174–75, 180
carnitine, 236
Carson, Richard, 292
causes
  biochemistry, 111–16
  debate over, 103–4
  genetics, 119–23

cell body, 108–9
central nervous system (CNS), 88, 104
cerebellum, 106
cerebral cortex, 105
cerebrum, 104
changes, making gradual, 185–86
chaos theory, 316
chaotic families, 140
childhood. See families; upbringing
children
  bipolar disorder in, 75–77, 80
  depression in, 74
chocolate, 177
cholesterol, 156, 179–80, 231
choline, 115, 228
chromium, 231
chronic adrenal insufficiency, 91
cingulate gyrus, 105
Citizens Commission on Human Rights (CCHR), 58
clinical social workers, 211
co-counseling, 222
cognitive-behavioral therapy (CBT), 135–36, 213
cognitive therapy, 135, 213
colors, 254
communication
  about feelings, 215
  about illness, 261–62
  family, 143–45
  helpful and hurtful, 319–20, 328
  without labeling, 149
community-based services, 340–41
Community Mental Health Centers Act, 333
confidence, 13–14
  lack of, 29–30
co-occurring conditions, 81, 84–102
  autoimmune disorders, 85–87
  cancer, 87–88
  endocrine disorders, 89–92
  infectious diseases, 92–93
  migraine headaches, 101
  neurological disorders, 93–95
  psychiatric disorders, 95–101
  relationship of, 101–2

tumors, 88–89
Cook, Ian, 351
Copeland, Mary Ellen, 248
copper, 232
corporal punishment, 146–50
corpus callosum, 107
corticotropin releasing hormone (CRH), 118, 156
cortisol, 91, 117–18, 155, 156, 157
cost, of treatment, 54
counseling, 210–11
  see also talk therapy
counselors, 212
  see also therapists
Cousin, Norman, 265
cravings, 177
creative therapies, 294–99
creativity
  inborn, 284
  madness and, 285–94
  medication and, 288–89
  realizing your, 292–93
  tapping into, 289–90
CT (computerized tomography), 70
Cushing's syndrome, 91
cyanocobalamin, 228
cyclic adenosine monophosphate, 115
cyclothymia, 74, 78

D
dance therapy, 295
DBSA (Depression and Bipolar Support Alliance), 221
deficiency needs, 167–68, 252
deinstitutionalization, 333
delusions, 80
dendrites, 109, 111
denial, 54
depression
  adolescent, 74
  beginning of, 34–35
  blues and, 52
  causes of, 27
  childhood, 74
  defined, 24
  experience of, 23–24, 32
  faith and hope during, 305
  signs and symptoms of, 24–34
    anger, 31
    apathy, 30
    appetite changes, 29
    despondency, 28–29

feeling overwhelmed, 27–28
frustration, 31
indecisiveness, 27–28
inexplicable aches and pains, 25–26
lack of confidence, 29–30
lack of feeling, 28–29
poor self-esteem, 29–30
self-destructive thoughts/actions, 33–34
sleep changes, 29
substance abuse, 32–33
useless actions, 30–31
warning signs of, 267–68
depressive episodes, 71, 72–74, 322
despondency, 28–29
diabetes, 91–92, 231
diagnosis
complications in, 81
criteria for, 77–78
difficulties in, 65, 347
factors in, 69–71
getting a, 67–71
Diagnostic and Statistical Manual of Mental Disorders (DSM), 70–71
diagnostic tests, 70
Dianetics (Hubbard), 58
diet
adjusting your, 174–80
natural foods in, 173
regular mealtimes and, 172–73
restrictions, MAOI, 181
dietary changes, 182
dietary recommendations, 180–81
dietary supplements, 225–43
amino acids, 235–39
cautions, 226, 230, 231, 234, 237, 239, 240, 241, 242
defined, 225–26
essential fatty acids, 239–40
herbs, 240–42
minerals, 231–35
new, 242–43
vitamins, 227–30
disbelief, 54
discipline, 145–50
dissociative identity disorder, 127
distant family, 140
distractibility, 15
DNA, 108–9

doctors
changing, 190
communicating with, 67–69, 202–5
finding right, 188–90
preparing to see, 67
referrals for, 188–89
types of, 66
dopamine, 97, 113
dosage adjustments, 199–200
drama therapy, 295
drug abuse, 19–20, 32–33, 96–97, 122–23
drugs, avoiding, 182–83
DSM-IV, 70–71
dual diagnosis, 97
Duel Recovery Anonymous (DRA), 306
dysfunctional families, 139–41, 143–45
dysthymic disorder, 72–74

E
EA (Emotions Anonymous), 307
eating disorders, 98–99
EEG (electroencephalogram), 70
Egeland, Janice, 123
electroconvulsive therapy (ECT), 205–6
electroencephalogram (EEG), 170, 247
Ellis, Albert, 277
emotions
about treatment, 54
length of, 52
loss of control of, 32
mood disorders and, xiii–xiv
primary, 216
repressed, 209–10
secondary, 216–17
talking about, 215
employers, discussing illness with, 255–57
employment
conventional, 255–58
part-time, 258
rights, 257–58
self-, 259
volunteer, 259
endocrine disorders, 89–92, 116–17
endocrine glands, 116–17
endocrine system, 87, 89, 116–19, 156
energy, elevated, 14–15

enzyme, 112
epilepsy, 93–94
essential fatty acids, 179–80, 239–40
estrogen, 118, 202
euphoria, 11–12
evil spirits, 304, 332
exercise, 183–85, 264
explanatory style, 130–31
expressive therapies, 294–99
Eysenck, Hans, 126

F
faith, 305
families
analysis of, 141–43
behavior patterns from, 138
communication in, 143–45
discipline in, 145–50
dysfunctional, 139–41
fair fighting in, 145
functional, 138–39
risks in, 119–23
family therapy, 214
fats, 179–80
fear, of treatment, 53
feelings
lack of, 28–29
nature of, 216–17
overwhelmed, 27–28
talking about, 215
feng shui, 254
fiber, 178–79
fighting, fair, 145
first-degree relatives, 122
first messengers, 113–15
flight-or-flight response, 114
focus, lack of, 15
folic acid (folate), 228
Food Guide Pyramid, 180
foods, natural, 173
fructose, 174–75
frustration, 31

G
gamma-aminobutyric acid (GABA), 236
gender, 77
generalized anxiety disorder, 96
general practitioners, 66
genetics
medication and, 201
mental illness and, 119–23
personality and, 126–27
ginkgo, 240
glia, 108
glucose, 92, 172

glutamic acid, 236
glutamine, 236
glycine, 236
goals/goal setting, 271–76
  areas, 273
  evaluating, 276
  exercises, 274
  falling short of, 275–76
  guidelines for, 272–73
  prioritizing, 273–74
  reasons for, 272
  rewarding self for meeting, 275
  value-based, 273–74
Gold, Mark, 90
Goldberg, Natalie, 298
government programs, 341
G-proteins, 109
G proteins, 115
grandiosity, 14
gratitude journals, 313
grief, 32, 54–55
group therapy, 219–20
growth needs, 167, 169
guided imagery, 281–83
guilt, 31

H
half-lives, 199, 353–54
hallucinations, 80
happiness, versus manic euphoria, 12
Hashimoto's disease, 85
help
  for someone with a mood disorder, 318–30
  when to seek, 320–21
  words that, 319–20
hemoglobin, 232
hepatitis C, 92–93
herbs, 240–42
Hierarchy of Needs, 167–69, 254, 317
hippocampus, 106–7, 157
Hippocrates, 125
Hirschfeld, Robert, 334
histadine, 237
histrionic personality disorder, 129
HIV, 85–86
Hobson, Charles, 154
Holmes, Thomas, 154
home environment, 253–54
homelessness, 338–39
homeopathic medicine, 243
homeostatis, 169
hope, 305

hormone replacement therapy (HRT), 202
hormones
  about, 77
  neurotransmitters and, 116
  sex, 118–19
  stress, 117–18
  that affect moods, 117–19
  thyroid, 118
hospitalization
  helping someone cope after, 326–30
  involuntary commitment, 59, 324–26
  protecting your rights during, 59–61
  as treatment option, 207–8
  voluntary commitment, 59, 324
  when it is necessary, 323–26
Hubbard, L. Ron, 58
humor
  healing power of, 265
  laughter clubs, 266
  therapeutic, 265–66
Huntington's disease, 94
hypercortisolism, 91
hypersexuality, 17–18
hyperthyroidism, 89–90
hypnotics, 198, 355
hypocortisolism, 91
hypomania
  childhood and adolescent, 76
  defined, 10
  signs and symptoms of, 10–22
  warning signs of, 267–68
hyposexuality, 25
hypothalamus, 107, 156
hypothyroidism, 89–90, 116

I
immune system, 85
impulsiveness, 16
indecisiveness, 27–28
infectious diseases, 92–93
inhibition, lack of, 16
inositol, 228
insoluble fiber, 178
insomnia, 14, 29
insulin, 92, 172–73, 231
insurance problems, 339–40
interpersonal therapy, 212–13
ion channels, 109
iron, 232

J
jails, 341–42
Jamison, Kat Redfield, 285, 287–88
Johnson, Catherine, 127
journaling, 296, 313

K
Kaplan, Bonnie, 242
kava, 241
kindling, 157–58, 195–96
Kübler-Ross, Elisabeth, 133–34, 216, 304, 316–17

L
ladder of inference, 143–44
language, people-first, 5–6
laughter clubs, 266
learned helplessness, 131–32
Life Is Good (Shreeve), 313
lifestyle adjustments, 251–69
  to activity levels, 262–64
  developing new routine, 262–69
  developing supportive relationships, 260–62
  home environment, 253–54
  making gradual, 185–86
  reducing stress, 264–67
  safe environments, 253–60
  starting out, 252–53
  work environment, 255–60
light therapy, 247–49
limbic system, 106–8, 245–46
lithium, 115, 119, 157, 185, 191, 195–96
Living Without Depression and Manic Depression (Copeland), 248
Lorenz, Edward, 316
Ludwig, Arnold, 288
lupus, 86–87
Lyme disease, 93
lysine, 237

M
magnesium, 232
Maier, Steven, 131–32
major depressive disorder, 72–74
managed care, 339–40
manganese, 232
mania
  adolescent, 76
  beginning of, 22
  childhood, 76

defined, 10
experience of, 9–10
faith and hope during,
305–6
signs and symptoms of,
10–22
aggression, 12–13
anger, 12–13
appetite changes, 14
bizarre thoughts/behav-
iors, 20–21
confidence, 13–14
distractibility, 15
elevated energy and
activity, 14–15
euphoria, 11–12
hypersexuality, 17–18
impulsiveness, 16
lack of focus, 15
lack of inhibition, 16
optimism, 11
racing thoughts, 15–16
rapid and erratic speech,
15–16
risky behaviors, 16–18
self-esteem, 13–14
sleep needs, 14
substance abuse, 18–20
violence and, 13
Manic Depressives Anony-
mous (MDA), 307
manic episodes, 9–10, 71,
74–76, 323
see also hypomania; mania
Manning, Martha, 206
MAOIs (monoamine oxidase
inhibitors)
about, 356
cautions, 199
diet restrictions, 181
tyrosine and, 239
use of, 112, 198
Maslow, Abraham, 167–69,
300–1, 310
Maslow's Hierarchy of
Needs, 167–69, 254, 317
massage, 245
Matthews-Simonton,
Stephanie, 281
McEwen, Bruce, 157
McGraw, Phillip, 276
mealtimes, regular, 172–73
medical information, 204–5
medications
addiction and, 191–92
anti-anxiety agents, 198,
355

antidepressants, 79, 115,
196–98, 356–57
antipsychotics, 196, 358
cautions, 199
clarifying, with doctor,
202–3
classes of, 194–99
combining, 201–2
creativity and, 288–89
dislike of, 54
dosage determinations,
352–53
effectiveness of, 194
generic, 203
genetics and, 201
half-lives, 195, 199, 353–54
hypnotics, 198, 355
individual differences in,
193–94
informing other doctors
about, 204–5
managing, 202–5, 328
managing costs of, 204
meals and, 173
mood-stabilizing agents,
195–96, 358–59
myths and questions about,
190–94
new, 350–51
over-the-counter, 182
patience with, 200–1
personality changes and, 191
remembering, 205
resisting, 190
side effects from, 192–94,
224–25
switching, 194
synaptic cleft and, 110
table of, 355–59
titrating, 199–200
weakness myth and, 191
meditation, 313–15
melatonin, 248
Mental Health Bell, 333
mental health organizations,
343–44
mental health professionals
experiences with, 26–27
for treatment, 66–67
mental illness
accepting, 51–53
causes of, 103–4
defined, 52
discussing with others,
261–62
helping someone with,
318–30

myths about, 4–5, 345–50
naysayers and, 57–58
versus normalcy, 52–53
religion and, 304
stigma of, 331–39
suicide and, 51
upbringing and, 137–50
violence and, 336
metabolism, 118
migraine headaches, 101
Miller, Alice, 146
mimicking conditions,
84–85
see also co-occurring conditions
mineral deficiencies, 234
minerals, 231–35
mixed episodes, 78–79
monoamine oxidase, 112
monoamine oxidase
inhibitors (MAOIs), 112,
181, 198, 199, 239, 356
mood disorders
artistic people and, 299
creativity and, 285, 287
defined, 66
diagnosis of, 67–71, 81
genetic link of, 119–23
helping someone with,
318–30
life changes and, 251–69
milder forms of, 55–56
public figures with, 286
religious beliefs and,
305–6
risks of untreated, 49–51
types of, 71–81
visualization for, 282
see also bipolar disorder
moods
biochemistry and, 115–16
defined, 52
monitoring your, 268–69
as warning sign, 321
mood-stabilizing agents,
195–96, 358–59
mood-stabilizing anticonvulsants, 196
movement therapy, 295
MRI (magnetic resonance
imaging), 70
MSG (monosodium gluta-
mate), 236
multiple sclerosis, 94
music therapy, 296
myelin, 94, 232
myoinositol, 115

N

NAMI (National Alliance for the Mentally Ill), 221
narcissistic personality disorder, 129–30
NaSSAs, 356
natural foods, 173
nature, communing with, 311–12
NDRIs, 356
needs, hierarchy of, 167–69, 254, 317
negative ion generators, 249–50
neuroleptics, 196
neurological disorders, 93–95
neuronal structure, 108–11
neurons, 108–11, 119
neuropeptides, 113
neurosyphilis, 93
neurotransmitters, 80, 110, 111–16
New Age thinkers, 58, 271, 276
niacin, 227
nicotine, 182–83
NMHA (National Mental Health Association), 221
nonaerobic exercise, 183
Noonday Demon, The (Solomon), 30
noradrenaline, 114
norepinephrine, 114
normalcy, 52–53
Norman, Warren, 125
nucleus accumbens, 107
nutrition, 172–82
  artificial sweeteners, 176–77
  caffeine, 178
  chocolate, 177
  dietary recommendations, 180–81
  fats, 179–80
  fiber, 178–79
  MAOI diet restrictions, 181
  natural foods, 173
  regular mealtimes and, 172–73
  sugar, 174–75

O

obsessive-compulsive disorder (OCD), 95–96
omega fatty acids, 179, 239–40
optimism, 11

overactivity, 262–63
overprotective families, 140
overwhelmed, feeling, 27–28

P

pancreas, 92
panic disorder, 96
Parkinson's disease, 94–95
patients, former, 57
patothenic acid, 227
Pearce, Anna, 201
people
  discussing illness with, 261–62
  negative, 260
  supportive, 254, 260–62
people-first language, 5–6
perfect families, 140
perfectionism, 132–34
personality
  bipolar disorder and, 127
  changes, medication and, 191
  concepts, 130–36
  defined, 125
  disorders, 128–30
  genetic contributions to, 126–27
  theories, 125–26
PET (positron-emission tomography), 70
pets, 262
phenylalanine, 237
phosphomonoesterase, 115
phosphorus, 232–33
phototherapy, 247–49
pineal gland, 107–8, 117
pituitary gland, 107–8, 117
poetry therapy, 296
pons, 105–6
postsynaptic neuron, 110, 111, 112
posttraumatic stress disorder (PTSD), 96, 159–60
potassium, 233
potential, achieving your, 300–2
Power of Attorney for Health Care, 60
prayer, 308–9
prefrontal cortex, 105
premenstrual dysphoric disorder (PMDD), 99–100
premenstrual syndrome (PMS), 99–100, 172
presynaptic neuron, 110, 111
prison, 341–42
problem-solving tips, 267

promiscuity, 17–18
prostaglandins, 239
protein, 180–81
protein kinase C, 115
pschopharmacologists, 188
psychiatric disorders, co-occurring, 95–101
psychiatric nurses, 188, 211
psychiatrists, 188, 211
psychodynamic therapy, 213, 214
psychoeducation, 212
psychologists, 211
psychomotor agitation, 115
psychoneuroimmunology, 246
psychosis, 80
psychotherapy. *See* talk therapy
psychotropic medications. *See* medications
punishment, 145–46
  see also discipline
pyridoxine, 227–28

Q

quiet time, 312–13

R

racing thoughts, 15–16
rages, 13
Rahe, Richard, 154
rapid cycling, 79–80
rapid transcranial magnetic stimulation (rTMS), 206
rate of concordance, 122
Ratey, John, 127
receptors, 109
Recovery, Inc., 221
reference daily intakes (RDIs), 226
referrals, 188–89, 217–18
relationships
  supportive, 260–62
  toxic, 260
relaxation, 313–15
religion
  benefits of, 305
  evolving views of, 310–11
  organized, 304–5
  spirituality and, 303
  support groups and, 306–9
religious beliefs, 305–6
religious upbringing, 309–10
research, 350–51
reticular activating system (RAS), 106
reuptake, 112

rheumatic diseases, 86–87
riboflavin, 227
rights, protecting your, 59–61
rigid beliefs, 135–36
risky behaviors, 16–18
Rosenthal, Norman, 248

S

saccharin, 176
SAD. *See* seasonal affective disorder
safe environments, 253–60
SAM-e (S-adenosylmethionine), 241
SARIs, 356
schizoaffective disorder, 80
schizophrenia, 65, 100–1
school, returning to, 259
scientologists, 58
seasonal affective disorder (SAD), 80, 172, 248, 250
second-degree relatives, 122
second messengers, 113, 115–16
selenium, 233
self-destructive thoughts/actions, 33–34
self-employment, 259
self-esteem
    corporal punishment and, 146–50
    mania and, 13–14
    poor, 29–30
self-fulfillment, 300–2
self-talk, negative, 276–77
Seligman, Martin, 131–32
Selye, Hans, 265
"Serenity Prayer", 308–9
serotonin, 101, 114–15, 232, 238
sex drive, 17–18, 25
sex hormones, 118–19
sexual dysfunction, 192–93
Shadow Syndromes (Ratey and Johnson), 127
shock therapy, 205–6
Shreeve, Caroll McKanna, 313
side effects
    from medications, 192–94
    relief from, 224–25
signs and symptoms
    of bipolar disorder, 75
    of dysthymia, 73
    of major depression, 73
    of mania/hypomania, 10–22

of stress, 158–59
Simonton, Carl, 281
sleep
    decreased need for, 14
    during depressed period, 29
    importance of, 169–72
    tips for, 170–71
    as warning sign, 320–21
sleep–wake cycle, 114–15
SNRIs, 356
social anxiety disorder, 96
Social Readjustment Rating Scale, 154
social rhythms therapy, 213
social skills training, 213
social workers, 211
sodium, 233
Solomon, Andrew, 30
soluble fiber, 178
spanking, 146–50
SPECT (single photon emission computed tomography), 70
speech, rapid and erratic, 15–16
spelt, 175
spinal cord tumors, 88–89
spirituality
    connecting with your, 311–17
    religion and, 303
SSRIs (selective serotonin reuptake inhibitors), 112, 357
St. John's wort, 241–42
state, 52
stevia, 175
stigma
    historical perspective on, 332–34
    of mental illness, 331–39
    present-day, 334–37
    results of, 337–39
    of treatment, 53
    working to overcome, 342–44
stress
    about, 151–52
    chronic, 156–57
    good and bad, 153
    kindling and, 157–58
    personal experiences of, 161–62
    physical nature of, 156–57
    positive aspects of, 155
    posttraumatic stress disorder (PTSD), 159–60

reducing, 264–67
    reducing workplace, 259–60
    relaxation techniques for, 313–15
    short-term, 156
    signs and symptoms of, 158–59
    sources of, 154–55
    trauma and, 159–60
stress hormones, 117–18
Stress of Life, The (Seyle), 265
stressors, 152, 154–55
substance abuse, 18–20, 32–33, 44, 96–97, 122–23
substantia nigra, 107
sucralose, 176–77
sugar, 174–75
suicide
    asking about, 47
    attempt, 39–42
    contemplation of, 33–34, 36–42, 39
    legacy of, 46
    mental illness and, 51, 336–37
    religion and, 304
    risk of, 40
    seriousness of, 346
    substance abuse and, 44
    teen and adolescent, 37
    those left behind by, 42–47
    warning signs of, 38
Sultanoff, Steven, 265–66
supplements. *See* dietary supplements
support groups
    12-step programs, 221–22, 306–9
    cautions, 222
    co-counseling, 222
    finding right, 222–23
    first-time visits to, 223
    religious, 306–9
    sponsored by nonprofits, 220–21
    for support person, 328–29
supportive people, 254, 260–62
surroundings
    home, 253–54
    work, 255–60
symptoms, communicating your, 67–68
synapses, 110, 111, 119
synaptic cleft, 110
syphilis, 93

systemic lupus erythematosus (SLE), 86–87

T

tai chi, 315
talk therapy, 209–23
  about, 210
  benefits of, 187
  co-counseling, 222
  communication in, 215
  group therapy, 219–20
  individual therapy, 210–19
  options, 212
  support groups, 220–23
  therapists for, 211–12
  types of, 212–14
  see also therapists
Taming Your Gremlin (Carson), 292
tardive dyskinesia, 192
taurine, 238
teen suicide, 37
television viewing, 33
temperament, 124–25
  bipolar disorder and, 127
  genetic contributions to, 126–27
  see also personality
terminals, 109
terminology, 51–52
tests, 70
tetracyclic antidepressants, 197, 357
thalamus, 107
therapists
  finding right, 217–19
  relationship with, 214
  role of, 214–15
  types of, 211–12
  working with, 219
therapy. *See* talk therapy
thiamine, 227
thoughts
  bizarre, 20–21
  racing, 15–16
  self-destructive, 33–34
thyroid disorders, 89–90
thyroid gland, 117
thyroid hormones, 118
thyroid releasing hormone (TRH), 118, 156
Toastmasters, 153, 266
tobacco, 182–83
Touched with Fire (Jamison), 285, 287
toxic relationships, 260
trait, 52
tranquility corners, 313

transcendence, 317
transcranial magnetic stimulation (TMS), 206
trauma
  defined, 159
  personal experiences of, 161–62
treatment
  admitting need for, 55
  advocating for better, 342–44
  alternative, 224–50
  electroconvulsive therapy (ECT), 205–6
  find effective, 58
  health professionals for, 66–67
  helping others deal with your, 55–58
  helping someone get, 321–23
  herbal, 240–42
  hospitalization, 59–61, 207–8
  posttraumatic stress disorder (PTSD), 159–60
  preparing for, 67
  prison-based, 341–42
  recognizing need for, 48–49
  reasons for putting off, 53–55
  risks of not seeking, 49–51
  shortages, 339–41
  transcranial magnetic stimulation (TMS), 206
  types of, 187–88
  vagal nerve stimulation (VNS), 207
  when to seek, 65–66
  see also medications
tricyclic antidepressants (TCAs), 79, 197, 357
tryptophan, 238
tumors, 88–89
Tunnel and the Light, The (Kübler-Ross), 133–34, 316–17
12-step programs, 221–22, 306–9
twins, 122
tyramine, 181
tyrosine, 239

U

Undercurrents (Manning), 206
unemployment, 337–38
unipolar disorder

age of onset of, 76
defined, 71
depressive episodes and, 72–74
treatment of, 197
unrealistic expectations, 134–35
upbringing, 137–50
  analysis of, 141–43
  bad-parenting myth, 137–38
  discipline and, 145–50
  dysfunctional families and, 138–39
  in functional family, 138–39
  religious, 309–10

V

vagal nerve stimulation (VNS), 207, 247
verbal abuse, 148–49, 260
vesicles, 110, 111
violence, 13, 336
Viscott, David, 216, 217
visualization, 281–83
vitamin C, 228–29
vitamin D, 229
vitamin deficiencies, 230
vitamin E, 229
vitamins, 227–30
volunteer work, 259

W

warning signs, 81–83, 267–68
weight gain, 192–93
Weiner, Bernard, 217
What Color Is Your Parachute? (Bolles), 301–2
Whybrow, Peter, 65–66
Wilson, Steve, 266
words, helpful and hurtful, 319–20, 328
work environment, 255–60
worry, reducing, 266–67
writer's block, 297–98
writing therapy, 296–99

X

Xanax, 192

Y

yoga, 315
Yudofsky, Stuart, 187

Z

zinc, 233